MOTIVATIONAL INTERVIEWING

MOTIVATIONAL INTERVIEWING

Preparing People to Change Addictive Behavior

WILLIAM R. MILLER
University of New Mexico
U.S.A.

STEPHEN ROLLNICK
Whitchurch Hospital
Cardiff, Wales

and National Drug and Alcohol Research Centre
Sydney, New South Wales, Australia

THE GUILFORD PRESS
New York   London

© 1991 The Guilford Press
A Division of Guilford Publications, Inc.
72 Spring Street, New York, NY 10012

Printed in the United States of America

This book is printed on acid-free paper.

Last digit is print number: 9 8

Library of Congress Cataloging-in-Publication Data
Miller, William R.
    Motivational interviewing: preparing people to change addictive
behavior / William R. Miller, Stephen Rollnick.
        p.   cm.
    Includes bibliographical references and index.
    ISBN 0-89862-566-1   ISBN 0-89862-469-X (pbk.)
    1. Compulsive behavior—Treatment.   2. Substance abuse—Treatment.
3. Compulsive behavior—Patients—Counseling of.   4. Substance
abuse—Patients—Counseling of.   I. Rollnick, Stephen, 1952–   .
II. Title.
    [DNLM: 1. Behavior Therapy.   2. Compulsive Behavior—therapy.
3. Interview, Psychological.   4. Motivation.   5. Substance
Dependence—therapy.   WM 176 M652m]
RC533.M56   1991
DNLM/DLC
for Library of Congress   91-16597
                                                              CIP

To my mother, Hazel Marie Reitz Miller, who shared with me by example the kind of love, patience, and faith that can transform lives.

—W. R. M.

To my dear parents, Sonia and Julian Rollnick.

—S. R.

Contributing Authors

Steve Allsop, DipAlcStud, Director of Education and Research, Western Australia Alcohol and Drug Authority, Perth, Western Australia

Amanda Baker, MPsychol, Clinical Psychologist, National Drug and Alcohol Research Centre, University of New South Wales, Sydney, New South Wales, Australia

Alison Bell, RGN, RPN, Clinical Nurse Specialist, National Drug and Alcohol Research Centre, University of New South Wales, Sydney, New South Wales, Australia

Joseph P. Blount, PhD, Assistant Professor of Psychology, Widener University, Chester, Pennsylvania

W. Miles Cox, PhD, Director, Addictive Behaviors Research Center, and Associate Professor of Psychology, VA Medical Center, The Chicago Medical School, Chicago, Illinois

Carlo C. DiClemente, PhD, Associate Professor, Department of Psychology, University of Houston, Houston, Texas

Julie Dixon, RGN, Clinical Nurse Specialist, National Drug and Alcohol Research Centre, University of New South Wales, Sydney, New South Wales, Australia

Michael J. Dougher, PhD, Associate Professor, Department of Psychology, University of New Mexico, Albuquerque, New Mexico

Randall J. Garland, MA, Twin Lakes Correctional Center, Monroe, Washington

Rosemary Kent, MSW, Lecturer in Alcohol Intervention (Counselling), Alcohol Interventions Training Unit, School of Continuing Education, Rutherford College, University of Kent at Canterbury, Canterbury, Kent, England.

Eric Klinger, PhD, Professor of Psychology, University of Minnesota, Morris, Minnesota

William R. Miller, PhD, Professor, Departments of Psychology and Psychiatry, and Director, Research Division, Center on Alcoholism, Substance Abuse, and Addictions, University of New Mexico, Albuquerque, New Mexico

Stephen Rollnick, MSc, DipPsychol, Principal Clinical Psychologist, Whitchurch Hospital, Cardiff, Wales, and Visiting Research Fellow, National Drug and Alcohol Research Centre, University of New South Wales, Sydney, New South Wales, Australia

Bill Saunders, MPhil, Associate Professor, Addiction Studies Unit, Curtin University of Technology, Perth, Western Australia

Tim Stockwell, PhD, Associate Professor, Deputy Director, National Centre for Research into the Prevention of Drug Abuse, Curtin University of Technology, Perth, Western Australia

Gillian Tober, BA (Hons), Head of Training, Leeds Addiction Unit, and Honorary Lecturer, Department of Psychiatry, University of Leeds, Leeds, West Yorkshire, England

Henck P. J. G. van Bilsen, Psychotherapist and Behavior Therapist, Head of Child Guidance Clinic, Institute for Child and Adolescent Psychology, Rotterdam, The Netherlands

Celia Wilkinson, BSc (Hons), Research Associate, Addiction Studies Unit, Curtin University of Technology, Perth, Western Australia

Allen Zweben, DSW, Associate Professor, School of Social Welfare, University of Wisconsin—Milwaukee, Milwaukee, Wisconsin

Preface

People change in many different ways and for a multitude of reasons. The psychology of change is a broad and fascinating subject in its own right. In one sense, in fact, psychology *is* the science of change.

This book represents one aspect of the larger topic of change. As therapists, we are fascinated by what motivates change in people struggling with personal problems. It is a common problem for people to seem "stuck," to persist in patterns of behavior that clearly harm them and those around them. It is an old complaint: "I do not understand my own actions. For I do not do what I want, but I do the very thing I hate" (Romans 7:15, Revised Standard Version).

Nowhere is this problem more clearly seen than in what have come to be called the "addictive behaviors": alcohol and other drug abuse, eating disorders, pathological gambling, and other compulsions (Miller, 1980; Peele, 1985). They represent what Orford (1985) has called "excessive appetites." A defining characteristic of addictive behaviors is that they involve the pursuit of short-term gratification at the expense of long-term harm. Often the person is quite aware of damaging consequences, and has resolved to control or abandon the addictive behavior, yet time and again returns to the old familiar pattern. The addictive behaviors are chronic relapsing conditions (Brownell, Marlatt, Lichtenstein, & Wilson, 1986; Marlatt & Gordon, 1985).

This problem is by no means restricted to the addictive behaviors. A central characteristic of the neuroses, as Freud and his students described them, is their self-defeating nature. Books and self-help programs abound to help people with motivational problems that are variously described as difficulties of procrastination, self-esteem, self-assertion, positive thinking, and "getting unstuck" (e.g., Simon, 1988). Within religious contexts, conceptions of sin often emphasize the struggle of immediate gratification against higher values. Our colleague Tim Stockwell once quipped that "*Life* is a chronic relapsing condition."

What we hope to offer in this book is a clear understanding of how people can be trapped by ambivalence, and how those who want to help them can strengthen their motivation for change. The audience to whom we have addressed ourselves here consists of our professional colleagues: counselors, psychologists, members of the clergy, social workers, physicians, nurses, and any others whose work includes therapeutic engagement with people in need of change. The principles and approaches we describe are more broadly applicable in fields such as business, education, and management, but our focus here is on the therapeutic context. Most of our discussions and examples are explicitly directed to the addictive behaviors, because our own treatment and research have centered in this area, and it was in working with problem drinkers that the concept of motivational interviewing was developed. Nevertheless, we hope that the ideas and approaches we present will be helpful in working with a wide range of clients and problem areas.

Motivational interviewing is an approach designed to help clients build commitment and reach a decision to change. It draws on strategies from client-centered counseling, cognitive therapy, systems theory, and the social psychology of persuasion. The appearance of a motivational interviewing session is quite client-centered; yet the counselor maintains a strong sense of purpose and direction, and actively chooses the right moment to intervene in incisive ways. In this sense, it combines elements of directive and nondirective approaches. It can be integrated with a broad range of strategies, and can also be used to prepare a motivational foundation for other approaches (e.g., behavioral training, cognitive therapy, attending Twelve-Step groups, taking medication).

The theoretical basis of motivational interviewing lies in two broad areas. It draws heavily on the construct of "ambivalence" and the conflict between indulgence and restraint that is so clearly seen in the addictive behaviors (Orford, 1985). Failure to change a behavior that is causing problems is a phenomenon that extends well beyond the addictions, however, and the immobilizing effects of ambivalence can be seen in many spheres. A more general conceptual base, then, is found in theory and research on "self-regulation" (Kanfer, 1987; Miller & Brown, 1991). Strategies of motivational interviewing can be understood within this broad framework; they draw on principles of social, cognitive, and motivational psychology.

A few additional comments are in order. First, we present motivational interviewing as *one* approach, not as the *only* correct and proper way to proceed with clients. Although we have found this approach to be useful with many different types of people and problems, there are surely those for whom a different strategy would be more effective. Nothing works for everyone, and current knowledge of how to match clients with optimal intervention styles is quite imperfect. Similarly, we believe that not all counselors can use this approach well. In teaching motivational interviewing, we have found that trainees vary widely in how readily they can learn, apply, and be comfortable with this approach. It represents something of a polar opposite from an authoritarian, confrontational style. Some clinicians seem to "recognize" motivational interviewing and take to it quickly as a natural style for their work. Others perceive it to be a frustrating, slow-paced, ineffectual approach. Such differences are to be expected.

The unusual authorship of this volume deserves comment. We set out only to write a clear explanation of the whys and hows of motivational interviewing. That book is found in the first 12 chapters of this volume, which are our original work. As we wrote, however, we realized that over the years we have had many companions on the journey, and we decided to invite a number of these colleagues to contribute their own perspectives, based on their pioneering work with motivational interviewing. The result is Part III, in which 17 clinicians describe their applications of motivational interviewing in Australia, England, The Netherlands, Scotland, and the United States.

A word of informed consent: This approach is likely to change you. The style that we offer here specifically avoids argumentative persuasion, and instead operationally assumes the validity of clients' subjective experiences and perspectives. This aspect involves listening to, acknowledging, and practicing acceptance of (though not acquiescence to) a broad range of client concerns, opinions, preferences, beliefs, emotions, styles, and motivations. We find that this approach has had the effect, on us and on our students, of opening up a broader range of acceptance of human experiences and choices. This is, we believe, an enriching change, and one that deepens self-acceptance as well. Nevertheless, it can also be disquieting and draining at times to maintain this degree of openness to the validity and integrity of others' perspectives, which carries with it a regular questioning and re-evaluation of one's own understanding. One does not emerge unchanged from the practice of motivational interviewing.

Finally, we tender a caution. In what follows, we argue that your personal style can have dramatic effects on people's motivation and change. The principles and strategies that we describe are explicitly intended to help you facilitate change in others. Our research and experience tell us that these are powerful processes. To the extent that this is so, the inherent risks and responsibilities of power must be taken seriously when one sets out on this path. Do not be enchanted by the processes themselves. There is a temptation to become fascinated with the strategies and their influence. When power becomes a focus in itself, energy is channeled into weaponry, influence into control, investment into greed, and healing into self-aggrandizement. Our concern ought not to be with our own power, but with our clients. Therapists have the unique privilege of sharing intimately in many lives at moments of transformation, in a role that blends agent and wide-eyed witness of change. The human processes described in the chapters that follow are change-empowering indeed, as water, air, and sunlight are vital elements in photosynthesis. The growth, even the life of plants can be altered by providing or depriving them of such conditions. We wish you the joy of the gardener, whose pleasure and purpose are found in using skill to nourish life and growth for which the gardener is never the source, but ever a vital participant.

Acknowledgments   We wish to express our appreciation to Professor Nick Heather and the staff of the National Drug and Alcohol Research Centre in Sydney, for their hospitality throughout our time in Australia, during which we met and began this collaboration. Thanks are also due to Eva Congreve for her library support, and to Steve Allsop, Lea Greenaway, Rosemary Kent, and Bill Saunders for their helpful suggestions. Finally, we acknowledge our gratitude to our many clients and students, who have taught (and continue to teach) us that which we now seek to share with you.

WILLIAM R. MILLER
STEPHEN ROLLNICK
Sydney, New South Wales, Australia

Contents

MOTIVATIONAL INTERVIEWING

PART ONE

BACKGROUND

1

The Atmosphere of Change

Men's courses will foreshadow certain ends, to which, if persevered in, they must lead. . . . But if the courses be departed from, the ends will change. Say it is thus with what you show me!
                    —Ebenezer Scrooge to the Ghost of Christmas Yet to Come,
                    in Charles Dickens, *A Christmas Carol*

Healers in all ages have sought to understand and to create the conditions that lead to beneficial change. Precisely what therapeutic steps are taken depend upon the assumptions of those involved. In the prescientific history of medicine, a wild array of cures were prescribed, including bleeding, heating or chilling the body, applying leeches, inducing insulin shock, dunking or spinning the person, inducing vomiting, raising blisters, exorcism, and administering many natural powders and potions. Some of these treatments were effective in some cases. It happened on occasion that the prescribed cure was appropriate for the particular affliction because of biomedical principles that had not yet been discovered. Most of the benefit from such ministrations, however, is now thought to be attributable to common "placebo" factors underlying treatment (Shapiro, 1971).

Yet simply to rename certain healing effects as "placebo" or "nonspecific" is not to understand or explain them. Substantial changes are often observed following the administration of a placebo or minimal intervention, often rivaling in magnitude the effects of "treatment." Faithful compliance with placebo treatment has been found to be predictive of favorable outcome (e.g., Fuller et al., 1986). What is going on here? If benefit is not due to the "specific" effects of treatment, what accounts for change?

Consider another piece of the puzzle. Research indicates that across a broad range of schools of therapy, certain characteristics of *therapists* are associated with successful treatment. Therapists working in the same setting and offering the same treatment approaches show dramatic differences in their rates of client dropouts and successful outcomes. The apparent variations in effectiveness among therapists within specific treatment approaches sometimes exceed those among different treatment modalities (e.g., Luborsky, McLellan, Woody, O'Brien, & Auerbach, 1985; Miller, Taylor, & West, 1980). A majority of client dropouts at a particular clinic may occur within the caseloads of a few staff members (Greenwald & Bartmeier, 1963; Raynes & Patch, 1971; Rosenberg, Gerrein, Manohar, & Liftik, 1976; Rosenberg & Raynes, 1973; Schorer, 1965), and therapist characteristics predicting high dropout rates may be as subtle as vocal tone (Milmoe, Rosenthal, Blane, Chafetz, & Wolf, 1967). In sum, the way in which a therapist interacts with clients appears to be nearly as important as—perhaps more important than—the specific approach or school of thought from which she or he operates.

This suggests that therapist style, a variable often ignored in outcome research, is a major determinant of treatment success (Cartwright, 1981). A *majority* of variance in treatment outcome cannot be accounted for, even by a combination of client pretreatment and posttreatment characteristics and the specific treatment events offered (e.g., Cronkite & Moos, 1980). Recent studies suggest that a substantial proportion of this unexplained variance may be related to therapist style characteristics (e.g., Luborsky et al., 1985). A study at the University of New Mexico found that about two-thirds of the variance in 6-month drinking outcomes could be predicted from the degree of empathy shown by therapists during treatment (Miller et al., 1980). Therapist empathy still accounted for half of the variance in outcomes at 12 months, and a quarter of variance at 24 months after treatment (Miller & Baca, 1983). Similar effects of therapist empathy have been reported in other studies (e.g., Miller & Sovereign, 1989; Valle, 1981).

Specifying Nonspecifics

This is not a new insight. For decades it has been recognized that "nonspecific" factors contribute to treatment. The original use of this term implied that such factors are not specific to particular treatment methods, but cut across all styles of therapy. They are, in essence, those mysterious common healing elements presumed to be present in all forms of therapy.

But there is nothing necessarily mysterious about "nonspecifics." Viewed in another way, this term simply means that these determinants of outcome have not yet been adequately specified. "Nonspecifics" are *unspecified* principles of change. If these factors account for a large part of treatment success, then it is important that they be specified, researched, discussed, and taught. It is not a safe assumption that all therapists somehow know and practice these principles. To say that these principles of change are important, regardless of specific orientation, does not imply that they are manifested equally in all therapists or treatment approaches. In fact, therapists vary dramatically in their effectiveness, and specific treatment approaches or philosophies differ in the extent to which they foster certain therapist styles (Luborsky et al., 1985).

It appears that therapist style characteristics manifest themselves relatively early in the treatment process (Davies, 1979, 1981), and indeed can have a significant impact within a single session (Chafetz, 1961; Chafetz et al., 1962; Miller & Sovereign, 1989). The therapeutic relationship tends to stabilize relatively quickly, and the nature of the client–therapist relationship in early sessions predicts treatment retention and outcome (Luborsky et al., 1985; Tomlinson, 1967).

Critical Conditions of Change

The most clearly articulated and tested theory regarding critical therapist conditions for change is that of Carl Rogers (1959). Rogers asserted that a client-centered interpersonal relationship, in which the therapist manifests three crucial conditions, provides the ideal atmosphere for change. Within the context of such a safe and supportive atmosphere, he maintained, clients are able to explore their experiences openly and to reach resolution of their own problems. The therapist's role, in this view, is not a directive one of providing solutions, suggestions, or analysis. Instead, the therapist need only offer the three critical conditions to prepare the way for natural change: accurate empathy, nonpossessive warmth, and genuineness. The key insights of Rogers have been well translated into practice by his students and by other, more recent writers (Egan, 1982; Gordon, 1970; Ivey, 1980, 1982; Truax & Carkhuff, 1967).

Subsequent evidence has supported the importance of these conditions of change, particularly accurate empathy. This condition should not be confused with the meaning of "empathy" as *identification* with the client, or as the sharing of common past experiences. In fact, a recent personal history of the same problem area (e.g., alcoholism) may compromise a counselor's ability to provide the critical conditions of change, because of overidentification (Manohar, 1973). What Rogers defines as "accurate empathy" involves skillful reflective listening that clarifies and amplifies the client's own experiencing and meaning, without imposing the therapist's own material (Gordon, 1970). (We discuss this skill in detail in Chapter 6.) Manifestation of these critical conditions—especially accurate empathy—has been found to promote therapeutic change in general (Truax & Carkhuff, 1967; Truax & Mitchell, 1971), and recovery from addictive behaviors in particular (Luborsky et al., 1985; Miller et al., 1980; Valle, 1981).

The Evolution of Confrontation

Where Did We Go Wrong?

This picture of the conditions that create a favorable atmosphere for change stands in sharp contrast to approaches often advocated (particularly in the

United States) for treating people with alcohol problems and other addictive behaviors. Consider this quote, from the front page of *The Wall Street Journal*, describing a representative confrontational intervention directed at an executive:

> They called a surprise meeting, surrounded him with colleagues critical of his work and threatened to fire him if he didn't seek help quickly. When the executive tried to deny that he had a drinking problem, the medical director . . . came down hard. "Shut up and listen," he said. "Alcoholics are liars, so we don't want to hear what you have to say." (Greenberger, 1983, p. 1)

Some therapy groups, particularly those organized around a Synanon therapeutic community model, have employed what is called "attack therapy," "the hot seat," or "the emotional haircut." Here is a sample from the lips of Chuck Dederich, founder of Synanon, to a Mexican-American addict:

> Now, Buster, I'm going to tell you what to do. And I'll show you. You either do it or you'll get the hell off Synanon property. You shave off the moustache, you attend groups, and you behave like a gentleman as long as you live here. You don't like it here? God bless you, I'll give you the same good wishes that I gave other people like you when they left and went off to jail. That's the way we operate in Synanon; you see, you're getting a little emotional surgery. If you don't like the surgery, fine, go and do what you have to. Maybe we'll get you again after you get out of the penitentiary or after you get a drug overdose. "Nobody tells me what to do!" Nobody in the world says that except dingbats like dope fiends, alcoholics, and brush-face-covered El Gatos. (Yablonsky, 1989, p. 122)

Approaches such as these would be regarded as ludicrous and unprofessional treatment for the vast majority of psychological or medical problems from which people suffer. Imagine these same words being used as therapy for someone suffering from depression, anxiety, marital problems, sexual dysfunction, schizophrenia, cancer, hypertension, heart disease, or diabetes. Aggressive confrontational tactics have been largely reserved for those suffering from alcohol and other drug problems, and for certain other groups such as criminal offenders.

It is commonly believed that such individuals *need* this different kind of treatment, and are not affected by ordinary therapeutic principles and processes. Confrontation of this harsh variety has been believed to be uniquely effective—perhaps the only effective strategy for dealing with alcoholics and addicts. Yet confrontational strategies of this kind have not been supported by clinical outcome studies. Therapist behaviors associated with this approach have been shown to predict treatment failure, whereas accurate empathy—an almost exact opposite of hostile confrontation (Gordon, 1970)—is associated with successful outcomes. Confrontational group therapy, in fact, has been found to yield more harmful and adverse outcomes than alternative approaches (Lieberman, Yalom, & Miles, 1973), and may be particularly damaging for individuals with low self-esteem (Annis & Chan, 1983). There is, in short, no persuasive evidence that aggressive confrontational tactics are even helpful, let alone superior or preferable strategies in the treatment of addictive behaviors or other problems.

Where did we go wrong? How did we come to believe that a certain class of human beings is possessed of a unique condition that requires us to use aggressive confrontation if we wish to help them? How did it become believable, justifiable, and acceptable to rely upon such hostile tactics for addressing certain addictive behaviors, when these same approaches would be seen as reflecting at best poor judgment (if not malpractice) in treating most other psychological and medical problems?

These tactics are sometimes associated with and attributed to the Twelve-Step fellowships, perhaps because treatment programs that have used them have also commonly embraced the philosophy of Alcoholics Anonymous (AA) or Narcotics Anonymous (NA). Yet this kind of coercive confrontation is wholly at odds with the origins of AA, as reflected in the writings of Bill Wilson (Alcoholics Anonymous, 1976). AA is meant to operate by attraction and support: "Recovery begins when one alcoholic talks with another alcoholic, sharing experience, strength, and hope" (p. xxii). Wilson advocated an approach to life that "would contain no basis for contention or argument. . . . Most of us sense that real tolerance of other people's shortcomings and viewpoints and a respect for their opinions are attitudes which make us more useful to others" (pp. 19–20). Writing on how to work with alcoholics, Wilson advised:

> Let him steer the conversation in any direction he likes. . . . You will be most successful with alcoholics if you do not exhibit any passion for crusade or reform. Never talk down to an alcoholic. . . . He must decide for himself whether he wants to go on. He should not be pushed or prodded. . . . If he thinks he can do the job in some other way, or prefers some other spiritual approach, encourage him to follow his own conscience. We have no monopoly on God; we merely have an approach that worked with us. (Alcoholics Anonymous, 1976, p. 95)

Clearly, Bill Wilson did not favor coercive, directive, and authoritarian tactics in dealing with alcoholics. These are, in fact, anathema to the gentle approach and spiritual way of life he outlined in "the big book."

Motivation as a Personality Problem

A key assumption underlying aggressive confrontational strategies is that alcoholics (drug addicts, offenders, etc.)—*as a class*, and as an inherent part of their condition—possess extraordinarily high levels of certain defense mechanisms, which render them inaccessible by ordinary means of therapy and persuasion. It has been believed that these are deeply ingrained in such individuals' personality and character. This assumption appears to have arisen from psychodynamic thinking, which viewed alcohol and other drug problems as symptomatic of a personality disorder (Clancy, 1961; DiCicco, Unterberger, & Mack, 1978; Moore & Murphy, 1961). The disorder was believed to be reflected in excessive reliance upon some of the more primitive ego defense mechanisms described by Anna Freud (1948). This view was adopted and espoused by influential early professionals in the alcoholism field, such as psychiatrist Ruth Fox (1967), who summarized her clinical experience in psychodynamic terms: "Most patients refuse to face their alcoholism for many years, using the defense mechanisms of denial, rationalization, regression, and projection" (p. 772). The alcoholic, she wrote, "builds up an elaborate defense system in which he denies that he is alcoholic and ill, rationalizes that he needs to drink for business or health or social reasons, and projects the blame for the trouble he is in" (p. 771). These alleged attributes came to be seen as universal, inherent elements of the character structure of alcoholics and drug addicts, and substantial impediments to recovery (e.g., Clancy, 1961). "The layers of denial in alcoholism run deep and present an almost impenetrable wall" (DiCicco et al., 1978, p. 600).

Once the assumption of pernicious inherent defense mechanisms is accepted, the question follows: How should one deal with such robust and formidable defenses? The processes through which the recovering person must pass came to be described in such terms as "surrender," "accepting powerlessness," and "reduction of ego" (Cavaiola, 1984; Clancy, 1964; Tiebout, 1953, 1954; Wilson, 1977). These concepts arose with or evolved from the AA idea that an alcoholic naturally "hits bottom" in the course of his or her drinking career. Gradually this idea of hitting bottom came to be reformulated as a developmental crisis (Bateson, 1971) that might be precipitated or hastened by intervention strategies (DiCicco et al., 1978). The perceived need for "surrender" suggested the tactic of attacking defenses. The stage was set for the entry of confrontation.

This idea of using confrontation to crush defenses was particularly championed by Vernon Johnson (1973), and came to be associated with a broad and influential treatment philosophy known as "the Minnesota model." Legitimate interest in the biomedical "disease" aspects of addictive behaviors became confused with the belief that chemical dependency represents a unique *personality* disease that renders sufferers qualitatively different from normal individuals or those with other problems, and incapable (by virtue of denial) of seeing reality.

> The primary factor within [alcoholism] is the delusion, or impaired judgment, which keeps the harmfully dependent person locked into his self-

destructive pattern. . . . The alcoholic evades or denies outright any need
for help whenever he is approached. It must be remembered that he is not
in touch with reality. (Johnson, 1973, p. 44)

This condition can be seen as justifying the use of unusually aggressive
treatment strategies and, by virtue of the poor judgment supposed to inhere
in the condition, coercive intervention.

However, the approach espoused by Johnson (1973) is in fact a broad
one, in which confrontation is defined as "presenting a person with himself
by describing how I see him" (p. 121). Johnson explicitly emphasized the
importance of empathic listening, and described a form of counseling that is
more compassionate than aggressive. Programs espousing the Minnesota
model have more recently repudiated aggressive confrontation and emphasized gentler approaches (Hazelden Foundation, 1985; Johnson Institute,
1987). It appears, then, that responsibility for the practice of aggressively
confrontational counseling tactics cannot be assigned to Johnson, the Minnesota model, or AA.

There seems to be no single clear historic source for the aggressively
confrontational tactics that sometimes dominate addiction treatment programs. Certainly a strong emphasis on ego reduction through confrontation
is found in Synanon, which was founded by an alcoholic recovering through
AA, and became a prototype for therapeutic communities (Yablonsky, 1965,
1989). Proponents of Synanon and the similar Daytop model, working with
younger drug addicts, developed and promoted approaches that manifest
the more authoritarian, aggressive, and coercive meanings often associated
with the term "confrontational."

Such confrontational approaches, reflected in the examples provided
earlier, do not arise from any coherent theoretical understanding of the
addictive behaviors. They are inconsistent with the precepts of AA (Alcoholics Anonymous, 1976) as outlined by Bill Wilson, and violate the empathic tone of Johnson's (1973) writings. They appear to have arisen gradually in *practice*, guided in part by the vaguely psychodynamic belief that
alcoholics and others with drug problems are characterized by "an addictive
personality" or unusually "strong defenses."

The Search for an Addictive Personality

Curiously, this idea of a common alcoholic or addictive personality is
supported neither in the original writings of AA, nor by five decades of
psychological research (Miller, 1976). Vaillant (1983), tracing a group of
men over 40 years of development, found no distinctive personality traits
predictive of adult alcoholism. When defense mechanisms have been opera-

tionally defined and specifically examined, denial has been found to be no more characteristic of alcoholics than of nonalcoholics (Chess, Neuringer, & Goldstein, 1971; Donovan, Rohsenow, Schau, & O'Leary, 1977; Skinner & Allen, 1983). Individual-difference measures of denial within alcoholic populations have also yielded curious results. Successful outcomes have sometimes been related to *higher* levels of pretreatment denial (O'Leary, Rohsenow, Schau, & Donovan, 1977) and nonacceptance of the label "alcoholic" (Orford, 1973). Trait denial has been reported to *increase* from the beginning to the end of treatment (Baumann, Obitz, & Reich, 1982). In sum, there is not and never has been a scientific basis for the assertion that alcoholics (let alone people suffering from *all* addictive behaviors) manifest a common consistent personality pattern characterized by excessive ego defense mechanisms.

Denial need not be defined as a personality trait. It may, alternatively, be seen merely as refusal to admit problems, even conscious deception and lying. Is problem recognition prognostic of good outcome? Studies have found acceptance of self-labeling as "alcoholic" to be unrelated to treatment outcome (Lemere, O'Hollaren, & Maxwell, 1958; Trice, 1957), or even negatively related to recovery (Orford, 1973). A high level of problem recognition is common among unremitted alcoholics (Polich, Armor, & Braiker, 1980). Again, it has not been shown that individuals with alcohol and other drug problems display pathological lying or an abnormal level of self-deception; nor does it appear to be the case that self-labeling promotes recovery.

To summarize, research does *not* support the belief that there is a common personality core or set of robust defenses that is characteristic of people suffering from alcohol and other drug abuse. If such people show consistencies of behavior (such as resistance or defensiveness) in the counselor's office, it appears that they do not possess these consistencies before walking through the door. Importantly, the combative intervention strategies suggested by this model appear to be generally ineffective.

The Self-Fulfilling Prophecy

How, then, have professionals become so convinced that alcoholics and other drug abusers are characterologically denying, lying, rationalizing, evasive, defensive, and resistant people and need to be treated as such? Yablonsky (1989), for example, opined: "Almost all substance abusers in the early phase of the addiction process, when confronted about their addiction deny they are addicted" (p. 4). If the consistency does not result from a pervasive personality pathology within this population, then how do these perceptions arise?

There are several possibilities. One is that the observation is simply erroneous, but is maintained by processes of selective (mis)perception. Chapman and Chapman (1967) described the phenomenon of "illusory correlation," whereby people can form an inaccurate conviction that two events are associated with each other. A common example is the mistaken belief that a particular response to Rorschach's inkblot test is indicative of a certain pathological condition. Thus it was incorrectly believed for some time that people who reported water percepts in Rorschach's test had alcoholic tendencies (Griffith, 1961). Such beliefs are notoriously difficult to remove. Once the belief has been established, it is reconfirmed by at least occasional observation of cases where the two events *do* coincide, while inconsistent cases are ignored or forgotten. Racial prejudices can be maintained by this same process. Thus the belief in the stereotypic "resistant, denying alcoholic" may be maintained by the salient memory of particular *cases* who illustrate these characteristics. The anecdotal basis of much clinical instruction in this area readily lends itself to such error: An example becomes a principle.

But selective perception is not the only means by which the denial myth may be perpetuated. Such perceptions may be based upon regular, repeated observations of actual behaviors that conform to the belief system. That is, clients may truly and frequently show behaviors consistent with the clinical impression of "denial." One way in which this may occur is that *normal* behaviors may be misinterpreted as abnormal and indicative of pathology. Orford (1985), for example, maintained that normal psychological phenomena such as ambivalence (see Chapter 4) are often labeled as pathological when they are associated with addictive behaviors. That is, experiences and behaviors that follow ordinary principles of psychology are mistakenly interpreted as special symptoms indicative of unique addictive pathology (e.g., denial, craving, loss of control).

Still another possibility is that the interpersonal style and context of addictions counseling *create* behavioral consistencies in clients through predictable psychological processes. Psychological "reactance," for example, is a predictable pattern of emotion and behavior that occurs when an individual perceives that his or her personal freedom is being reduced or threatened (Brehm, 1966; Brehm & Brehm, 1981). When a person is accused of possessing an undesirable characteristic or identity ("You're a liar" or "You are an alcoholic"), or is told that he or she *must, should,* or *cannot* do something, the response is predictable. The person is likely to argue with (deny) the accuracy of what has been said, and to assert his or her personal freedom. This reaction may be particularly strong when the topic is one about which the person is ambivalent (Miller, 1983). This phenomenon is by no means unique to the addictive behaviors; it is a general psychological principle.

The point, however, is that certain kinds of counseling strategies—particularly those that are more directive, coercive, or confrontational—are quite likely to *evoke* reactance in most people. Consider what happens if these strategies are employed by a counselor who suspects clients to be "in denial." The counseling tactics in themselves pull for resistance in a client. When such reactance is shown, however, it confirms in the counselor's mind both the client's diagnosis and the counselor's general belief that clients of this type characteristically deny and resist. This is the familiar psychological phenomenon of "self-fulfilling prophecy" (Jones, 1977).

That this is a very real possibility was demonstrated by Patterson and Forgatch (1985). Observing a recorded series of family therapy sessions, they classified all therapist and client behaviors and examined interrelationships. They found that therapist attempts to teach and confront were associated with higher levels of client resistance. In a subsequent experiment, they had therapists switch back and forth between high and low levels of confrontation, alternating these styles in blocks of about 12 minutes within sessions. Clients' resistance behaviors increased substantially during the confrontational periods, and dropped when the therapists changed style. Using this same system for recording behaviors of therapists and clients, Miller and Sovereign (1989) found that problem drinkers *randomly* assigned to confrontational counseling showed much higher levels of resistance (arguing, changing the subject, interrupting, denying a problem) than did those given a more client-centered motivational interviewing approach. In this same study, therapist behaviors during a single session were highly predictive of clients' drinking more than a year later. The more a therapist had confronted, the more a client was drinking a year later; the more the therapist had been supportive and listening, the more the client changed.

This, then, offers a rather disturbing alternative explanation of how it is that a particular client population may show high levels of "denial," even though this is not generally characteristic of such clients outside the treatment context. From the research evidence available, the denial hypothesis—that alcoholics or "chemically dependent" people *as a class* evidence particular personality abnormalities or unusually high levels of certain defenses—is a myth. Whether it is maintained by illusory correlation, misconstrual of normal ambivalence, or self-fulfilling prophecy, the evidence simply does not support it. What a client *does* typically bring to counseling is ambivalence (see Chapter 4), and it is the therapist's handling of such ambivalence that influences the degree of client resistance and change. The powerful denial myth from the drug counseling field offers a more general and humbling warning to clinicians: that it is possible to become quite convinced of mistaken beliefs, even ones that ultimately lead toward countertherapeutic attitudes and approaches.

Confrontation: A Goal, Not a Style

Some of the confusion in this area probably arises from the multiple ways in which people have used the term "confrontation." In one sense it connotes the heavy-handed and coercive tactics of Synanon, Daytop, and Scared Straight. It suggests uneven power—an authoritarian one-up pounding the truth into a defiant one-down. This is a style that complements personal or societal attitudes of anger toward the one-downs, and individual needs for power or abasement.

Yet in a different sense, confrontation is a *goal* of all counseling and psychotherapy, and is a prerequisite for intentional change. "The goal of the intervention," says Johnson, "is to have him see and accept enough reality so that, however grudgingly, he can accept in turn his need for help" (1973, p. 51). More generally, the purpose of confrontation is *to see and accept reality*, so that one can change accordingly. This may or may not happen in the context of counseling. Certainly it occurs outside treatment. Coming face to face with a disquieting image of oneself may be the precipitating force in many changes that occur without formal intervention (Orford, 1985).

In this larger sense, confrontation is a goal, a purpose, an aim. It is part of the change process, and therefore part of the helping process. Viewed in this way, confrontation is a goal in many different forms of treatment for a wide variety of problems (Prochaska & DiClemente, 1984). This kind of awareness-raising "confrontation" is quite consistent with the client-centered philosophy of Carl Rogers, who sought to provide people with a therapeutic atmosphere in which they could safely examine themselves and change. It is found in schools of psychotherapy that emphasize insight. To see one's situation clearly is a first step in change. This is the goal of confrontation.

The question, then, is this: What are the most effective ways for helping people to examine and accept reality, particularly uncomfortable reality? It is to this question that we turn in Chapter 2.

2

What Motivates People to Change?

Cut yer name across me backbone,
　　Stretch me skin across a drum,
Iron me up to Pinchgut Island
　　From today till Kingdom Come!
I will eat your Norfolk Dumpling
　　Like a juicy Spanish plum,
Even dance the Newgate hornpipe,
　　If you'll only give me rum!

　—19th-century Australian convict song,
　　quoted in Robert Hughes, *The Fatal Shore*

Motivation as a State

In Chapter 1, we have questioned a common assumption, particularly in the field of addictive behaviors, that resistance is the result of pernicious personality traits (e.g., "denial") and that clients are inherently unmotivated to change. We have pointed to research evidence indicating that factors sometimes called "nonspecifics" are important determinants of whether and how much change occurs, and have indicated that therapist style characteristics influence client motivation and outcomes. It seems clear that a person's motivation for change is affected by a variety of conditions outside his or her skin.

We suggest, then, that motivation should not be thought of as a personality problem, or as a trait that a person carries through the counselor's doorway. Rather, motivation is a *state* of readiness or eagerness to change, which may fluctuate from one time or situation to another. This state is one that can be influenced.

One helpful model of how change occurs has been developed by psychologists James Prochaska and Carlo DiClemente (1982). These researchers have sought to understand how and why people change, either on their own or with the assistance of a therapist. They have described a series of stages through which people pass in the course of changing a problem.

These stages seem to apply equally well to self-change and to therapy-assisted change. That is, in or out of therapy, people seem to pass through similar stages and to employ similar processes of change. Within this approach, motivation can be understood as a person's present state or stage of readiness for change. It is an internal state influenced by external factors.

The "wheel of change" derived from the Prochaska–DiClemente model can be drawn with four, five, or six stages. We have chosen the five-part wheel shown in Figure 2.1, with a sixth stage (precontemplation) lying outside the wheel. Before we describe the six specific stages of change, notice several aspects of this wheel. First, the fact that it *is* a wheel, a circle, reflects the reality that in almost any change process, it is normal for the person to go around the process several times before achieving a stable change. In their initial research with smokers, for example, Prochaska and DiClemente found that smokers ordinarily went around the wheel between three and seven times (with an average of about four) before finally quitting for good. This wheel also thereby recognizes relapse as a normal occurrence or stage of change. We sometimes tell our clients, "Each slip or relapse brings you one step closer to recovery." This is not, of course, meant to be an encouragement to relapse; rather, it is a realistic perspective to keep them from becoming disheartened, demoralized, or bogged down when a relapse occurs. By discriminating different stages of readiness for change, this model also implies that a counselor should take different approaches with a client, depending upon where she or he is in the process of change (Davidson, Rollnick, & MacEwan, 1991). Different skills are needed, for example, in working at the contemplation and at the action stages. We believe that

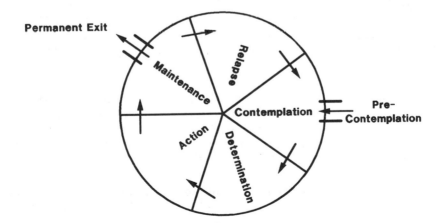

FIGURE 2.1. Prochaska and DiClemente's six stages of change.

problems of clients' being "unmotivated" or "resistant" occur when a counselor is using strategies inappropriate for a client's current stage of change.

The entry point to the process of change (which is here drawn as lying outside the wheel) is the "Precontemplation" stage. At this point the person is not yet considering the possibility of change. Before the first time around the wheel, the person has not even contemplated having a problem or needing to make a change. A person who is approached at this stage and told he or she has a problem may be more surprised than defensive. Needless to say, precontemplators seldom present themselves for treatment. They may come under coercion, though by this time they are more likely to be defensive contemplators. The very use of the term "precontemplator" assumes that someone else knows of the person's problem, even though he or she is unaware of it. Such people may be identified, for example, during a routine medical examination; from elevated blood test scores indicative of liver damage from excessive drinking (Kristenson, Ohlin, Hulten-Nosslin, Trell, & Hood, 1983); or through a questionnaire-based screening procedure (Chick, Lloyd, & Crombie, 1985; Wallace, Cutler, & Haines, 1988). A person in the precontemplation stage needs information and feedback to raise his or her awareness of the problem and the possibility of change. Giving prescriptive advice at this stage can be counterproductive (Rollnick & MacEwan, 1991).

Once some awareness of the problem arises, the person enters a period characterized by ambivalence: the "contemplation" stage. The contemplator both considers change and rejects it. Allowed to talk about the problem area without interference, the contemplator is likely to go back and forth between reasons for concern and justifications for unconcern. This is a normal and characteristic stage of change, though sometimes its manifestations are misattributed to pathological personality traits or defense mechanisms. The contemplator's experience may be described as a kind of seesawing between reasons to change and reasons to stay the same (we say more about this in Chapter 4). A problem drinker in the contemplation stage, for example, may say something like this:

> I don't think I really have a "problem" with drinking. Probably I do drink too much for my own health, but I don't drink any more than my friends do. Sometimes I feel pretty bad the next morning, and it worries me when I can't remember things now and then. But I'm not an alcoholic. I can quit drinking whenever I want to, and I don't miss it.

The contemplator simultaneously (or in rapid alternation) experiences reasons for concern and for unconcern, motivations to change and to continue unchanged. The counselor's task at this stage is to help tip the balance in favor of change. It is common for people to come for consultation in the contemplation stage, and it is here that motivational interviewing may be particularly useful. A counselor who launches into strategies appropriate for the action stage at this point is likely to engender resistance.

From time to time the balance tips, and for a span of time the person's statements reflect a good deal of what might be judged to be "motivation." At this "determination" stage, a client may say things like these:

- I've *got* to do something about this problem!
- This is serious! Something has to change.
- What can I do? How can I change?

We think of the determination stage as something like a window of opportunity, which opens for a period of time. If during this time the person enters into action, the change process continues. If not, the person slips back into contemplation. The counselor's task when a client is in the determination stage is not one of motivating so much as matching—helping him or her find a change strategy that is acceptable, accessible, appropriate, and effective. Phase II strategies of motivational interviewing (see Chapter 9) are especially relevant here.

The "action" stage is what people most often think of as counseling or therapy. Here the person engages in particular actions intended to bring about a change. These efforts may or may not be assisted by formal counseling. Most people who quit smoking, for example, do so on their own, without treatment of any kind. The goal during this stage is to produce a change in the problem area.

Making a change, however, does not guarantee that the change will be maintained. Obviously, human experience is filled with good intentions and initial changes, followed by minor ("slips") or major ("relapses") steps backward. During the "maintenance" stage, the challenge is to sustain the change accomplished by previous action, and to prevent relapse (Marlatt & Gordon, 1985). Maintaining a change may require a different set of skills and strategies than were needed to accomplish the change in the first place. Quitting a drug, reducing drinking, or losing weight is an initial step, followed by the challenge of maintaining abstinence or moderation.

Finally, if "relapse" occurs, the individual's task is to start around the wheel again rather than getting stuck in this stage. Slips and relapses are normal, expected occurrences as a person seeks to change any long-standing pattern. The counselor's task here is to help the person avoid discouragement and demoralization, continue contemplating change, renew determination, and resume action and maintenance efforts. These stages and the corresponding counseling tasks are outlined in Table 2.1.

TABLE 2.1. Stages of Change and Therapist Tasks

Client stage	Therapist's motivational tasks
Precontemplation	Raise doubt—increase the client's perception of risks and problems with current behavior
Contemplation	Tip the balance—evoke reasons to change, risks of not changing; strengthen the client's self-efficacy for change of current behavior
Determination	Help the client to determine the best course of action to take in seeking change
Action	Help the client to take steps toward change
Maintenance	Help the client to identify and use strategies to prevent relapse
Relapse	Help the client to renew the processes of contemplation, determination, and action, without becoming stuck or demoralized because of relapse

Motivation as a Behavior Probability

Yet what *is* motivation? A counselor often judges a person's "motivation" from a number of behaviors such as the following:

- Agreeing with the counselor
- Accepting the counselor's diagnosis (e.g., admitting that he or she is "alcoholic")
- Expressing a desire or need for help
- Appearing to be distressed about his or her condition
- Following the counselor's advice

Conversely, a counselor may tend to judge as "unmotivated" (or "resistant" or "in denial") a person who does the following:

- Disagrees with the counselor
- Refuses to accept the counselor's diagnosis or judgment
- Expresses no desire or need for help
- Appears undistressed about his or her current condition
- Does not follow the counselor's advice

Warren Farrell once mused that disagreeing with one's therapist is called "denial," and if one later comes to agree with the therapist it is called "insight." The point is that we often judge clients' motivation by what they *say*.

Yet our greater concern as therapists is usually with what clients *do*. The verbal statements that cause a client to be judged as "motivated" are no guarantee that the client will actually change. As we have noted in Chapter 1, there is little evidence that accepting a diagnosis (e.g., "I am an alcoholic") is predictive of recovery. Many unrecovered individuals freely admit their problems or accept a diagnostic label, and many others recover without consciously endorsing a sick role or diagnosis and asking for help. It is no news that people often say one thing and do another.

What *does* appear to predict change is a person's actual adherence to advice or a plan. Those who faithfully take a prescribed medication, for example, are considerably more likely to recover than those who do not comply with advice, even when the "medication" is a placebo with no active ingredients (e.g., Fuller et al., 1986). Following the therapist's advice or, more generally, adhering to a systematic program for change is associated with successful outcomes.

This suggests a more specific and pragmatic understanding of motivation. If a key dimension of motivation is adherence to or compliance with a change program, then motivation may be thought of as a *probability* of certain behaviors. This is, in many ways, a more practical and more optimistic approach than viewing motivation either as a personality trait or as a general internal state of readiness. Psychologists have learned a great deal about how to *change* behavior probabilities. A century of research on learning has given us a range of conceptual models and practical tools for increasing or decreasing the likelihood that specific behaviors will occur.

If we take this pragmatic approach, "motivation" can be defined as *the probability that a person will enter into, continue, and adhere to a specific change strategy* (Council for Philosophical Studies, 1981; Miller, 1985b). Notice how specific this definition is. A given individual may well be motivated to participate in one form of treatment but not another, to work on one problem but not another, or to continue seeing one particular therapist but not another. Perhaps something called "treatment" is unacceptable, but the person is motivated to join a self-help group. This specificity is readily confirmed by clinical experience, and further clarifies that motivation is not a general trait existing within the skin of the individual, but depends on the context. It shifts the emphasis from the passive adjective "motivated" to the active verb "motivate." Motivation becomes an important part of the counselor's task. It is the counselor's responsibility not only to dispense advice, but to *motivate*—to increase the likelihood that the client will follow a recommended course of action toward change. From this perspective, it is no longer sensible for a therapist to blame a client for being unmotivated to change, any more than a salesperson would blame a potential customer for being unmotivated to buy. Motivation is an inherent and central part of the professional's task.

Effective Motivational Approaches

This raises a practical question: What strategies can a counselor use to enhance motivation for change? If motivation is a behavior probability, then it is reasonable to look for specific techniques that increase the probability of change behaviors. There is a very large research literature on what motivates people for change and treatment, which has been reviewed in detail elsewhere (Miller, 1985b). We summarize this literature here by describing eight general motivational strategies. No one of these strategies is magic. Effective approaches typically combine several of these motivational strategies, as we discuss in Chapter 3. For now, however, we present these eight building blocks, which (conveniently for mnemonic purposes) run alphabetically from A through H:

Giving ADVICE
Removing BARRIERS
Providing CHOICE
Decreasing DESIRABILITY
Practicing EMPATHY
Providing FEEDBACK
Clarifying GOALS
Active HELPING

In this chapter we provide only an introduction to these strategies. The practical, "how-to" clinical applications are developed in Part II of this book, where these general themes are woven together into the systematic approach of motivational interviewing.

Giving ADVICE

One element that stimulates a change is clear advice. Although we have great respect for the insights and approaches of Carl Rogers, a wholly nondirective strategy can leave a client confused and floundering. Well-timed and tempered advice to change can make a difference. For example, brief and systematic advice from a physician has been found to increase (albeit modestly) the likelihood that medical patients will stop smoking or change their alcohol use (Chick et al., 1985; Elvy, Wells, & Baird, 1988; Kristenson et al., 1983; Russell, Wilson, Taylor, & Baker, 1979; Wallace et al., 1988). In other studies with patients visiting a hospital emergency room for alcohol-related illnesses and injuries, a single session of counseling advice increased the rate of returning for treatment from 5% to 65% (Chafetz, 1961; Chafetz et al., 1962) and from 6% to 78% (Chafetz, 1968; Chafetz et al., 1964). Advice alone is not likely to be sufficient to induce change in a majority of individuals, but the motivating influence of clear and compassionate advice should not be overlooked.

The elements of effective advice are being clarified through current research. At a minimum, advice should (1) clearly identify the problem or risk area, (2) explain why change is important, and (3) advocate specific change. Providing the individual with specific alternative strategies for change may help him or her follow the advised course of change. Brief advice interventions are discussed in more detail in the next chapter.

Removing BARRIERS

A second effective motivation approach is to identify and remove significant barriers to change efforts. A contemplator, for example, may be willing to consider entering treatment, but also may be inhibited or discouraged from doing so by specific practical barriers (e.g., cost, transportation, child care, shyness, waiting time, or safety concerns). One study found that attendance at aftercare meetings could be predicted from the distance a person had to travel in order to attend (Prue, Keane, Cornell, & Foy, 1979). Such barriers may interfere not only with treatment entry, but with change efforts more generally. Effective motivational counseling helps a client to identify and overcome these inhibiting factors. Once such barriers are identified, the counselor's task is to assist the client in practical problem solving. How could these barriers be overcome? If the client has regular child care responsibilities, how can the children be cared for while the parent is attending treatment? If the person needs transportation or is reluctant to go alone, what alternatives are available?

A good example of the power of simple strategies for overcoming barriers is provided in a report by Sisson and Mallams (1981). Their goal was to motivate clients to begin attending Alcoholics Anonymous (AA) meetings. One group was given the usual encouragement: an explanation of the importance of attendance, a schedule of available meeting times and places, and exhortation to attend. A second group, chosen at random, received systematic help in overcoming barriers to attendance. While the client was in the office, the counselor placed a prearranged telephone call to an AA member, who then spoke to the client, offering to provide transportation and to accompany him or her to the first meeting. They agreed on a meeting time, and the member obtained the client's telephone number in order to place a reminder call on the evening before the agreed-upon meeting. The results could not have been more marked. Every client in the latter group attended AA; in the former (encouragement) group, not a single client made it to the first AA meeting.

Most barriers have to do with *access* to treatment or other change strategies. Some, such as economic and transportation factors, are very tangible. The accessibility of buildings to handicapped persons is another obvious example. Other access factors are less tangible but also significant: delays, comfort, a sense of belonging, cultural appropriateness. Long delays in a waiting room or assignment to a waiting list can discourage participation. It may be better to offer clients an effective brief intervention, such as the type we describe in Chapter 3, than to place them on a waiting list for treatment (e.g., Harris & Miller, 1990; Sanchez-Craig, 1990; Schmidt & Miller, 1983).

Special barriers may need to be addressed in dealing with men versus women, or different age groups (e.g., youths, the elderly) and ethnic/racial populations. Such special populations may not require unique *treatment* approaches so much as efforts to ensure that effective treatment is provided in an accessible, comfortable, and appropriate manner. Child care during treatment is an access issue for many women. Transportation and safety may be special concerns for the elderly. Language and cultural sensitivity are issues in counseling people from different racial and cultural backgrounds.

Finally, some barriers to change are more attitudinal than overt. A person may fear that changing will result in adverse consequences (Hall, 1979) or cut off important sources of positive reinforcement. An individual's circle of friends or cultural context may encourage the perception that the "problem" behaviors are really quite normal and acceptable, and that no change is needed. Removal of these barriers to change may require more cognitive and informational strategies.

Providing CHOICES

Few people like to be told what to do, or forced to take a particular course of action. In fact, resistance can be expected when a person perceives that his or her freedom is being limited or threatened (Brehm, 1966; Brehm & Brehm, 1981). Intrinsic motivation is enhanced by the perception that one has freely chosen a course of action, without significant external influence or coercion (Deci, 1975, 1980; Parker, Winstead, & Willi, 1979). A counselor who wishes to enhance motivation for change, then, is well advised to help clients feel their freedom (and indeed responsibility) of personal choice.

This assumes that there are alternatives available to the individual. Perceived choice is not encouraged in a system where people are coerced to take a particular course of action, or in programs where a relatively standard treatment is provided for all clients (Orford & Hawker, 1974). Offering clients a choice among alternative approaches may decrease resistance and dropout, and may improve both compliance and outcome (Costello, 1975; Kissin, Platz, & Su, 1971; Parker et al., 1979; Sanchez-Craig, 1990). Similarly, client motivation may be enhanced by acknowledging freedom of choice with regard to treatment goals. Insistence on a particular treatment goal, despite the client's perceptions and wishes, can compromise motivation and outcome (Sanchez-Craig & Lei, 1986; Thornton, Gottheil, Gellens, & Alterman, 1977).

Decreasing DESIRABILITY

In the contemplation stage, a person is weighing the benefits and costs of change against the merits of continuing as before. It is as though there were a motivational balance (see Figure 2.2) between factors favoring the status quo and those favoring change (Janis & Mann, 1977). Motivation strategies for the contemplation stage, then, involve removing weights from the status quo side of the balance, and increasing weights on the change side of the scales.

One kind of weight on the status quo side has to do with perceived costs or risks of changing. (This is the focus of our discussion above on removing barriers to change.) Equally important, however, is another kind of weight favoring the status quo: the perceived desirability of present behavior. It is a safe assumption that a behavior pattern persisting despite negative consequences is maintained by other positive incentives. It is not necessary that these be true or accurate positive consequences—only that the person perceive and believe that the behavior has positive rewards. Brown and her

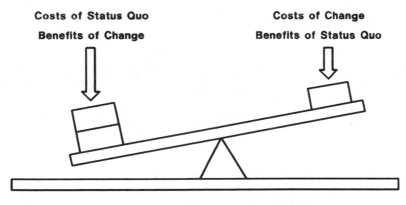

FIGURE 2.2. Contemplation: cost–benefit balance.

colleagues have demonstrated, for example, that perceptions of positive effects from alcohol predict early onset of drinking among youths, problematic drinking among adults, and relapse among alcoholics after treatment (Brown, 1985; Brown, Goldman, & Christiansen, 1985; Brown, Goldman, Inn, & Anderson, 1980; Christiansen & Goldman, 1983; Christiansen, Goldman, & Inn, 1982; Christiansen, Smith, Roehling, & Goldman, 1989).

An important motivational task for the counselor, then, is to identify the client's positive incentives for continuing his or her present behavior. How and why is this behavior desirable to the client? Once these positive incentives are clarified, the counselor can seek effective approaches for decreasing, undermining, or counterbalancing them.

It should not be expected, however, that simple rational reflection on these factors will induce change. Summarizing his review on this topic, Moskowitz (1989) concluded, "Logical introspection regarding the costs and benefits of substance use has not been found to be highly predictive of subsequent use. . . . Evaluation studies have found this approach to be ineffective in influencing values organization, self-esteem or behavioral adjustment" (p. 68). Behavior is more likely to be altered if affective or value dimensions of desirability are affected (Leventhal, 1971; Orford, 1985; Premack, 1970; Rokeach, 1973).

Various strategies are available for decreasing the perceived desirability of a problem behavior. The incentive value of behaviors can be directly diminished by aversive counterconditioning methods such as covert sensitization (Elkins, 1980; Rimmele, Miller, & Dougher, 1989), but this constitutes a treatment approach that already requires substantial commitment to change. A more general counterbalancing approach is to increase the person's awareness and salience of adverse consequences of the behavior (Karoly, 1980). Several of the motivational interviewing strategies presented in Part II of this book are directly applicable to this goal.

Changes may also be made in social contingencies that decrease the positive consequences and increase the negative consequences of the problem behavior. We have argued that motivation does not lie solely within the individual, but is affected by the person's relationships and environment. Suppose that a client named David is drinking heavily, experiencing alcoholic blackouts, missing days of work because of hangovers, and ignoring his family. How motivated would he be to change under each of these two conditions?

(A) David has a large group of friends who all drink in the same manner, and who assure him that blacking out and passing out are "just part of having a good time" and nothing to worry about. His employer also drinks a fair amount, and looks the other way when David calls in sick.

His wife does her best to keep the family functioning, and tries not to "rock the boat" or make David angry.

or

(B) David's friends are becoming concerned about his drinking, and express these worries to him in a caring manner. His employer has taken notice of his poor attendance record, and calls him in: "I really don't want to lose you, David, and I'm willing to do whatever I can to help you work out this problem, but if things don't change I'm going to have to let you go." His wife is also telling David that things have to change: "I love you, and I'm willing to go to counseling with you if that will help, but we can't go on like this. If you don't do something about your drinking, we can't stay together."

The point of these two examples is to illustrate how the same person with the same type of problem can be more or less inclined to do something about it, depending upon his or her situation. If the people in his or her life make it easier to continue a problem by making it seem normal, trying to ignore it, or protecting the person from its consequences, change is less likely, If, in contrast, those around the person express concern, offer help, and reinforce the negative consequences of the problem, motivation for change is increased. Sisson and Azrin (1986) reported success with a procedure for counseling the spouses of uncooperative alcoholics. The spouses were counseled to stop what might be called "enabling" behaviors, withdrawing all positive reinforcement when the alcoholics were drinking and ceasing to protect the alcoholics from the negative consequences of drinking. Relative to a control group, which evidenced very little change, the motivational counseling group showed marked decreases in drinking even before the alcoholics agreed to enter treatment, which occurred after seven spouse counseling sessions on average. Others have used the threat of job loss or legal sanctions to coerce treatment (Freedberg & Johnston, 1978; Gallant et al., 1973; Rosenberg & Liftik, 1976). Strategies that impose aversive consequences, however, are vulnerable to collapse if the contingency cannot be maintained (Rosenberg & Liftik, 1976), and are likely to evoke resistance and discourage intrinsic motivation for change.

Practicing EMPATHY

For decades, treatment professionals have written about the importance of such therapist characteristics as warmth, respect, supportiveness, caring, concern, sympathetic understanding, commitment, and active interest (Chafetz, 1959; Davies, 1981; Malcolm, 1968; Mann, 1950; Swenson, 1971; Truax & Carkhuff, 1967). A well-researched therapist characteristic in this domain is accurate empathy (Rogers, 1959). In Chapter 1 we have discussed evidence that therapeutic empathy is a factor that favors motivation for change. Experimental and correlational studies have shown that an empathic therapist style is associated with low levels of client resistance and with greater long-term behavior change (Miller & Sovereign, 1989; Miller, Taylor, & West, 1980; Patterson & Forgatch, 1985; Valle, 1981).

As we have indicated earlier, this kind of empathy is not an ability or tendency to *identify* with a person's experiences. Rather, it is a specifiable and learnable skill for *understanding* another's meaning through the use of reflective listening, whether or not you have had similar experiences yourself. Although a therapist skilled in empathic listening can make it look easy and natural, in fact this is a demanding counseling style. It requires sharp attention to each new client statement, and a continual generation of hypotheses as to the underlying meaning. Your best guess as to meaning is then reflected back to the client, often adding to the content of what was overtly said. The client responds, and the whole process starts over again. Reflective listening is easy to parody or do poorly, but quite challenging to do well. It is, as we discuss in Chapter 6, a key element of style in motivational interviewing.

Providing FEEDBACK

If you don't know where you are, it's difficult to plan how to get somewhere else. People sometimes fail to change because they do not receive sufficient feedback about their current situation. Clear knowledge of the present situation is a crucial element of motivation for change. Check-ups that provide drinkers with information about how alcohol is harming them, for example, have been found to yield long-term changes in alcohol use (Kristenson et al., 1983; Miller & Sovereign, 1989).

Such feedback can come in many ways. Expressions of concern from family and friends represent one form of feedback (Johnson, 1973). Clients can also be given feedback through the results of objective tests, as we discuss in Chapter 7. Keeping a self-monitoring diary (e.g., recording every drink taken) is still another form of feedback that has been found to have an impact (Miller & Muñoz, 1976). Simply stepping on the scales provides feedback about body weight. An important motivational task of the counselor, then, is to provide clear feedback about a client's current situation and its consequences or risks.

Clarifying GOALS

Feedback alone, however, is not enough to precipitate change. Feedback must be *compared* with some standard. It is this process of self-evaluation—

comparing perceived status with personal standards—that influences whether or not change will occur (Kanfer & Gaelick, 1986; Miller & Brown, in press). Thus, if the person lacks a clear goal or standard, feedback may be of no use.

Onc important element here is what the person perceives to be normal and acceptable. Antisocial behaviors that are rejected by society in general may be regarded as normal and praiseworthy within a delinquent subculture. Alcohol abuse and its consequences are condoned and normalized among circles of heavily drinking friends.

Helping people to set clear goals has been found to facilitate change (Locke, Shaw, Saari, & Latham, 1981). It is important, however, for a person to see the goal as realistic and attainable. Otherwise little or no effort will be made to reach the goal, even if it is acknowledged to be important (Bandura, 1982). Likewise, goals are of little use if the person lacks feedback about his or her present situation. Goals and feedback work together in creating motivation for change.

Active HELPING

The final motivational building block that we discuss here is an active helping attitude. From your perspective as a therapist, this means being actively and affirmatively interested in your client's change process. Although in one sense it is true that change is your client's decision, it is also true that you can have a great influence on how this decision is made.

Two general themes here are taking the therapeutic initiative and expressing your caring. If, for example, a client misses a session, what should you do? One way of thinking is that you should wait for the client to take the responsibility of getting in touch and rescheduling. In an active helping approach, however, you would take the initiative and express your caring about what happens to your client. A simple way to do this is to make a telephone call or send a handwritten note. The same principle applies after a first consultation: Should you wait to see whether the client comes back, or take some caring initiative? Again, the principle of active helping would suggest that you do the latter. Follow-through contacts with clients are discussed in detail in Chapter 6 of this book.

Another area where this approach seems to make a difference is making a referral. If you wish, for example, to refer someone for treatment, what should you do? Is it best to place the telephone call for him or her, or to provide the agency name and number and leave the person with the responsibility to make contact? Conventional wisdom sometimes favors the latter. These two options were compared in a random assignment experiment (Kogan, 1957). Of those given the telephone number, 37% made contact;

when the counselor took initiative to place the referral call for the client, 82% completed the referral.

Some counselors are reluctant to take the initiative in these ways because they are concerned about adopting an enabling role or taking responsibility for their clients' change. The concept of "enabling," however, refers to actions taken by another that make it easier for the person to continue problematic behavior and to escape its adverse consequences. If a simple caring letter or telephone call can double, triple, or quadruple the chances of a client's continuing with counseling and change efforts, in what way does this constitute harm to the client? As for being responsible, our inclination is first to engage and retain the client in counseling, *then* to worry about encouraging responsibility! More often than not, caring initiative is better than passivity.

Putting the Ingredients Together

So far we have given you some ingredients of motivational intervention, but not a recipe for how to combine them. Knowing what ingredients to use is a good beginning, but to make bread you must also know when and how to mix them, how long to knead the dough and to let it rise, and how long and at what temperature to bake it. Any baker knows that some of this knowledge comes with experience, and there is room for artistic variation, but there are basic guidelines that one must follow for success. There is a tolerable range in the ratio of flour to other ingredients. If you leave out the yeast or kill it with hot water, nothing rises. There are limits on how warm the oven can be. At different altitudes, you have to adjust the recipe. To learn to bake, it may be helpful to see pictures of finished products, to understand the basic chemistry of baking, to learn the general guidelines to follow in mixing and handling ingredients, to get some tips on how to perform each step, and to hear about what can go wrong and how to deal with common problems.

That is what we propose to do through the remaining chapters of this book. In Chapter 3 we show you some "finished products"—relatively brief interventions that were apparently successful in motivating change in problem drinkers—and analyze their contents. In Chapter 4, the last chapter of introductory background, we discuss the "basic chemistry" of motivation, through the dilemma of ambivalence. Then in Part II, we turn to practicalities. Chapter 5 lays out the essential principles of motivational interviewing. Chapters 6–9 cover the "how-to" aspects of various steps, and Chapter 10 explains typical problems that are encountered and ways to deal with them. Chapter 11 provides an extended case example, illustrating how the strategies of Chapters 5–10 are applied in practice. In Chapter 12, we offer some guidelines for teaching motivational interviewing. Finally, in Part III, other professionals discuss their experience in applying motivational interviewing in a variety of settings and populations, and offer their own clinical perspectives on the practice of motivational counseling.

3

Brief Intervention:
More Pieces of the Puzzle

Things do not change: We change.
—Henry David Thoreau, *Walden*

Self-Change

In Chapter 2 we have outlined six stages of change, and described eight motivational elements that seem to help people progress through these stages. Prochaska and DiClemente, the creators of the transtheoretical model from which these stages are derived, originally developed them to describe steps through which people pass in the course of self-change, without the assistance of formal treatment (Prochaska & DiClemente, 1982). Their work in the subsequent decade indicated that these same stages of change occur in or out of therapy (Prochaska & DiClemente, 1984). That is, people seem to go through the same sequence of change stages, whether or not they are receiving the help of a therapist.

This raises an important and, for some, surprising point: Most people who change their addictive behaviors, such as smoking or drinking or illicit drug use, do so on their own with no formal treatment. That this is necessarily so can be seen by examining (1) the population prevalence rates of current and former users, (2) the rates of change in these behaviors over time within a general population, and (3) the relatively small number of people who receive formal treatment for these problems (Cahalan, 1987; Peele, 1985). Most people who quit smoking do so on their own with no formal help. Most people who have problems with alcohol are found, years later, to have resolved or reduced their problems, and only a small minority of these do so with the help of treatment (Fillmore, 1975; Sobell, 1991). Among soldiers in Vietnam, a majority of regular heroin users abruptly gave up or changed their habit upon their return home (Robins, Helzer, & Davis, 1975).

How do such changes occur? When self-changers are asked why and how they did it, they commonly reply that they "just decided." Some describe specific events that shocked them, and caused them to see themselves and their habit in a new light (Premack, 1970). Some relate religious experiences, interactions with family and friends, or life transitions as triggers for their change (Knupfer, 1972; Saunders & Kershaw, 1979). In many cases, however, there is a common thread of *decision* running through the stories of self-changers. Things may have happened around them, but something also happened *inside* them to set off a change.

Too often, counselors overlook or underestimate the importance of this decision process. Faced with a suffering client or family, there is a temptation to rush right to the action stage in the Prochaska–DiClemente model. Armed for action, the counselor begins prescribing goals and strategies for change. Then comes the "Yes, but . . ." of contemplation, which often is understood by the counselor as resistance. As we have discussed in Chapter 1, if the counselor presses against this resistance, the contemplator's likely response is reactance, and a self-perpetuating cycle has begun. Resistance is encountered when the counselor uses strategies inappropriate for the client's current stage of change.

The crucial point to remember is that *decision* is an important part of change. As Syme (1988) and Rollnick (1985) have argued, counseling strategies that focus immediately on *how* to change (action) may be detrimental by distracting the client (contemplator) from the crucial issue: *commitment* to change. This can be a particularly important point for physicians and other primary care workers to understand, as they encounter health problems requiring behavior change (Rollnick & MacEwan, 1991). This issue is considered in Chapters 10 and 14.

The Impact of Brief Interventions

This brings us to another persistent finding in addictions treatment research. Research teams in Canada (Zweben, Pearlman, & Li, 1988), England (Orford & Edwards, 1977), New Zealand (Chapman & Huygens, 1988), Norway (Skutle & Berg, 1987), and the United States (Miller & Taylor, 1980; Miller, Taylor, & West, 1980) have found that relatively brief interventions of one to three sessions are comparable in impact to more extensive treatments for alcohol problems. Other recent research has shown brief interventions to be substantially more effective than no treatment in altering problem drinking, including studies from Scotland (Chick, Lloyd, & Crombie, 1985; Heather, Campion, Neville, & Maccabe, 1987), England (Anderson & Scott, 1990; Wallace, Cutler, & Haines, 1988), New Zealand (Elvy, Wells, & Baird, 1988), Sweden (Kristenson, Ohlin, Hulten-Nosslin, Trell, & Hood, 1983), and the United States (Harris & Miller, 1990), as well as a major study conducted by the World Health Organization in 11 nations (Babor, Korner, Wilber, & Good, 1987; Saunders, 1987). Accordingly, brief motivational intervention has been proposed as a viable outpatient treatment approach in its own right (Edwards & Orford, 1977; Heather, 1989; Ritson, 1986; Sanchez-Craig & Wilkinson, 1989), and was identified by the Institute of Medicine (1989) as a high-priority area for future research on the treatment of alcohol-related problems.

It appears, then, that relatively brief counseling can have a substantial impact. Those receiving well-planned brief counseling show much more improvement than those given no counseling at all. In some studies, the effects of such brief intervention appear comparable to the results of more extensive treatment. What can be learned from these findings?

One thing these studies indicate is that the critical conditions for precipitating change may be contained—at least for some clients—in a relatively brief span of counseling, shorter than is usually thought of as constituting "treatment" (Orford, 1986). Successful brief interventions have typically included no medications, skill training, conditioning, or psycho-therapy—alternative strategies that can be of benefit in the treatment of addictive behaviors (Cox, 1987; Hester & Miller, 1989). It appears that the primary impact of brief interventions is *motivational*. Their effect, we believe, is to trigger a decision and commitment to change (Miller & Brown, 1991; Miller, Sovereign, & Krege, 1988). The nature of the sample selection procedures (e.g., medical screening) used in many studies of brief intervention is likely to yield a high percentage of precontemplators and early contemplators, for whom the key challenge is to foster decision and commitment. Once this motivational decision has been made, the person may proceed to apply his or her own natural skills to accomplish a change.

Active Ingredients of Effective Brief Counseling

If effective brief interventions contain the critical elements that trigger motivation for change, what are these elements? Miller and Sanchez (in press) analyzed the content of brief counseling strategies that were studied in the outcome research described above. They described six counseling elements that appeared to be the common and "active ingredients" in effective brief interventions. These are summarized in the acronym "FRAMES."

F: Feedback

Effective brief interventions have typically included a structured and often comprehensive assessment, through which the client is given feedback of his or her current status (e.g., Kristenson et al., 1983; Miller & Sovereign, 1989; Orford & Edwards, 1977). We have found that even when such feedback is not formally structured, the very process of conducting a thorough assessment provides the client an opportunity to reflect in detail upon his or her present situation. As discussed in Chapter 2, feedback can be a potent element in motivation for change. In Chapter 7, we discuss in greater detail how to use assessment results in this manner.

R: Responsibility

A second element commonly included in brief interventions has been an emphasis on the client's personal responsibility for change. Often this has been made explicit (e.g., Edwards & Orford, 1977) through messages such as this:

> It's up to you to decide what to do with this information. Nobody can decide for you, and no one can change your drinking if you don't want to change. It's your choice, and if change is going to happen, you're the one who has to do it.

In other cases, the message of self-responsibility has been more implicit, as in providing the client with a self-help manual and instructing the client to use it on his or her own (e.g., Heather, Whitton, & Robertson, 1986; Miller, Gribskov, & Mortell, 1981).

A: Advice

A third common element has been clear *advice* to the client to make a change in drinking. Sometimes such advice has been the prescription of a specific goal, such as total abstinence (e.g., Edwards et al., 1977). In other cases, the admonition has been to eliminate hazardous drinking, but the specific goal has been left to the client's discretion (e.g., Kristenson et al., 1983). In still other cases, the advice given has been to seek further treatment, and motivational interventions have been quite successful in accomplishing such referrals (Chafetz, 1961; Elvy et al., 1988). Even simple advice from one's primary care physician can induce a small percentage of patients to give up an addictive behavior (Burnum, 1974; Russell, Wilson, Taylor, & Baker, 1979).

M: Menu

Another approach is to offer clients a menu of alternative strategies for changing their problem behavior. Prescribing a single goal or approach runs the risk that a client will find the offering unacceptable. Providing a range of options, on the other hand, allows an opportunity for clients to select strategies that match their particular needs and situations (Miller & Hester, 1986b). Furthermore, selection of one's own approach from among options has the effect of enhancing perceived personal choice and control. When a person perceives that he or she has freely chosen a course of action, it is more likely that the person will persist and succeed (Deci, 1980; Kopel & Arkowitz, 1975; Miller, 1985b).

E: Empathy

As discussed earlier, therapist empathy has been found to be a potent determinant of client motivation and change (e.g., Miller et al., 1980; Valle, 1981). Effective brief interventions have typically emphasized the empathic nature of therapeutic intervention (e.g., Chafetz, 1961; Edwards & Orford, 1977). Even when clients in brief interventions are "confronted" with feedback or given direct advice, this can be done in a highly empathic manner (Miller, 1983; Miller & Sovereign, 1989).

S: Self-Efficacy

One more common emphasis in effective brief interventions has been on reinforcing the client's self-efficacy, hope, or optimism. The concept of "self-efficacy" was first described by Bandura (1977, 1982), and refers to a person's belief in his or her ability to carry out or succeed with a specific task. In this case, the goal is to persuade the client that he or she *can* make a successful change in the problem area. The more general theme of hope and optimism, however, is much older, and has long been recognized as an important element in healing (Frank, 1973; Miller, 1985a). If a person is persuaded of a serious and threatening condition, but perceives no way in which change is feasible, the result is likely to be defensiveness (e.g., denial, rationalization) rather than behavior change (Rogers & Mewborn, 1976). It is also worth mentioning here that the *therapist's* belief in the client's ability to change can also be a significant determinant of outcome (e.g., Leake & King, 1977).

These six elements, then, seem to be promising building blocks for constructing motivational interventions. Though they were derived from the outcome literature on brief interventions, they do, as you may recognize, overlap with the eight motivational intervention elements described in

Chapter 2. The key point here is that these conditions for motivating change can be captured in relatively brief spans of counseling.

Motivation as an Interpersonal Interaction

There is, for our present purposes, at least one more important lesson to be learned these from studies of effective brief interventions. Across these studies, which have been conducted in many nations, clients who received brief counseling showed patterns of motivation and change very different from the behavior of those not receiving it. In comparison with randomly chosen control groups, they were substantially more likely to seek further treatment (Chafetz, 1961, 1968), to decrease their drinking (Elvy et al., 1988; Harris & Miller, 1990; Miller et al., 1988; Wallace et al., 1988), and to reduce alcohol-related problems (Babor et al., 1987; Chick et al., 1985; Kristenson et al., 1983; Saunders, 1987). In these studies, such changes did not occur at the same rate without the face-to-face brief counseling intervention. Although change can occur with truly impersonal self-help approaches (e.g., Heather et al., 1986), in these studies the difference occurred in relation to an *interpersonal interaction.*

It matters not only *whether* a person interacts with a counselor, but *what* the counselor does during their exchange. Overtly directive and confrontational therapist styles, for example, tend to evoke high levels of client resistance (Patterson & Forgatch, 1985), whereas a more empathic style is associated with little resistance and better long-term change (Miller & Sovereign, 1989).

This reinforces a point raised in our first two chapters: that motivation for change does not simply reside within the skin of the client, but involves an interpersonal context. Relatively brief interactions with skilled counselors in these studies apparently made a difference in people's motivational states, which in turn were reflected in long-term behavior change. It is encouraging, in fact, that such brief contacts can alter the course of problem behaviors. More systematic motivational counseling may yield even larger effects. As a therapist, you are not a passive observer of your clients' motivational states. You are an important determinant of your clients' motivation. "Lack of motivation" is a challenge for your therapeutic skills, not a fault for which to blame your clients. Our purpose in this book is to help you strengthen your skills to meet this challenge.

That is the task we address in Part II. Before we do, however, there is one more important conceptual piece to put into place.

4

Ambivalence: The Dilemma of Change

"Why are you drinking?" demanded the little prince.
"So that I may forget," replied the tippler.
"Forget what?" inquired the little prince, who already was sorry for him.
"Forget that I am ashamed," the tippler confessed, hanging his head.
"Ashamed of what?" insisted the little prince, who wanted to help.
"Ashamed of drinking!" The tippler brought his speech to an end, and shut
    himself up in an impregnable silence.
And the little prince went away puzzled.
"The grown-ups are certainly very, very odd," he said to himself.
           —Antoine de Saint-Exupéry, *The Little Prince*

I Want To, but I Don't Want To

As should be clear from the first three chapters of this book, counselors have a surprising amount of freedom to affect the responsiveness and motivation of their clients. We have described, for example, how a confrontational interviewing style can create or exacerbate problems of "denial" and "resistance." On the positive side, there clearly is much that can be done to enhance a person's readiness for change. We turn now to a consideration of motivation from the viewpoint of the client, who is obviously more than just a passive recipient of the counselor's therapeutic style.

People struggling with addictive problems usually enter counseling with fluctuating and conflicting motivations. They want to, but they don't want to. This conflict, which can be called "ambivalence," often pervades early counseling sessions. The person says "I've come for help," yet in the next sentence adds, "but it's not that serious." A mood of vulnerability can shift to one of defiance and back again within a few minutes. Perhaps it is this fluctuating readiness to consider change that makes people with addictive problems so sensitive to the way in which they are approached by a counselor. This conflict, which is by no means unique to addictive problems, is now explored in some detail before we move on to the principles and strategies of motivational interviewing.

36

Encountering Ambivalence

Feeling two ways about something or someone is a common experience. Indeed, a person who feels no ambivalence about anything is hard to imagine; feeling 100% clear about something important is probably more exceptional than normal. This phenomenon often plays a key role in psychological problems. A person suffering from agoraphobia, for example, may say, "I want to go out, but I'm terrified that I will lose control." So, too, a person who is socially isolated, unhappy, and depressed may suffer from ambivalence: "I want to be with people and make closer friendships, but I don't feel like an attractive or worthwhile person." With some psychological problems, the part played by ambivalence is even more striking. A person having an extramarital affair vacillates between spouse and lover in an intensely emotional ambivalence. A compulsive hand washer or checker desperately wants to avoid going through this disabling ritual time and time again, yet feels driven toward it by fear.

When it comes to the addictive behaviors, this kind of conflict clearly plays a central role (Orford, 1985). Problem drinkers, addicts, bulimics, and pathological gamblers often recognize the risks, costs, and harm involved in their behavior. Yet they are also quite attached and attracted to the addictive behavior, for a variety of reasons. To complicate the conflict further, they typically are not exactly sure what they should *do* about their situation! They want to drink (or smoke, or purge, or gamble), but they don't want to. They want to change, and they don't want to.

Counselors who treat addictive behaviors sometimes misinterpret this conflict as a personality problem. A counselor who hears some manifestation of the common ambivalence, "I want to, but I don't want to," may assume that there is something wrong with the client's judgment or mental state. The client's uncertainty is viewed as abnormal or unacceptable, and as a sign of poor motivation. A sensible conclusion from this line of reasoning is that the client needs to be educated and persuaded regarding the adverse consequences of his or her problem.

What happens next? The counselor attempts to persuade the client that the problem is serious and must be changed. This represents one side of the conflict from which the person already suffers, and the client's response is almost completely predictable. Faced with the "You should change" side of the conflict, the client gives voice to the other side: "Yes, but . . ." This signals something for the counselor: "Aha! This client is in denial." If the counselor therefore escalates by arguing more "persuasively," the client counters with still stronger reasons why the behavior is attractive or acceptable, the problem "isn't that serious," and change is not required (confirming the counselor's diagnosis of pernicious "denial"). They are, in essence, acting out the client's conflict.

This may seem harmless enough, but as we explain in Chapter 6, this strategy is often counterproductive, yielding exactly the *opposite* result from what the counselor intends. There are well-demonstrated social-psychological reasons why this is so. For now, suffice it to say that this confrontation–denial spiral is often countertherapeutic.

Instead of viewing ambivalence as a "bad sign" and trying somehow to persuade the client to change his or her mind, we hope to demonstrate the fruitfulness of regarding it as normal, acceptable, and understandable. This leads to an entirely different manner of dealing with clients in conflict. Fewer communication problems and power struggles occur, once the counselor understands the normality of ambivalence and the way it works. Instead of attacking the mythical "denial" monster, the counselor sees more clearly the complexity of the client's dilemma, and makes moves that are more like a friendly game of chess than a frontal assault on a castle. This approach, in turn, evokes less resistance from the client and facilitates progress in counseling. In one sense, motivational interviewing centers around the management of ambivalence in counseling.

Understanding Ambivalence

The Heart of the Problem

In addition to these practical merits, we believe that there is another, equally important reason for adopting an accepting attitude toward ambivalence. In many cases, *working with ambivalence is working with the heart of the problem*. One reason why brief interventions (see Chapter 3) may work so well is that they help people to get "unstuck" from their ambivalence—to make a decision and move on toward change. The often-discussed "problem of motivation" in addictions counseling can be understood as a manifestation of client ambivalence (Davies, 1979, 1981). The more firmly problem drinkers believe that alcohol offers them positive rewards, the more likely it is that they will relapse after treatment (Brown, 1985). Indeed, unless a client is helped to resolve the "I want to but I don't want to" dilemma, progress is likely to be slow-going and short-lived.

Ambivalence is a state of mind in which a person has coexisting but conflicting feelings about something. In the case of addictive behaviors, the person is typically ambivalent about engaging in the behavior in question (eating, drinking, smoking, gambling, etc.) versus resisting it. Many people experience little or no serious conflict about whether to have a drink, enter a lottery, or eat fattening food; they are in a state of balance or equilibrium. Other people, however, experience severe conflict about engaging versus resisting. Orford (1985) puts it this way:

The difference is between behaviour which is mostly kept within moderate limits by a variety of discriminations and restraints, and behaviour which relatively frequently gives rise to the information that the behaviour is "in excess." . . . This "information" may be conveyed by other people, by a mismatch between awareness of one's own behaviour and some idea about proper or ideal behaviour, or through bodily state or by some other means. At one end of a continuum lies unremarkable behaviour characterized by relatively little inclination and requiring little obvious restraint to keep it within bounds. At the other end lies behaviour which excites much emotion and arouses much comment, which seems to be characterized by a powerful drive, and which calls for relatively vigorous efforts at control. (p. 233)

Attachment

How does such conflict develop? Certainly it exists in degrees, and seems to increase (and decrease) over time. One obviously important ingredient is the emergence of *attachment* to the behavior. This makes it more difficult for the person to resist or move away from the behavior. There are various ways in which such attachment occurs. We cannot undertake a comprehensive review here, but we discuss a few attachment processes by way of illustration.

One familiar process is pharmacological dependence. In the case of certain drugs (such as alcohol, nicotine, and heroin), physical changes can occur whereby the body adapts to the presence of the drug. When the drug is subsequently withdrawn, the body goes into a rebound state of maladjustment, and it takes time to readjust. For the drinker, this rebound process varies from a mild morning-after hangover to severe delirium tremens.

A related phenomenon is tolerance. Over time, the person requires a larger "dose" of the drug or behavior to experience the same desired effect. A normal dose that is sufficient for other people is not enough. This phenomenon of accelerating need is not limited to drug use, but can be observed in a range of other addictive behaviors (Peele, 1985; Peele & Brodsky, 1975).

Learning or conditioning patterns can also be quite powerful sources of attachment to problematic behaviors. Sexual deviations can be established and strengthened by repeated pairing of masturbation with particular fantasies, stimuli, or situations. Physical and behavioral changes occur in heavy drinkers (and in laboratory animals given regular doses of alcohol) when they are given a drink that they *believe* contains alcohol, even if it is alcohol-free (Marlatt & Rohsenow, 1980). The relaxation and conviviality of the "happy hour" or local pub can come to be associated with alcohol. Hundreds of thousands of times, smokers take a puff of a cigarette and almost immediately deliver a dose of nicotine to the brain. These habitual aspects can be strong sources of attachment to addictive behaviors.

People may also use addictive behaviors as a means of coping—a pattern known as "psychological dependence" (Miller & Pechacek, 1987). They come to rely upon a drink (or sweets, or smoking, etc.) to help them deal with difficult or unpleasant states. It helps them relax, get to sleep, feel comfortable, forget, talk to people, feel powerful, be sexually disinhibited, or feel better. Over time, it becomes difficult to cope *without* the addictive behavior, and this is another source of attachment.

The Approach–Avoidance Conflict

The idea of "conflict" has been an important concept in many psychological theories, and conflicts have been described as coming in three varieties. In the "approach–approach" conflict, the person is torn between two equally attractive alternatives, and the important choice factors are positive. If one has to have a conflict, this is probably the kind to choose. An example is deciding which of two exciting and rewarding job offers to accept. The "avoidance–avoidance" conflict, in contrast, involves having to choose between two evils—two (or more) possibilities each of which involves significant fear, pain, embarrassment, or other negative consequences. This is being caught "between a rock and a hard place," or "between the devil and the deep blue sea." In a congested city, for example, one may have to choose between parking far away from one's destination or risking payment of an expensive ticket.

The grand champion conflict, however, is the "approach–avoidance" type. This kind of conflict seems to have special potential for keeping people "stuck" and creating stress. Here the person is both attracted to and repelled by a single object. The term "fatal attraction" has been used to describe this kind of love affair: "I can't live with it, and I can't live without it." In alternating cycles, the person indulges in and then resists the behavior (relationship, person, object). The resulting yo-yo effect is a classic characteristic of the approach–avoidance conflict. The resemblance of this conflict situation to the addictive behaviors is apparent (Orford, 1985). Our point is that this is not a unique characteristic of addictive behaviors. Ambivalent cognitions, emotions, and behaviors are a normal part of any approach–avoidance conflict situation.

The Decisional Balance

A helpful way of illustrating the ambivalence conflict involves the metaphor of a balance or seesaw (Janis & Mann, 1977). The person experiences competing motivations because there are both benefits and costs associated with both sides of the conflict. This has been illustrated in Chapter 2 (see Figure 2.2). (Keep in mind that this is not an *explanation* of addictive behaviors, but only a descriptive framework that we believe to be helpful.) There are two kinds of weights on each side of the balance. One has to do with the perceived benefits of a particular course of action (such as continued drinking). The other has to do with the perceived costs or disadvantages of an alternative course of action (such as stopping drinking). Another aspect of this balance is that in an approach–avoidance conflict, as the weight begins to tip one way, the person tends to focus on (and shift weights to) the opposite side.

Another way of illustrating this is through a "balance sheet," which can be used to specify what a person perceives to be the benefits and costs associated with a behavior (cf. Orford, 1985). An example is shown in Table 4.1, again with regard to drinking behavior. As shown here, the balance sheet (and hence the nature of a person's ambivalence) may be quite complex. It can comprise a set of pros and cons for each of the options open to the person. It is important to note, by the way, that the person may experience ambivalence no matter which option is currently being favored. If someone is abstaining, for example, he or she may feel ambivalent about this particular state—there will be costs and benefits associated with it. Such a person, whether he or she is aware of this or not, has particular expectations about what the positive and negative effects would be of an alternative choice (e.g., drinking), and the person is likely to feel ambivalent about this option as well. How these competing forces balance out at a given point in time will determine whether the person indulges or resists. The expectations illustrated in Table 4.1 are those of the client, and the counselor may choose to examine the validity of some of them in more detail. As we discuss further in Chapter 7, the balance sheet can be used with motivational interviewing to penetrate this state of ambivalence, to clarify the competing motivational factors, and to encourage the person to consider the possibility of change.

A serious danger in a model of this kind is oversimplification. We do not mean to imply that clients are always (or even usually) consciously aware of this balancing process, or that when they are made aware, they will proceed like accountants toward rational decisions. The elements of this balance sheet, unlike the books or inventory of a business, do not add up in simple fashion. The value of each item may shift over time. Elements in the lists are linked together, and a change in one causes shifts in others. Almost by definition, a client's balance sheet will be full of contradictions: "I know it's bad for me, but I like it." "It doesn't make sense, but we all do it." "Sometimes I stop myself, and other times I want to but I just don't care." For both client and counselor, ambivalence can be confusing, frustrating, and difficult to understand.

TABLE 4.1. A Decisional Balance Sheet

Continuing to drink as before		Making a change in my drinking	
Benefits	Costs	Benefits	Costs
Helps me relax	Could lose my marriage	Happier marriage	What to do about my friends
I like getting high	Bad example for children	More time for family	Won't have a way to relax
	Damaging my health	Feel better	
	Spending too much money	Helps money problems	
	Damaging my brain		
	Might lose my job		
	Wasting my time/life		

Yet it is important to persist despite these obstacles, for, if we are correct, ambivalence is often the very heart of the problem. Counseling within this framework can require considerable patience and tolerance for ambiguity. It also helps to have a profound respect for your clients, as well as a "love of the game" itself—a fascination with the intricacies of each new person and situation.

Some Complications of Ambivalence

We have already presented ambivalence as a complex phenomenon, with costs and benefits attached to each alternative, of which the client (and counselor) may or may not be aware. We now call a few other general characteristics of ambivalence to your attention, because they may help you make sense of what could otherwise seem strange and pathological. Remember that these are not unique to the addictive behaviors. They are qualities that occur with ambivalence in many contexts, and are discussed in greater depth by Orford (1985).

Values

Never assume that clients will view a given cost or benefit in the same way that you do. A stomach problem caused by drinking may be viewed with alarm by some, whereas others may regard it as something that they "just put up with." The threat of fines and imprisonment will deter many from engaging in illegal behavior, but for others it is just a risk that is part of the cost of doing business. What is highly valued by some (e.g., being healthy, employed, popular, slim, or pious) will be of little importance to others.

Expectancies

Beyond their values, people also have particular expectancies about the likely results, both positive and negative, of certain courses of action. These expectations can have a powerful effect on behavior. Someone who desperately wants to quit smoking may still make no effort to do so, in the belief that all such efforts are futile. Gamblers may not want to consider quitting because they believe (rightly or wrongly) that whatever the merits of abstaining, gambling is the greatest source of excitement they have ever known. An abstainer may think regularly about how wonderful it would be to have his or her favorite drug again, and so may be drawn back toward relapse (Brown, 1985; Cummings, Gordon, & Marlatt, 1980). Drinkers may resist abstinence in spite of the ravages of alcohol abuse, because they fear that without alcohol they simply could not cope with life (Hall, 1979).

Self-Esteem

The importance even of commonly valued goals (such as personal health) can be undermined by poor self-esteem. From the depths of depression, a client may acknowledge: "Yes, I know that I'm killing myself, but so what?" Sometimes the bolstering of self-esteem is a necessary prerequisite to motivation for change (Miller, 1983). Happily, some of the key elements of motivational interviewing to be described in Part II (e.g., accurate empathy) can also be useful in supporting client self-esteem.

Social Context

Social and cultural factors affect people's perceptions of their behavior, as well as their evaluation of its costs and benefits. Thus even across different neighborhoods and social groups within the same city, people may hold very different views regarding the pros and cons of behavior. In the United Kingdom, for example, the social meaning and value of drinking in rounds can vary dramatically among pubs in the same locality, or even within the same pub. In certain American communities and subgroups, drinking that results in a memory blackout, fighting, vomiting in the street, and passing out in one's car is regarded as just a normal part of a good time on a Friday night. Stealing, missing work, taking risks, and using drugs are much more acceptable within some subgroups than others. A client's motivational system cannot be understood outside the social context of family, friends, and community.

Paradoxical Responses

An increase in a particular cost of a behavior does not necessarily mean that change is more likely. The opposite can occur. Orford (1985) provides an example wherein increased nagging of an overeater by family members had the opposite effect from what the family intended. Far from reducing the eating, the nagging amplified the person's anxiety, and eating increased in response to this discomfort. In his historical account of Australia's first century as a British penal colony, Hughes (1987) recounts how convicts endured savage beatings and torture to continue smoking tobacco. The chilling song lyric quoted at the beginning of Chapter 2 reflects similar persistence. This convict song defiantly expresses a willingness to risk torture (Pinchgut Island was a bare rock in the middle of Sydney Harbour, where convicts were chained without food—hence the name—and exposed to the elements for long periods), flogging (a "Norfolk Dumpling" was a whipping of 100 lashes with the steel-tipped "cat-o'-nine-tails"), and even execution (the "Newgate hornpipe" refers to the dancing of a hanged man's legs in midair) in order to get rum. Clinicians know all too well that people with alcohol and drug problems can similarly persist in their habits despite incredible personal suffering and losses. Obviously, a simple increase in painful consequences is not always successful in stopping such behaviors. Sometimes such consequences only seem to strengthen and entrench a behavior pattern.

How can such a seemingly paradoxical response occur? The theory of psychological reactance, discussed in Chapter 1, would predict an *increase* in the rate and attractiveness of a "problem" behavior if a person perceives that his or her personal freedom is being threatened. Secondary effects of a change within the person's social environment may also account for detrimental shifts. For instance, the breakdown of the person's marriage—seemingly a terrible cost—may deprive him or her of the only social support that served to deter an addictive behavior, resulting in ever greater excess (Orford, 1985). If all other sources of reinforcement are blocked, a person may persist in seeking the one remaining reward, albeit at great cost. Such seemingly paradoxical responses are neither mysterious nor uniquely pathological. They are, in some circumstances, quite understandable and predictable (cf. Cahoon, 1968).

Impaired Control

It has long been recognized that the addictive behaviors are often accompanied by some impairment of self-control processes that normally restrain people's behavior. Faced with a balance sheet strongly favoring change, and despite clearly stated intentions, a person may persist in a harmful behavior through a breakdown of normal self-regulation processes (Miller & Brown, 1991). This is not a hopeless situation by any means. It does mean, however, that beyond the building of motivation, the individual will need additional supports to establish and maintain a new course of behavior.

This list of characteristics and complications of ambivalence is not comprehensive. It is meant only to be illustrative of the complexity of the phenomenon of ambivalence in a counseling context. To be sure, there are many gaps in present knowledge about conflict and how people change. Yet in spite of these complexities and unanswered questions, the counselor who is mindful of ambivalence as a normal and key phenomenon can still work with conflict in a constructive way.

We close this chapter, therefore, with a brief accounting of the general clinical implications of the model we have proposed (cf. Orford, 1985). In Part II, we build upon this framework by describing the specific principles (Chapter 5) and strategies (Chapters 6–10) of motivational interviewing.

Working with Ambivalence

Ambivalence is a normal and common component of many psychological problems. In the addictive behaviors, it is a central phenomenon. It does not arise from a uniquely pathological ("addictive") personality, nor from disordered character defense mechanisms (such as denial, rationalization, and projection). Rather, the person can be thought of as caught in an approach–avoidance conflict. It is unhelpful to think of a person as "poorly motivated." The challenge is to discover how you can help to strengthen the person's motivation for change.

It is important, then, to understand the elements of this conflict, which will be unique for each client (though there are certain similarities across clients). You should not assume that you already know the costs and benefits in a particular client's situation, or the relative importance that the client assigns to these factors. Discovering and understanding these motivations is an important part of individual assessment. It is also important to understand each client's outcome expectations for different courses of action—what would happen if he or she continued on the present course, if he or she abstained, and so forth.

Clients will obviously vary in the extent to which they have understood their ambivalence. In the language of Prochaska and DiClemente, this is how far the person has progressed into the contemplation stage. As a counselor, you should be careful not to jump too far ahead. For example, a heavy drinker may enter counseling in the throes of marital conflict, assuming that the marriage is the problem and that drinking is simply a means of relieving stress. Such a person may need time to consider other aspects of the problem and may, with regard to drinking, be a precontemplator. Pressuring such a person to make a change in drinking is jumping too quickly and too far ahead—a recipe for resistance. In contrast, an ambivalent smoker who comes to a doctor with "chest trouble" might readily acknowledge that his or her health is endangered, yet may feel concerned about coping with social situations without smoking. This person appears to have moved further into the process of contemplation—he or she understands some of the elements of the conflict, and may well respond to careful questioning about "What's the next step?" (see Chapter 9). The former individual (the drinker) seems less acutely ambivalent, and the conflict itself is more complex. It can be useful to view the precontemplation and contemplation stages (see Chapter 2) as a continuum. In moving from precontemplation into contemplation, the person becomes more aware of conflict and experiences greater ambivalence. As this ambivalence is understood and worked through (with or without counseling), the person moves closer to determination and decision making. This working through of ambivalence is a central goal of motivational interviewing.

How you respond as a counselor to ambivalence is crucial. There is a confrontation–denial trap into which clients and counselors can easily fall. In this trap, the counselor takes responsibility for the pro-change side of the client's conflict, and the client is left to defend the status quo. It is important to avoid falling into this easy trap, and we shortly explain how.

Ambivalence is not wholly rational. In focusing on motivational ambivalence, it is especially important to remain attuned to your client's feelings, values, and beliefs. The empathic skills described in Part II represent excellent tools for doing so.

Finally, working through ambivalence is only part of the picture. Motivational interviewing promotes the client's *readiness* to change, to try various courses of action that can lead to recovery and health. Sometimes it is enough to help clients break through ambivalence, and they proceed to change on their own from there on (see Chapter 3). Sometimes it is necessary to provide additional skills, helps, and strategies for change (Hester & Miller, 1989), which are beyond the scope of this book. What we hope to do is to help you strengthen your skills for moving clients out of the precontemplation and contemplation stages, and into readiness for change. Direct persuasion and confrontation are usually not the best strategies for accomplishing this. We believe that counselors can take a different and powerful approach in dealing with ambivalence. How this is done is the subject of Part II.

PART TWO

PRACTICE

5

Principles of Motivational Interviewing

If you treat an individual as he is, he will stay as he is, but if you treat him as if he were what he ought to be and could be, he will become what he ought to be and could be.

—Johann Wolfgang von Goethe

The original concept of motivational interviewing grew out of a series of discussions with a group of Norwegian psychologists at the Hjellestad Clinic near Bergen. They asked one of us (Miller) to demonstrate how he would respond to particular problematic situations they were encountering in treating people with alcohol problems. As he demonstrated possible approaches, they asked excellent questions: "Why did you say that instead of something else? What were you thinking when you said that? Why did you remain silent? What is it that you are trying to *do* with the client? Why didn't you push harder at that point? Where are you going with this line of questions? Why didn't you just tell him what he should do?" The result was a first statement of principles and strategies of motivational interviewing (Miller, 1983).

In the ensuing years, much progress has been made toward clarifying and specifying processes of motivational interviewing. Important clinical applications have been undertaken in Australia, Britain, Canada, The Netherlands, Scandinavia, and the United States, and some of these are reflected in Part III of this book. A number of evaluations of motivational counseling strategies have been completed (as reported in Part I), and others are underway.

From its beginning, motivational interviewing has been *practical* in focus. The concept arose from the practical questions of clinicians. Its principles have emerged from our own experience in working with hundreds of people with alcohol and other problems, and in this sense it has been taught to us by our clients. It has been enthusiastically adopted by clinicians in a broad range of cultures because—they tell us—of its applicability and practical utility.

But what *is* motivational interviewing? We begin this chapter by providing a statement of what we perceive motivational interviewing to be, and how it differs from other approaches. Then we proceed to outline five key principles of this approach.

What Is Motivational Interviewing?

Motivational interviewing is a particular way to help people recognize and do something about their present or potential problems. It is particularly useful with people who are reluctant to change and ambivalent about changing. It is intended to help resolve ambivalence and to get a person moving along the path to change. For some people, this is all they really need. Once they are unstuck, no longer immobilized by conflicting motivations, they have the skills and resources they need in order to make a lasting change. All they need is a relatively brief motivational boost (see Chapter 3). For others, motivational interviewing is only a prelude to treatment (though an important one). It creates an openness to change, which paves the way for further important therapeutic work.

In motivational interviewing, the counselor does not assume an authoritarian role. One avoids the message that "I'm the expert and I'm going to tell you how you need to run your life." Responsibility for change is left with the individual (which, by the way, is where we think it *must* lie, no matter how much therapists may debate about what we can "make" or "allow" or "permit" our clients to do). Our clients are always free to take our advice or not. This certainly does not mean that therapists are helpless or powerless. To the contrary, some research indicates that therapists exert a surprising amount of influence over whether or not their clients change!

The strategies of motivational interviewing are more persuasive than coercive, more supportive than argumentative. The counselor seeks to create a positive atmosphere that is conducive to change. The overall goal is to increase the client's intrinsic motivation, so that change arises from within rather than being imposed from without. When this approach is done properly, it is the *client* who presents the arguments for change, rather than the therapist. Motivational interviewing employs a variety of strategies, some of them derived from client-centered counseling, to accomplish this. In contrast to more aggressive styles, the counselor may at times appear relatively inactive. Yet the motivational interviewer proceeds with a strong sense of purpose, clear strategies and skills for pursuing that purpose, and a sense of timing to intervene in particular ways at incisive moments.

Differences from Three Other Styles

Confrontation-of-Denial Approaches

In Part I we have described how motivational interviewing differs from traditional strategies that are predicated on the assumption of "confronting denial." These contrasts have already been discussed in detail, but it may be useful to summarize these points here. A list of contrast points is provided in Table 5.1.

Skill-Training Approaches

A second general counseling orientation with which motivational interviewing can be contrasted is a directive approach that emphasizes skill training. The term most often used for this approach is "cognitive–behavioral." Such skill-training strategies assume that the client is already in the "action" stage

TABLE 5.1. Contrasts between Confrontation of Denial and Motivational Interviewing

Confrontation-of-denial approach	Motivational interviewing approach
Heavy emphasis on acceptance of self as having a problem; acceptance of diagnosis seen as essential for change	De-emphasis on labels; acceptance of "alcoholism" or other labels seen as unnecessary for change to occur
Emphasis on personality pathology, which reduces personal choice, judgment, and control	Emphasis on personal choice and responsibility for deciding future behavior
Therapist presents perceived evidence of problems in an attempt to convince the client to accept the diagnosis	Therapist conducts objective evaluation, but focuses on eliciting the client's own concerns
Resistance is seen as "denial," a trait characteristic requiring confrontation	Resistance is seen as an interpersonal behavior pattern influenced by the therapist's behavior
Resistance is met with argumentation and correction	Resistance is met with reflection
Goals of treatment and strategies for change are prescribed for the client by the therapist; client is seen as "in denial" and incapable of making sound decisions	Treatment goals and change strategies are negotiated between client and therapist, based on data and acceptability; client's involvement in and acceptance of goals are seen as vital

TABLE 5.2. Contrasts between Skill Training and Motivational Interviewing

Skill-training approach	Motivational interviewing approach
Assumes that the client is motivated; no direct strategies are used for building motivation	Employs specific principles and strategies for building client motivation for change
Seeks to identify and modify maladaptive cognitions	Explores and reflects client perceptions without labeling or "correcting" them
Prescribes specific coping strategies	Elicits possible change strategies from the client and significant others
Teaches coping behaviors through instruction, modeling, directed practice, and feedback	Responsibility for change methods is left with the client; no training, modeling, or practice
Specific problem-solving strategies are taught	Natural problem-solving processes are elicited from the client and significant others

and is motivated for change. The emphasis is on teaching the person *how* to change, rather than building commitment (the *why*) to change. Unlike motivational interviewing, these approaches are often highly prescriptive, offering specific directions, instructions, and assignments. Although motivational interviewing can be used as a preparation for skill training, the approaches are readily differentiated. The key points of contrast are shown in Table 5.2.

Nondirective Approaches

Motivational interviewing incorporates many of the insights and strategies described by Carl Rogers, but it differs in several ways from a classic "Rogerian" style, as well as from other nondirective (e.g., existential) approaches. Although motivational interviewing can be accurately described as client-centered, it is quite directive. The counselor typically has a clear goal (e.g., to change drinking and reduce alcohol-related problems) and pursues systematic strategies to achieve that goal. The counselor's own feedback and advice are given. Empathic reflection is used selectively, to reinforce certain points while de-emphasizing others. Furthermore, as we discuss shortly, the counselor is often working actively to *create* discomfort and discrepancy, rather than passively following the client's own offerings. These differences are summarized in Table 5.3.

TABLE 5.3. Contrasts between Nondirective and Motivational Interviewing Approaches

Nondirective approach	Motivational interviewing approach
Allows the client to determine the content and direction of counseling	Systematically directs the client toward motivation for change
Avoids injecting the counselor's own advice and feedback	Offers the counselor's own advice and feedback where appropriate
Empathic reflection is used noncontingently	Empathic reflection is used selectively, to reinforce certain processes
Explores the client's conflicts and emotions as they exist currently	Seeks to create and amplify the client's discrepancy in order to enhance motivation for change

Five General Principles

To help you see the forest before we get to the trees, we now outline five broad clinical principles underlying motivational interviewing. These incorporate but differ from the principles first outlined by Miller (1983). They are as follows:

1. Express empathy.
2. Develop discrepancy.
3. Avoid argumentation.
4. Roll with resistance.
5. Support self-efficacy.

We explain these five basic principles in this chapter, saving the "how-to" strategies for Chapters 6–10.

1. Express Empathy

An empathic therapist style is one essential and defining characteristic of motivational interviewing. As we have discussed in Part I, the therapeutic skill of "accurate empathy," as described by Carl Rogers, has been shown to be predictive of success in treating problem drinkers. This style of empathic warmth and reflective listening is employed from the very beginning and throughout the process of motivational interviewing.

The attitude underlying this principle of empathy might be called "acceptance." Through skillful reflective listening, the therapist seeks to understand the client's feelings and perspectives without judging, criticizing, or blaming. It is important to note here that acceptance is not the same thing as agreement or approval. It is possible to accept and understand a client's perspective but not to agree with it. Nor does an attitude of acceptance prohibit the therapist from differing with the client's views. The crucial attitude is a respectful listening to the client with a desire to understand his or her perspectives. Paradoxically, this kind of acceptance of people *as they are* seems to free them to change, whereas insistent nonacceptance ("You're not OK; you have to change") can have the effect of keeping people as they are. This attitude of acceptance and respect also builds a working therapeutic alliance, and supports the client's self-esteem—an important condition for change (Miller, 1983).

An empathic therapist seeks to respond to a client's perspectives as understandable, comprehensible, and (within the client's framework, at least) valid. Ambivalence is accepted as a normal part of human experience and change, rather than seen as a pathological trait or pernicious defensiveness. Reluctance to give up a problem behavior is to be expected at the time of treatment; otherwise, the person would probably have changed before this point. The client is not seen as uniquely pathological or incapable. Rather, the client's situation is understood as one of being "stuck" through understandable psychological principles.

PRINCIPLE 1: EXPRESS EMPATHY.
Acceptance facilitates change.
Skillful reflective listening is fundamental.
Ambivalence is normal.

---

2. Develop Discrepancy

We certainly do *not* mean that the general goal of motivational interviewing should be to have clients accept themselves as they are and stay that way. Neither do we advocate using reflective listening simply to follow clients wherever they happen to wander. A person who presents with a health-threatening drug habit can be motivated to change that habit. This certainly does involve, in at least one sense of the term, "confronting" the client with an unpleasant reality. The question is how best to accomplish this.

A second general principle of motivational interviewing is thus to create and amplify, in the client's mind, a discrepancy between present behavior and broader goals. In the original exposition of motivational interviewing, Miller (1983) described this as creating "cognitive dissonance," borrowing a concept introduced by Festinger (1957). A more general and, we believe, a better way to understand this process is simply as a discrepancy between where one is and where one wants to be. This can be triggered by an awareness of the *costs* of the present course of behavior. When a behavior is seen as conflicting with important personal goals (such as one's health, success, family happiness, or positive self-image), change is likely to occur. Consider this example given by Premack (1970) of a man who

> dates his quitting [smoking] from a day on which he had gone to pick up his children at the city library. A thunderstorm greeted him as he arrived there; and at the same time a search of his pockets disclosed a familiar problem: he was out of cigarettes. Glancing back at the library, he caught a glimpse of his children stepping out in the rain, but he continued around the corner, certain that he could find a parking space, rush in, buy the cigarettes, and be back before the children got seriously wet. The view of himself as a father who would "actually leave the kids in the rain while he ran after cigarettes" was . . . humiliating, and he quit smoking. (p. 115)

No one "confronted" this man. No one else may have known what a significant event was occurring in his life. But in fact he was confronted by an unpleasant reality about himself, and it triggered a change. This kind of story—in which a life event changes one's perception of a habit—is common in the reports of people who have quit using alcohol, tobacco, or other drugs on their own. It is difficult, of course, for a therapist to arrange for such an event to occur. The *principle*, however, is one that is quite central to motivational interviewing. Motivation for change is created when people perceive a discrepancy between their present behavior and important personal goals (Miller, 1985b).

Many people who seek consultation already perceive some discrepancy between where they are and where they want to be. Yet they are also ambivalent, caught in an approach–avoidance conflict. A goal of motivational interviewing is to *develop* discrepancy—to make use of it, increase it, and amplify it until it overrides attachment to the present behavior. The strategies of motivational interviewing seek to do this *within* the client, rather than relying primarily upon external motivators (e.g., pressure from the spouse, threat of unemployment, or court-imposed contingencies). This involves clarifying important goals for the client, and exploring the consequences or potential consequences of his or her present behavior which conflict with those goals. When successfully done, motivational interviewing changes the client's perceptions (of discrepancy) without creating a feeling of being pressured or coerced.

The general approach is one that results in the *client's* presenting the reasons for change, rather than the counselor's doing so. People are often more persuaded by what they hear themselves say than by what other people tell them. When motivational interviewing is done well, it is not the therapist but the client who gives voice to concerns (e.g., "This problem is more serious than I realized") and intentions to change (e.g., "I've got to do something about this").

PRINCIPLE 2: DEVELOP DISCREPANCY.
Awareness of consequences is important.
A discrepancy between present behavior and
     important goals will motivate change.
The client should present the arguments for
     change.

---

3. Avoid Argumentation

A third important principle of motivational interviewing is that the counselor avoids arguments and head-to-head confrontations. The least desirable situation, from this viewpoint, is one in which the counselor is arguing that the client has a problem and needs to change, while the client is defending an opposite viewpoint. This is a trap that we discuss in detail in Chapter 6.

Motivational interviewing *is* confrontational in its purpose: to increase awareness of problems and the need to do something about them. A casual observer of this counseling approach, however, would not be likely to label it as "confrontational." One experienced therapist in a workshop we were offering called it "soft confrontation." It is this gently persuasive style that is a hallmark of motivational interviewing.

Direct argumentation tends to evoke reactance from people; that is, it results in their asserting their freedom to do as they please. The more you tell someone "You can't," the more likely she or he is to respond "I will." Strongly defending a position (e.g., "You have a problem and you've got to change") is likely to elicit opposition and defensiveness from the client. As we have discussed in Part I, client resistance is strongly affected by how the therapist responds, and resistance during treatment is predictive of failure to change. For these reasons, it is a general goal in motivational interviewing to avoid approaches that evoke client resistance. When resistance is encountered, the therapist shifts strategies.

One place where arguments are quite likely to emerge, particularly in counseling addictive behaviors, is in regard to the applicability of a diagnostic label. Some counselors place great importance on a client's willingness to "admit" to a label such as "alcoholic." (In fact, in most other problem areas there is usually little emphasis placed on a client's acceptance of a diagnostic label.) Trying to force a client to accept such a label can be countertherapeutic, however, and there is no evidence to suggest that recovery is promoted by persuading people to admit to a diagnostic label. Within Alcoholics Anonymous (AA), the emphasis has been more on self-recognition than on coerced admission. Bill Wilson wrote, "We do not like to pronounce any individual as alcoholic, but you can quickly diagnose yourself" (Alcoholics Anonymous, 1976, p. 31). No doubt some people do find it an important turning point when they first accept their problem. Our point here is that there is no particular reason why the therapist should badger clients to accept a label, or exert great persuasive effort in this direction. van Bilsen and van Emst (1986) observed, "Our experience was that we were often fighting against our clients instead of motivating them for change" (p. 707). Accusing clients of being "in denial" or "resistant" or "addicted" is more likely to increase their resistance than to instill motivation for change. We advocate starting with clients wherever they are, and altering their self-perceptions not by arguing about labels, but through substantially more effective means.

PRINCIPLE 3: AVOID ARGUMENTATION.
Arguments are counterproductive.
Defending breeds defensiveness.
Resistance is a signal to change strategies.
Labeling is unnecessary.

---

4. Roll with Resistance

If you don't argue, then what *do* you do? Jay Haley and other pioneers in the field of strategic family therapy have spoken of "psychological judo." They refer to the kinds of martial arts in which an attack is not met with direct opposition (as in boxing), but rather the attacker's own momentum is used to good advantage. It makes no difference what one throws at a master of this art. All blows fall on empty air, and the harder one attacks, the faster one falls into nothing.

This is not to say that the master is passive. Not at all. He or she *adds to* the momentum—a little spin, a glance to the side, an extra tug. The fall is inevitable, but the master is in control of *where* the other person lands. Often it is not where the person intended to land, and there may be the surprise of "How did I get over here?"

Any analogy can be taken too far. Motivational interviewing is not like combat; it is not about winning and losing. The client is not an opponent to be defeated. Yet the illustration of rolling with resistance is useful. We explain in Chapter 8, for example, how statements that a client offers can be turned or reframed slightly to create a new momentum toward change. The object in motion is not a body but a perception. The client starts by throwing out present perceptions, and finds (if the counselor, the "master," is skillful) that they come down in a new place.

There is also an element of great respect for the client. What to do about a problem, if anything, is ultimately the client's decision. Reluctance and ambivalence are not opposed, but are acknowledged by the therapist to be natural and understandable. The counselor does not *impose* new views or goals. Rather, the client is invited to consider new information and is offered new perspectives. "Take what you want and leave the rest" is the permissive kind of advice that pervades this approach. It's an approach that is hard to fight against.

In motivational interviewing, the counselor also commonly turns a question or problem back to the client. It is not the therapist's job to generate all the solutions. Doing so, in fact, allows the client to dismiss each idea with "Yes, but . . ." It is assumed that the client is a capable individual, with important insight and ideas for the solution of his or her own problems. Rolling with resistance, then, includes involving the client actively in the process of problem solving.

PRINCIPLE 4: ROLL WITH RESISTANCE.
Momentum can be used to good advantage.
Perceptions can be shifted.
New perspectives are invited but not imposed.
The client is a valuable resource in finding
    solutions to problems.

---

5. Support Self-Efficacy

A fifth important principle of motivational interviewing involves the concept of "self-efficacy." As discussed in Chapter 3, self-efficacy refers to a person's belief in his or her ability to carry out and succeed with a specific task. Self-efficacy is a key element in motivation for change (Bandura, 1977, 1982; Rogers & Mewborn, 1976) and a good predictor of treatment outcome with addictive behaviors (Condiotte & Lichtenstein, 1981; DiClemente, 1981; DiClemente, Prochaska, & Gilbertini, 1985; Godding & Glasgow,

1985; Solomon & Annis, 1990; Wilkinson & LeBreton, 1986). A therapist may follow the first four principles outlined above, and persuade a person that he or she has a serious problem. If, however, the person perceives no hope for change, then no effort will be made, and the therapist's efforts have been in vain.

Although the term "self-efficacy" is relatively recent, healers have long recognized that hope and faith are important elements of change (Frank, 1973; Miller, 1985a; Shapiro, 1971). The therapist's own expectations about a client's chances for recovery can have a powerful impact on outcome (Leake & King, 1977; Parker, Winstead, & Willi, 1979). A general goal of motivational interviewing is to increase the client's perceptions of his or her capability to cope with obstacles and to succeed in change (Miller, 1983).

In presenting our first principle—"Express empathy"—we have discussed the importance of supporting self-esteem, the person's general self-regard. Although self-efficacy can be influenced by general self-esteem, the former is much more specific. Essentially, self-efficacy means confidence in one's ability to cope with a specific task or challenge. A client may, for example, suffer from very low self-esteem, but nevertheless may be persuaded that it is possible and within his or her ability to change a particular problem. Even approaches such as AA, which emphasize personal powerlessness over a problem, also stress that it is within the person's own power to change—in this case, by deciding to turn over control to a higher power, to take control by giving up control (Baugh, 1988). The overall message here is "You can *do* it. You can succeed."

There are various messages that support self-efficacy. One is an emphasis on personal responsibility (discussed, along with self-efficacy, in the "FRAMES" model of Chapter 3). The person not only *can* but *must* make the change, in the sense that no one else can do it for him or her. Motivational interviewing does not foster hope that the therapist will change the client. "I will change you" is not the intended message. A more appropriate message is "If you wish, I will help you to change yourself." A client may also be encouraged by the success of others. Contact with former clients as models can be helpful in this regard (Zweben & Li, 1981), but counselors also use accounts of the numbers of people who have succeeded in changing, or specific success stories. Still another helpful fact is the number of different approaches that are available and that have been shown to be helpful (e.g., Hester & Miller, 1989). Even a series of treatment failures need not be viewed as cause to abandon hope. It can be understood as this particular person's not yet having found the right approach. Given the range of different and promising treatment options, the chances of any given individual's finding something that works are quite good (Miller & Hester, 1986b). This is one emphasis within the "menu" element of the FRAMES model.

PRINCIPLE 5: SUPPORT SELF-EFFICACY.
Belief in the possibility of change is an
   important motivator.
The client is responsible for choosing and
   carrying out personal change.
There is hope in the range of alternative
   approaches available.

Summary

These five broad principles underlie the specific strategies that we describe
in the next five chapters. We have discussed them apart from practical
"how-to" elements, in order to give you a larger context regarding the "why"
of practice. These principles bespeak a more general philosophy behind
motivational interviewing. We believe that each person possesses a powerful
potential for change. Your task as a therapist is to release that potential, to
facilitate the natural change processes already inherent in the individual. In
this approach, the client is treated with great respect, and as an ally rather
than an opponent. Motivational interviewing is about helping to free people
from the ambivalence that entraps them, yielding repetitive cycles of self-
defeating or self-destructive behavior. It is more than a set of techniques for
doing counseling. It is a way of *being* with clients, which is probably quite
different from how others may have treated them in the past. This way of
being is not the whole story of change. There are many specific treatment
strategies that can be quite helpful as people pursue the course of change
(e.g., Garfield & Bergin, 1986; Hester & Miller, 1989). Motivational interviewing is intended to get the person unstuck, to start the change process
happening. Once begun, change may occur rapidly with relatively little
additional assistance (see Chapter 3), or it may require a long span of
therapeutic direction and support.

   We turn now to six chapters on specific strategies of motivational
interviewing. In the first of these, Chapter 6, we introduce strategies that are
important from the outset, and that can help you avoid some common traps
that await you. These strategies are most appropriate for *buiding motivation*
to change, the first of two major phases of motivational interviewing. In
Chapter 7 we explain ways in which pretreatment assessment results can be
used as motivational feedback, and explore ways to assess readiness for
change. Chapter 8 provides strategies for recognizing and coping with client
resistance, particularly during the first phase of motivational interviewing. Then in Chapter 9, we proceed to discuss strategies appropriate for
strengthening commitment to change, the second phase of motivational

interviewing. Chapter 10 explores a few typical but difficult situations that can arise in the application of motivational interviewing, and ways in which these special challenges can be met. Finally, in Chapter 11, we describe a practical case from start to finish, in order to illustrate how the strategies of motivational interviewing are interwoven.

6

Phase I: Building Motivation for Change

What you need, in trying to help people, are the qualities of a good bartender—sympathy, willingness to listen, and intuition.
       —Frank Buchman, quoted in Garth Lean, *Frank Buchman: A Life*

Starting a counseling process is not unlike starting a game of chess. Everything is neat and ordered to begin with, yet within minutes both players can become immersed in complexity. One cannot know beforehand exactly what moves should be made, but a clear idea of the overall game plan is of great benefit. The number of specific situations that one can face is nearly infinite; yet one can know beforehand a set of general strategies that are quite helpful in coping with the complexities of play. Part of this knowledge involves understanding what *not* to do, particularly at the outset. It also includes recognition of common problems and traps that may be encountered, and how to prevent or at least recover from them. There are different approaches for opening, middle game, and endgame, although the strategies overlap.

   The overall goal in this first phase of counseling is to *build motivation for change*. The assumption here is that the client is ambivalent, and in the contemplation or even precontemplation stage. This chapter contains some opening strategies for motivational interviewing that will allow you to put into practice the principles outlined in Chapter 5. We explain some traps that can be encountered early in motivational interviewing, and use specific examples of counseling dialogue to illustrate how counselors can succumb to or surmount these pitfalls. First, however, we want to say a few things about the opening session, and some common traps into which counselors can fall at the very beginning.

About the First Session

The very first session can be crucial, setting both the tone and the expectations for counseling. The therapist's actions even in a single session can have a powerful influence on client resistance and long-term outcome (Miller & Sovereign, 1989). It is important, then, to adopt the proper approach right from the beginning, and to avoid falling into several traps that can quickly undermine progress.

The Question–Answer Trap

At the beginning of a counseling process, it is easy to fall into a pattern wherein the counselor asks questions and the client gives short answers. This is similar to what may occur when a physician conducts a general health screening: The patient responds "Yes" or "No" to a long survey of potential problem areas. This can happen in part because the counselor feels a need for specific information. It may also be a response to anxiety—either in the counselor, who wants to keep control, or in the client, who is more comfortable with the safe predictability of this passive role. In tone, the "expert" counselor controls the session by asking questions, while the client merely responds with appropriate short answers. Here is an example:

THERAPIST: You're here to talk about your gambling, is that right?

CLIENT: Yes, I am.

T: Do you think you gamble too much?

C: Probably.

T: What is your favorite game?

C: Blackjack.

T: Do you usually drink when you gamble?

C: Yes.

T: Have you ever gone seriously into debt because of gambling?

C: Once or twice, yes.

T: How far into debt?

C: Once I had to borrow $8,000 to pay off a debt.

T: Are you married?

C: No, I'm divorced.

T: How long ago were you divorced?

C: Two years ago.

And so it can happen. There are several negative aspects of this trap. First, it teaches the client to give short, simple answers, rather than the kind of elaboration you will need for motivational interviewing. Second, it implies an interaction between an active expert and a passive patient: If you just ask enough questions, then you will have the answer. It also affords little opportunity for the client to explore and to offer self-motivational statements, which we soon describe as a crucial process in motivational interviewing.

This trap is relatively easy to avoid. We recommend having clients complete a precounseling questionnaire to give you the specific information you may need at the outset, and saving the other specifics for later. This saves you going through an inventory of short-answer questions. The open-ended questions and reflective listening strategies explained later in this chapter are also very helpful in getting around the question–answer trap.

There is, however, a subtler form of this same trap, which involves open-ended questions. The optimal approach is usually to ask an open-ended question, then to respond to the client's response *not* with another question, but with reflective listening. The use of a series of open-ended questions without sufficient reflective listening can have a very similar effect to that of a series of closed questions. The client is directed into a passive, question-answering role. As a general rule, avoid asking three questions in a row.

The Confrontation–Denial Trap

For purposes of motivational interviewing, the confrontation–denial trap is the most important trap to avoid, and a common trap it is. Therapists fall into it through their own good intentions, and through a faulty understanding of motivational processes. If a therapist makes the wrong openings, most clients will readily play along with the pattern.

How does this trap happen? The familiar script is that the counselor detects some information indicating the presence of "a problem" (e.g., "alcoholism"), begins to tell the client that he or she has a serious problem, and prescribes a particular course of action. The client then expresses some reluctance about this, making statements along two general lines: (1) "My problem isn't really *that* bad," and (2) "I don't really need to change that much."

This is actually quite predictable. If, as we assume, people usually enter counseling in a state of ambivalence, they feel two ways about their situation: They want it, and they don't want it. They think maybe they should change, and yet they are reluctant to give up their present pattern. They are in conflict. If the counselor argues for one side of the conflict, it is very likely that the client will give voice to the other side. Here is a sample:

THERAPIST: Well, it seems to me that you have a serious drinking problem. You're showing a lot of the signs of alcoholism.

CLIENT: What do you mean?

T: Well, you've had an alcoholic blackout, you're uncomfortable when you can't drink, and you're losing control of your drinking.

C: But a lot of people I know drink just like I do.

T: Maybe so, maybe not. But we're not talking about other people, we're talking about you.

C: But I don't think it's that serious.

T: Not serious! It's just sheer luck that you haven't been arrested or killed somebody driving after drinking.

C: I told you, I can drive just fine. I've never had a problem.

T: And what about your family? They think you're drinking too much, and they think you ought to quit.

C: Oh, Fran came from a family of teetotalers. There's nothing wrong with me. They think anybody who has three drinks is an alcoholic.

From the viewpoint of motivational conflict, presented in Chapter 4, this pattern is quite predictable and understandable. By taking responsibility for the "problem–change" side of the conflict, the therapist elicits oppositional "no-problem" arguments from the client.

What happens next? The therapist may regard the client's reactions as proof of the "alcoholic trait of denial," which confirms the diagnosis. Within this view, the appropriate response is to turn up the heat—to confront the client's denial all the more aggressively (see Chapter 1). The result of this is also rather predictable: As the therapist argues one side more adamantly, the client will defend the other with greater vigor. It is a familiar script, and probably one that the client has been through before with others.

If the client begins to feel trapped, the phenomenon of psychological reactance (see Chapter 1) may also be evoked: The person asserts freedom to do as he or she pleases. The end result is an escalating head-to-head power struggle. The more the therapist confronts, the more the client becomes resistant and unwilling to change (Miller & Sovereign, 1989). Clients in this situation can literally talk themselves out of changing. Hearing themselves vigorously arguing that they don't have a problem and don't need to change, they become convinced. Few people enjoy losing an argument or being proved wrong.

This is the confrontation–denial trap. It can occur at any stage in counseling, but it is particularly common in the early phase, where it can set a very unhelpful tone. It can focus on any of a wide range of topics, not just whether or not the person has "a problem." In fact, this trap can emerge any time the counselor is arguing with a client. Two of the central strategies of motivational interviewing—reflective listening and eliciting self-motivational statements—are good approaches for preventing this problem. The strategies for dealing with resistance that we present in Chapter 8 are also helpful in avoiding this trap.

The Expert Trap

The enthusiastic and competent counselor can unwittingly fall into the expert trap by conveying the impression of having all the answers. Like the question–answer trap, its most common effect is to edge clients into a passive role, which is inconsistent with the basic approach of motivational interviewing—giving people the opportunity to explore and resolve ambivalence for themselves. A sincere desire to help can lead a counselor to try to "fix" the situation for a client, to prescribe answers and solutions. There is a time for expert opinion (see Chapter 9), but the focus in this approach is first on building the client's own motivation. This is not likely to happen if the client is placed in the role of passive recipient of expert advice.

The Labeling Trap

Counselors and clients can also easily be ensnared by the issue of diagnostic labeling. Counselors sometimes believe that it is terribly important for a person to accept the counselor's labeling ("You're an alcoholic," "You're in denial," etc.). Because such labels often carry a certain stigma in the public mind, it is not surprising that people with reasonable self-esteem resist them. As we have discussed earlier, there is little apparent value in pressuring people to accept such labels, and the Alcoholics Anonymous (AA) philosophy specifically recommends against such labeling of others.

Often there is an underlying process in a labeling debate. It may be a power struggle in which the counselor seeks to assert control and expertise, or a judgmental communication. For some clients, even a seemingly harmless reference to "your problem with . . . " can elicit feelings of being cornered and uncomfortable. The danger, of course, is that the labeling struggle evokes resistance from the client, which in turn hinders progress. Since there are no important clinical advantages in imposing a label, the risk of descending into a confrontation–denial loop is simply not worth taking.

We recommend, therefore, that you *de-emphasize labeling* in the course of motivational interviewing. Problems can be fully explored without attaching labels that evoke unnecessary resistance. If the issue of labeling never comes up, it is not necessary to raise it. Often, however, a client will raise the issue, and how you respond can be quite important. We recommend a combination of reflection and reframing—two techniques to be discussed later. Here is a brief example.

CLIENT: So are you implying that I'm an addict?

THERAPIST: No, I really don't care that much about labels. But it sounds like you do, that it's a worry for you.

C: Well, I don't like being called an addict.

T: When that happens, you feel like saying that your situation really isn't that bad.

C: Right! I'm not saying that I don't have any problems . . .

T: But you don't like being labeled as "having a problem." That sounds too harsh to you.

C: Yes, it does.

T: That's pretty common, as you might imagine. Lots of people I talk to don't like being labeled. There's nothing strange about that. I don't like people labeling me, either.

C: I feel like I'm being put in a box.

T: Right. So let me tell you how I see this, and then we'll move on. To me, it doesn't matter what we *call* a problem. I don't care if we call it "addiction" or "problems" or "Fred," for that matter. We don't have to call it anything. If you'd like a label, I could give you one, but that's not important to me. What really matters is to determine how your use of cocaine is harming you, and what, if anything, you want to do about it. That's what I care about.

As a final note, we would add that we also see no strong reason to *discourage* people from accepting a diagnosis if they are so inclined. Members of AA, for example, often report that it was important for them to recognize and accept their alcoholism. There is little point in opposing such self-acceptance. Our emphasis here is not to get into debates and struggles over labels.

The Premature-Focus Trap

Even if the counselor avoids arguments and labels, resistance may result if client and therapist wish to focus on different topics. In addictions counseling, for example, it is not uncommon for the therapist to want to hone in quickly on the client's alcohol and other drug use and related problems, while the client wishes to discuss a broader range of concerns. A struggle may ensue regarding how much attention should be paid to what the counselor perceives to be "the problem." Indeed, in the client's mind, alcohol/drug use may be a relatively small part of the picture, and it may not be clear whether and how this is related to the client's larger concerns. If the counselor presses too quickly to focus the discussion on addiction, the client may be put off and become defensive. Other clients, however, present their drinking or drug use as a primary concern. In this case, early focusing is quite appropriate. The point is to avoid becoming engaged in a struggle about the proper topic for early discussion. Starting with the client's concerns, rather than those of the counselor, will ensure that this does not happen.

The Blaming Trap

Still another obstacle that can be encountered in the first session is a client's concern with blaming. Whose *fault* is the problem? Who's to blame? If this issue arises and is not dealt with properly, needless time and energy can be wasted on defensiveness. The obvious key here is that blame is irrelevant. Usually this can be dealt with by reflecting and reframing the client's concerns. If this problem arises, for example, the client may be told,

> It sounds like you're worried about who's to blame here. I should explain that counseling is not about deciding who is at fault. That's for the courts. Counseling has a "no-fault" policy. I'm not interested in looking for who's responsible, but rather what's troubling you, and what you might be able to do about it.

Concerns about blame may also be prevented by offering a brief structuring statement at the beginning of counseling. If the client has a clear understanding of the purpose of counseling, worries about blaming may be averted.

Opening Structure

Clients come to counseling with widely varying expectations. They may come expecting to be criticized, healed, advised, questioned, listened to, blamed, taught, medicated, or consoled. Prospective clients enter treatment with widely differing expectations, fears, hopes, and concerns. For this and other reasons, it can be useful at the outset to provide the client with a simple and brief structuring of the first session, and of counseling in general. A good structuring statement can set the client's mind at rest and get counseling off to a good start. Some elements that may be included in a good structuring statement are as follows:

- The amount of time you have available
- An explanation of your role and goals
- A description of the client's role
- A mention of details that must be attended to
- An open-ended question

Here is an example:

> We have about an hour together now, and in this time I want to get a beginning understanding of what brings you here. I'll probably spend most of this time listening, so that I can understand how you see things and what your concerns are. You must also have some hopes about what will and won't happen here, and I'll want to hear about those. Toward the end of this hour I'll need to ask you for some specific information that I need, but let's just get started now. What's on your mind? I understand that you have some concerns about your use of tranquilizers. . . .

Five Early Strategies

The first four strategies described below are derived largely from client-centered counseling, although in motivational interviewing they are used for a particular purpose—that of helping clients to explore their ambivalence and express reasons for change. The fifth strategy is more directive and is specific to motivational interviewing. It integrates and guides the use of the other four strategies.

1. Ask Open-Ended Questions

During the early phase of motivational interviewing, it is important for the therapist to establish an atmosphere of acceptance and trust, in which the client will explore his or her problems. This means that the *client* should do most of the talking at this stage, with the counselor listening carefully and encouraging expression. The first four of these five early strategies directly support this goal.

One way to begin this process is to ask early questions in a way that encourages the client to do most of the talking. Short-answer questions are necessary in most sessions, but should not be emphasized during the early phase of motivational interviewing. It is better to begin with *open-ended* questions—ones that cannot easily be answered with a brief reply. Such questions open the door for the client to explore. Some clients come in almost bursting to talk, and it takes only a simple invitation to elicit their story. Others are more guarded and require encouragement. How you respond to the client's initial answers will strongly influence what happens next, but that is taken up below. Our interest here is in how to ask good open-ended questions.

If you know in advance or otherwise sense that the client has clear concerns to talk about, a simple opening of the door may suffice. Here are some examples:

- I assume, from the fact that you are here, that you have some things you want to talk over with a counselor. What would you like to discuss?
- I'd like to understand how you see things. What's brought you here? What's been the problem?
- I understand that you have some concerns about drinking. Tell me about them.
- You said on the telephone that you have been using drugs for a long time, and you wanted to talk about it. Fill me in. Why don't you start from the beginning, when you first used drugs, and bring me up to date?

In discussing a focal problem with more ambivalent clients (e.g., ones in the early contemplation stage), it can be useful to ask for both sides of the coin, or to ask a connected cluster of more neutral-sounding questions. Some therapists prefer to ask clients first what they have liked about their current ("problem") behavior, and then what the negative side includes. Here are some possible openings:

- Tell me about your use of cocaine. What do you like about it? And what's the other side? What are your worries about using it?
- Tell me what you've noticed about your drinking over the years. Have you seen any changes in your drinking and how it affects you? What have you noticed that might concern you, or that has concerned other people?
- I understand that you're here to talk about your gambling. So help me see the whole picture here. What do you enjoy about gambling, and what's the darker side?

Obviously, people will vary in how they react to opening questions such as these. Some will respond eagerly to the opportunity to talk about their difficulties. In such cases, your job is a matter of guiding the person in this exploration, using the strategies described in this and subsequent chapters. Others will volunteer relatively little, and may change the subject or head off into one of the traps described earlier. These questions are only door-openers, which provide opportunities for using other strategies.

2. Listen Reflectively

Perhaps the most challenging skill in motivational interviewing is that of reflective listening. In popular conceptions, listening just involves keeping quiet and hearing what someone has to say. The crucial element in *reflective* listening, however, is how the counselor *responds* to what the client says. Thomas Gordon (1970) has outlined 12 kinds of responses that are *not* listening:

1. Ordering, directing, or commanding
2. Warning or threatening
3. Giving advice, making suggestions, or providing solutions
4. Persuading with logic, arguing, or lecturing
5. Moralizing, preaching, or telling clients what they "should" do
6. Disagreeing, judging, criticizing, or blaming
7. Agreeing, approving, or praising
8. Shaming, ridiculing, or labeling
9. Interpreting or analyzing
10. Reassuring, sympathizing, or consoling
11. Questioning or probing
12. Withdrawing, distracting, humoring, or changing the subject

These responses have also been called "roadblocks" because they get in a client's way. In order to keep exploring in the same direction, the client has to deal with the roadblock and go around it. Roadblocks have the effect of blocking, stopping, diverting, or changing direction. They all imply an uneven or "one-up" relationship. A counselor who responds with one of these is not listening—at least not in the sense of reflective listening. Rather, the counselor is keeping quiet just long enough to think of a response from the list above, and then offering it. The underlying message is "Listen to *me*; I know best." Instead of continuing to explore the path, the client then has to deal with the roadblock. Consider this unhelpful "therapist" talking to a client who feels two ways about an important decision. (The number of each corresponding roadblock from the list above is given in parentheses.)

CLIENT: I just don't know whether to leave him or not.
THERAPIST: You should do whatever you think is best. (#5)

C: But that's the point! I don't know what's best!

T: Yes, you do, in your heart. (#6)

C: Well, I just feel trapped, stifled in our relationship.

T: Then you should separate for a while and see how you feel. (# 3)

C: But I love him, and it would hurt him so much if I left!

T: But if you don't do it, you could be wasting your life. (#2)

C: But isn't that kind of selfish?

T: It's just what you have to do to take care of yourself. (#4)

C: I just don't know how I could do it.

T: I'm sure you'll be fine. (#10)

This client has not been helped to explore ambivalence, but instead is prematurely pressed toward one resolution. The "counselor" in this situation has never really listened, has never given the client a chance to keep on talking and exploring. The client's time has been spent dodging roadblocks.

But what else is there? If one avoids all 12 roadblocks, what is there left to say? We don't mean to imply that it is *wrong* to use these 12 responses. There is a time and a place for each of them. We *do* mean to say that reflective listening is something different from these ways of responding. It has been extensively described by Rogers (1957), Truax and Carkhuff (1967), Gordon (1970), Ivey (1980), and Egan (1982), among others.

The essence of a reflective-listening response is that it makes a guess as to what the person *means*. Before a person speaks, he or she has a certain meaning to communicate. This is coded into words, often imperfectly. The listener has to hear the words accurately and then decode their meaning. That means there are three steps along the way where communication can go wrong: coding, hearing, and decoding (Gordon, 1970; Miller & Jackson, 1985). The reflective listener forms a reasonable guess as to what the original meaning was, and gives voice to this guess in the form of a *statement*.

A statement? Why not a question? After all, the listener is not sure whether the guess is correct. The reason is very practical: A well-formed reflective statement is less likely to evoke resistance. *Asking* about meaning, through questioning, seems to distance clients from experiencing it. They step back and begin to ask if they really do or should feel what they have expressed. The difference is subtle, and not everyone notices it. Consider the difference in sound between these reflections:

You're feeling uncomfortable?
You're feeling uncomfortable.

You're angry with your mother?
You're angry with your mother.

The difference is an inflection. The voice tone goes up at the end of a question, gently down at the end of a statement. Reflective-listening statements should usually turn *down* at the end.

In order to offer reflective listening, you first must train yourself to *think* reflectively. This includes the realization that what you *believe* or *assume* people mean is not necessarily what they really mean. Most statements can have multiple meanings. Emotion words such as "depressed" or "anxious" have very different meanings to different people. What could it mean for a person to say, "I wish I were more sociable"? Here are some possibilities:

I feel lonely and I want to have more friends.
I get very nervous when I have to talk to strangers.
I should spend more time getting to know people.
I would like to be popular.
I can't think of anything to say when I'm with people.
People don't invite me to their parties.

To think reflectively is to make this process more conscious. In fact, when you hear a statement, you consider what it might mean, and you choose what you believe to be the most likely meaning. Many people then act as if this *were* the actual meaning of the statement. Reflective listening is a way of checking, rather than assuming that you *know* what is meant.

Reflective listening, then, involves making a statement that is not a roadblock, but rather a *guess* about what the person means. Usually, but not always, the subject of the sentence is the pronoun "you." Here is an extended example from a counseling session with an ambivalent problem drinker. For illustrative purposes, every therapist sentence in this segment is a reflective-listening statement.

CLIENT: I worry sometimes that I may be drinking too much for my own good.

THERAPIST: You've been drinking quite a bit.

C: I don't really *feel* like it's that much. I can drink a lot and not feel it.

T: More than most people.

C: Yes. I can drink most people under the table.

T: And that's what worries you.

C: Well, that and how I feel. The next morning I'm usually in bad shape. I feel jittery and I can't think straight through most of the morning.

T: And that doesn't seem right to you.

C: No, I guess not. I haven't thought about it that much, but I don't think it's good to be hung over all the time. And sometimes I have trouble remembering things.

T: Things that happen while you're drinking.

C: That, too. Sometimes I just have a blank for a few hours.

T: But that isn't what you meant when you said you have trouble remembering things.

C: No. Even when I'm not drinking, it seems like I'm forgetting things more often, and I'm not thinking clearly.

T: And you wonder if it has something to do with your drinking.

C: I don't know what else it would be.

T: You haven't always been like that.

C: No! It's only the last few years. Maybe I'm just getting older.

T: It might just be what happens to everybody when they reach 45.

C: No, it's probably my drinking. I don't sleep very well, either.

T: So maybe you're damaging your health and your sleep and your brain by drinking as much as you do.

C: Mind you, I'm not a drunk. Never was.

T: You're not that bad off. Still, you're worried.

C: I don't know about "worried," but I guess I'm thinking about it more.

T: And wondering if you should do something, so that's why you came here.

C: I guess so.

T: You're not sure.

C: I'm not sure what I want to do about it.

T: So if I understand you so far, you think that you've been drinking too much and you've been damaging your health, but you're not sure you want to change that.

C: Doesn't make much sense, does it?

T: I can see how you might feel confused at this point.

Notice that the therapist does not insert roadblocks throughout this process. It would have been easy to substitute some of the roadblocks for these reflections. This is avoided, however, because the purpose is to elicit self-motivational statements from the client.

Reflective-listening statements can be quite simple. Sometimes the mere repetition of a word or two will keep the client moving (in the example above, the first reflection could have been "Too much . . ."). A more sophisticated reflection substitutes new words for what the client has offered, or makes a guess about the unspoken meaning. Sometimes it is helpful, too, to reflect how the client seems to be *feeling* as he or she speaks.

Reflection is not a passive process. The counselor decides what to reflect and what to ignore, what to emphasize and de-emphasize, what words to use in capturing meaning. Reflection can be used to reinforce certain aspects of what a person has said, or to alter its meaning slightly. These applications of reflection are discussed in Chapter 8. We advise that reflective-listening statements should constitute a substantial proportion of counselor responses during the early phase of motivational interviewing. In particular, self-motivational statements should be reflected back. In this way, clients hear their own statements twice.

Reflection is particularly important following open-ended questions. Once you have asked an open question, respond to the client's answers with reflective listening. Because questioning is a much less demanding skill (for the counselor) than empathic listening, it is easy to fall into the question–answer trap, asking a series of questions instead of reflecting the client's statements. This may evoke resistance more than self-motivational statements. Remember, then, to follow up a question with reflective listening.

3. Affirm

It can also be quite helpful to affirm and support your client during the counseling process. This can be done in the form of compliments and statements of appreciation and understanding. The process of reflective listening can be quite affirming in itself, but direct affirmations have a place in counseling, too. Here are some examples:

> I appreciate how hard it must have been for you to decide to come here. You took a big step!
> I think it's great that you want to do something about this problem.
> That must have been very difficult for you.
> You're certainly a resourceful person, to have been able to live with the problem this long and not fall apart.
> That's a good suggestion.
> It must be difficult for you to accept a day-to-day life so full of stress. I must say, if I were in your position, I would also find that difficult.

I guess that's why you're here—because you don't want to accept that kind of stress any more.

It seems like you're a really spirited and strong-willed person in a way. You enjoy being happy with other people, and making them laugh. In that way, it's hard to think about giving up drinking.

You're certainly having to cope with a lot of problems right now—more than most people. I can understand how sometimes you want a "lift" so badly, you want a release from it all.

4. Summarize

A fourth strategy to use early and throughout motivational counseling is summarizing. Summary statements can be used to link together material that has been discussed. When you are eliciting a client's self-motivational statements, for example, it is wise to summarize periodically:

So thus far you've said that you are worried with the *amount* that you are drinking, relative to other people, and how much you're spending on it. You're not sure what it means that you can drink so much more than other people without seeming to be affected. You're concerned that your drinking is damaging your memory, and that it keeps you from normal sleeping. What else?

Such periodic summaries reinforce what has been said, show that you have been listening carefully, and prepare the client to move on. They also allow a client to hear his or her own self-motivational statements a third time!

Linking summaries can be especially helpful in expressing a client's ambivalence. The typical experience of ambivalence is to vacillate back and forth between reasons to change and reasons to stay the same. A summary statement is one way to allow a person to examine the positives and negatives *simultaneously*, acknowledging that both are present. Linking phrases, such as "on the one hand . . . on the other" and "at the same time," can be useful:

It sounds like you're torn two ways. On the one hand, you're very worried that drinking is hurting your family, and that your work is being affected as well. You're especially surprised that two different friends in the same week told you they are concerned about your drinking. At the same time, you certainly don't think of yourself as an alcoholic, and you find that you can go for a week at a time without drinking, without any bad effects. This must be puzzling for you.

Other sources of information can be incorporated into a summary as well. Results of objective assessment (see Chapter 7) and information from the courts or family members can be combined with the client's own statements.

At the end of the first session, and at other points during motivational counseling, it is useful to offer a major summary, pulling together what has transpired thus far. Again, it should be noted that in giving such summaries, you must decide what to include and to emphasize. When you are introducing such a major summary, it is helpful to use a prefacing statement that announces what is to follow. Here is an example of a fairly complete summary at the end of a first session:

> Our hour is running out, and I'd like to try to pull together what you've said so far, so we can see where we are and where we're going. Let me know if I miss anything important that we've covered. You came in because your husband is concerned about your drinking and your marijuana smoking. If he hadn't pushed you, you might not have come right now, but you've been very open in exploring this, and I admire you for that. I asked you about problems in your life that you think could be related to alcohol and marijuana, and you mentioned several. You've been feeling quite depressed and tired, and as we discussed, alcohol is a depressant. You said you are having a lot of trouble concentrating, and that you're feeling as if you aren't motivated to do anything in your life. Again, rightly, you think this might be linked to your drinking and smoking, although you think that's not the whole picture. You resent your husband's sending you here, in a way, because you think he has a part in these problems too. The tests that you completed indicate that you have developed a fairly significant dependence on alcohol and, to a lesser extent, on marijuana, and that's a problem that can keep growing if you don't do something about it. When you were arrested that one time 2 years ago, your breath test showed that you were over .20, which is really quite intoxicated, even though you weren't feeling drunk. We talked about how this kind of tolerance is in itself a risk factor. You're also worried that you're not the kind of mother you want to be, in part because of drinking and smoking, and you don't want your kids to grow up with drug problems. Your doctor told you that your stomach problems are probably caused, or at least made worse by, your drinking. At the same time, you have liked alcohol and marijuana because you use them to relax and to get away from some heavy family stresses. You're not sure how you could handle life without drinking and smoking, and so you're not sure what to do. Is that a fair summary so far? What have I left out?

This kind of summary is a good way to draw the first session to a close. Notice the collaborative tone, allowing the client to add to or correct your summary. A somewhat shorter form of the same statement can be used to begin the next session, building upon progress made earlier. A major summary of this kind is also used at the transition point from the first to the second phase of motivational interviewing (see Chapter 9).

5. Elicit Self-Motivational Statements

The preceding four strategies are fundamental to motivational interviewing. If these were the only strategies employed, however, it would be quite easy to become stuck in ambivalence. It is necessary, therefore, to have a guiding strategy to help clients resolve their ambivalence. That is the underlying purpose of the fifth strategy. The other four strategies can all be applied in this goal-directed approach.

In one sense, motivational interviewing is the opposite of a confrontation-of-denial approach, in which the therapist promotes the "problem-change" position and the client defends against it. We believe that such a confrontational approach is often detrimental, precisely because it causes the client to defend a "no-problem" position. Our goal is to have the client give voice to exactly the opposite kinds of statements. *In motivational interviewing, it is the client who presents the arguments for change.* It is the counselor's task to facilitate the client's expression of these self-motivational statements (Miller, 1983).

Self-motivational statements fall into four general categories. The first of these is *problem recognition.* (It is often a desire for problem recognition that leads counselors into labeling struggles, but the imposition of labels is usually an ineffective strategy.) Some examples of desirable problem recognition statements from clients are as follows:

> I guess there's more of a problem here than I thought.
> I never really realized how much I am drinking.
> This is serious!
> Maybe I *have* been taking foolish risks.
> I can see that in the long run, my gambling is going to do me in.

A second and related kind of self-motivational statement is *expression of concern* about perceived problems. This is often communicated nonverbally, through the client's facial expressions, sighs, tears, or gestures. Some verbalizations of this kind are these:

> I'm really worried about this.
> How could this happen to me? I can't believe it!
> I feel pretty hopeless.

The third type of self-motivational statement is direct or implicit *intention to change.* This can be expressed in the person's taking action as an initial step to change (e.g., taking disulfiram) or in stated intentions to do so. A few examples of the latter are as follows:

I think it's time for me to think about quitting.
I've got to do something about this.
This isn't how I want to be. What can I do?
I don't know how I'm going to do it, but I've got to make a change.
How do people quit a habit like this?

Finally, self-motivational statements can express a theme of *optimism* about change. Such statements reflect an ability to make a difference (self-efficacy) in the problem area. Here are a few statements of this kind:

I think I can do it.
Now that I've decided, I'm sure I can change.
I'm going to overcome this problem.

These four kinds of statements reflect cognitive (recognition, optimism), affective or emotional (concern), and behavioral (intention to act) dimensions of commitment to change. From our perspective, every statement of this kind tips the balance a little further in the direction of change.

Some people walk through the counselor's door already saying things like this, and only need some help in confirming their commitment and planning a course of action. But how can a counselor evoke such statements from more ambivalent clients? This is one of the key skills of motivational interviewing.

Evocative Questions

A very direct approach is simply to ask the client for such statements. Open-ended questions can be used to explore the client's own perceptions and concerns. Don't ask *whether* the person has such concerns (e.g., "Do you think that you have a problem with drugs?"). Assume that the person is feeling ambivalent and that he or she *does* have such concerns. Open-ended questions for evoking each of the four categories of self-motivational statements are suggested in Table 6.1.

When the client offers a self-motivational statement, even tentatively, reinforce it nonverbally (e.g., with head nods) as well as verbally with reflective listening or a supportive statement (e.g., "I can see how that would concern you" or "That must be difficult for you"). Whether a client will continue offering self-motivational statements and exploring ambivalence and discrepancy depends largely on how you respond. It is important, therefore, to respond in a manner that communicates acceptance, reinforces

TABLE 6.1. Sample Questions to Evoke Self-Motivational Statements

1. Problem Recognition

What things make you think that this is a problem?

What difficulties have you had in relation to your drug use?

In what ways do you think you or other people have been harmed by your drinking?

In what ways has this been a problem for you?

How has your use of tranquilizers stopped you from doing what you want to do?

2. Concern

What is there about your drinking that you or other people might see as reasons for concern?

What worries you about your drug use? What can you imagine happening to you?

How do you feel about your gambling?

How much does that concern you?

In what ways does this concern you?

What do you think will happen if you don't make a change?

3. Intention to Change

The fact that you're here indicates that at least a part of you thinks it's time to do something. What are the reasons you see for making a change?

What makes you think that you may need to make a change?

If you were 100% successful and things worked out exactly as you would like, what would be different?

What things make you think that you should keep on drinking the way you have been? . . . And what about the other side? What makes you think it's time for a change?

What are you thinking about your gambling at this point?

What would be the advantages of making a change?.

I can see that you're feeling stuck at the moment. What's going to have to change?

4. Optimism

What makes you think that if you did decide to make a change, you could do it?

What encourages you that you can change if you want to?

What do you think would work for you, if you decided to change?

---

self-expression, and encourages continued exploration. Your responses should be encouraging, and should not imply that you are accumulating evidence to use against the client. The goal is to reinforce the client's self-motivational statements and to encourage him or her to continue.

Once the process has begun, straightforward encouragement to continue is often effective. The general form here is "What else?"

What else have you noticed or wondered about?

What other concerns have you had?

What are some other reasons why you may need to make a change?

What other things have people told you?

Why else do you think you could succeed?

> What other problems have you had?
> What else worries you about your drinking?

Remember that the overall purpose here is for the client to take responsibility for the "problem–change" side of the conflict. Periodic summaries of the client's self-motivational statements can be useful in moving the process along.

The Decisional Balance

As mentioned earlier, it can be helpful to have clients discuss the positive as well as the negative aspects of their present behavior. They may be asked, for example, to say or list what they *like* about their drinking or drug use, as a preface to inquiring about the negative side. This has the advantage of getting clients talking and feeling comfortable, as well as of clarifying both sides of the ambivalence. It can be useful to fill out a decisional balance sheet, like the one shown in Chapter 4 (see Table 4.1), to allow a client to see the full picture. Additional strategies can then be used to strengthen motivations for change. Often, however, simply talking about the negative side of the conflict leads directly to expressions of concern about it.

Elaboration

Once a motivational topic has been raised, it is useful to ask the client to elaborate. This helps to reinforce the theme and to elicit further self-motivational statements. One good way of doing this is to ask for specific examples, and for clarification as to why (how much, in what way) each one is a concern. Here is a demonstration:

CLIENT: One place where I see a problem is money.

THERAPIST: In what way is that a concern for you?

C: Well, I've been spending a lot of money on drugs and not paying my bills.

T: Give me an example.

C: Just last week I went through about $400. I get started and I just keep going.

T: And it really adds up. How else does it affect your money?

C: I do stupid things when I'm high.

T: For example . . .

C: I lent $300 to this guy I met. I'll never see that again. And I buy things I don't need.

T: Such as . . .

C: A watch. One time I bought myself this really good watch. At least I *thought* it was a good watch. I spent a lot on it.

T: How much does this money issue concern you?

C: It's getting to be a big problem. I've got people coming to the door, calling on the telephone, sending nasty letters. I've got to do something.

T: And it sounds like you think your use of drugs is part of your money troubles.

C: A big part. Yes.

In the early stages of motivational interviewing, a useful target for elaboration is a typical day or session of use. Asking in detail about behavior and mood changes, for example, can highlight the positive reasons for using alcohol or other drugs; areas of concern also emerge quite naturally from such discussion.

Using Extremes

Clients can also be asked to describe the extremes of their concerns, to imagine worst consequences. Some questions of this type are as follows:

- What concerns you the *most*?
- What are your worst fears about what might happen if you don't make a change?
- What do you suppose are the worst things that might happen if you keep on the way you've been going?

Looking Back

Sometimes it is useful to have the person remember times before the problem emerged, and to compare these with the present situation. Here are some examples:

- Do you remember a time when things were going well for you? What has changed?
- What were things like before you started drinking so heavily? What were *you* like back then?
- Tell me about how you two met each other, and what attracted you to each other back then. What was it like?
- What are the differences between the Pat of 10 years ago and the Pat of today?
- How has your use of drugs stopped you from growing, from moving forward?

Looking back at past substance use often brings out the observation that the person's tolerance has markedly increased. This can be used as a powerful motivator if the counselor reframes this phenomenon as a danger sign, along the lines described in Chapter 8.

Looking Forward

Helping people to envision a changed future is another approach for eliciting self-motivational statements. Here you ask for the client to tell you how it might be after a change:

- If you do decide to make a change, what are your hopes for the future?
- How would you like things to turn out for you?
- I can see that you're feeling really frustrated right now. How would you like things to be different?
- What are the options for you now? What could you do?
- What would be the best results you could imagine if you make a change?

Exploring Goals

Yet another approach is to ask the client to tell you what things are most important in his or her life. (This can overlap nicely with the "looking forward" process.) What values or goals does this person hold most dear? Rokeach (1973) has described a simple procedure for assessing personal value hierarchies, whereby a set of cards describing possible values are arranged in rank order, according to which value the person prizes most highly. From the perspective of motivational interviewing, the purpose of this exploration is to discover ways in which the problem behavior is inconsistent with or undermines important values and goals for the client. When the highest or most central values and goals have been defined, you can ask how the problem you are discussing (e.g., drinking) fits into this picture. For a drinker, it would be possible to insert a card labeled "drinking" in the set to be sorted by Rokeach's method—a strategy that in itself can provoke useful discussion with a client. The central point here is to explore and develop themes of discrepancy between these important goals and the present problem behavior.

Paradox

Sometimes a skillful therapist can make use of paradox to encourage self-motivational statements. The term "paradox" can refer to a number of different therapeutic tactics, but in this context we mean that the counselor subtly takes on the role of the "no-problem" side of the client's conflict. By stating this side of the conflict, the therapist intends to evoke the opposite— namely, statements of problem recognition, expression of concern, intention to change, and optimism. Here are a few examples of how a counselor might take on this role:

> You've come all the way down here to talk to me about this, but you haven't convinced me yet that you've got a real concern. Is that *all*?
>
> Let me tell you something that concerns me. A program like this one requires a lot of motivation and effort. We don't really want to start working with somebody until they're sure they need to change, and frankly, I'm not sure about you. As I listen to you, I'm not convinced you're motivated enough.
>
> I'm not sure you believe you could change even if you wanted to.

There is a clear test of whether such a strategy is working: If it evokes self-motivational statements from the client, it is working. But beware—paradoxes can backfire.

Sometimes a paradoxical evoking strategy can be used very directly, with the client's full awareness and participation. With certain clients, this can be quite beneficial and engaging:

> One thing that I find is helpful is to clarify the real reasons for change. I've heard from you some of the reasons why you are reluctant to think about making a change, and now I have a suggestion. I want to have a little debate with you. I will defend the position that you don't really have a problem and don't need to change, and I'd like you to do your best to convince me otherwise. Do you understand? I'm going to be you, and your job is to persuade me that there really is a problem here that I need to examine and do something about. OK?

Clients sometimes need extra encouragement to get rolling with a role play of this kind. Have the client speak in "you" language, while you as the counselor speak in "I" language and voice the client's prior "no-problem" arguments. Here's how it might go:

THERAPIST: I just can't see what you think is the problem here. I drink just the same as my friends.

CLIENT: Well, you certainly drink more than a lot of your friends, and then some of your friends are pretty heavy drinkers themselves.

T: But that doesn't mean we've got a problem. I mean, what's the harm in having a drink?

C: It's not having *a* drink that's harmful. But you're the last to leave the party. (*Out of role:*) Am I doing OK?

T: (*Out of role:*) You're doing great. But don't go easy on me. Don't let me get away with anything. OK?

C: OK

T: (*In role:*) Well, I can handle it! I can drink all night and still not be drunk.

C: But what about the next morning . . . ?

Over time, the therapist allows the client to "persuade" him or her that there is reason for concern. This technique is not appropriate for every client, but it can be an appealing, even entertaining way to externalize and examine the ambivalence. At the same time, it is evoking many self-motivational statements from the client, who must defend the presence of harm and the need for change.

The eliciting of self-motivational statements is a very important strategy for developing discrepancy. Hearing oneself make statements such as these tends to increase awareness of the discrepancy between one's goals and present actions. The greater this discrepancy, the greater the motivation for change. The first four strategies for early motivational interviewing can be integrated into the development of discrepancy by (1) asking open-ended questions that pull for self-motivational statements; (2) reflecting back, sometimes selectively, the self-motivational aspects of what a client has said, which allows the client to hear it a second time; (3) affirming and reinforcing the client for making self-motivational statements; and (4) offering periodic summaries of self-motivational themes that the client has offered, allowing the client to hear them once again as statements that he or she has made. Other strategies, such as objective feedback (see Chapter 7), can also serve to increase perceived discrepancy (Miller, 1983). Phase I of motivational interviewing focuses primarily on building motivation through the amplification and clarification of discrepancy.

Realize that the eliciting of self-motivational statements can be important not only in early sessions, but throughout counseling. Ambivalence does not usually disappear, but only diminishes. The evoking of self-motivational statements can serve as a continuing reminder of the reasons for commitment to change.

Follow-Through Contact

The risk of a client's dropping out of treatment is highest following the first session. In some studies, the dropout rate in alcoholism treatment has been well over 50%. The strategies outlined above may be helpful in reducing dropout, but one additional step has been shown to increase significantly the rate of clients' returning for further treatment. This is a simple follow-through contact.

In one study (Koumans, Muller, & Miller, 1967), alcoholics who made an initial contact with a psychiatric clinic were divided into two groups. The first 50 received only the ordinary referral procedures, whereas the next 50 received a single telephone call after their consultation. Of these two groups, 8% versus 52% returned for treatment, most of them within 1 week. That is, a single further contact increased the return rate by more than six times. In another study (Koumans & Muller, 1965), 50 alcoholics randomly selected after initial consultation to receive "a personal letter expressing concern for the patient's well-being and repeating our invitation to return for further assistance" were compared with 50 others receiving no letter. The return rates for outpatient treatment were 50% and 31%, respectively.

Simple follow-through contact can also be effective in preventing treatment dropout. One clinic (Nirenberg, Sobell, & Sobell, 1980) found that when clients failed to keep an appointment, a personal telephone call (but not standard letters) reduced the dropout rate from 92% to 60%. When the follow-through letter was changed from an impersonal format to one more clearly expressing an interest in the client, a letter alone reduced dropout from 96% to 66%. Panepinto and Higgins (1969) likewise found that a follow-through letter after the first missed appointment reduced early dropout from 51% to 28%. Intagliata (1976) found that telephone contacts nearly doubled the rate of aftercare attendance in alcoholics discharged from inpatient treatment. In short, simple expressions of caring and interest can have a major effect on a client's "motivation" to return for treatment (cf. Wedel, 1965).

We have thus far discussed ways to enhance client motivation during early contacts and sessions. In Chapter 7 we consider how information from a more careful assessment can be incorporated into the process of motivational interviewing.

7

Using Assessment Results

O wad some Pow'r the gifie gie us
To see oursel[ve]s as others see us!
It wad frae monie a blunder free us . . .

—Robert Burns, "To a Louse"

Most treatment programs include some form of pretreatment evaluation. The purposes of such assessment are several, and include (1) screening for problems; (2) establishing a diagnosis; (3) establishing eligibility and appropriateness for treatment; (4) understanding the individual more comprehensively; and (5) determining which form of treatment, if any, is most appropriate (Jacobson, 1989a). To the extent that treatment is individualized, a careful evaluation can help to determine optimal goals and strategies (Glaser et al., 1984; Gottheil, McLellan, & Druley, 1981; Miller, 1989b; Miller & Hester, 1986b).

There is, however, another important potential use of pretreatment assessment that is too often overlooked. This is to use evaluation results as part of motivational counseling. Providing the client with a thorough summary of findings can be very helpful in building motivation and strengthening commitment for change. In this chapter, we discuss several issues of individual evaluation, including (1) how to prepare clients for assessment, (2) what dimensions to include in a comprehensive pretreatment evaluation, (3) how to assess motivation itself, and (4) how to present your findings in a motivational manner.

Presenting Assessment

In the dimmest view, pretreatment assessment is seen by both counselor and client as an annoying set of hurdles and obstacles that must be crossed before treatment can commence. Such a view assumes that the evaluation is of no use in planning treatment—a sad commentary on the extent to which we may fail to individualize treatment according to the person's particular needs (Orford & Hawker, 1974). If assessment is presented in this light, both counselor and client are likely to approach it grudgingly and perhaps not very seriously, with a hope to have it behind them as soon as possible.

We commend to you an entirely different way of thinking about assessment and presenting it to your clients. The opening assumption here is that without a careful evaluation, you do *not* already know everything you need to know about a client. If you believe otherwise—that you can proceed confidently into treatment without bothering about evaluation—we urge you to reconsider. Such a view implies either that "one treatment fits all," or that your personal intuition is sufficient for all needs. A careful assessment is essential in the development of an appropriately individualized plan for change. How to conduct such an assessment and when to do it constitute the subject of the discussion that follows.

From the beginning, assessment should be presented to the client in a *motivational* fashion. It is a way of finding out what problems (if any) need to be addressed, and how best to begin. To the person who is unconvinced that there is any problem at all, you can say, "Perhaps you are right. I certainly don't know without more information. Let's do a careful evaluation, and see what we find." At the other end of the spectrum is the person who is well aware of problems and convinced of the need for immediate treatment. To this person you can say, "I'm glad that you recognize your problems and want to do something about them now. Let's get started by doing a careful evaluation, so that we will know where to begin, and exactly what problems we're dealing with. Otherwise, it's like a surgeon trying to operate while blindfolded." Whatever position the person occupies along this pretreatment motivational continuum, the truthful purpose of evaluation is to provide important additional information. And in any case, the findings of the evaluation can be shared with the client.

One practical question is the timing of assessment. Some programs require applicants to complete assessment before seeing a therapist. There are several disadvantages to this procedure. The importance of assessment may not be apparent to the client, who therefore does not take it seriously and may respond carelessly or defensively. Assessment can be seen as an obstacle to what brought the client in, and dropout may occur. The assessment-first approach also establishes a somewhat impersonal tone at the very outset of consultation. Furthermore, it provides no opportunity to assess the client's special needs for assessment or crisis intervention.

We recommend, therefore, that a client's treatment experience should begin with a motivational interview, following the guidelines described in Chapter 6. This establishes a personal working relationship and provides a motivational basis on which to ask the client to complete assessment. Details required for initial paperwork can be obtained via brief preconsultation questionnaires, or toward the end of the initial consultation.

Dimensions for Assessment

There are many alternative approaches and instruments that can be used in pretreatment assessment of alcohol and other drug abuse. These have been reviewed in detail elsewhere (Donovan & Marlatt, 1988; Jacobson, 1989a, 1989b; Lettieri, Nelson, & Sayers, 1985; Lettieri, Sayers, & Nelson, 1985; Sobell, Sobell, & Ward, 1980), and their discussion is beyond the scope of this book. For present purposes, we only discuss eight major domains that we believe should be covered in a comprehensive evaluation. Of course, it is not feasible for all counseling agencies to assess all of these domains. A workable assessment plan must take into account the types of clients served and the available resources.

1. Alcohol/Drug Use

The most obvious dimension is the client's use of alcohol and other drugs. This means determining *which* drugs the client uses (including legal drugs such as tobacco and caffeine, as well as prescription medications) on a regular or periodic basis. More detailed approaches can be used to establish the amount and frequency of such use (e.g., Miller & Marlatt, 1984; Sobell et al., 1980). It can also be useful to have the client keep self-monitoring records of use for a period of time before and during treatment (e.g., Miller & Muñoz, 1982; Wilkinson & LeBreton, 1986).

2. Life Problems

A second important dimension is a survey of problems that are occurring in the person's life, whether or not these are regarded as "related to" alcohol or other drugs. This will include a review of possible negative consequences of alcohol/drug use. This is typically the emphasis in popular screening questionnaires such as the Michigan Alcoholism Screening Test (Selzer, 1971) and the CAGE (Mayfield, McLeod, & Hall, 1974). It can be very useful, however, to survey life problems more broadly, in order to identify other difficulties that may have an impact on treatment and recovery (Miller & Marlatt, 1984).

3. Dependence Syndrome

Current diagnostic thinking focuses on a "dependence syndrome" associated with the use of certain drugs (American Psychiatric Association, 1987; World Health Organization, 1982). Among the commonly recognized elements (Edwards & Gross, 1976) are (1) greater predictability of use, (2) greater urgency or priority given to use, (3) increased tolerance, (4) repeated withdrawal symptoms, (5) use of the drug to relieve withdrawal symptoms, (6) a sense of compulsion or craving to use, and (7) a rapid reestablishment of addiction when the person resumes use after a period of abstinence. The severity of dependence is regarded to be an important indicator of treatment outcome, and can be measured in various ways (Jacobson, 1989a). Drug tolerance (e.g., being able to "hold your liquor") is a common phenomenon that many clients readily report, and that can be reframed to induce motivation for change (see Chapter 8).

4. Functional Analysis

The first three dimensions discussed above basically ask "How much?" and "With what complications?" A different and important question is "Why?" From a motivational perspective, this question explores the positive incentives for continuing the current pattern.

The term "functional analysis" refers to an examination of the relationship between a behavior and the environment. More specifically, a functional analysis explores (1) the particular stimuli or situations that *precede* the behavior (antecedents), and (2) the events that typically *follow* the behavior (consequences). For example, a person may use alcohol or another drug in particular situations (e.g., when unable to sleep or when feeling anxious) in hopes of obtaining specific effects (e.g., getting to sleep, feeling more relaxed). A functional analysis examines such antecedents and consequences, in order to clarify the "meaning" of the behavior to the individual (Miller & Muñoz, 1982).

Functional analysis is important in understanding a client's motivation for use and for change. Some of the motivational assessment approaches discussed below are tools in this regard. The related concept of "psychological dependence" refers to ways in which a person relies upon a drug for coping purposes (Miller & Pechacek, 1987). If you are going to encourage a person to give up a drug, it is important to understand and address these issues, as well as to ensure that he or she has alternative skills for coping without the drug (Annis & Davis, 1989; Marlatt & Gordon, 1985). Otherwise, the person is at higher risk of relapse.

5. Biomedical Effects

Alcohol and other drug abuse can clearly have adverse effects on physical health. For this reason, it is wise to include biomedical measures in a comprehensive evaluation. Common approaches include blood chemistries, a general systems review, blood pressure screening, and the LeGo examination (Babor, Kranzler, & Lauerman, 1989; National Council on Alcholism, 1972). The extent of such screening will be affected by cost considerations and the typical medical severity of the population.

6. Neuropsychological Effects

Brain impairment is commonly associated with alcohol abuse, and appears to occur earlier and more frequently than clinical damage to other physical systems (Miller & Saucedo, 1983; Parsons, Butters, & Nathan, 1987; Wilkinson, 1979). A full neuropsychological test battery is costly and time-consuming, but briefer sets of measures can be employed to screen for cognitive difficulties. Feedback of impairment on such measures can provide a potent motivational boost, because such information is novel and not available to the person from ordinary daily experience (Miller & Sovereign, 1989; Miller, Sovereign, & Krege, 1988). Memory difficulties are common, including the classic alcoholic "blackout," and should be queried during any evaluation of problem drinkers. It must be noted that neuropsychological impairment often clears substantially during the first month of abstinence in dependent alcoholics; thus it is prudent in such cases to delay assessment, in order to avoid the effects of acute intoxication and detoxification. On the other hand, testing after prolonged abstinence is likely to underestimate the impairment characteristic of the individual when drinking.

7. Family History

It can be useful to inquire about problems that have been experienced by the client's biological relatives. Risk for alcohol problems appears to be influenced in part by genetic factors. We recommend inquiring about relatives who have experienced problems with alcohol or other drugs (Miller & Marlatt, 1984; Schuckit, 1984). Other potentially important patterns in family history include affective disorders (such as major depression), antisocial personality, and attention deficit disorder (e.g., Tarter, McBride, Buonpane, & Schneider, 1977; Winokur, Reich, Rimmer, & Pitts, 1970).

8. Other Psychological Problems

Finally, abuse of alcohol and other drugs is often associated with additional psychological problems. Some such difficulties are directly linked to the drug use, and disappear or diminish when the primary problem is treated. Often, however, other problems persist or worsen, even during long periods of abstinence. Rates of depression, anxiety disorders, psychoses, suicide, antisocial personality, attention deficit problems, marital and sexual problems, and social skill deficits are all elevated among alcohol and other drug abusers. For this reason, it is wise to screen for other psychological concerns. Because such problems are exacerbated by active alcohol/ drug use and may clear during recovery, however, it is wise to conduct this evaluation after the individual has been free of abuse for at least 1 month.

Comprehensive Assessment

The eight dimensions outlined above pose a substantial challenge for counselors. Each of these is an important area for assessment. Although there is some overlap among these dimensions, knowing about any one domain tells you relatively little about the other seven. We have treated people with high consumption (1) and dependence (3), but surprisingly few overt life problems (2), and little or no evidence of biomedical (5) or neuropsychological impairment (6). In medical settings, one sees what Jellinek (1960) called "beta alcoholics"—people with biomedical problems related to alcohol, without significant life problems or dependence. In essence, all combinations of elevations are conceivable. Unless you assess a dimension directly, you are unaware of the person's status on it.

Yet in reality, time is limited, and assessment is costly. A thorough assessment of all eight dimensions could take days (cf. National Council on Alcoholism, 1972). An ideal approach would sample each of these dimensions in a relatively efficient manner. There are various questionnaires (Horn, Wanberg, & Foster, 1987) and interview protocols (Addiction Research Foundation, 1985; Miller & Marlatt, 1984; Schuckit, 1984) designed to do this. Some dimensions, however, cannot be validly assessed through self-report items (e.g., liver function or cognitive impairment).

Comprehensive assessment offers several advantages. It provides important knowledge of the range of dimensions on which impairment can occur. It also permits tailoring of treatment to the needs and characteristics of the individual. Pretreatment scores can be compared with status on these same dimensions after treatment, to assess and document improvement. Finally, a broad-based assessment allows you to give the client a thorough review of his or her status on a wide range of measures—a process that can be very helpful in building motivation for change (Miller & Sovereign, 1989).

Assessment of Motivation

Although motivation has been widely discussed as a critical issue in the treatment of addictive behaviors, until recently there have been few efforts to *measure* this important dimension. The direct assessment of motivation could be added to the list above as a ninth important dimension for evaluation. The reason for direct assessment is simple: A client's motivation for change may not be clear even if all eight other dimensions are assessed.

Therapists have most often assessed motivation informally, judging from such client behaviors as agreement with the therapist, acceptance of diagnosis, expressed desire for help, apparent distress, and compliance with advice (Miller, 1985b). With the exception of compliance with advice, however, these behaviors are of little value in predicting change.

Two major approaches have been developed thus far for the direct assessment of motivation. One of these focuses on the client's perceived benefits versus harm from present behavior. The second explores the client's self-acknowledged readiness for change.

Decisional Balance

The idea of a decisional balance (Appel, 1986; Janis & Mann, 1977) has been discussed in Chapter 2. The notion here is that motivation for change occurs as the perceived costs of a behavior begin to outweigh the perceived benefits (see Figure 2.2 in Chapter 2). It is important to realize that this is not a simple matter of the *number* of positive versus negative factors. It is conceivable, for example, that a client may have many negatives that nevertheless are counterbalanced by one very strong and important positive motivation.

One common approach is to assess what the person perceives to be the negative consequences of the addictive behavior. Common screening instruments (e.g., the Michigan Alcoholism Screening Test) include such items, although they are typically intermixed with signs of dependence and reports of seeking treatment.

Less common is a systematic assessment of what the client perceives to be the benefits of the addictive behavior. These are motivations for continued use. The Alcohol Expectancy Questionnaire (Brown, Christiansen, & Goldman, 1987) offers a related assessment of what reinforcing effects the person expects from alcohol.

A balancing between these two sets of factors can be done in several ways. A decisional balance sheet can be constructed to summarize the client's perceived positive versus negative effects. A simple balance sheet can be prepared for a client by drawing a line down the middle of a blank sheet of paper and listing the pros and cons of continued use, as well as the reasons for and against change, on the two sides. An example is shown in Chapter 4 (Table 4.1).

It is worth saying here that the construction of a decisional balance sheet is not merely a passive assessment of current motivation. It is likely to *influence* motivation. A systematic survey of negative versus positive motivations, for example, may help the client clarify for the first time the relative weight of these factors. Thus the very assessment of motivation can cause it to change. This underlines what we have discussed earlier—that motivation is a dynamic state or process, rather than a static personality trait.

Readiness to Change

Another approach is to ask the client directly about willingness or readiness to change. Several different concepts can be involved here: (1) the person's judgment of a need for change; (2) the perceived possibility of changes occurring; (3) the individual's self-efficacy for change; and (4) the person's stated intention to change in the future, or within a specific period of time. These constructs are often blended in general questions about change. (Note the overlap of these concepts with the types of self-motivational statements that we recommend eliciting from clients in early interviewing; see Chapter 6.)

A conceptual context for judging change readiness is provided by the Prochaska and DiClemente (1984) transtheoretical model of stages of change. These authors have developed the University of Rhode Island Change Assessment (URICA), an instrument for measuring general stages of change, without specific reference to addictive behaviors. A parallel instrument, the Stages of Change Readiness and Treatment Eagerness Scale (SOCRATES), assesses the Prochaska–DiClemente stages of change with regard to alcohol or other drug abuse (Montgomery et al., 1990).

Personalized Feedback

Motivation for change is promoted when people perceive a discrepancy between where they are and where they want to be. Personal feedback of results from objective tests and measures can be persuasive input for convincing clients that they are not where they ought to be.

The general approach that we recommend is to provide clients with their own scores on a range of measures related to the problem area (e.g., drinking). Each score is accompanied by an explanation, as well as a comparison of the client's score with normative or other interpretive information. Kristenson, Ohlin, Hulten-Nosslin, Trell, and Hood (1983), for example, gave medical patients information about their levels of gamma-glutamyltransferase (GGT), a liver enzyme that indicates excessive drinking. These patients were given the information that their levels were above the normal range, and that such elevations are predictive of long-term risks for disease and premature death. Notice that both the personal score and the interpretive information are crucial. Explaining to people that elevated GGT levels are risky is of little interest unless the person knows that his or her own level is elevated. Similarly, telling someone his or her level of GGT is not interesting information unless the person has something with which to compare it. Giving personal scores *and* interpretive information is what can set up a motivational discrepancy.

One example of this feedback strategy is the Drinker's Check-up program, which was developed at the University of New Mexico. It was advertised to the general public through announcements like this one, which appeared in local newspapers:

> The University of New Mexico is offering a free Drinker's Check-up for people who would like to find out whether they are being harmed by their own use of alcohol. The Check-up is not part of any treatment program, and is not intended for alcoholics. Rather it is an informational health service. Participants will not be labelled or diagnosed, and consultation is completely confidential. Objective personal feedback of results will be provided. It is up to the participant to determine what, if anything, to do about the feedback received. (Miller & Sovereign, 1989, p. 223)

People who referred themselves for the Check-up were, almost without exception, significantly impaired by alcohol, but had rarely considered or entered treatment before. In two controlled studies, problem drinkers showed significant reductions in their drinking after receiving the Check-up (Miller & Sovereign, 1989; Miller et al., 1988). This same strategy can be used at the outset of treatment to enhance motivation for change.

We recommend the structured feedback of assessment results. This can be done by providing clients with an explanatory report of their results (Miller et al., 1988). We emphasize that this report is not simply handed to the client. Rather, it is reviewed in person by a knowledgeable counselor, point by point, using a motivational interviewing style.

The basic approach is that of helping the client to understand somewhat complicated results. The counselor specifically avoids using these results to "prove" anything, or to pressure the client to accept a diagnosis or prescribed course of action. Each result is described, along with the information needed to understand what it means. When asked for an opinion, the counselor offers one, but always within a context that allows the client to form his or her own conclusions. Results can be presented with a prefatory comment that underlines this freedom of choice:

> I don't know what you will make of this result, but . . .
> This may or may not concern you . . .
> I don't know whether this will matter to you, but . . .

Any "scare tactic" tone is avoided. In fact, clients are usually quite interested in and concerned with such feedback, without needing much encouragement in this direction from the therapist. If anything, an overbearing counselor style is likely to diminish the client's openness to feedback.

Another important point in giving such feedback is to solicit and reflect the client's own reactions. We find it much more effective to elicit clients' own concerns than to tell the clients what they ought to feel. As noted above, the review of personal assessment results is a rich opportunity for eliciting self-motivational statements. In the course of reacting to their feedback, clients are likely to make statements that acknowledge problems or reflect consideration of change. This can be encouraged by asking for a client's reactions during the feedback process:

> What do you make of this?
> Is this what you expected?
> I'm giving you a lot of information here. What are you thinking at this
>   point?
> How do you feel about this?

A sensitive counselor can also pick up and respond to the client's nonverbal reactions during feedback. These may include a shaking of the head, a scowl or frown, a sigh, a low whistle, raised eyebrows, or tears. Reflective listening is an excellent way to respond to both verbal and nonverbal reactions to feedback. Here are a few possible examples:

> This really took you by surprise—it wasn't what you expected.
> Looks like this is hard for you to hear.
> I imagine this is a little scary.
> You're starting to wonder what you can do about this.
> I guess it must be hard to see this, because in a way you can hear your
>   wife saying, "I told you so."
> It's hard to believe.
> This must be disturbing or confusing for you.

We would add, too, that this kind of feedback can evoke strong emotional reactions in some clients, and counselors should be prepared to deal with these (see Chapter 10). Fears and tears are not unusual when people receive intensive personal feedback regarding risk and problems.

At the end of an assessment feedback period, it is very useful to summarize what has transpired (see Chapter 6). Such a summary should include the following elements: (1) the risks and problems that have emerged from assessment findings; (2) the client's own reactions to the feedback, including self-motivational statements that have been made; and (3) an invitation for the client to add to or correct the summary. This summary often represents the turning point between Phase I and Phase II of motivational interviewing, and it can be useful to proceed directly into strategies for strengthening commitment. These are presented in Chapter 9. But first, we turn to a discussion of how to deal with client resistance when it emerges during either phase of motivational counseling.

8

Dealing with Resistance

You're kind of young yet, and we don't know if you've had enough.
—Dr. Bob to Clarence S., quoted in Ernest Kurtz,
Not-God: A History of Alcoholics Anonymous

The Therapist's Role in Resistance

How one deals with resistance is a crucial issue in motivational interviewing. This is one of the ways in which the approach we are describing is dramatically different from a traditional confrontational strategy (see Chapter 5). An important goal of motivational interviewing, in fact, is to *avoid* eliciting or strengthening resistance. The more a client resists, the less likely it is that the client will change (Miller & Sovereign, 1989). High resistance is also associated with treatment dropout (Chamberlain, Patterson, Reid, Kavanagh, & Forgatch, 1984). The clients of a skillful motivational counselor show realtively low levels of resistance.

Implicit in this argument is another working assumption of motivational interviewing: that *client resistance is a therapist problem*. Perhaps this seems an overstatement. For example, some clients may be highly resistant no matter what therapeutic approach is taken; there are exceptions to every rule. It is also clear that level of client resistance is influenced by factors other than the therapist. Agency-referred clients, for example, have been reported to show more initial resistance than self-referred clients (Chamberlain et al., 1984).

Research does indicate, however, that the extent to which clients "resist" is powerfully determined by therapist style. This finding is not due just to differences between therapists. Dramatic differences in client resistance have been shown when the *same* therapists take different approaches with clients (Miller & Sovereign, 1989), or even switch styles within the same session (Patterson & Forgatch, 1985). The lesson here is that counselors can change their style in ways that will decrease (or increase) client resistance. It is desirable to evoke low levels of client resistance, because this pattern is associated with long-term change (Miller & Sovereign, 1989).

This is an important point. It means that you can judge your success in counseling, in part, from the extent to which your clients show resistance—the less, the better. In this way, your clients will give you feedback about the effectiveness of your own motivational interviewing. This is a great advantage in learning how to adapt this approach in your own work. If you get resistance, shift strategies.

This chapter has only two goals. First, we offer a simple and very practical definition of resistance, and teach you how to recognize it. Then we discuss some general strategies that can be used when you encounter resistance. These strategies can be useful both in Phase I when building motivation for change, and in Phase II, which is discussed in Chapter 9. Resistance is often encountered during the very first session, and so these strategies can be important from the outset. The peak of resistance may occur during the middle phase of counseling (Chamberlain et al., 1984). In Phase II, when commitment is being strengthened and a change plan negotiated, the skillful handling of resistance can also be crucial. The material discussed in this chapter, then, is important throughout the process of motivational interviewing.

Recognizing Resistance

Some therapists believe that resistance occurs because of a client's personality characteristics. Older psychodynamic theories, for example, view resistance as symptomatic of unconscious conflicts that are established during childhood. In this view, resistance walks through the door with the client.

In Chapter 1 we have questioned this view, which attributes resistance wholly to the client's characteristics. Instead, we have argued that resistance arises, to a significant extent, from the interpersonal interaction of therapist and client. A change in therapist style results in a change in client resistance. This is a very practical, here-and-now view of resistance. It means that there is something you can *do* about it.

But what *is* resistance? From our perspective, resistance is observable behavior that occurs during treatment. It signals the therapist that the client is not keeping up. From the perspective of the Prochaska–DiClemente model, it may mean that the therapist is using strategies that are inappropriate at the client's present stage of change. In a way, it is the client's way of saying, "Wait a minute. I'm not with you. I don't agree." The therapist's general task at this point is to double back, find out where the client is, and work at that point. To do this, you need to be able to recognize resistance when it is happening.

An Oregon research group devised a clever and helpful system for observing client resistance behavior during treatment sessions (Chamberlain et al., 1984). It was revised slightly for use in research on the treatment of alcohol problems at the University of New Mexico (Miller, 1986). In this system, there are four major categories of client resistance behaviors. All four of these have been found to be predictive of long-term drinking behavior (Miller & Sovereign, 1989). These categories are shown in Table 8.1.

To be sure, these categories can overlap. Unless you are undertaking detailed research, it is not so important to clarify exactly which category is the right classification for a particular client response. The point is that responses of these kinds can be considered resistance, and indicate that the client is moving away from the direction of change.

Opposite to resistance behaviors are the self-motivational statements described in Chapter 6. We have found that a motivational interviewing style evokes high levels of self-motivational statements and relatively little resistance, whereas a confrontation-of-denial style evokes high levels of resistance and few self-motivational statements (Miller & Sovereign, 1989).

Resistant responses are quite normal during counseling, and their initial occurrence is not reason for concern. It is a problem, however, if such responses persist or escalate as the client's general pattern throughout a session or a course of treatment. It is largely your behavior as the therapist that determines whether initial reluctance will turn into patterned and persistent resistance. It is how you *respond* to client resistance that makes the difference, and that distinguishes motivational interviewing from other approaches.

Strategies for Handling Resistance

Simple Reflection

One good general strategy is to respond to resistance with nonresistance. A simple acknowledgment of the client's disagreement, emotion, or perception can permit further exploration rather than defensiveness, thus avoiding the confrontation–denial trap. A reflective-listening statement will often suffice for this purpose. Sometimes a small shift in emphasis can also be accomplished through reflection. Here are some examples, with codes that indicate the corresponding category of resistance in Table 8.1.

CLIENT: I'm not the one with the problem. If I drink, it's just because my husband is always nagging me. (*3a, blaming*)

THERAPIST: It seems to you that the real reason you drink so much has to do with problems in your marriage.

TABLE 8.1. Four Categories of Client Resistance Behavior

1. Arguing. The client contests the accuracy, expertise, or integrity of the therapist.
    1a. *Challenging*. The client directly challenges the accuracy of what the therapist has said.
    1b. *Discounting*. The client questions the therapist's personal authority and expertise.
    1c. *Hostility*. The client expresses direct hostility toward the therapist.
2. Interrupting. The client breaks in and interrupts the therapist in a defensive manner.
    2a. *Talking over*. The client speaks while the therapist is still talking, without waiting for an appropriate pause or silence.
    2b. *Cutting off*. The client breaks in with words obviously intended to cut the therapist off (e.g., "Now wait a minute. I've heard about enough").
3. Denying. The client expresses an unwillingness to recognize problems, cooperate, accept responsibility, or take advice.
    3a. *Blaming*. The client blames other people for problems.
    3b. *Disagreeing*. The client disagrees with a suggestion that the therapist has made, offering no constructive alternative. This includes the familiar "Yes, but . . .", which explains what is wrong with suggestions that are made.
    3c. *Excusing*. The client makes excuses for his or her own behavior.
    3d. *Claiming impunity*. The client claims that he or she is not in any danger (e.g., from drinking).
    3e. *Minimizing*. The client suggests that the therapist is exaggerating risks or dangers, and that it "really isn't so bad."
    3f. *Pessimism*. The client makes general statements about self or others that are pessimistic, defeatist, or negativistic in tone.
    3g. *Reluctance*. The client expresses reservations and reluctance about information or advice given.
    3h. *Unwillingness to change*. The client expresses a lack of desire or an unwillingness to change, or an intention not to change.
4. Ignoring. The client shows evidence of not following or ignoring the therapist.
    4a. *Inattention*. The client's response indicates that he or she has not been following or attending to the therapist.
    4b. *Nonanswer*. In answering a therapist's query, the client gives a response that is not an answer to the question.
    4c. *No response*. The client gives no audible or nonverbal reply to a therapist's query.
    4d. *Sidetracking*. The client changes the direction of the conversation that the therapist has been pursuing.

Note. Adapted from a behavior coding system developed by Chamberlain, Patterson, Reid, Kavanagh, and Forgatch (1984).

C: This says that I'm as addicted as the average person in treatment, but that can't be right. I can quit any time I feel like it. (*3b, disagreeing*)

T: This is confusing. You can't see how it could possibly be true.

C: Who are you to tell me what to do? What do you know about smack? You've probably never even smoked a joint! (*1b, discounting*)

T: Sounds like you're pretty angry at me.

C: I don't want to quit! (*3h, unwillingness*)

T: You don't think that would work for you.

C: I couldn't change even if I wanted to. (*3f, pessimism*)

T: You can't see any way that you believe in, and you might fail if you tried.

Amplified Reflection

A related and very useful approach is to reflect back what the client has said in an amplified or exaggerated form—to state it in an even more extreme fashion than the client has done. If successful, this will encourage the client to back off a bit, and will elicit the other side of the client's ambivalence. This must be done artfully, however, because a sarcastic tone or *too* extreme an overstatement may itself elicit a hostile or otherwise resistant reaction.

CLIENT: I couldn't just quit. What would my friends think? (*3g, reluctance*)
THERAPIST: In fact, it might be hard for you to change at all.

C: I can hold my liquor just fine. I'm still standing when everybody else is under the table. (*3d, claiming impunity*)

T: So you really have nothing to worry about; alcohol can't hurt you at all.

C: My wife is always exaggerating. I haven't ever been *that* bad. (*3e, minimizing*)

T: It seems to you she doesn't have any reason to be concerned about you.

C: That can't be right. I don't drink that much. (*1a, challenging*)

T: You think maybe there's something wrong with the test, or with our calculations.

C: Those studies about cancer don't really prove anything anyway. (*1b, discounting*)

T: As you see it, lung cancer doesn't have anything to do with smoking. It just happens.

We emphasize that responses should be made in a straightforward, supportive manner. A vocal tone of sarcasm, incredulity, or impatience could recast your response as hostile, and thus elicit client resistance.

Double-Sided Reflection

Another approach within the realm of reflective listening is to acknowledge what the client has said, and add to it the other side of the client's ambivalence. This requires the use of material that the client has offered previously, though perhaps not in the same session. Here are some examples:

CLIENT: I'm not an alcoholic. It's just that Pat used to be married to an alcoholic, and thinks that anybody who overdoes it now and then has a problem. (*3a, blaming*)

THERAPIST: You can see that sometimes you have trouble with drinking too much, but it seems to you that Pat is making too much of it.

C: I don't smoke any more than most of my friends. What's wrong with smoking a joint now and then? (*3c, excusing*)

T: I can see how this must be confusing for you. On the one hand you've told me how you're concerned about your smoking and how it affects you, and on the other it seems like you're not using any more than your friends do. Hard to figure it out!

C: I know that what you want is for me to give it up completely, but I'm not going to do that! (*3h, unwillingness*)

T: You can see that there are some real problems here, but you're not willing to think about quitting altogether.

C: OK, maybe I've got some problems with drinking, but I'm not an alcoholic. (*3e, minimizing*)

T: You don't have any problem seeing that your drinking is hurting you, but you surely don't want to be labeled.

Shifting Focus

A different approach is to shift the client's attention away from what seems to be a stumbling block standing in the way of progress. This amounts to going around barriers rather than trying to climb over them. Such detouring can be a good way to defuse resistance when encountering a particularly difficult issue.

CLIENT: OK, maybe I've got some problems with drinking, but I'm not an alcoholic. (*3e, minimizing*)

THERAPIST: I don't think that's the issue at all, and I don't want you worrying about it. It's not important to me whether or not you want to think of yourself as alcoholic. I *am* worried, though, as you are, about some of the things that seem to be happening in your life. Tell me a little more about . . .

C: I know that what you want is for me to give it up completely, but I'm not going to do that! (*3h, unwillingness*)

T: Hey, slow down! We're just sitting down at the beginning of the game, and you're already trying to guess the final score! I'm certainly not ready to jump to any conclusions at this point. We don't know enough yet to even *talk* about quitting, so don't get stuck or worried over that. OK? What we need to do right now is . . .

Agreement with a Twist

Another way of rolling with resistance is to offer initial agreement, but with a slight twist or change of direction. This retains a sense of concurrence between therapist and client, but allows the therapist to continue influencing the direction and momentum of change.

CLIENT: Why are you and my wife so stuck on my drinking? What about all *her* problems? You'd drink, too, if your family were nagging you all the time. (*3a, blaming; 3c, excusing*)

THERAPIST: You've got a good point there, and that's important. There *is* a bigger picture here, and maybe I haven't been paying enough attention to that. It's not as simple as one person's drinking. I agree with you that we shouldn't be trying to place blame here. Drinking problems like these *do* involve the whole family. I think you're absolutely right.

Emphasizing Personal Choice and Control

As we have noted earlier, resistance sometimes arises from the phenomenon of reactance (see Chapter 1). When people think that their freedom of choice is being threatened, they tend to react by asserting their liberty (e.g., "I'll show you; nobody tells me what to do"). This is, again, a common and natural reaction to the perceived loss of freedom, and not a uniquely pathological condition associated with addictions. Probably the best antidote for this reaction is to assure the person of what is certainly the truth: that in the end, it is the client who determines what happens. An early assurance of this kind can diminish reactance. Here are some possible counselor statements:

> What you do with this information is completely up to you.
> Nobody can change your drinking for you. It's really your decision.
> I can't decide for you, and I can't change you, even if I wanted to. You're a free person, and it's up to you.
> If you decide that you don't want to change, then you won't. If you want to change, you can. It's your choice.

Reframing

Yet another approach in dealing with resistance is to reframe information that the client is offering. This is particularly useful in a situation where a client is offering arguments that serve to deny a personal problem. This approach acknowledges the validity of the client's raw observations, but offers a new meaning or interpretation for them. The client's information is recast into a new form, viewed in a new light that is more likely to be helpful and to support change.

An almost universal opportunity for reframing with problem drinkers is offered by the phenomenon of relative tolerance. It is very common for heavy drinkers to report that they are less affected by alcohol than other people. They can drink large quantities without feeling or showing the degree of intoxication that would normally be expected. Over a career of heavy drinking, this capacity tends to increase (up to the point where liver damage becomes significant, and metabolic tolerance drops). Tolerance occurs for several reasons. Over months or years of heavy drinking, the human body develops some capacity to process alcohol more rapidly. This upward adjustment in alcohol metabolism is quite limited, however, and does not account for a substantial drop in reactivity to intoxication. Mostly, tolerance amounts to a failure to *feel* or *show* the high level of alcohol that is actually in the bloodstream. This occurs through a combination of learning and conditioning, adaptation of body tissue, and an insensitivity to alcohol's effects that may be partly inherited. What this means is that problem drinkers regularly consume quantities of alcohol that are large enough to do substantial damage to the body, but do not feel or show it. In essence, they lack the normal warning systems that protect most people from drinking to excess. Here, then, is the opportunity for reframing. Many problem drinkers regard the ability to "hold their liquor" as a sign that they are safe, more able to drink with impunity than most people. This information suggests exactly the opposite: that alcohol tolerance is a risk factor. Here is an example of reframing:

THERAPIST: So something else you've noticed about your drinking is that you can really hold your liquor, so to speak. You can drink a lot more than most people without feeling or looking drunk. You've even been able to fool people, so that they can't tell how much you've had to drink.

CLIENT: Right. I've always been like that.

T: I don't know if you know this or not—many people don't—but that *is* a reason for concern. You see, ordinary people will have one or two drinks, and then they start to feel the effects and something happens. They don't want any more. Something tells them that they've had enough. But some people, unfortunately, have what we call a high tolerance. They don't have the normal built-in warning systems. Maybe they're born without them, maybe they lose them or ignore them—nobody is sure why it happens. The result, however, is that they damage themselves without realizing it.

C: But if I'm not feeling anything, how can I be drunk?

T: Imagine this: that suddenly you lose all sense of pain. Never again in your life will you feel any physical pain. The sensation is gone. Is that good or bad?

C: Mostly good, I guess.

T: Many people would think that would be wonderful, an incredible blessing. But in fact it would be a curse. Your health and your life would be in great danger. The first warning you would have that your hand is on a hot stove would be the smell of the smoke. You could strain or break your limbs and go on using and damaging them, because you wouldn't realize what was happening. You wouldn't have the pains that are early warnings of tooth decay or illness, and by the time you discovered the problem it could be too late to do anything about it. People with a high tolerance for alcohol are like that. They drink large amounts of alcohol, enough to do serious damage to their bodies, but don't feel or show their intoxication. The people around them can't see it as easily, because they don't look drunk. They damage themselves because they're missing the normal warning signs. What you're talking about is not your body's ability to get rid of alcohol at superhuman speed. The alcohol is there, doing its damage. What you're talking about is tolerance, the lack of this warning system. And that's reason for concern.

This extended example shows how reframing can involve some detailed teaching—the communication of new information that the client needs in order to understand his or her situation in a new light. Sometimes reframing is much simpler, however, and can be accomplished with a few sentences. Here are two more examples:

C: My husband is always nagging me about my drinking. That's all he ever talks about—always telling me I'm an alcoholic.

T: It sounds like he really cares about you, and he's very concerned about you. I guess he expresses it in a way that you're angry about, and that's too bad. Maybe we can help him learn to tell you in a better way that he loves you and is worried about you.

C: What's the use? I've tried to quit, and I think I'm hopeless. I'm tired. I'm worn out. I don't want to try any more.

T: It may seem a trite saying, that "It's always darkest before the dawn," but it's also true. When people are at their lowest point, at the bottom of the valley, it's hardest to see the light. I think that all of the effort you've put into trying shows how very much you *want* to recover. I admire you for that. So don't give it up now. You remember that wheel of change we talked about? Every time you go around it, you're one turn closer to getting off. You've discovered a lot of things that *don't* work for you. Now let's use that strong desire of yours, and move on to find what *will* work for you.

Therapeutic Paradox

The idea of presenting clients with a therapeutic paradox has become familiar through the writings of family systems therapists (e.g., Haley, 1963). We have briefly mentioned paradoxical strategies in Chapter 6, with regard to eliciting self-motivational statements.

As an approach for handling resistance, therapeutic paradox is somewhat more complex. It is designed to place the client in a position where opposition or resistance to the therapist results in movement in a beneficial direction. Some strategies of this kind are applicable within motivational interviewing. As mentioned earlier, however, we do regard paradoxical approaches as somewhat risky and requiring substantial skill. For this reason, we recommend that they be tried when other strategies have been used without success, and we advise caution in their application.

An example of a general therapeutic paradox is to "prescribe the problem." If all change efforts are met with opposition, the therapist can recommend that the client should continue on as before, without changing, or should even increase the behavior in question. This is not done in an angry, exasperated, "I give up" manner. Most often it is done in a calm, straightforward tone. Reasons can be given as a rationale for why the person should not change. Two examples:

(1) We've talked about the difficulties you've been having, and we've discussed quite a few different options that you have for changing. What strikes me is that none of the options appeal to you. You actually seem very happy with your old pattern, at least when you compare it with any alternative. It seems to me, then, that what you ought to do is to keep on exactly as before. There's no point in going to all the trouble of trying to change if what you really want to do is stay the same.

(2) You remember we talked about the pros and cons of drinking, and although you told me quite a few reasons why alcohol is causing you trouble, I think what I'm hearing is that for you the pros still outweigh the cons. You're quite happy drinking as you were, and don't really want to change. That's a choice which is yours to make, and perhaps that's what you should do. Clearly, it would be hard for you to change your drinking—maybe too hard for you. Maybe you couldn't even do it if you tried. The point is that it sounds like what you really want is to go on drinking as much as you were before, or more. Maybe that's what you need. Perhaps you really need alcohol to cope with life.

This latter example raises another element that is sometimes labeled "paradoxical," and that can be included in motivational interviewing. This is the element of challenge, with an implicit question as to whether the person is able to do something. A phrase such as "if you can handle it" may evoke self-motivational statements asserting the client's ability to change. Other examples include "I don't know whether this would be too difficult for you, but . . ." or "Maybe this is asking too much of you."

The complexities of therapeutic paradox have been discussed in detail elsewhere (Frankl, 1960; Haley, 1963; Stanton, Todd, & Associates, 1982). We mention this approach here only to say that a therapist skillful in its use may be able to employ it within the context of motivational interviewing. Again, however, we advise caution.

Handling Missed Appointments

Any counselor knows that it is not uncommon for clients to miss appointments and to terminate counseling at an early point. There are a number of reasons why this may occur. Dislike of or alienation from the counselor is one possibility likely to be minimized if you are following the processes of motivational interviewing. Interestingly, exactly the opposite can be a problem as well. If the client has come to like and respect you, he or she may avoid coming back in order not to disappoint you with reports of relapse or indecision. The only remedy for this that we know is what Carl Rogers (1957) termed "unconditional positive regard"—the communication of acceptance and respect, regardless of what a client expresses. You can tell your clients quite directly that you want to see them again no matter what they decide, and that you care about them and want to help no matter how badly things may seem to be going.

Sometimes a client misses sessions because he or she is ambivalent about continuing toward change. Such ambivalence is normal, but unless you intervene to resume contact, the client may opt for passive avoidance, and ambivalence ends the treatment process.

Another reason why clients drop out, however, is that they perceive they have received enough of what they wanted. Clients who stop complying with treatment procedures (e.g., keeping self-monitoring cards or reading a self-help book) may be doing at least as well as those who continue to comply with treatment recommendations (e.g., Miller, 1978; Miller & Taylor, 1980). Dropout, then, is not necessarily bad news. In Chapter 3 we have reviewed a number of studies showing that brief motivational counseling alone is enough to initiate change for many clients.

We believe that the strategies outlined in this book should help to reduce client dropout, and there is already evidence that therapist style makes quite a difference (Miller, 1985b). Yet it is impossible to prevent dropout, and it is unrealistic to expect that you can. Some clients don't come back as planned. You *can*, however, respond in a helpful way when a client misses an appointment. Don't sit passively by and wait for the client to contact you. As discussed in Chapter 6, a simple personal note (not a form letter) or a telephone call when an appointment is missed may as much as double the chances that the client will return (Intagliata, 1976; Nirenberg, Sobell, & Sobell, 1980; Panepinto & Higgins, 1969; Wedel, 1965).

The Drama of Change

Resistance is a key to successful treatment if you can recognize it for what it is: an opportunity. In expressing resistance, the client is probably rehearsing a script that has been played out many times before. There is an expected role for you to play—one that has been acted by others in the past. Your lines are predictable. If you speak these same lines, as others have done, the script will come to the same conclusion as before.

But you can rewrite your own role. Your part in the play need not be the dry, predictable lines that your client may be awaiting. Therapy is, in a way, like improvisational theater. No two sessions run exactly the same way. If one actor changes role, the plot is headed off in a new direction. In the words of Ebenezer Scrooge, "if the courses be departed from, the ends will change."

Resistance is often the life of the play. It is the twist that adds drama and excitement to the plot. Viewing resistance as a perverse character flaw is a sad mistake. Resistance lies at the very heart of interplay. It arises from the motives and struggles of the actors. It foreshadows certain ends to which the play may or may not lead. The true art of therapy is tested in the recognition and handling of resistance. It is on this stage that the drama of change unfolds.

9

Phase II: Strengthening Commitment to Change

It takes two to speak truth—One to speak, and another to hear.
—Henry David Thoreau, *A Week on the Concord and Merrimack Rivers*

Recognizing Readiness for Change

The first phase of motivational interviewing involves building motivation for change. This takes much longer with some clients than with others. In the language of the Prochaska–DiClemente stages, some clients are beginning in precontemplation, and some are in early contemplation. Others enter treatment already voicing determination to change and needing relatively little motivation building.

There comes a point when it is time to shift strategies—when the goal changes from building motivation (Phase I) to strengthening commitment (Phase II). At this point the client is ready to change, but has not yet made a firm decision or commitment to do so. Salespeople recognize a comparable point in selling: when the customer has privately decided to make a purchase, and they shift strategies toward closing the sale. A leading trainer once told us that this is the most critical period in a sale, and that the main task at this point is to help the person confirm and justify the decision that has been made. Knowing exactly when to shift strategies is one of the skills that separates successful from unsuccessful salespeople. Similarly, in cooking, there are crucial timing judgments to be made: when the liquid has boiled sufficiently, how long to knead the bread dough and let it rise before baking, or when the candy is hot enough to set. Proceeding either too soon or too late can spoil the recipe.

Don't worry about this too much. We doubt that there is often an exact, ideal moment. The contemplation stage seems more like a long continuum, ranging from early to late readiness for change. We do believe that once a person has reached the late contemplation or determination stage, there is a certain window of time during which change should be initiated. How long this window stays open will vary widely, but the recognition of an important discrepancy is just too uncomfortable to sustain forever. If change isn't begun, the person is likely to start using defenses to decrease the discomfort (rationalizing, minimizing, denying, forgetting, projecting, etc.). It is important to recognize when the window is open, so that you can help the client to start stepping through it.

What are the signs of an open window? Good research is needed here. At present, we can offer some of the cues that we have used in intuiting when to shift from Phase I to Phase II (see Table 9.1). Not all of these will happen in all or even most cases, but they are possible signs of readiness for change. When there are such indications of readiness, it is time to shift direction to the new goal: strengthening the client's commitment. This can be a useful process even when a client enters treatment apparently having already decided to change. The strategies presented in this chapter are appropriate for strengthening commitment, once a client has entered the later contemplation stage and seems to have sufficient motivation to move on toward action.

This can be quite an enjoyable part of the process. Phase I of motivational interviewing can be slow and hard work—a bit like slogging up a mountain in snowshoes. Once this hard work is done, Phase II may proceed much more easily—like skiing down the other side. To be sure, there are hazards on the way down, and we begin by discussing a few of these. Nevertheless, the going tends to be faster and more pleasant. There is a sense of companionship with the client, a feeling of sitting next to the person and sorting out which way to go, then moving on together. At the top of the mountain, the main task is to persuade the client to come with you down the other side, rather than staying there and ultimately deciding to backtrack down the way you came. When you reach Phase II, most of the hard work of motivational interviewing is done. It remains for the client to put on the skis, pick an appropriate slope, make that fateful decision to push off, and enjoy the journey down while avoiding its rocks, moguls, and chasms. As the therapist, you can be a guide throughout this process.

Phase II Hazards

As noted above, there are a few hazards for the therapist in negotiating the slopes of Phase II. Here are three to beware.

Underestimating Ambivalence

It is very tempting to assume that once your client is showing signs of readiness for change (Table 9.1), the decision has been made and it's all

TABLE 9.1. Signs of Readiness for Change

1. *Decreased resistance.* The client stops arguing, interrupting, denying, or objecting.
2. *Decreased questions about the problem.* The client seems to have enough information about his or her problem, and stops asking questions. There is a sense of being finished.
3. *Resolve.* The client appears to have reached a resolution, and may seem more peaceful, relaxed, calm, unburdened, or settled. Sometimes this happens after the client has passed through a period of anguish or tearfulness.
4. *Self-motivational statements.* The client makes direct self-motivational statements (see Chapter 6), reflecting recognition of a problem ("I guess this is serious"), concern ("This worries me"), openness to change ("I need to do something"), or optimism ("I'm going to beat this").
5. *Increased questions about change.* The client asks what he or she could do about the problem, how people change if they decide to, or the like.
6. *Envisioning.* The client begins to talk about how life might be after a change, to anticipate difficulties if a change were made, or to discuss the advantages of change.
7. *Experimenting.* If the client has had time between sessions, he or she may have begun experimenting with possible change approaches (e.g., going to an Alcoholics Anonymous meeting, going without drinking for a few days, reading a self-help book).

downhill from there on. This confuses the decision process with a big-D *D*ecision. Most decisions to change are not made suddenly, once and for all. People often enter into the action stage with still quite a lot of ambivalence. They take their first tentative steps while they are still not sure which way they want to go. Sometimes they seem to have progressed well into the journey, only to turn around and double back. There is a great risk, then, of becoming overeager at the first signs of a shift toward change. In our alpine analogy, the client in this situation may be like the reluctant student who has finally built up the courage to get to the top, only to be dragged by the instructor to the edge of what seems the steepest and most menacing slope. The same care and style that characterizes Phase I should be maintained during Phase II, and indeed throughout the counseling process. Ambivalence does not disappear after the decision is made to begin the change process. This issue is discussed further in Chapter 24.

Overprescription

A second danger in Phase II is to prescribe a plan that is unacceptable to the client. There can be a tendency to say, "Now that you're ready to change, here's what you have to do." This violates the client-centered tone of motivational interviewing, and runs the risk of undoing the progress that has been made. There is no point in carefully building a client's motivation, only to offer a plan that is unacceptable. Sometimes one can run into difficulty even when making what seems a simple suggestion. The client responds, "Yes, but that won't work because . . ." and adopts the passive role of someone who is waiting for solutions to be provided by the expert. The Phase I emphasis on personal responsibility and choice extends to Phase II and the negotiation of change strategies.

Insufficient Direction

The opposite risk is to provide the client with too *little* direction. The question "What can I do?" is better answered by alternatives than by reflection. If a wholly nondirective approach is sustained at Phase II ("So you're wondering what you can do"), the client may flounder. The strategies that we now describe are meant to guide you between the two extremes of rigid prescription and insufficient direction. The goal is to channel the client's motivation into a workable plan for change, and to strengthen the client's commitment for carrying out that plan.

Recapitulation

A first step in making the transition to Phase II is to summarize once again the client's current situation, as reflected in your interactions thus far. This is meant to have the effect of drawing Phase I to a close. The length of your summary will depend upon the complexity of the client's situation. It is wise to begin with a statement announcing that you are attempting to draw together everything you have discussed, for the purpose of evaluating what to do next. Your recapitulation should include as many of the following elements as possible:

1. A summary of the client's own perceptions of the problem, as reflected in his or her self-motivational statements.
2. A summing-up of the client's ambivalence, including what remains positive or attractive about the problem behavior.
3. A review of whatever objective evidence you have regarding the presence of risks and problems.
4. A restatement of any indications the client has offered of wanting, intending, or planning to change.
5. Your own assessment of the client's situation, particularly at points where it converges with the client's own concerns.

The purpose of this summary is to draw together as many reasons for change as possible, while simultaneously acknowledging the client's reluctance or ambivalence. The recapitulation is used as a final preparation for the transition to commitment, and leads directly into the key questions.

Key Questions

Consistent with the tone of Phase I, clients are not told what they have to do, but rather are asked what they want to do. Timing is important here. These questions should be asked at a point when a client is likely to be at a peak of problem awareness. Thus it is important to recognize when you have reached this peak.

Key questions are open-ended. They cannot be answered with a simple "Yes" or "No." They get the client thinking and talking about change. The central theme of key questions is "the next step." Typically, they are asked immediately after the recapitulation, but they can be useful throughout Phase II. Some examples of key questions are presented in Table 9.2.

The client's answers to key questions are met, as before, with reflection. This serves to clarify the client's thoughts and to encourage further exploration. Reflection can also be used selectively to reinforce self-motivational statements that are offered (Chapter 6) and to deal with resistance that may arise (Chapter 8). The client's personal responsibility, freedom, and choice can be emphasized again during this process. Be careful not to shift wholly into a problem-solving mode. The strategies from earlier chapters continue to be useful during Phase II.

TABLE 9.2. Possible Key Questions

What do you think you will do?

What does this mean about your drinking?

It must be uncomfortable for you now, seeing all this. . . . What's the next step?

What do you think has to change?

What could you do? What are your options?

It sounds like things can't stay the way they are now. What are you going to do?

Of the things I have mentioned here, which for you are the most important reasons for a change? . . . How are you going to do it?

What's going to happen now? Where do we go from here?

How would you like things to turn out for you now, ideally?

What concerns you about changing your use of drugs?

What would be some of the good things about making a change?

Information and Advice

Often during this phase, the client will ask you for information or ideas. It is quite appropriate in this circumstance to offer your own best advice. It is important, however, to guard against falling into the "Yes, but . . ." pattern, which is really a variation on the confrontation–denial trap. In this script, the counselor gives information and the client says what is wrong with it, or the counselor offers an idea, and the client responds by saying why it will not work. A few rounds of this can set a deadly pattern.

There are several ways to guard against this. First, do not be too eager to offer advice. Wait for a direct invitation or request for information. Play a bit "hard to get," evoking from the client additional requests and permission for your advice:

> I'll be happy to give you some ideas, but I don't want to get in the way of your own creative thinking, and *you're* the expert on you.
> I'm not sure you really want my advice. Maybe you have some ideas of your own about what to do.
> Of course I can tell you what I think, if you really want to know. But I don't want you to feel like I'm telling you what you have to do. Would my opinion really make a difference to you?

Second, qualify any suggestions that you make. It can be useful to present advice in a deliberately nonpersonal way, allowing the client to judge how it fits his or her situation. Here are some prefacing comments to accomplish this:

> I don't know if this would work for you or not, but I can give you an idea of what has worked for some other people in your situation.
> This may or may not make sense to you, but it's one possibility. You'll have to judge whether it applies to you.
> I can give you an idea, but I think you'd have to try it out to see if it would work for you.
> All I can give you, of course, is my own opinion. You're really the one who has to find what works for you.
> Some people have . . . [make suggestion]. I wonder whether that would work for you?

A third useful approach is to offer not one, but a *cluster* of options. There is evidence that when people choose a course of action from among alternatives, they are more likely to adhere to it and succeed (Miller, 1985b). This further avoids the easy "Yes, but . . ." pattern in which the client rejects suggestions one at a time:

Well, there really isn't any one way that works for everybody. I can tell you about approaches that other people have used successfully, and you can see which of those might fit you best.
Let me describe a number of possibilities, and you tell me which of these makes the most sense for you.

It is also possible to elicit requests from the client for information and advice. This can be done, for example, in Phase II after offering a closing summary. You might say something like this: "We've talked over quite a bit of material here, and you seem to have been giving this a lot of thought. I wonder if there is anything you'd like to ask me, or that you've been wondering about." This may evoke requests for more information about material discussed in Phase I, or for advice regarding change options. If you are asked something that you do not know, feel free to say that you don't know but will find out for the client.

Negotiating a Plan

Through the client's responses to key questions and your own provision of information and advice, a plan for change may begin to emerge. The development of this plan is a process of negotiation that involves (1) setting goals, (2) considering options, and (3) arriving at a plan.

1. Setting Goals

Motivation is driven by a discrepancy between a person's goals and his or her present state. A first step in instigating change, then, is to set clear goals toward which to move. Key questions in this regard might be as follows:

How would you like for things to be different?
What is it that you want to change?
If you were completely successful in accomplishing what you want now, what would be changed?
Let's take things one step at a time. What do you think is the first step?

This brings us to the probability that the client's goals may not correspond with your own. For example, you may want a particular client to swear off alcohol and all other psychoactive drugs for the rest of her life, whereas she may be more concerned about improving her marriage and, at most, reducing her drinking to a moderate level. How do you deal with this situation?

The fact is that you cannot impose your own goals on a client. You can offer your best advice, but the client is always free to accept or disregard it. Arguing and insisting are more likely to evoke defensiveness than agreement. Again, it makes little sense to work within a motivational interviewing strategy during Phase I, only to alienate the client with a rigidly prescriptive style in Phase II. It is far better, we believe, to maintain a strong working alliance with the client, and to start with the goals toward which he or she is most eager to make progress. If these goals are misguided, it will become apparent soon enough.

An issue over which counselors and clients often disagree is the desirability of quitting "cold turkey." Commonly the counselor wants total abstinence right now, and the client refuses or resists. In this case, it is possible to negotiate goals that represent progress toward recovery, albeit not all that the counselor may hope for in the end. Miller and Page (in press) have described three "warm turkey" alternatives to immediate abstinence: (1) a negotiated period of trial abstinence, (2) a process of gradual tapering down toward abstinence, and (3) a period of trial moderation. In cases where problems are less severe, moderation may be an appropriate starting goal (Miller, 1987), although even in this situation many clients may opt for abstinence in the long run (Miller, Leckman, Delaney, & Tinkcom, in press). The point is to *stay with* the client, defining acceptable and attainable goals that represent progress toward recovery.

Remember to keep a broad view in discussing goals. Although there may appear to be a focal problem, the client is likely to have wider goals that are important to discuss. As discussed in Chapter 6, awareness of these larger goals can be helpful in building motivation for change. You may also want to suggest additional goals that you believe are important to the client's welfare and change efforts (e.g., to get a job, to stop sharing needles).

One way to evaluate whether a chosen goal is achievable is to ask the client to consider the consequences of taking this particular course of action. A client may well have concerns that have not been expressed. Some possible questions are as follows:

> How would your life be different if you followed this idea and quit altogether?
>
> You have said you would like to cut down, so let's talk about that for a while. How do you think this would work?
>
> So that's your goal. What can you think of that might go wrong with this plan?
>
> If you succeeded in achieving this goal, what else do you think might happen? What might be good, and what might be not so good, about reaching this goal?

This often leads naturally to the second step: considering how the client might go about achieving the goal. Success is not simply a matter of "will-power" once the goal is set. There are usually things that the client can do to increase the chances of success. Before proceeding, however, make sure the goal seems right. If the client is expressing serious concerns about the achievability or desirability of the goal, you need to do more work before proceeding. The issue of goals in motivational counseling is discussed further in Chapter 19.

2. Considering Change Options

Once clear goals have been defined, the next step is to consider possible methods for achieving the chosen goals. A review of alternative treatment modalities is beyond the scope of this volume (see Cox, 1987; Garfield & Bergin, 1986; Hester & Miller, 1989), but three general points are worth considering here.

First, the treatment outcome literature in many fields points to a menu of promising approaches. With psychological problems, it is rarely the case that there is one and only one treatment of choice. In the treatment of addictive behaviors in particular, there is no single outstandingly effective approach. Instead, we are blessed with a range of options that have been found, in controlled research, to be effective methods for some populations (Holder, Longabaugh, Miller, & Rubonis, in press; Miller & Hester, 1986a). This means that you can, in good conscience, discuss a variety of options with the person who wants to make a change. This offers the added advantage of enhancing the client's motivation through personal choice of strategies. The idea of a menu of options from which the client chooses (Ewing, 1977) is quite consistent with motivational interviewing.

Second, there is a growing literature on how to match people to optimal treatment strategies (Finney & Moos, 1979; Gottheil, McLellan, & Druley, 1981; Hester & Miller, 1989; Miller & Hester, 1986b; McLellan, Woody, Luborsky, O'Brien, & Druley, 1983). Familiarity with this literature is an important asset in helping clients to select the right approach the first time. Choosing an inappropriate strategy can result in treatment failure and discouragement. Although the client still may not choose to follow your counsel, it is possible to offer advice based on the available research regarding what works for whom.

Third, despite your best collective efforts, the client may not choose the right approach the first time. It is important to prepare clients for this possibility. Relapse is a normal part of recovery (Marlatt & Gordon, 1985). It is typical for people to go around the Prochaska–DiClemente "wheel" several times before getting off. Here are some points that might be made in introducing this idea during Phase II:

> The truth is that there is no one approach that is best for everybody. What works for some is unacceptable or ineffective for others. What's encouraging is that there are quite a few different ways that have been shown to be promising. The question now is which ones would be best for you. We can talk about the options if you want, and I would certainly try to help you find the right approach the first time. But if you try one way and it doesn't seem to be working, don't be discouraged. It might only mean that it isn't the right approach for *you*. With so many possibilities, you're bound to find something that works for you, and I'm willing to stay with you until you do. Do you want to hear about the possibilities?

In describing alternative goals or approaches, it is usually best to avoid professional jargon and technical names. Available options should be described in language that is understandable to the client and relevant to his or her concerns. Tell the client what a strategy is intended to do, how it works, what is involved, and what to expect. Ask whether the client has any questions about each option, and generally reserve choice and negotiation until you have reviewed the menu.

As different possible courses of action are discussed, ask for the client's best guesses as to what would happen with each alternative. This is also an opportunity to review what the client perceives to be the likely outcomes if *nothing* is done, which represents another option. In this process, you are searching for change strategies with which to begin. Ideally, these are approaches that the client believes in or views optimistically. The viability of change options can be explored by asking questions that help the person to examine the consequences of possible changes. For example:

> You say that what you really need to do is learn to say "No" when people offer you a drink. What do you think would happen if you did that?
> You would like to do something about feeling lonely at night, so that you don't have to sit there thinking about taking drugs to comfort yourself. What sorts of things could you do instead? How do you think they would turn out?

3. Arriving at a Plan

This discussion leads directly toward the negotiation of a plan for change. It can be useful to fill out, for or with the client, a change plan worksheet, summarizing the client's responses to items such as these:

- The most important reasons why I want to make a change are . . .
- My main goals for myself, in making a change, are . . .
- I plan to do these things in order to reach my goals:
  Plan of Action   *When*

- The first steps that I plan to take in changing are . . .
- Other people could help me in changing in these ways:
  Person   *Possible ways to help*

- I hope that my plan will have these positive results:

On the basis of your discussions, summarize a plan that seems to fit with the client's goals, needs, intentions, and beliefs. This is best done in "you" language. Here is an example:

> Let me see if I can summarize where you are, then. You wanted to know about different ways that people can change their drinking, and we've talked about a number of possibilities. You're thinking that you may need to quit completely in the long run, but you're really not ready to do that without first giving moderation a good try. You considered different options and decided that you'd like to work with me on the approach called "self-control training." We should be able to tell in 6–8 weeks whether that will work for you, and you thought that would tell you what you want to know. Even if you decide then that what you want to do is quit, cutting down is a reasonable step on the way. So what you are going to do is read this material I've given you, begin keeping daily records, and come back next Tuesday to get started. We also discussed bringing Jan along to that session, and you thought that would be a good idea. You're still a little nervous about this plan, I think, but you do see that you need to make a change, and this sounds like the one you've chosen. Have I missed anything?

Endgame

Eliciting Commitment

The plan summary may bring you right to the point of commitment. This involves getting the client's approval of and agreement to the plan, and deciding on immediate steps to be taken. Verbal agreement may be as simple as asking, "Is this what you want to do?" and getting a "Yes." It can be useful to explore what reluctance the client still has about this plan, and to use Phase I strategies to resolve ambivalence.

Commitment to a plan can be enhanced by making it public. If a spouse or other loved one is present in the session, the commitment is made with that person's knowledge and consent. You may ask the client to visit, write, or telephone other people to let them know about the decision, and to ask for their help. Such a telephone call may be made during the counseling session. If the client has had contact with other staff members within the clinic, you may ask permission to share the client's positive plan with them, or even call them into the session to have the client share it. The more the client verbalizes the plan to others, the more commitment is strengthened. There is also the very real benefit of recruiting the help and support of others. If it appears that telling others may be difficult or risky, rehearse this with the client during the session.

Transition to the Action Stage

Commitment is also reflected in action. It may be possible to plan immediate steps that can be taken to implement (and consolidate) the plan. If a client agrees to take disulfiram (Fuller, 1989), for example, steps can be taken to obtain the prescription immediately. Some clinics are well enough organized to provide an immediate medical screening and prescription, so that the client can take the first disulfiram tablet before leaving the building. Making even a small financial investment in the plan (e.g., buying a book, paying for a prescription) may help to confirm it. If the spouse is participating in sessions, specific steps can be negotiated for his or her role in implementing the plan (e.g., Sisson & Azrin, 1989).

The point is to arrive at a clear plan, to obtain the client's verbal decision to follow the plan, to reinforce the client's decision, and to initiate immediate steps for implementing the plan. This obviously enters into what Prochaska and DiClemente have called the "action" stage—taking steps to accomplish change. Their research indicates that there is usually no clear line between contemplation and action. In the later contemplation stage people begin trying steps to change, and during the initial action phase people are usually still somewhat ambivalent and contemplating (DiClemente & Hughes, 1990). This is a good reminder that the strategies of motivational interviewing are not to be abandoned once the action stage has been entered (see Chapter 24). As we have said at the outset, this is a way of *being* with clients that can characterize the counseling process from start to finish.

If a client is not ready to make a commitment, you should not press. It is better to roll with this process and say, "If you're not ready yet, then I don't want you to make a commitment. This is too important to decide now. Go home and think about it, and we can talk about it more next time." In this case, *do* maintain contact with the client. An active therapist role at this point (e.g., a simple note or telephone call) may reduce the likelihood that the client will drop out of the change process.

10

Typical and Difficult Situations

Anyone who willingly enters into the pain of a stranger is truly
a remarkable person.
　　　　　　　　—Henri J. M. Nouwen, *In Memoriam*

In the preceding chapters, we have described the principles and strategies
that characterize motivational interviewing. The remaining two chapters of
Part II and all of Part III are intended to help you implement this approach
in practice. Chapter 11 offers an extended clinical example to show how the
material from Chapters 5–9 can be woven together to form the unique
tapestry of an individual case. Chapter 12 discusses the practicalities of
teaching motivational interviewing. The chapters of Part III discuss different applications of this approach to specific problems and populations. In
the present chapter, we discuss some special situations that often arise in the
practice of motivational interviewing, and that can pose difficulties or
dilemmas for the counselor.

Working with Spouses

Clinicians differ in their opinions about whether and how to involve a
client's spouse in motivational interviewing. Particularly if the spouse has
been pressuring the client to seek help, it can be useful to meet with the
client alone in order to build an atmosphere of trust and support. A
confrontational spouse can evoke resistance just as a confrontational counselor can, and the participation of such a spouse in counseling may interfere with the strategies of motivational interviewing (e.g., eliciting self-
motivational statements from the client). For these and other reasons,
some counselors prefer to work with the client alone during motivational
interviewing.

　　On the other hand, the spouse can be an important source of information, motivation, and support for change (e.g., Sisson & Azrin, 1986).

Furthermore, a confrontational spouse is likely to evoke resistance to change outside of sessions as well as during them. If the spouse participates in counseling, the therapist has the opportunity to observe and alter disruptive communication patterns. Strategies of motivational interviewing can be employed to build the spouse's motivation for and commitment to change. A skillful counselor can involve a spouse in ways that enhance the client's own motivation.

Many of the skills required for involving a spouse in motivational interviewing are the same as those needed for successful couples counseling (e.g., O'Farrell & Cowles, 1989). We discuss here only a few special issues that can arise. The topic of spouse involvement in motivational interviewing is further discussed by Allen Zweben in Chapter 16.

Averting Destructive Communication Patterns

Couples in distress often rely upon very negative communication styles, rich in criticism, defensiveness, and fault finding. The blaming trap is a particular risk when counseling a couple, and it is useful to clarify early that blame is unhelpful. It is also important during early sessions to keep couples from reverting to hurtful arguments and accusations. A motivational interviewing approach seeks to maintain a positive and problem-solving focus.

One way to prevent negative communication is to maintain control of the session. Ask specific (but open-ended) questions, and keep the client and spouse on the topic. Include questions likely to evoke positive statements from each about the partner. Maintain a balance of "air time," so that when one partner has responded, you turn to the other and ask for his or her perceptions and feelings. Offer a clear statement of the spouse's role as a caring helper.

If negative communications emerge, interrupt them early. A good approach is to acknowledge the person's feelings and perceptions, perhaps with a bit of reframing, and then to redirect them along a more helpful route. It can also be useful to explore the consequences of negative communications. Here is an example:

CLIENT: I guess I overdo it sometimes, but I don't really think I have a "problem" with drinking.

WIFE: How can you sit there and say that you don't have a drinking problem? Are you blind? Last week . . .

THERAPIST: (*Breaking in, to wife*) Excuse me. I know how very concerned you are about Jim, and I admire you for that. I know that you care a lot, and it's hard for you not to jump in like that. I imagine you've had arguments like that before.

C: Lots of times.

T: (*To wife*) And what has usually happened? Has there been a good result?

W: We have a big fight. Usually I wind up angry and crying, and he keeps drinking.

T: Exactly. So I don't want you to do the same here. (*To client*) How do you feel when she says something like that to you?

C: It makes me mad, and I feel more like drinking.

T: A little backed into a corner, maybe.

C: Yeah. And then it's like, "I'll show her."

T: (*To wife*) Now I don't want you to feel blamed here, either. This isn't anybody's fault. It's a pattern that people often fall into when they care about each other and don't know what to do. The point is that it doesn't help, and we need to try something different. I know that you care. Jim knows that you care. I do want to hear what both of you have to say, and in fact I'm going to ask more about what you've observed in just a few minutes. But to get somewhere new, you have to try a different way. (*To client*) Now, Jim, you were starting to tell me what you've noticed about your drinking. . . .

Eliciting Self-Motivational Statements

Although a client's spouse is sometimes more eager for a change than the client is, frequently the spouse is also quite ambivalent—wanting but also not wanting. This ambivalence may have to do with the client's problem, the relationship, treatment, personal involvement, or even problems of the spouse's own (e.g., the spouse also takes drugs). Do not, therefore, assume that the spouse is committed to change. Rather, explore ambivalence and build motivation for change.

The strategies for doing so are the same as those used in motivational interviewing with the client (Chapters 5–9). In particular, it is useful to evoke from the spouse some self-motivational statements paralleling those you seek from the client. Here are some sample questions that can be used for this purpose during Phase I:

How has this affected you?
What would be the best effects, do you think, if your spouse made a change?

What do you like best about your spouse when he [or she] isn't
     drinking?
What things do you see that worry you the most?
What concerns do you have that make you think it's time for a change?
What things give you hope that your spouse could change?
In the feedback that I have presented, what concerns you most?
What do you think will happen if your spouse doesn't change?

The spouse's answers to these questions are responded to with reflection,
and can be incorporated into periodic summaries that you offer during
sessions. Other Phase I strategies (e.g., reframing, affirming, double-sided
reflection, emphasizing personal choice) can be applied directly in working
with the client's spouse.

Phase II

Similarly, there are spouse parallels for most of the strategies used with
clients during Phase II (Chapter 9). Some key questions for the spouse may
include the following:

How would you like for things to turn out?
What do you think this means about your wife's [husband's] drinking?
In what ways could you help your spouse to make a change?
What do you think is the next step?

The spouse can be involved in evaluating alternative goals and strategies, as
well as in arriving at a plan for change. The spouse not only provides input
to this process, but serves as a witness to the client's own commitments. You
can help the client and spouse to negotiate the spouse's role in the change
process, and plan for how to proceed if the initial strategy is not successful.
A spouse can often provide valuable practical help and support in carrying
out a change.

Significant Others

Our discussion here has focused on the client's spouse, but similar approaches can be employed to involve significant others in treatment. If the
client does not have a primary partner, it may be helpful to have the client
bring along a close friend, parent, coworker, or family member to serve in a
supportive role. The ideal individual is one who cares about the client,
knows about the problem, is willing and resourceful enough to help, and has
frequent contact with the client.

Unilateral Counseling of Significant Others

It is common for a counselor to be consulted by a concerned spouse or family member before the "client" is willing to seek help. In this case, it is feasible to conduct motivational interviewing with the spouse or family members alone, paving the way for eventual counseling of the person for whom they are concerned. Sisson and Azrin (1986) studied a unilateral counseling approach that focused on building spouses' motivation for change and negotiating strategies whereby the spouses could (1) reduce their partners' drinking, and (2) facilitate entry into treatment. Within an average of seven sessions with the spouses, most of their partners had entered treatment and had cut their drinking in half even before starting treatment. Phase I and Phase II motivational interviewing strategies, then, can be used with a spouse or significant other alone, as a preparation for counseling.

The Coerced Client

A different set of challenges is posed by people who are coerced into treatment—for example, by a court of law or by the threatened loss of employment. In these circumstances the issue of coercion can hang like a cloud over the counseling process. What happens if you attempt to use motivational interviewing with coerced clients?

One crucial distinction is whether you are an agent of the coercing body (e.g., the court, the employer). If not, it can be much easier to make progress by initially dissociating yourself from the coercion process. The client may well enter the first session feeling angry, resentful, and disinclined to admit a problem or to consider a change in behavior. These, we suggest, are good reasons to use motivational interviewing, considering the alternatives. If you set out to confront the reluctance directly, or to persuade this person that he or she really *does* have a problem and needs to change, both you and the client will fall readily into a confrontation–denial trap (see Chapter 6). Instead, stay close to one of the cornerstones of motivational interviewing—that clients are at liberty to do whatever they wish to do, and it is not your job to convince them otherwise. When you are emphasizing personal control in this way, it is important not to be defensive or patronizing. Rather, state it as a matter of fact, and then indicate clearly your willingness to help if a client wishes. Here is an example of how this may be said:

> You and I both know that the court required you to come here. If I were in your place, I'd probably be feeling angry about that, resenting having to be here. That's a normal feeling in your spot, and perfectly under-standable. What I want to explain to you is that I am not a part of the

court. My job is to help people change. It's not my job to make you admit anything or change anything. I couldn't do that even if I wanted to—only you can decide what you're going to do. I also want to emphasize that you don't have to be here. As I understand your situation with the court, you have to do *something* in the way of counseling or risk some penalties, but that doesn't mean you have to be *here*. You have other options, and if you'd rather do something different or talk to somebody else, I'll help you explore the possibilities. My job is helping people who want to explore their situation, and to consider making a change. How does that sound to you?

Because of the reactance evoked by coercion, mandated clients may offer much more resistance during the early phase of counseling, requiring more time devoted to Phase I (Chapter 6) and to defusing resistance (Chapter 8). A broad assessment (Chapter 7) can be especially helpful as a base for Phase I discussion, particularly if it includes measures less subject to falsification. The involvement of a spouse or significant other may be helpful. The key point is to emphasize the client's personal choice and control within the confines of the mandate. One choice every client has, in fact, is to ignore the mandate and accept the consequences. Beyond this, the processes of motivational interviewing are largely the same with coerced clients. If you are not an agent of the coercing body, you can detach yourself, (at least to some extent) from the coercive process. It is important to be clear, however, about the ways in which you *are* required to be involved with the coercing body (e.g., reporting attendance to the court or employer). The extent and limits of such involvement should be specified, as well as the implications for client confidentiality.

If on the other hand, you *are* working as a direct agent of the mandating body (e.g., to determine and report to the court the client's extent of problem and need for treatment), communication with the client can be tainted by this special role, which carries with it an element of supervisory responsibility. For example, monitoring someone's progress in keeping within the law after release from jail is not readily conducive to creating a trusting relationship. Probation officers often encounter this problem when trying to address personal issues with their clients. Here, it is quite easy to fall into the familiar pattern of using confrontation, which often forms the understandable backdrop to so much of a probation officer's interaction with clients. Agents of the law are accustomed to asking direct questions and seeking straight answers. Unfortunately, the likely outcome will be a confrontation–denial trap.

Using motivational interviewing in this context requires a fairly substantial shift in the direction and tone of an interview. The counselor is well advised to make this shift explicit through the use of an appropriate reframing statement (see Chapter 8). This can only be done if the counselor has moved toward establishing a frank and trusting relationship with the client. Here is an example:

> Part of my work has to do with seeing that people stay out of trouble, but there's another equally important side to my job, which is the counseling side. I think it's important for you to feel able to talk to me about other personal things, whatever they are. This part of my job does not involve checking up on people, but simply helping them to solve problems and be more independent.

Even if this initiative succeeds, the counselor is still likely to encounter resistance, in the form of reluctance to discuss problems openly or a general feeling of hopelessness. Again a reframing statement can be useful, to reinforce the client's autonomy and stress the need to develop internal controls in the face of external ones:

> I can see that this is a difficult situation for you. So much of your time in the last few weeks has been spent dealing with things that have control over you—the police, jail, and even coming to see me. We need to turn that around if we can, and see what you can do to control things yourself, so that you feel in charge of your own life.

Broaching the Subject

This raises another issue: how to introduce a "problem" topic for discussion when the individual is unaware of it (precontemplation) or reluctant to consider it (early contemplation). This most often arises in the office of a physician, probation officer, member of the clergy, psychologist, psychiatrist, counselor, or other health care worker. Usually the biggest initial obstacle to helpful discussion is how to broach the subject and initiate some form of constructive dialogue.

We believe that motivational interviewing strategies can be particularly useful here. The general approach is to ask open-ended questions that allow exploration of the person's motivational state without generating significant resistance. This is also helpful in dealing with individuals who are volunteering little, in that short answers are more difficult to give in response to open-ended questions. Just how to phrase these questions depends upon the client and the context. With some people in some situations you can be reasonably direct, whereas with others it can be a very delicate business. Here are a few examples:

Closed questions, likely to evoke resistance	Open-ended questions, to open discussion
You drink quite a bit, don't you?	Tell me about your drinking in a typical week.
It seems like you have a problem with gambling; don't you agree?	What do you enjoy about gambling?
Don't you think that your cocaine habit is a big cause of this problem?	How does cocaine fit in here?

It is helpful, too, to ask such questions in a matter-of-fact manner. The topic can follow on a series of other topics, being introduced as a natural and routine subject for discussion. Avoid nonverbal cues that give particular emphasis to the new topic or that communicate discomfort (e.g., looking down, shifting posture). Vocal tone should be normal and relaxed. In short, the introduced topic should flow continuously from prior discussion. Often it is useful to start by discussing the client's presenting problems and concerns, and then to explore the relationship between these and the subject you wish to broach.

Equally important is how you respond to the client's initial statements in response to such questions. Early Phase I strategies (reflective listening, affirmation, summarizing) are crucial to establishing a comfortable basis for further discussion.

Shortage of Time

Nonspecialists have numerous other priorities besides counseling for behavior change in an individual. Finding enough time to spend with a needy person is a constant dilemma for many busy professionals, including physicians, members of the clergy, attorneys, and probation officers. It is important to remember, however, that sometimes a relatively brief intervention can nudge someone toward behavior change. A likely explanation for this, as we have discussed in Chapter 3, is that a brief intervention serves to trigger a decision and commitment to change.

Motivational interviewing need not be a lengthy process. Sometimes a few carefully timed, incisive questions and some good reflective listening can trigger motivation for change; in other cases it takes longer. Whatever your time frame, however, we suggest that motivational interviewing provides a good framework for maximizing the potential for change in most interviewing situations. How to do this, while making the most of the time available, is the biggest challenge.

One obstacle to overcome in motivational interviewing, especially when time is short, is your own sense of urgency. There can be a sense of "I don't have time for this! I've got to get the job done quickly." Although listening may seem a good thing to do if you have lots of time, there is a tendency to think that when time is limited (as it generally is), you just have to confront people and tell them what to do. The problem, however, is that people's reactions to such strategies tend to be the same, whether or not time is limited. Confrontational/directive approaches tend to evoke resistance rather than change. Surely an important goal, even (perhaps especially) in a brief contact, is "First, do no harm." If all you have is a short time in which to make an impact, seek at least not to do any damage by entrenching resistance and discouraging change. In fact, a brief application of the strategies outlined in Chapters 6–9 may be quite helpful.

Motivational interviewing in a short time (e.g., a single interview) revolves around a compressed progression through Phase I and Phase II. Typically, this begins with sensitive questioning and reflection (Phase I), encouraging the person to articulate self-motivational statements and the arguments for change. After a period of motivation building, the intervention proceeds into key questions designed to evoke problem solving and commitment to change. An example of such brief intervention within a general medical practice is given in Chapter 14.

Exploring Emotions

The exploration of personal issues, problems, and ambivalence can open up deep emotion. We have found that motivational interviewing not uncommonly evokes distress or tears. Counselors find that in following the strategies of motivational interviewing they sometimes feel weighed down by the sadness of their clients; they are unsure about where to go next and whether they are doing "the right thing."

How important is such emotional expression, and how can you deal with this kind of situation? To begin with, it would be misguided to take the view that emotional expression has no part in motivational interviewing. If sadness, frustration, anxiety, or anger is related to a client's problem, then it is part of the process. On the other hand, it is not the aim of motivational interviewing to evoke emotional expression as an end in itself. There is no evidence thus far to suggest that overt emotional expression or "breaking down" is a necessary precondition for change. Therefore, we take a cautious view on this matter.

The crucial question is whether exploring a particular issue or emotion will aid the process of building motivation for change. Sometimes it will be constructive to pursue strong feelings; at other times it will not. This is a matter of judgment and timing. For example, a man who is often angry at his spouse for complaining about his behavior may not benefit from exploring this, particularly if it leads into the blaming trap described in Chapter 6. However, a person who is drinking or taking tranquilizers in response to sadness about a loss may well benefit from exploring this fairly early in counseling (Miller & Pechacek, 1987).

A key is how to deal with emotional exploration without sinking into a mire and losing your sense of direction in counseling. It is important to remember that motivational interviewing is not a nondirective approach in which the counselor simply follows the client wherever he or she goes. As the counselor, you control the direction of a session and keep it within constructive bounds in building motivation for change. Sensitive observation of the client will often indicate the right time to consider a change of direction. At this point the goal should be to lift the person gently out of the immediacy of the experience, and to help him or her integrate it into the larger journey toward change. A good way of doing this is to use skills described in Chapter 6: reflective listening, affirming, summarizing, and eliciting self-motivating statements. Here is an example, taken from midway through a 54-year-old man's second session:

THERAPIST: It sounds as if quite a lot has happened to you these last few months.

CLIENT: (*Visibly upset*) Yes, that's right. When the doctor told me I could never work again, I was very depressed. It's the most terrible thing that can happen to a man like me. Then when he said I might be seriously ill, I went into shock. Someone like me can't sit around doing nothing. I can't take this. (*He weeps.*)

T: Things look awfully black to you right now.

(*Client continues weeping; therapist waits silently for about 1 minute.*)

C: I'm sorry about this. It's the first time I've ever cried in front of someone else.

T: It's OK. You're going through a terribly difficult time. I'm here to help you.

C: I just feel so bad. My wife doesn't know what to do with me, moping around the house all day. She said I should come and see someone like you.

T: I'm glad you did. How are you feeling right now?

C: (*Wiping his eyes and beginning to move out of his tearfulness*) Well, it does help to talk to someone. Only my wife knows what I am going through. I haven't told my family or my friends that I will never be going back to work. They think I am just off work because of a little illness.

T: Then you've been bearing most of this burden on your own.

C: Yes, that's right. Sometimes I feel like giving up.

T: Well, I think it's good that you have allowed yourself to talk to me like this. You have been carrying this burden on your shoulders for months now, and I can understand how upset you feel about it all. I can also see better now where the drinking fits into the picture, and why it's increased in recent months. I guess there must be times when drinking feels like your only consolation.

C: It does. Sometimes it feels like a trap I'm in. Without the alcohol and those few hours a day in the pub, I don't know what I would do.

T: So in some ways the drinking is a comfort, and in other ways you think it's trapping you. How is it like a trap? What concerns you most about your drinking?

C: Well, I'm a proud man, and I like to work hard. I don't like to do nothing, and I can't just drink all the time. . . .

This example illustrates the use of Phase I skills to bring someone through an emotional episode and back into a constructive process of exploration and change. The sensitive handling of moments like this can bring counselor and client closer together, strengthening the working relationship through which motivation emerges.

In sum, emotional experience is a natural part of motivation. We do not regard emotional expression as essential for change to occur, though exploration of feelings related to a problem area may facilitate change. The essential strategies of motivational interviewing can be used to maintain the direction of a session while handling emotion in a caring and sensitive manner.

Life in Chaos

Another complexity, in seeking to evoke change in a particular area, is posed by a client whose whole life seems to be in chaos. Attempts to deal with what you perceive to be the focal problem may be met with various versions of the message "You don't understand." From the client's perspective, no piece of the puzzle (e.g., drinking) captures the "black hole" scope of the situation. *Everything* is wrong.

One likely possibility in this situation, of course, is that you truly *don't* yet understand the full picture. The client's message is a plea for further reflective listening. It is not likely to be fruitful to argue with the client to do things your way. Shifting direction in motivational interviewing is accomplished by gradual turning, not abrupt pushing. A first level of response to this situation, then, is to offer further reflective listening as you help the client construct a more complete picture.

There may come a point, however, when your judgment is that the way out of the "black hole" is through resolving a particular aspect of the problem. The question is how to get your client moving in this direction without evoking "You don't understand" resistance. Again, we believe that the key is skillful use of strategies already discussed. The principal maneuver here is to offer a summary statement that both acknowledges the complexity of the client's situation (and feelings) and reframes it in solvable terms. This is then followed by key questions that direct attention and movement in the desired direction.

Here is a clinical example with a 35-year-old woman who came with multiple life problems, including a disintegrating marriage, a demanding 2-year-old, a critical boss, panic attacks, and tightening agoraphobia. Concerned with her escalating use of tranquilizers, her physician referred her for counseling as a condition of continuing her prescription. Initial attempts to discuss her tranquilizer use evoked protestation that this was "the least of my worries" and only a necessary by-product of all her other concerns. The counselor spent a full session exploring her major problem areas, responding primarily with reflective listening. This process continued during the second session, toward the end of which this transition was offered:

> I can see how you have felt completely overwhelmed by your situation. Your husband doesn't seem to understand you, and hasn't offered much help in taking care of your child, who seems to need a lot of loving from you. On the job you're getting mostly criticism, and your work seems to be going downhill. That seems partly to be related to how bad you feel in the morning, and to your feeling worn out most of the time. It's like you're running out of fuel. On top of that, you're having these terrifying experiences where you feel like you're dying, and you're starting to feel scared about leaving the house and your child. It's understandable that until you find a way to deal with all of this and get your stress level down, you're desperate for anything that seems to offer a little rest and peace. You're also frightened that in spite of everything you're doing, all of this seems to be getting worse, more out of control. I think you've been very strong to deal with all this as well as you have. How do you think the tranquilizers fit in here?

This summary reframed the tranquilizers as part of a deteriorating problem that needed other solutions. Rather than telling her that the tranquilizers were causing or contributing to the problem, the therapist asked her to explore how they fit into the picture. This opened the door for exploring ambivalence and evoking self-motivational statements. The point is not to discount how a client sees his or her situation, but to acknowledge that perception and then focus attention on constructive steps toward change.

Sidetracking

A similar approach can be used to cope with the more common and less complicated problem of sidetracking during an interview. A client may wander off into a subject that the therapist does not regard to be productive. This may occur through natural associations, or it may be an intentional refocusing by the client on a more desirable or important topic. In the latter case, it is useful to offer an acknowledging summary of what the client is saying, and then to redirect the client to the topic of concern. This is easier to do if you and the client have explicitly agreed about the topic of consultation, in which case it is a matter of relating the sidetrack back to the main topic. If the client regards a different topic to be more urgent, the strategy outlined above can be followed.

Not all sidetracking is motivated resistance. Some people simply enjoy telling stories and providing great detail. Some think in wide associations or are easily distracted, and so readily wander off into tangential topics. Again we emphasize that motivational interviewing is *not* nondirective, and it is not necessary to follow wherever the client leads. Sometimes a simple redirection will suffice ("I think you started this story as an example of what concerns you about your drinking. What else have you noticed?"). Sometimes it is necessary to interrupt (politely) an extended monologue ("That sounds like a long story, and I want to make sure we have enough time today to focus on what brought you here. Let's go back, then, to . . ."). In any case, the strategy is to point the client back in the right direction, and to restart the process with an open-ended question. If this process evokes resistance, use the skills presented in Chapter 8.

Detoxification

One more question that has arisen, as we have offered and taught motivational interviewing, is that of how this process works when a client needs detoxification from alcohol or other drugs. Two major concerns arise here: (1) How able is the client to respond to this approach during acute detoxification? (2) When during a course of detoxification is it best to begin motivational interviewing? These are both empirical questions best answered by careful research, but we can offer a few comments in the interim.

Without question, clients are often cognitively impaired during acute detoxification, and show substantial recovery of function during the first few weeks of sobriety. The characteristic types of cognitive impairment may be expected to interfere with learning and self-regulation (Wilkinson, 1991; Wilkinson & Sanchez-Craig, 1981). For this reason, some have argued that treatment interventions, particularly those involving complex cognition, be delayed until the detoxification process has been completed. We believe there is merit to this argument, and that motivation built up and commitments made during the early weeks of detox may not hold. On the other hand, incentives for change may be particularly salient during the detoxification period, when discomfort is often high. The degree of cognitive impairment during a period of detox is highly variable across individuals, some of whom may respond well to earlier interventions. Furthermore, it is a common observation that when detoxification is offered apart from treatment, relatively few clients are "motivated" enough to make the transition from detox to a recovery program. These factors argue against waiting until the end of detoxification to begin motivational interviewing. Our own advice is to try this approach as early as common sense tells you it may be feasible. The detox period may be a particularly *good* time to build motivation and commitment with some individuals. Neither should this be a one-time effort. The process of motivational interviewing can be extended throughout detoxification. You may anticipate a need for bolstering of motivation for change as detox concludes and discomfort subsides. If detox is conducted apart from treatment, specific supplementary procedures may be used to increase the likelihood of referral completion (Kogan, 1957; Sisson & Azrin, 1986; Sisson & Mallams, 1981).

11

A Practical Case Example

The practice of motivational interviewing involves a creative integration of the strategies we have outlined. As in the game of chess, there are no standard scripts that can be followed. Each case is novel and poses unique challenges.

For this reason, we have hesitated about offering a "sample case" from start to finish. There is a limited amount that can be learned from observing a single game of chess or a single clinical example. No particular case can demonstrate the rich variety of situations and problems you will face, nor the range of ways in which these challenges can be met. Still, we have thought it helpful to provide a detailed example of how motivational interviewing proceeds. This *exact* approach may not be well suited to other individuals, but it does illustrate how the strategies of motivational interviewing are interwoven in actual practice.

The case to be described is that of a 38-year-old photographer who came for consultation about his drinking. He had never sought help for alcohol problems before, and was in the early contemplation stage. He was not at all certain that he needed help or a change. Two events had precipitated his coming. The first was a check-up by his physician, in response to some stomach pains he had been having. Based on this examination, the physician had told him that both his complaints and his blackouts suggested that he was drinking too much, and recommended that he see a specialist. Second, when he discussed this with his wife, she voiced her own concern that his drinking was getting out of hand. The combination of these comments was enough to prompt him to make an appointment.

THERAPIST: Good morning. Please have a seat here. I believe you wanted to talk about some concerns with your drinking. We have about 45 minutes today, and mainly I want to hear about your situation and your concerns. I'll need to get some specific information from you later, but right now perhaps you could start by telling me what concerns you about your drinking.

The therapist began with a brief structuring statement and an open-ended question.

CLIENT: Well, I'm not really sure if it's a problem at all. My wife seems to think that I drink too much. My doctor did some blood tests, and he told me those showed I am probably drinking too much. *Probably*, he said, but ever since I told my wife about that, she's been worried about my drinking. So I told her I would come here, but I'm not really sure I should be here.

The client immediately expressed ambivalence and some defensiveness.

T: So at least two other people, your wife and your doctor, have been worried that maybe alcohol is harming you. But I wonder: What have *you* noticed yourself? Is there anything that you have observed about your drinking over the years that might be reason for concern? Tell me something about your drinking.

A simple reflection.

It would have been easy here to fall into the question–answer trap, by asking a series of specific questions. Instead, the therapist asked a cluster of open-ended questions.

C: I guess maybe I drink more than I used to. My wife says I've been drinking more over the past few years.

T: So one thing you've noticed is that you are drinking more now than you used to. What else?

Reflection and "what else?".

C: I can't really think of anything else. It doesn't really affect me much. I don't really get *drunk* very often.

T: So although you know that your drinking has gone up over the past few years, it doesn't really seem to affect you more.

Reflection.

C: Right. I can drink all night and it doesn't make me drunk. Other guys have trouble keeping up with me.

T: That's interesting. What do you make of that?

C: I think it runs in my family. My dad was like that. He could drink most guys under the table, and it never seemed to bother him.

T: He *was* like that. Is he still living?

C: No, he died of a heart attack a few years ago. But that was after he had stopped drinking.

T: Why did he stop?

Useful information, but a risk of too many specific questions.

C: My mother wanted him to. He used to tell people that he quit for his health—that he wanted to lose some weight, and beer has a lot of calories.

T: So you think your drinking has been increasing over the years, and you've noticed that alcohol doesn't seem to affect you as much as it does other people. And you think that might be something that runs in your family.

A linking summary of self-motivational themes offered thus far, picking up a possible motivational theme related to the father's drinking.

C: Is that possible?

T: Yes, it is, and that may be important. Is there anything else you've noticed, any other way in which your drinking seems like your father's?

It was a bit early for extended information. The therapist gave a short answer and returned to eliciting self-motivational statements.

C: Lately, there have been some times when I can't remember things that happened. I'll be drinking at a party, and the next morning I can't remember getting home. It's not too pleasant to wake up and have no idea where you left your car.

T: That can be scary, especially the first few times it happens. Give me an example.

Reflection of feeling, and request for example to elicit further self-motivational statements by elaboration.

C: About 2 weeks ago, I was out with Bob, and I guess I drank a little more than usual. We

were playing billiards, with loser buying
rounds. When I woke up in the morning, I
couldn't think of where my car was, and I remembered starting this one game but I
couldn't remember how it ended. I looked out
the window and my car was in the driveway,
and I guess I drove it there. I felt terrible.

T: In what way?   *Another request for elabora-*
                                                        tion.

C: Well, I wondered if I had done anything stupid. I guess I could wake up in jail.

T: For driving while intoxicated, you mean?

C: I don't usually get that drunk, but probably
that time I was.

T: What else bothered you that morning?

C: I know that it happened to my dad, too. He
told me about it.

T: So it worries you that the same thing is hap-   *The therapist stayed with re-*
pening to you, too. What do you think it   *flecting and eliciting.*
means?

C: I don't know. I haven't really thought about
that. And I remember he'd get up in the
morning looking pretty shaky, and needing a
drink.

T: You feel that way yourself sometimes.

C: No, I don't think I ever feel like I need a
drink. But I have felt pretty bad some morn-
ings. I don't drink in the morning, though.

T: That's a rule you've kept for yourself.

C: Yes, except on rare occasions. I don't think
it's good to drink in the morning.

T: Why is that?

C: I've noticed that I feel better; it gets rid of the
hangover. That could get to be a bad habit. I
usually just tough it out and it goes away.

T: When you stop to think about it, then, there   *Another summary, drawing*
are several things you've noticed. Your drink-   *together the major self-moti-*
ing seems to be going up over the years, and   *vational themes that had*
you know that you've driven sometimes when   *emerged.*

you've had too much. Your wife is concerned about you, as your mother was about your father, and your doctor has told you that it's affecting your health. You've noticed that, like your father, you can drink quite a bit without feeling intoxicated, and you've been having these problems with your memory. You've had some bad hangovers, and you notice that if you drink some more in the morning you feel better. Which of these things concern you the most?

C: My health, I suppose.

T: So if you thought that you were harming your health, that would worry you. What else concerns you?

C: I don't like not remembering things.

T: That doesn't seem normal to you.

C: No. But I don't think I'm an alcoholic. I've known some alcoholics, and I'm not like that. *The labeling trap opened up.*

T: Your situation doesn't seem that bad to you. *Reflection.*

C: No, it doesn't. I've quit drinking for weeks at a time with no problem. And I can have a couple of drinks and leave it alone. I have a good job and family. How could I be an alcoholic?

T: That must be confusing to you, as you think *Reflection of feeling, and a* about it. On the one hand you can see some *double-sided reflection.* warning signs that you are drinking too much, and you worry about that. On the other hand, you don't seem to fit how you picture an alcoholic.

C: Right. I mean I've got some problems, but *The client responded by ac-* I'm not a drunk. *knowledging both sides.*

T: And so thus far it hasn't seemed like you needed to do anything about it. But now you're here. Why now?

C: It just seemed like I ought to talk to somebody. I don't want to ignore this. I saw what happened to my dad, and I don't want that to happen to me and my family.

T: Your family is really important to you.   *Reinforcing an important*
                                                          goal.

C: I love my wife and my son.

T: And it sounds like they love you, too. Your
    wife cared enough to tell you how worried she
    is about your drinking. And though you don't
    see yourself as an alcoholic, you're a little
    worried, too.

C: Yes, I guess so.

T: It must have been a difficult thing for you to   *Affirmation.*
    decide to come here. You must care quite a
    bit about yourself and your family, and I re-
    spect you for being so open here. It's not an
    easy thing that you are doing.

C: It was hard. I didn't really want to come at   *Labeling trap again.*
    first. But do you think I'm an alcoholic?

T: That's a word that means many things to dif-   *A "Yes" here could have led*
    ferent people. I don't want you to worry   *to argumentation and resis-*
    about what to call yourself. What matters,   *tance. Instead the therapist re-*
    really, is that we take a good close look at   *framed the issue, and shifted*
    what's going on here. I can see why you're   *the focus back to the task at*
    concerned, and I'd like to help you find out   *hand: exploring drinking and*
    what risk you might be facing, and what—if   *its effects.*
    anything—you could do about it.

C: What do you think I should do?

Commentary   This is an example of the process of eliciting self-motivational statements, as a means for building motivation during Phase I.
Most of the therapist's responses up to this point were in the form of
questions to elicit self-motivational statements or reflective listening to
reinforce them. At many points where it might have been tempting to begin
"confronting," the therapist retained a generally empathic stance and
avoided argumentation. Clients are often surprised and relieved at this;
instead of resisting, they tend to be willing to continue their self-evaluation
process. Self-motivational statements are reinforced by reflection and periodic summarizing.

     At this point, the client asked an important question: "What do you
think I should do?" The therapist had to make a decision here. Was there
enough of a motivational base to begin discussing strategies for change? If
this had been an office consultation with a physician, where time was quite
limited, this could well have been a one-time opportunity; it might have

been best to proceed toward strengthening commitment and negotiating a plan (Phase II). The risk, however, was that not enough Phase I work had been done, and the therapist would be put in the role of making suggestions that the client would reject (a form of the confrontation–denial trap). In this case, the client was consulting a specialist, and it was therefore possible to engage him in a longer counseling process. One option was to continue the present interview with Phase I strategies, accumulating further self-motivational statements that could be used to develop discrepancy. Another was to use the base that had been established to involve the person in a more detailed assessment (Chapter 7), which in turn would provide more material to discuss. The therapist chose the latter route and offered a transition to structured assessment.

C: What do you think I should do?

T: There are quite a few possibilities, and I could help you think about your options right now if you want. But if you want my opinion, I think that first we ought to get a better picture of your present situation. What you have told me so far raises a few concerns, but we really don't know enough yet to make good decisions. What I would suggest, then, is that we take some time for a good check-up. There are some questionnaires you could answer, and I'd also like to spend a couple of hours with you getting more helpful information. After that, when we have a clearer picture of exactly what is happening in your life, we can focus on your options. What do you think? Are you interested enough to spend 2 or 3 hours finding out more about yourself?

The client completed three paper-and-pencil questionnaires at home: the Alcohol Use Inventory (Horn, Wanberg, & Foster, 1987), and two instruments to assess motivation for change, the University of Rhode Island Change Assessment (URICA) and the Stages of Change Readiness and Treatment Eagerness Scale (SOCRATES) (see Chapter 7). The therapist administered the Brief Drinker Profile interview (Miller & Marlatt, 1984) and a brief neuropsychological test battery. In addition, a blood sample was drawn and analyzed via a broad serum chemistry screen. It is possible, of course, to conduct an assessment that requires less time and expense. The key here was to provide structured feedback to the client, along with information to allow interpretation of personal results (Chapter 7). Here is a portion of the subsequent interview, in which this feedback was provided. The client was provided with a written report to follow as the therapist reviewed the findings.

T: I appreciate the time and care that you took with these tests. What I want us to do this morning is to review the results together. First, you remember that we went through a typical week and added up your drinking. That came out to about 53 standard drinks a week, with one "drink" here being a regular glass of beer or wine, or about an ounce of liquor. If you compare that to the whole population, you're drinking more than 95% of adults. What do you think about that?

This typifies the style for presenting results. The client's score was presented, relative to normative data. Rather than being told what to think or how to feel about the result, the client was asked for reactions, which were then reflected.

C: It seems like a lot. I never really added it up before, but I don't think of myself as a heavy drinker.

T: You're surprised.

Instead of confronting, the therapist used simple reflection.

C: Yes! I know that when you were asking me about how much I drink usually, it sounded like a lot. But I drink about the same as my friends do.

T: So this is confusing for you. On the one hand you can see that it's a lot, and it's more than 95% of people drink. Yet it seems about normal among your friends. How can both things be true?

Double-sided reflection.

C: I guess I can drink with the top 5%.

T: Your friends are really heavy drinkers.

The therapist would have done better to understate this reflection.

C: I don't know about "heavy." I guess we drink more than our share.

T: We also have a computer program that estimates blood alcohol levels based on drinking patterns. Most social drinkers stop somewhere between 20 and 50 on this scale. Fifty here is the same as .05, which is enough to impair driving. Our estimate is that you get up around 179 units, or .179, in the course of a typical week of drinking. That's over three times the upper limit for most drinkers, and well up into the legal intoxication range for impaired driving.

C: You mean every week?

T: From what you told me, yes. I believe there are three nights a week when you get up around this level.

C: That can't be right. I never even feel drunk. I drive home all the time, and I've never had a problem.

Resistance: Challenging.

T: It seems to you that something must be wrong with the computer.

Amplified reflection.

C: Well, no, but I don't ever feel that drunk.

T: And you can't see how you could have that much alcohol in your body without feeling it.

C: Is that possible?

T: Not only that, it's common among heavy drinkers. It's called "tolerance," though most people call it "being able to hold your liquor." We talked about that the first time I saw you.

C: So I can drink a lot and not feel it?

T: That's right. You can have a fairly high blood alcohol level—enough to affect your driving and even do damage to your internal organs—but not feel like you're intoxicated.

C: So I'm driving around legally drunk three times a week?

T: That's how it looks. What are you thinking about that?

C: I guess I've been lucky.

T: Now this score is for those heavier drinking times we talked about. On one of those weekends, we estimate, you get up as high as 220 units, or .22. That makes sense, because that's the range in which memory blackouts sometimes occur.

C: Wow!

T: That seems high to you.

C: Yeah, I just . . . I never thought about it.

T: Well, that's why we're doing this, and I appreciate how honestly you answered these questions. I can see, though, that this is hard for you. I've been through this with a lot of people, and it's tough to look at yourself in the mirror like this. Do you want to go on?

Affirmation.

C: OK.

T: This next one is a rough measure of alcohol's effects in your life, the number of places it has caused problems. Your score of 18 falls in the middle of the range that we call "significant problems"—not quite severe, but more than just mild or moderate effects.

The score being presented here was that for the Michigan Alcoholism Screening Test (Selzer, 1971), which is part of the Drinker Profile (Miller & Marlatt, 1984).

C: Uh-huh.

T: Does that make sense to you?

C: About right, I guess.

T: OK. I don't know what you'll make of this next result. This reflects the degree to which you are depending on alcohol, becoming dependent on it. Your score here is at the bottom of the range we call "definite and significant symptoms of dependence." Roughly, that means that you are starting to show some of the common signs of alcohol dependence, though you still have a way to go before getting into severe problems.

C: You mean I am addicted?

T: It's not as simple as either you are or you aren't addicted. Dependence is something that happens gradually, in steps or degrees. This tells you about how far along that path you've gone. It says there is definitely something happening here, that you are starting to show early signs of dependence on alcohol.

C: I don't like that at all.

T: You don't like the idea of being dependent on alcohol.

C: On anything!

T: You like to be in charge of yourself, in control.

C: Yes.

T: Well, we're not talking about severe prob- | *Here the therapist took a slightly*
lems yet. Dependence increases over the years, | *paradoxical tone, voicing the*
sometimes at a fast rate, sometimes more | *"maybe it's not so bad" side of*
slowly. You're just in the middle range now. | *the client's ambivalence, and*
But it looks like that one hit you pretty hard. | *then ending with a reflection.*

C: (*Silent for some time*) Let's go on to the next one.

T: I'm worried that I'm going a little too fast for you. This is difficult, and I don't want to give you too much at once. Do you want some more time to take this in or talk about it?

C: No, it's OK. Let's go ahead.

Commentary The therapist continued with feedback from the questionnaires and from the serum chemistry profile, which reflected moderate elevations in liver enzymes. Finally, neuropsychological test results were presented, again reflecting patterns of impairment typical among problem drinkers.

This feedback process can be a very difficult one for a client, and therapist empathy is needed throughout this phase. Tears and distress are not unusual. Feedback of this kind contributes powerfully to the development of discrepancy and of the perception that a change is needed. Resistance is commonly encountered in response to some results, and should be dealt with sensitively (see Chapter 8). At the conclusion of this process, a therapist invites a client to ask any questions, then summarizes the feedback and integrates it with the client's own stated concerns. This recapitulation prepares the way for asking key questions (Chapter 9).

T: We've covered a lot of ground. I wonder if | *An invitation to receive infor-*
there's anything you'd like to ask me—any- | *mation and advice.*
thing you've wondered about so far, or some-
thing you'd like to know.

C: Yes. Is this something I could have inherited from my father?

T: There is some evidence that people can in-
herit a predisposition to have alcohol problems. It's not quite as simple as inheriting a
condition called "alcholism." It's a bit more
like hereditary risk for high blood pressure or
heart disease. Your blood pressure is determined in part by genetics, but is also influenced by your diet and exercise, your stress
level, your use of salt, and so on. Drinking is
like that, too. Men who have biological relatives with drinking problems seem to have a
higher risk themselves. And tolerance is also a
risk factor.

C: So I have a higher risk, then.

T: That's it, really. You have more reason than
most people to be careful about your drinking. Anything else you're wondering about?

C: I guess not.

T: Then let me try to summarize where we are,   *Recapitulation.*
and you can tell me if I've left anything out.
You came here partly at the urging of your
wife, partly because of your doctor, and
partly because you were concerned about
your own drinking, though you hadn't really
thought much about it before. You were
aware that your drinking has been going up
over the years, and now it's over 50 drinks in
a typical week. You were also aware that you
drink more than other people, and you seem
to have a substantial tolerance for alcohol.
You can drink a lot of it without feeling
drunk, even though—as we discussed today—
you must have enough alcohol in your bloodstream to affect you and do some damage.
You want to take care of yourself, and you
are concerned for your own health. The blood
tests that we did suggest that your body is
being damaged by your drinking—which is
what your physician had told you. You've already piled up some problems related to
drinking, and there are some indications that
you are starting to become dependent on al-

cohol, particularly when you want to socialize or change how you feel. At the same time, you don't think of yourself as an alcoholic, and in the past you've assumed that if you're not an alcoholic you have nothing to worry about in regard to drinking. You don't like the idea of being dependent on anything. You've had some bad hangovers, and you're concerned about alcohol's effects on your memory, and your test scores indicate that your concerns are well founded. Your scores resemble those of heavy drinkers, in sharp contrast to your otherwise very good intelligence. I know you've thought about how your drinking is looking like your father's in some ways, and that's a worry. We talked about your family history, and how you probably have a higher risk than most people for being harmed by alcohol. You especially want to make sure that your drinking doesn't hurt your family, because you know what that hurt is like. Is that a fair summary?

C: Yes, except that I didn't really think when I came here that I was drinking more than other people.

T: It had seemed to you that your drinking was perfectly normal.   *Amplified reflection.*

C: Well, maybe not normal, but not abnormal either. I just hadn't thought about it.

T: And now you are thinking about it. I've given you a lot of information, and some of it is fairly heavy. What do you make of all this?   *Key question.*

C: It's kind of depressing. I really didn't think I had a problem, at least not this bad.

T: This isn't what you expected to hear, and I can see how it must be upsetting for you. Let   *Reflection.*
me put this in perspective, though. On all of these measures, you are roughly in a twilight   *Reframing.*
zone, a border region. The good news is that you realized what was happening before any of these problems became severe. People who   *Supporting self-efficacy.*

make a change in their drinking, if they do it
in time, usually show quite a bit of improvement, and their test scores often go back to
normal. Other people wait until they have done
serious and irreversible damage. You didn't
wait. It's like so many other problems: the earlier you catch it, the better your chances are of
turning it around and staying healthy.

C: What would I do on the weekend if I gave   *Envisioning.*
   up alcohol? (*Grins*)

T: It's hard to imagine how different your life
   might be.

Commentary   Here was another choice point: The therapist had to
decide whether to press on toward setting goals, negotiating a plan for
change, and obtaining commitment. It would have been possible to continue
with Phase I strategies, perhaps by constructing a decisional balance sheet
with the pros and cons of change. The question was this: How ready was this
client for change? Several of the signs listed in Table 9.1 (Chapter 9) were
evident. There was little resistance, and the client was asking few questions
about the problem. He as offering some self-motivational statements,
though the therapist could at this point have sought to elicit more (e.g.,
"What do you think are the most important reasons for concern here? Of the
things we've talked about, what are the most important reasons for making
a change? What do you think will happen if you don't change your drinking?"). There was one indication of his envisioning how life might be
without alcohol. The client's nonverbal cues at this point also suggested a
kind of surrender, a sad resignation. The therapist decided to test the waters
with a key question on change.

T: So what does this mean about your drink-   *Key question.*
   ing? What happens now?

C: Well, I want to do *something*. I don't want
   to just let this go on.

T: What do you suppose that "something" is?   *Key question.*
   What's the next step?

C: I guess I have to do something about my   *The client opened up the ne-*
   drinking—either cut it down or give it up.   *gotiation process by discuss-*
                                                     ing goals.

T: One or the other.

C: Well, I can't just let it go! If I keep drinking, won't all of this get worse?

T: Probably.

C: Then something's got to change. I either cut down or quit.

T: What do you think about these two possibilities?

C: If I had my choice, I would prefer to just cut down. I'd like to drink sometimes.

T: Drinking is important to you.

C: Not *important*, really. It's just that I enjoy a drink, and I might feel strange sitting there with a Coke while everybody else is drinking.

Envisioning.

T: So it might be uncomfortable for you; you'd feel out of place.

C: Yes. That's not too serious, I guess. I'd just rather not give it up if I don't have to.

T: But if it were clear to you that you had to quit altogether, then you could.

Supporting self-efficacy.

C: Sure. If I knew I had to.

T: How can you find out?

C: I guess I try something and see if it works.

T: How much help would you want?

C: What kind of help?

T: I mean help from other people—support, counseling, ideas, that sort of thing. How much would you do it on your own, and how much would it help to have some support?

C: I don't know. I've never tried. I like to handle things myself, and I think I could do it, but maybe it would help to talk to somebody else about it too.

T: So you would be open to some support if you decide to change your drinking.

C: I think so, yes.

T: What do you think you will do?

C: You're the expert. What can I do?

T: I can tell you some things that other people
have tried successfully, but you're the expert
on you. All I can do is give you ideas. Maybe
some of them will make sense to you; maybe
none of them will. You're the one who has to
decide what to do. Do you want some ideas?

Introducing the "menu" concept.

Emphasizing personal control.

C: Yes.

T: First of all, there's your decision about cutting down versus quitting. Some people do
succeed in getting their drinking reduced to a
point that it no longer causes them problems.
Others find it's necessary or easier to abstain.
You're not sure which way to go.

C: No. What do you think?

T: This has to be your decision; I can't make it
for you. Are you sure you want my advice?

Emphasizing personal control.

C: Please. I don't have to take it just because
you say it.

T: OK. I guess if I were in your place, I might be
a bit worried about some of the findings we reviewed, like the effects on your liver and your
brain. The surest way to reverse those problems
and get them back toward normal is a period
of total abstinence, if you can handle it.

Personal challenge.

C: Oh, I can handle it all right. How long do
you think I ought to go on the wagon?

T: That's hard to say. At least long enough for
your body to get back to normal. I'd say that
3 months would be a good start. It might be a
good idea to repeat some of these tests after
that to see how you are doing.

C: And if I keep drinking, I won't get better?

T: I can't say for sure. You could take your
chances. But I do think that the surest and
quickest way to repair this damage would be
to take a vacation from alcohol. That's my
opinion. I don't know how that sounds to
you.

C: Then when I am healthy again, I can start
drinking again if I want to?

T: The fact is that you can start drinking any time you want to. Nobody can stop you. It's not a question of whether you *can*. The real question is what would happen. As I told you, some people are careful with their drinking and they manage. The danger, of course, is falling back into old habits and starting to drink in a way that endangers your health and your family again. But don't try to make that decision now. You can decide that after you've had your vacation. You might even find that you *like* not drinking!

Emphasizing personal control.

Delaying a decision.

C: And for now I should quit.

T: You asked me what I think. I didn't say you *should*, only that it's what I think would be the safest course. What you do is up to you. What do you think you'll do?

C: That seems best.

T: Then let me ask you this: What still stands in the way of your doing what you have decided to do? If you have decided to stop drinking for a period of time, what will make that hard?

C: My friends. A lot of the time I spend with them is drinking, and I don't know how I would handle that.

T: What could you do?

C: Maybe I spend more time with my friends who don't drink, or stay away from the bars and see them when they're not drinking.

T: Can you manage that?

Personal challenge.

C: I think so.

T: What else would be hard?

C: I *like* to drink. But I guess that's not a big problem. I just have to remind myself that it's important.

T: Let me ask you this: What do you think would happen if you *don't* change your drinking? What bothers you about that?

The therapist assumed that there was continuing ambivalence, and used this opportunity to reinforce motivation.

C: I guess all of those things we talked about could get worse—my liver, my brain, my memory. And I think my family would have a hard time—I don't like to think about losing them. Maybe even lose my job if it got bad enough. It's not very pleasant to think about.

T: How do you feel about drinking right this minute?

C: It doesn't seem very appealing.

T: One more thing. Usually there's a bigger picture than just drinking. How else would you like for things to be different? Are there other changes you would like to make?

C: I'd like to get along better with my wife.

T: So it might be good for the two of you to talk to somebody together, to work on your relationship. Would both of you be willing to do that?

C: I think so.

Commentary At this point, the therapist decided it was time to review with the client a range of options available to help him in carrying out his plan. The specifics would depend upon the alternatives available in the area. A variety of options were described to this client, including nondrinking support groups, disulfiram, covert sensitization (to overcome liking for alcohol), assertiveness training (especially for drink refusal), tapering versus "cold turkey" quitting, and marital counseling. The client expressed a preference to "do it on my own," but showed some interest in coming back for follow-up sessions with his wife. The therapist proceeded with a plan summary.

T: Let me see if I understand what you want to do for yourself, then. You've decided that what you want to do is take a break from alcohol for a period of at least 3 months, and you're going to go home and tell your wife. You thought it would be a good idea for the two of you to come back together, and to be able to check in with me on how you're doing. You like the idea of being able to accomplish this on your own, so for now you

don't want to use other kinds of support, like
the medication we discussed [disulfiram] or a
group. You did, say, though, that if it didn't
work out and you took up drinking again in
the next 3 months, then we would talk about
some additional support. You're going to
come back next Thursday with your wife, so
we can go over this plan with her, and then
we'll decide what to do from there. Is that
what you want to do?

C: Yes, I guess so.

T: You sound a little reluctant still, and I guess   *Reflecting the ambivalence.*
that's understandable. This is a big change for
you. What is there about this plan that you're
nervous about? Have I missed something?

C: I'm not really "nervous" about it. No, it's
OK. I was just thinking about some of the
good times I have.

T: And it's hard because you're weighing those   *Reframing.*
against your health and your family, and
good times to come. It's hard to let go.

C: But it's what I have to do.

T: No, you don't have to. It happens only if it's   *Emphasizing personal control.*
what you *want* to do. If you want it enough.
Is this what you *want*?

C: Yes. It is.

T: Then I'll see you and your wife on Thursday.

This is just one example of how motivational interviewing flows in
practice. There are many different approaches through which the basic
principles of motivational interviewing can be pursued. This case is illustrative of some of the choice points that arise, and how a skilled therapist might
proceed. The challenge to your creativity is in applying the general principles to each individual case.

12

Teaching Motivational Interviewing

Learning is nothing but discovery that something is possible. To teach means to show a person that something is possible.
—Frederick S. Perls, *Gestalt Therapy Verbatim*

Motivational interviewing involves the integration of a complex set of clinical skills, posing special challenges for trainers and supervisors. It is not an approach that can be acquired merely by reading or listening to lectures. For novices, it requires the learning of a set of integrated therapeutic skills, and the development of judgment regarding when and how to use them. For experienced clinicians, it may also involve the unlearning of familiar styles and habits in dealing with clients.

A key in acquiring the necessary skills for motivational interviewing is *practice with feedback*. Although many of the strategies appear logical and even easy, they prove challenging to implement in practice. That is why we have included this chapter, which is designed primarily to help professionals who wish to train others in motivational interviewing. We provide you with a structured and sequential series of exercises that we have developed through our own experience in teaching this approach over the past decade. These exercises make heavy use of role play in order to simulate practical conditions. Although we have offered workshops for 100 people or more, we recommend working with not more than 15–20 trainees at a time. This allows the trainer to circulate among pairs during dyadic exercises, and to provide some feedback to each individual in the course of a day-long workshop. The time required will vary, depending upon the level of prior experience of trainees; however, we recommend not less than 8–12 hours for an introductory workshop, ideally followed by supervised practice for shaping key skills. A series of five or more 3-hour training blocks can also be effective, allowing time for practice and integration between sessions.

The exercises that we present in this chapter follow the sequence of material presented in Chapters 5–9. They provide direct demonstrations of the traps that counselors can fall into, and of the core skills that characterize motivational interviewing. The menu of exercises that we provide here is long, and you will want to choose those that are most appropriate to the needs and experience of the trainees.

Some General Points

Qualities of the Trainer

A few words are in order about the qualities that make a good trainer of motivational interviewing. Needless to say, it is important for the trainer to have developed a high level of the skills that are being taught. This means having had substantial experience in applying motivational interviewing with a range of client groups, preferably with supervision and feedback. Trainees pose a wide range of questions, depending on their own needs and settings. Some of the issues you may encounter include the following:

- How can you use this approach with people who are required to come for treatment and don't want to be there?
- Isn't this really a middle-class style? How would it work with my clients, who are down and out?
- What do you do with a teenager who just won't talk?
- How would you handle a woman who doesn't think that alcohol is a problem for her, and who just wants to talk about her depression?
- What about working in a military setting, where I have to report any drug use to the client's commanding officer? How does that affect motivational interviewing?
- What happens if I just can't go along with the goal and the plan that a client wants to pursue?
- You seem to be talking about strategies to use at the beginning of treatment. Can you use this approach in aftercare?
- Most of my clients know perfectly well that they are drinking too much. They have lots of problems and can talk about them for hours. How would this work for them?

A good trainer, then, needs flexibility in applying these strategies in many different contexts.

The same qualities that make an effective motivational counselor are also helpful in training. Being a good trainer requires respect for individual differences, tolerance for disagreement and ambivalence, patience with gradual approximations, and a genuine caring for and interest in the people you serve. The trainer communicates enthusiasm and commitment in teaching this approach, but takes no offense at those who disagree and prefer other approaches. Motivational interviewing is not for everyone, and some counselors find that it does not fit their own style and skills. Good training, like good counseling, respects personal choice, with the attitude of "Take what you want and leave the rest." The skills and qualities of motivational interviewing can be demonstrated by the very manner in which you deal with your audience. There is a certain integrity to showing, in your own training manner, the very style you wish to impart.

About Role Play

Newcomers to role play sometimes express reservations about its artificial nature, feel reluctant to try something new in front of others, or complain that it is "a waste of time." Our own experience is that such trainees readily adapt to (and often enjoy) role play if the exercises are properly designed and presented. It may be helpful for you to communicate the following general principles to trainees:

- Role play is important because complex new skills are not established without practice. These exercises provide an opportunity to try out these skills in your own words and to receive feedback.
- No one should feel obliged to participate. Anyone can withdraw at any time. Being an observer is a very useful role.
- Role play is not the real thing, but it can be very close to it! When learning to fly, for example, one may first learn the basic information and principles, then practice in a flight simulator, then receive guided practice on a quiet airstrip before taking to the skies on one's own. So it is with counselor training.
- If any of you should feel upset during a role play, you should bring this to my attention. This does not happen often, and it is not something to be alarmed about—but let me know.
- Try to stay in role during the exercises. Don't step out of role to comment on what you're doing and discuss it. That will be done after each exercise in the debriefing period. Use your time for practice, and discuss it later.

In short, don't be intimidated or dissuaded by initial resistance to role playing. Such resistance is very common and is easily overcome. Role play is an essential element of training for a clinical approach of this complexity.

We recommend, when you are doing a series of role-play exercises with a group, that participants should change partners instead of doing all exercises with the same people. This provides a variety of experiences with the techniques being practiced.

About Videotaping and Supervision

Although it is not essential, the video recording of a role play can provide a useful window into the dialogue between "client" and "counselor." It offers trainees the unusual opportunity to "see ourselves as others see us." Sometimes watching oneself on videotape can do more to alter counseling style than hours of supervision. The ability to stop the action also permits discussion along the way of different strategies that can be used at key points. The videotape can take the place of the "observer" in some of the exercises presented in this chapter.

With trainees who have never been exposed to this technology, the use of a light-hearted warm-up exercise (see Exercise 2, below) is advisable. Having fun at first is a good way to begin. Remember that the first exposure to oneself on videotape can be devastating. Typically, the trainee over-attends to (and is overcritical of) minor personal mannerisms. One of us, in viewing his first videotaped counseling session, nearly left the field of clinical psychology! His embarrassment was exacerbated by a supervisor who, in reviewing the tape, stopped it frequently, mercilessly criticizing his errors before an audience of his peers. We urge you, then, to be sensitive to how aversive it can be to see oneself on videotape for the first time. Be very wary of focusing on negative aspects of a videotape, or allowing members of an audience to do so. Even when the use of the tape is in one-to-one private supervision, be conscientious about reinforcing positive aspects, keeping suggestions for change brief and specific, and concluding with positive input. This kind of "feedback sandwich"—positives, then suggestions for change, then positives—is generally a good approach in supervision. Remember, too, that learning is a matter of successive approximations. For any single session or role-play exercise, choose a particular priority for shaping, and don't try to repair all errors at once.

Self-Teaching Aspects

One substantial advantage in teaching motivational interviewing is the extent to which this can be a *self*-teaching approach once the essential perspectives and component skills have been established. Once trainees learn what to look for from clients, they continue to receive immediate feedback regarding their effectiveness. Correctly applied strategies for eliciting self-motivational statements will elicit self-motivational statements. Blunders elicit and reinforce resistance. Well-done reflective listening results in a client's continuing to explore openly. Most reflective-listening statements lead to feedback on the correctness of the reflection and further elaboration, which over time will shape the accuracy of the clinician's reflections. Roadblocks stop the process of self-exploration. A well-timed transition to Phase II leads to a commitment to change; a premature press for commitment yields resistance.

This means that an important aspect in training motivational interviewing is to teach clinicians the cues to which they should attend. Recognizing these cues in clients is a key in adjusting strategies within each case, and in improving one's own skills through clinical experience. (When an expert witness once bragged about having experience with 500 cases, the cross-examining attorney asked, "Is that 500 cases of new learning, or just 500 repetitions of the same thing?") Teaching people how to read feedback cues prepares them for continued learning in subsequent practice.

Laying the Foundation

Unless your audience is already familiar with the relevant research and theory, it is useful to begin by providing at least a brief conceptual context for training. Ordinarily, this should be contained within about 60–90 minutes. The elements of this rationale are provided in Chapters 1–4. Some of the key ideas are as follows:

- Therapist style is a powerful determinant of client resistance and change (Chapter 1).
- Confrontation is a goal, not a style (Chapter 1).
- Argumentation is a poor method for inducing change (Chapter 1).
- When resistance is evoked, clients tend not to change (Chapter 1).
- Client motivation can be increased by a variety of therapist strategies (Chapter 2).
- Even relatively brief interventions can have a substantial impact on problem behavior (Chapter 3).
- Motivation emerges from the interpersonal interaction between client and counselor (Chapter 3).
- Ambivalence is normal, not pathological (Chapter 4).
- Helping people resolve ambivalence is a key to change (Chapter 4).

This presentation serves as a preparation for the introduction of motivational interviewing as a style for avoiding resistance, resolving ambivalence, and inducing change. It can also be useful to explain the basic characteristics and goals of this approach, and to distinguish motivational interviewing from other approaches (Chapter 5).

The foundation of motivational interview is further developed by discussing the five basic principles (Chapter 5) and the traps into which counselors can fall, which disrupt the motivational process (Chapter 6). This serves as groundwork for an introduction of the five early strategies of Phase I (Chapter 6). A handout describing the principles and strategies can be useful.

An alternative, if you are less didactically oriented, is to present a step-by-step introduction using quick practical demonstrations in order to illustrate the basic principles. The following sequence takes about 60–90 minutes. The overview is built up on a large screen or blackboard, which is initially blank.

1. Write the word "ambivalence" on the board, then demonstrate in 2–3 minutes "how not to do it," using a volunteer "client" from the audience who feels ambivalent about something (e.g., moving to the country vs. staying in the city). Argue strongly in favor of one option. If time is available, it can be useful for trainees to try this themselves.

2. Elicit from trainees the basic observation that if the counselor argues for the advantages of one side, the client will present the disadvantages of that side and the advantages of the other. Had the counselor chosen to argue for the other side, the client would have taken the opposite position.

3. Conduct a second, more clinical "how not to do it" demonstration for 4–5 minutes with a fairly reluctant "client" coming for his or her first counseling session. Start off with the assumption that this person has a specific problem and needs to face up to it. Label the person early on and work hard to persuade him or her to "face up to reality." The client will become overtly resistant. Again, trainees can do this exercise themselves, time permitting. If you choose this option, brief those role-playing the counselor carefully, to ensure that they are confrontational. Build in as many of the traps as possible.

4. Elicit from trainees, and write up on the board, a list of traps into which the counselor(s) fell, and then the basic goal of motivational interviewing: to elicit from the ambivalent client the reasons for concern and the arguments for change. Attention is then turned to *how* one does this, and the basic principles of motivational interviewing are presented (Chapter 5), along with a listing of the five early strategies (Chapter 6).

5. Clarify any confusions about motivational interviewing at this stage, and point out that it is not primarily a nondirective approach. Although client-centered strategies are employed, the process of eliciting self-motivational statements is quite intentional and directive.

Opening-Strategy Exercises

Training proceeds into the five opening strategies presented in Chapter 6. We find it helpful to present them in the following manner.

1. Ask Open-Ended Questions

The first strategy—asking open-ended questions—can be introduced effectively with a demonstration. Ask a participant to role-play a client coming for a first counseling session. This may be facilitated by structuring a specific "client" role (e.g., specifying demographics, presenting picture, agency, etc.). Indicate that you will be doing the first few minutes of the interview twice, using different styles. (Alternatively, two different participants can be involved in similar client roles.) Demonstrate the initial minutes of the interview, first by asking many specific closed (short-answer or yes–no) questions, and responding to the client's answers with new closed questions. (This also provides an illustration of the question–answer trap.) Then, after 3–5 minutes, repeat the interview from the beginning; however, this time ask only open-ended questions, responding with reflection to the client's answers. Afterwards, discuss the two styles: First ask the "client(s)" to describe their reactions to the two styles, and then ask for the observations of the audience.

2. Listen Reflectively

We believe that reflective listening represents one of the most essential—and most challenging—skills to be mastered in learning this approach. A counselor who cannot offer skillful reflective listening simply cannot conduct motivational interviewing. Many trainees correctly regard this as a very basic skill, but incorrectly believe that they already "know how to do that." Some do, but we find that a majority of those we work with enter training without a high level of empathic skill. In any event, reinforcement of these skills is in order. The acquisition of good reflective listening is often a slow process, and trainees readily relapse into reliance on questions and more directive communications. For these reasons, we devote a substantial amount of time in training to the development of empathic listening abilities. In a shorter (e.g., 1-day) workshop, there is not enough time to work through all of the reflective-listening exercises below. You must therefore select particular exercises on which to focus, taking care to explain how components of reflective listening are required for and embedded in this sequence of skills.

The most basic level for training in reflective listening is nonverbal attending. This first exercise may or may not be essential, depending on the initial skill level of your trainees.

EXERCISE 1: NONVERBAL ATTENDING

Aim: To increase awareness and skillfulness in the use of nonverbal cues to communicate empathic listening.

Time: 10 minutes plus discussion.

Format: Have participants pair up. One partner serves initially as speaker and the other as listener. These roles are then reversed.

Trainee Preparation:

Discuss the importance of nonverbal cues in listening: "If you were to observe a good listener on videotape without sound, what would you see? What are the dos and don'ts of good nonverbal listening?" Points to cover (usually raised by the audience) are eye contact, facial expression, posture, and devoting full attention.

Commentary:

In addition to highlighting nonverbal listening skills, this exercise is also good in raising awareness of the many things the speaker *might* have said, had silence not been imposed. This aspect leads directly to Exercise 2.

Briefing:

Each participant should be prepared to talk for about 5 minutes on a specified topic. Choose and specify the topic, so that all speakers have the same set. Good choices are topics of personal history, which each person can describe in monologue for 5 minutes. Some possibilities are as follows:

- What it was like growing up in my home.
- What one of my parents (or someone else close to me) is like.
- How I came to be in my career/profession.

The speaker talks to the listening partner on this topic. The instructions to the partner are to listen carefully to what the speaker is saying, and to use *nonverbal* cues to communicate interest and attention. The listener may *not* speak or make any sound (e.g., "mm-hmm"). Tell participants to continue in role until you interrupt them and ask them to reverse roles after 5 minutes.

Debriefing:

In a large group, ask participants to comment on their experiences as speaker and listener. Speakers should discuss what listeners *did* that effectively communicated listening. Listeners should reflect on what they wanted to say during the silence, and relate it to the next exercise.

The next step is to teach what empathic listening is *not*. Discussion of Gordon's 12 "roadblocks" (Chapter 6) is an excellent vehicle for this purpose. A handout is helpful here.

A pretraining assessment can also be useful at this point. To do this, distribute a questionnaire before you begin to discuss reflective listening or roadblocks. The questionnaire contains 6–10 statements that might be made by a client or friend who is talking about personal material (for examples, see Miller, Hedrick, & Orlofsky, 1991, or Miller & Jackson, 1985). Trainees are asked to write *the next thing* they would say in response to these different statements, restricting themselves to one or two sentences. If this has been done earlier, trainees can examine their own questionnaires at this point to determine which of the roadblocks they are most likely to use.

The following exercise is a humorous way to teach the effects of roadblocking.

EXERCISE 2: ROADBLOCKS TO LISTENING

Aim: To raise counselors' awareness of common responses that are *not* reflective listening, and that block a speaker's free self-exploration.

Time: 15 minutes plus discussion.

Format: Trainees are arranged in pairs.

Trainee Preparation:
1. If time permits, it can be useful to conduct and discuss the pretraining assessment describe above, before the roadblocks are explained. Participants can then compare their own responses to the 12 roadblocks, to consider which they are most likely to be using at present.
2. Present Gordon's 12 roadblocks to reflective listening (see Chapter 6; see also Gordon, 1970; Miller & Jackson, 1985). Offer a sample communication—something that a client or friend might say to you—and have participants generate examples of each type of roadblock response. It is important to note that these 12 responses are not "wrong." Each has its place. The point is that these responses are different from and can obstruct reflective listening.
3. Have each participant be prepared to talk for 5–7 minutes on the topic "Something I feel two ways about." Ask speakers to choose a topic of some complexity, and in which they have some personal investment (e.g., not "I feel two ways about broccoli").

Commentary:
This is a light-hearted exercise that often generates quite a bit of laughter, but it is also very good in helping people become aware of ways in which they ordinarily obstruct the flow of communication.

Briefing:
1. Within each pair, one partner is designated to be the first speaker and the other the first listener.
2. The speaker's task is to talk on the assigned topic, "Something I feel two ways about," trying to explain this inner dilemma to the listener.
3. The listener's job is more challenging: In the course of a short span of time, he or she must fit in as many different roadblock responses as

possible. The listener can start with the ones he or she is "good" at, but should work for variety. It is helpful for participants to have a handout or visible listing of the roadblocks as an aid.

4. Tell the pairs to stay in role until you interrupt them (after 5–7 minutes), and then to switch roles. The former "listener" now becomes the speaker, and the former speaker offers roadblocks.

Debriefing:

In a large group, ask listeners to describe the experience of trying to communicate in the face of roadblocks. What happened? How did they respond? Discuss the feelings that are raised by roadblock responses, and the underlying messages that they communicate (e.g., "Listen to *me*; I know best").

At the end of this presentation and exercise, participants sometimes are wondering: "If none of those (which are most of what I do) are good listening, then what *can* I do?" This leads to the introduction of reflective listening and the next exercises.

EXERCISE 3: THINKING REFLECTIVELY

Aim: To raise counselors' awareness of the ongoing process of hypothesis generation and testing during reflective listening.

Time: 20 minutes plus discussion.

Format: Participants are arranged in groups of three.

Trainee Preparation:

1. Discuss the ways in which a person's meaning may be lost through the process of the speaker's *coding* meaning into words, the listener's *hearing* the actual words correctly, and the listener's *decoding* their meaning. A diagram and discussion of this process can be helpful (cf. Gordon, 1970; Miller & Jackson, 1985). The process of reflective listening is one that checks the listener's perceived meaning against the speaker's own meaning.

2. Have each participant be prepared to share at least three personal completions of the sentence "One thing that I like about myself is that I _____." These statements should emphasize relatively abstract personal characteristics (which lend themselves to greater ambiguity and discussion) rather than concrete attributes (e.g., "One thing that I like about myself is that I am tall").

Commentary:

This exercise teaches an approximation to reflective listening, and emphasizes how a listener can generate multiple hypotheses as to what a speaker may mean in any given statement.

Briefing:

1. Participants in each triad are to take turns, in rotation, saying one of their sentences to their two partners.

2. When a speaker has offered a sentence, the other two serve as listeners and respond by *asking questions* of this form: "Do you mean that you _____?"

3. The speaker responds to each such question *only* with "Yes" or "No." No additional elaboration is permitted.

4. Demonstrate this by offering a personal example to the audience, and having trainees ask you "Do you mean that you . . . ?" questions. Respond only with "Yes" or "No." Example:

YOU: One thing I like about myself is that I'm organized.

TRAINEE: Do you mean that you keep your desk tidy?

Y: No!

T: Do you mean that you manage your time well?

Y: Yes.

T: Do you mean that you always know where to find things?

Y: No.

T: Do you mean that you manage to get a lot done?

Y: Yes.

T: Do you mean that you are a good planner?

Y: Yes.

T: Do you mean that you're difficult to live with?

Y: . . . Yes.

5. Instruct the triads to begin this process, generating at least five different "Do you mean . . ." questions for each statement that is offered. When questioning for one statement seems to have reached an end, rotate on to the next person, who becomes the speaker while the other two generate questions. Ask groups to stay on task and not stop for discussion. Circulate among groups to reinforce, clarify, give examples, and make suggestions. Allow about 20 minutes for this exercise; adjust time as needed, depending on progress.

Debriefing:

In a large group, ask for comments on this experience. What did the participants learn? What surprises were there? What was it like to be the speaker? Usually there are comments here about the speaker's wanting strongly to elaborate and explain, which is a good illustration of how the reflective process—even at this simple level—pulls for more exploration. What problems were encountered? Highlight how many different meanings a seemingly simple statement can have (the number of different "Yes" answers), as well as the fact that many early guesses are wrong ("No" responses). Point out how each guess receives immediate feedback ("Yes" or "No") in this exercise, which also happens during good reflective listening.

With the background of how to *think* reflectively and generate alternative hypotheses about meaning, the next step is to teach trainees how to form good reflective-listening statements.

EXERCISE 4: FORMING REFLECTIONS

Aim: To help trainees learn how to form effective reflective-listening statements.

Time: 20 minutes plus discussion.

Format: Participants are arranged in groups of three.

Trainee Preparation:

1. Explain how good reflective-listening statements are very similar to, yet different from, the "Do you mean . . ." questions. They *do* offer a hypothesis about what the speaker means, but this is done in the form of a *statement* rather than a *question* (difference in inflection at the end of the sentence). Offer some sample sentence stems that can be used to start a reflection:

- It sounds like you . . .
- You're feeling . . .
- It seems to you that . . .
- So you . . .

The process, however, is the same as in Exercise 3: The listener makes a guess about the speaker's meaning and offers this to the speaker for response.

2. Have each participant be prepared to offer at least three different personal statements of the form "One thing about myself that I would like to change is. . . ." Again, avoid concrete attributes (e.g., ". . . my hair color").

Commentary:

It is a short step from the questions of Exercise 3 to reflection statements, but trainees often find this harder and need some coaching and encouragement. Circulate among groups, reinforce good reflection responses, make suggestions, and offer some reflections of your own if a group seems stuck. Attend to voice inflection at the end of reflection statements, and encourage a downturn in voice (statement) rather than upward inflection (question).

Briefing:

1. Participants in each triad are to take turns, in rotation, saying one of their sentences to their two partners.

2. When a speaker has offered a sentence, the other two serve as listeners and respond with reflective-listening statements.

3. The speaker responds to each statement with elaboration that probably includes but is not limited to "Yes" or "No." The next reflective-listening statement, then, takes this new information into account, adding a degree of complexity not present in Exercise 3.

4. Demonstrate this by having a trainee tell you one change statement. You respond only with reflective-listening statements, and continue this process several times. For example:

TRAINEE: One thing about myself that I would like to change is my moodiness.

YOU: You never know if you're going to be up or down.

T: No, it's not that. I can tell how I'm going to feel. It's just that I overreact to things.

Y: Even little things can upset you.

T: Sometimes, yes. Mainly I think I worry too much.

Y: You sit and fret about things too much.

T: Uh-huh. Often there's nothing I can do about it, but still I go over and over it in my mind.

Y: And that gets you moody.

T: Yes! I get myself all worked up, and I lose sleep.

Y: Even at night, you're worrying.

T: Yes. That's what I wish I could change.

5. Have the triads begin this process, designating one member as the first speaker. The two listeners offer *only* reflective-listening responses (no questions or other roadblocks), and the speaker elaborates. When a statement seems to have been understood, rotate on to the next person, who becomes the speaker while the other two respond with reflective listening. Ask groups to stay on task and not to stop for discussion. Circulate among groups to reinforce, clarify, and make suggestions. Allow about 20 minutes for this exercise; adjust time as needed, depending on progress.

Debriefing:

Discuss the exercise from the viewpoint of speakers and listeners. How did the speakers feel in this exercise, as compared to Exercise 3? How easy was it to generate reflective-listening responses? What difficulties were there?

Generating single reflective statements is easier than sustaining empathic listening in the context of conversation. The challenge here is the continual reflection of new meaning that is offered as a topic is explored. Because this is difficult, trainees will readily fall back on familiar alternatives to listening (e.g., asking questions). This exercise is designed to challenge trainees to rely more on empathic listening.

EXERCISE 5: SUSTAINED REFLECTIVE LISTENING

Aim: To give each trainee an opportunity to practice reflective listening as a dominant style in one-to-one conversation.

Time: 20 minutes plus discussion.

Format: Trainees are arranged in pairs.

Trainee Preparation:

Some of the finer points of reflection can be discussed in preparation for this exercise. The concept of *levels* of reflection may be helpful:

1. Repeating. The simplest reflection simply repeats an element of what the speaker has said.

2. Rephrasing. Here the listener stays close to what the speaker said, but substitutes synonyms or slightly rephrases what was offered.

3. Paraphrasing. This is a more major restatement, in which the listener infers the *meaning* in what was said and reflects this back in new words. This adds to and extends what was actually said.

4. Reflection of feeling. Often regarded as the deepest form of reflection, this is a paraphrase that emphasizes the emotional dimension through feeling statements, metaphor, etc.

In general, simpler (1 and 2) reflections are used at first, when meaning is less clear, and deeper reflections are ventured as understanding increases. Jumping too far beyond what was said, however, can turn into interpretation (a roadblock). You may also discuss here some of the variations (e.g., double-sided reflection) discussed in Chapter 8. Participants should be prepared, as in Exercise 2, to talk about "Something I feel two ways about." The same topic from Exercise 2 may be used.

Commentary:

Trainees who are relatively new to reflective listening find this exercise a difficult step and need encouragement. This is a place where individualized training is appropriate, if this is possible. Some trainees will do well at this stage and are ready to proceed onward; others will need additional practice and support. Ideally, trainees should become proficient in reflective listening before working on more complex applications. This is easier to accomplish in individual and small-group training than in larger workshops.

Briefing:

1. Participants in each pair decide who will be the first speaker. This person then talks to the listener about the chosen topic.

2. The listener's task is to respond *only* with reflective-listening statements. Although it would be natural to intermix reflection with other forms (e.g., questions), the listener is intentionally prohibited from using anything except reflection. This is done because without such prohibition, trainees tend to rely on old habits. The speaker responds to reflection by continuing to elaborate.

3. Ask trainees to stay in role, not discussing or breaking role until you interrupt them. After about 10 minutes, instruct the participants in each pair to switch roles.

4. Model this process. Have a trainee present an ambivalence topic to you, and show how to respond with 100% reflective listening. If appropriate, demonstrate a double-sided reflection.

Debriefing:

In a large group, ask participants to describe their experience as speakers and as listeners. How "natural" did it feel to the speakers and to the listeners? Compare the speakers' experience with that in Exercise 2, where the same task was used. How difficult a task was this for the listeners? When a listener voices difficulty with the task, ask his or her partner (speaker) about the experience. Often the speaking partner perceives the experience much more positively. Use the experiences of speakers to illustrate how clients respond to reflective listening.

Before making the transition back to motivational interviewing, you may find it useful to give trainees an opportunity for a more extensive practice with empathic listening, which intermixes reflections with other helpful responses. If training time is short, this exercise may be a lower priority.

EXERCISE 6: INTEGRATING REFLECTIVE LISTENING

Aim: To provide trainees practice at integrating reflective listening with other counseling skills.

Time: 30 minutes.

Format: Trainees are arranged in pairs.

Trainee Preparation:
Exercises 1–5. Each participant is asked to prepare to speak on a specified topic that can be explored for at least 15 minutes. An interesting example: "Describe an experience you have had that you believe would be quite difficult for another person to understand." The topic should be of sufficient complexity to allow 15 minutes of elaboration and exploration.

Commentary:
This is an additional practice that can be valuable in experiencing how the skill of reflective listening can be integrated with other counseling responses (questions, affirmations, etc.). A minimum of 15 minutes per speaker should be allowed, which with role switching requires at least 30 minutes. We recommend *not* circulating among pairs during this exercise, as it interrupts the flow of conversation.

Briefing:
1. Have each pair decide who will speak first.
2. The listener's task is (a) to use nonverbal and reflective-listening skills to attend to the speaker, and (b) to seek to *understand* the experience the speaker is describing. Other kinds of responses may be used by the listener as appropriate, but about 90% of responses should be reflective-listening statements.
3. Ask trainees not to break role or discuss the experience before you interrupt them. Allow at least 15 minutes before asking the partners to switch roles.

Debriefing:
Ask trainees to describe this experience. Ask for questions and reactions that have arisen through this exercise.

---

3. Affirm

The third of the five early strategies is affirming. Though easy to explain, it is too often neglected by counselors. Emphasize the importance of expressing genuine appreciation, understanding, support, and admiration for clients. Positive reinforcement is unlikely to be excessive.

4. Summarize

Explain how to use summary statements during and at the end of motivational counseling sessions. Emphasize (1) the drawing together of self-motivational statements (see Strategy 5); (2) capturing positive and negative aspects of ambivalence simultaneously, as in double-sided reflections; and (3) incorporating the information that is available (from assessment, other people, the courts, etc.). Summarizing is another opportunity for the trainees to hear what they have said and to put it all together. Show how summarizing is, in a way, an extended reflection of what has transpired thus far.

5. Elicit Self-Motivational Statements

In introducing the fifth strategy, explain the concept of "self-motivational statement" and give examples of the four types (Chapter 6). Emphasize that this is a central strategy in motivational interviewing, and that client self-motivational statements are one indication that the approach is being used properly. Provide examples of open-ended questions that can be used (Table 6.1), and review additional questioning strategies (e.g., elaboration, using extremes, asking for examples). Again, handouts can be helpful. This is also a useful place to discuss the concept of decisional balance (see Chapters 2, 4, and 7). Discuss how reflective listening and affirming can be used to reinforce self-motivational statements. Emphasize the importance of self-motivational statements in summarizing.

It is useful to tie together the five opening strategies at this point. One way to do this is by demonstration. You may role-play segments of an initial interview with a client, showing how the five early strategies can be interwoven. This opportunity can also be used for a brief demonstration of how *not* to do motivational interviewing (e.g., closed questions, confrontational argumentation, labeling, giving early advice, trying to teach and persuade). The "client" may be a volunteer from the audience or may be prearranged. It is wise to provide or negotiate a clear client scenario before beginning: for example, a client who (1) feels uncertain about whether he or she really has a problem, and (2) is unsure about whether counseling is a good idea in the first place. Provide additional input as to the kind of client, setting, and problem, according to the nature of your audience. An alternative is to use a demonstration videotape.

There are at least two ways to help trainees tie together the five early strategies through practice. One is to employ the "tag-team" and "fishbowl" training methods, described later in this chapter, in which a team of counselors works with a "client" under the trainer's direction. The other, illustrated in Exercise 7, is to divide trainees into small groups for an integrative role play.

EXERCISE 7: INTEGRATING FUNDAMENTAL SKILLS

Aim: To give trainees experience in intermixing the five early strategies of asking open-ended questions, eliciting self-motivating statements, listening reflectively, affirming, and summarizing.

Time: 15 minutes plus discussion.

Format: Trainees are placed in groups of three, with a "client," a "counselor," and an observer in each. If the number of trainees is not divisible by three, a fourth member can be added as an observer to one or two groups.

Trainee Preparation:

An introduction to the principles of motivational interviewing (Chapter 5; Exercises 1–6).

Commentary:

This exercise can be used to demonstrate and strengthen these five fundamental skills, which are used from the outset of motivational interviewing.

Briefing:

1. Have groups of three choose individual roles as "client," "counselor," and observer. Provide the "clients" with an outline of a role, which is not revealed to "counselors" and observers. Here is an example:

> Pat is a 29-year-old civil service clerk who has been married for 8 years and has one child, a 6-year-old daughter named Melissa. Pat was referred for evaluation when several marijuana cigarettes were discovered at work by a supervisor. In fact, Pat smokes marijuana only occasionally, but has been a heavy drinker for about 10 years. Starting with regular weekend intoxication at high school parties, Pat's drinking has gradually increased over the years, and now averages six beers a night (usually after work with friends), with more on weekends at home. Drinking has been a source of marital distress and arguments, and Pat has wondered sometimes whether this may be having a bad effect on Melissa. Nevertheless, Pat vigorously rejects any notion of being a "problem" drinker, let alone an "alcoholic": "I don't drink any more than my friends. Some of them drink a lot more than I do, and they're not alcoholics." Pat is angry and defensive about being forced to come for evaluation.

Pat's parents, both still alive, are nondrinkers by virtue of strong religious beliefs, which Pat rejects. An only brother, Michael (age 32), has had several drunk-driving arrests as well as one arrest for possession of marijuana. Michael's marriage ended in divorce, in part because of his drinking, and Pat admits that Michael "has a problem." The maternal grandfather died of liver disease before Pat was born.

Pat has privately wondered about drinking too much, and has had a few unsettling episodes of being unable to remember things that happened while drinking. Pat likes to drink before having sex, which has been another source of marital tension and arguments. Once Pat talked about drinking, half-jokingly, with a friend and drinking companion: "Maybe I overdo it sometimes. But I like how it feels, and when I'm in a bad mood I like to drink to mellow me out." The friend agreed that Pat's drinking is entirely normal, and that people are entitled to have a drink when they feel like it.

2. Provide the counselor with complementary instructions. Emphasize *open-ended* questions at the beginning of the session, eliciting self-motivational statements from the client, reflective listening, affirming, and summarizing. These instructions are not to be given to "clients" or observers. Here is an example of how "counselor" instructions could be given:

You are about to have a first session with Pat, a 29-year-old civil service clerk, who has been referred for evaluation after several marijuana cigarettes were discovered among Pat's materials at work. The supervisor who made the referral mentioned that Pat is known to stop regularly after work for beers with coworkers, and to "have quite a few." On the telephone, Pat was obviously angry about being forced to come to the clinic.

Use the basic opening strategies of motivational interviewing:

- Give a brief structuring statement as an opener.
- Start with open-ended questions.
- Elicit self-motivational statements.
- Respond with reflective listening.
- Affirm and support where possible.
- Summarize periodically.

Pursue the following as your goals:

1. To increase Pat's awareness of a problem and a need for change.
2. To prepare Pat to be open to assessment and feedback.

Observe Pat's responses to your various strategies. As a further learning experience, you may depart occasionally from the motivational interviewing strategies, and insert other strategies such as (but not necessarily limited to) these:

- Attempting to convince by argumentation.
- Suggesting that Pat has "a problem."
- Confronting denial or resistance head-on.
- Saying that Pat needs to make a change.

Notice how Pat responds to such tactics, and compare this with how Pat responds to motivational interviewing strategies. Be careful, however, to stay primarily with the basic motivational interviewing approach, and deviate only occasionally for purposes of observation. Conclude with a summary statement.

3. Ask the participants to continue their role play, without breaking role or discussing, until you interrupt them.

4. Allow 15 minutes for practice. Circulate among groups to observe, reinforce, and make suggestions.

5. When time is up and/or groups seem to be coming to a concluding point, interrupt the practice and reconvene as a whole group.

Debriefing:

In a large group, ask first for general comments from "clients," "counselors," and observers. How did the process go? What was it like from each perspective? Then ask for specific comments about each of the component skills practiced. How easy was it to do? How was it received? What problems were encountered? How did clients respond to various strategies? Comment positively on effective motivational interviewing that you observed. Express support for statements that reflect the difficulty of learning this approach or breaking old habits.

Middle-Game Exercises

As in the game of chess, the middle game offers the most complexity, and is most difficult to teach. The training technique of breaking into small groups can serve well in teaching opening strategies, but it breaks down as scenarios become more complicated. This is because trainer input is needed more directly and regularly as clinical complexity increases. Our experience is that if middle-game challenges are given to be role-played in dyads or triads, practice quickly becomes bogged down, and the groups revert to discussing difficulties or completely abandon the assigned task.

This has led us to employ a different approach in teaching strategies for handling resistance and managing the later part of Phase I. We use three component training techniques here:

1. Problem-solving discussion
2. Demonstration
3. The "fishbowl" technique

The intermixing of these strategies will depend in part on the size of the group being trained, and in part on the responsiveness of the group to each approach.

Problem-Solving Discussion

In the first approach, a group (which can be a small group or the entire group) is posed with a specific problem situation, and is asked to brainstorm possible responses. This works quite well in teaching alternative strategies for handling resistance. Our preferred approach is to present a triggering script (e.g., portraying a particular kind of resistance) and to ask group members to generate alternative responses. The group can then discuss what the likely outcome would be if each of the alternatives were to be pursued. Here is an example.

EXERCISE 8: RESPONDING TO RESISTANCE
Aim: To help trainees explore alternative responses to client resistance.

Time: 5 minutes per scenario, plus discussion.

Format: Trainees may be divided into small groups of three to five members.

Trainee Preparation:
    Exercises 1–7. Present an interpersonal model of resistance (Chapter 8). Describe four general categories of client resistance behaviors (Table 8.1), and describe alternative strategies for handling resistance: simple reflection, amplified reflection, double-sided reflection, shifting focus, agreement with a twist, emphasizing personal choice and control, reframing, and therapeutic paradox. Provide a listing of these strategies on a handout or visual display.

Commentary:
    We find that it does not work well to ask trainees to generate particular kinds of responses (e.g., "Give a double-sided reflection"). Rather, we present a client statement and ask for alternative ways of handling it. These can

then be compared with the list of alternative strategies, to determine where (and whether) they fit.

Briefing:

1. Provide triggering case scenarios, consisting of brief segments of clinical dialogue in which a client poses a certain form of resistance. These can be presented verbally or visually one at a time, or several can be included on a handout. Here are a few examples:

THERAPIST: It sounds like you have a number of concerns, then, about your drinking. What do you think is the next step?

CLIENT: Well, I don't think I need to quit drinking. I'm not an alcoholic, after all. (*minimizing*)

T: So you've been thinking a lot about your marriage, and you can see that something needs to be done.

C: I just don't think anything will help. I think it's probably too late. (*pessimism*)

T: What concerns do you have about your use of drugs?

C: I'm not concerned, really. Some people get hooked, but I'm not like that. They don't affect me that much. I just enjoy how I feel. (*claiming impunity*)

T: I can see this must be difficult for you.

C: How could you know? You've never been through what I'm going through. What do you know? (*discounting*)

Other examples can be crafted to suit the needs of a particular audience. It is important, however, to provide a range of different kinds of resistance, and to see that not all examples fall within the usual work experience of your audience. If problem-solving discussion is being done in a number of small subgroups, it is useful for one member of each group to have written scenarios from which to work. In this case, you should pace the progress of discussions from one scenario to the next, either by distributing scenarios one at a time or by announcing when discussion should advance to the next case.

2. Ask members of the group to generate alternative ways in which the therapist might respond to this example of resistance. If this is being done in small subgroups, have someone record the alternatives that are generated. Consider whether the suggestion fits into one of the discussed categories of strategies for handling resistance.

3. Discuss the likely result of each alternative that has been generated. What would the client be likely to say next? Which options seem most effective in minimizing resistance? Why?

Debriefing:

If this is done in subgroups, reconvene as a large group and have reporters from each group present options that were generated, until all unique options have been given. Repeat discussion (point 3 above) in the larger group.

The essential purposes of the problem-solving discussion are to engage trainees in the process of generating alternative strategies, and to help them see how these fit into the larger context of motivational interviewing. One reason to break into smaller groups for this process is the greater personal involvement it requires of each trainee. Large-group discussions of this kind can leave many people in a passive role, particularly if the group is larger than 10–15.

Demonstration

A second good training option is a demonstration of the approach to be learned. The simplest way to do this is for you to demonstrate therapeutic strategies, interacting with a volunteer from the audience who role-plays a client. This usually works well, but can also be a disaster, depending upon the "client." On occasion, a trainee will volunteer with an apparent agenda of showing that nothing you do will work. The audience then sees an unsatisfying drama rather than a demonstration of how clinical strategies are typically employed.

There are at least three alternatives. One is to have a member of the audience discuss a *real* personal situation, rather than role-playing a client. A trainee in one of our workshops, for example, volunteered to discuss his smoking as part of a demonstration of Phase I strategies. Not only did the demonstration work well, but the trainee quit smoking immediately after the workshop! If a member of the audience is willing to engage in such a personal discussion, it lends a "real-life" integrity that may be lacking in a role play. A second option is to select an assistant to help in the role play, and review the role in advance. In this way you can design specific aspects of the role, including the severity of the problem and the kinds of resistance to be offered. The third and most dependable possibility is to show a demonstration videotape, which highlights the specific problems and strategies you wish to illustrate.

Any of these three types of demonstrations can lead to group discussion about how the case was handled, what mistakes were made, what other approaches might have been taken, and so on. Trainees often find it quite helpful to observe an example of how to apply the strategies they are learning.

The "Fishbowl" Technique

A third and very interesting option for demonstrating complex clinical processes is the "fishbowl" technique, which combines elements of problem-solving discussion and demonstration. This option has the advantages of a live demonstration, while affording you much more control over its course.

In essence, a triggering script is used to begin a role-play dialogue between a client and a counselor, *both* of whom are trainees. You serve as a coach and director for this interaction, stopping the action, asking for discussion or suggestions, going back for "retakes" to try a new approach, and so forth. The rest of the participants gather around the demonstration (hence the name "fishbowl"), but also have active involvement in the process. A good introduction of this approach is as follows: "We're going to create a demonstration together. We'll try out some of the strategies, make mistakes, go back and try alternatives. The purpose is not to have a perfect demonstration, but rather to wrestle with the complexities of using these strategies."

Trainees typically volunteer to play the client role more readily than they do the therapist role. An emphasis that "We *want* you to make mistakes" can help. It is also useful to change therapists once or more during such a demonstration, and to indicate that this will be done. An effective way to accomplish this is a "tag-team" approach, in which three counselors are seated opposite a client. One counselor begins, proceeding until he or she feels stuck, at which point he or she tags the next counselor, who takes over. This adds an element of fun, takes each counselor off the hook, and keeps all three quite alert. Most importantly, however, you must guard against criticism of a role-playing counselor, who is in a rather vulnerable position. Positive reinforcement is in order. You should point out effective aspects of the counselor's approximations, and the "client" and audience can be asked to do the same.

If you prepare a set of cue cards naming various strategies for dealing with resistance (e.g., "double-sided reflection"), you can "send in a play" by holding up a card for the counselor to see. Realize, however, that it is often difficult for a trainee to formulate a specific strategy that you prescribe. An alternative is to stop the action, discuss the strategy you have in mind, and then resume.

Don't allow fishbowl sessions to go on for long segments without interruption and discussion. The usefulness of this approach is not in watching a full-length demonstration, but in being able to stop the action, back up, and try something different. If he or she is willing, the same counselor can try a different approach that has been suggested, or a new counselor can take over at your discretion. You can step into the counselor role yourself as necessary, but your most valuable role is as director, maintaining close control. Acknowledge the difficulty of being in the counselor's seat, and note how much easier it is (in truth!) to see alternatives when one is outside the fishbowl. When a problem or trap is encountered, it is possible to stop the action and ask observers to suggest alternative ways in which to proceed.

This technique is difficult to do without a strong director. If you have a number of potential facilitators in a larger group, you may be able to break into groups of 10–15 for simultaneous fishbowls, all of which work from the same case scenario. The large group can then reconvene to discuss what happened with the same case in each group.

Endgame Exercises

Phase II of motivational interviewing (see Chapter 9) focuses upon the process of moving toward decision making. This phase requires the use of additional strategies for strengthening commitment. These strategies are usually much easier than those needed in the middle-game period (the later portion of Phase I). For this reason, we find that practice in small groups is again feasible at this point.

EXERCISE 9: STRENGTHENING COMMITMENT

Aim: To give trainees the opportunity to practice Phase II strategies—to use a closing summary with key questions that open up the issues of change, and to negotiate a plan in which realistic goals are set for review at a later stage.

Time: 20 minutes plus discussion.

Format: Participants are arranged in groups of three.

Trainee Preparation:
    Knowledge of the earlier phases of motivational interviewing (Chapters 5–8), and introduction to the strategies for strengthening commitment (Chapter 9).

Commentary:
    In the language of chess, this is an "endgame" exercise, in which matters are coming to a head and activity is focused on a narrower set of

permutations. While groups are practicing, circulate among the triads with encouragement, suggestions, and problem solving. If there is time, this exercise can be repeated three times, so that all members of each triad have the opportunity to practice in the counselor role.

Briefing:

1. Provide trainees with an *overview* of the process of strengthening commitment. This may include a handout describing the various stages of negotiation outlined in Chapter 9. Trainees should also be reminded:

- The other strategies of motivational interviewing are not abandoned in this phase, but are used throughout, particularly to re-examine ambivalence whenever this becomes apparent.
- The process of negotiating a plan does not take place at any particular point (e.g., at the end of the first session); it may take a number of sessions.

2. Provide each participant with a written case study appropriate to the audience, which includes some basic information about the background of the client and his or her progress in counseling. This description should end at the point where the counselor and client are ready to raise the question "What next?" Here is an example:

> Mrs. Evans, a 60-year-old widow, fell off a ladder at home and was admitted to a hospital, where she first made contact with an alcohol counselor. After being discharged, she has returned for a number of further sessions. Initially fearful about being told to stop drinking completely, she has responded well to questions about how *she* views her situation. It emerged that she is worried about her drinking sometimes. However, with her children living away from home, she feels most reluctant to abandon her regular social activity at the club, where most of her drinking is done. She has an occasional memory blackout, but has a rule not to drink before 3:00 in the afternoon. Her average daily intake is about six glasses of wine. The counselor asks her whether there is anything else to discuss, and she shakes her head; she is noticeably quieter than usual. She seems ready to make a decision, but also feels somewhat confused about what to do.

3. Ask participants to read the case description you provide, and then present them with guidelines for the role play:

- Establish roles for counselor, client, and observer.
- Begin with the counselor's closing summary, and follow up with the use of one or more key questions.

- Proceed onward, as possible, toward negotiation of a plan for change.
- The counselor should be careful not to go too fast; remember also that the client should be the one to articulate what the next step should be.
- The client should react spontaneously; it should be borne in mind that the client still feels confused about what to do.
- The observer should pay careful attention to the pace of the interview, and should also write down any useful key questions or other strategies.

4. Ask the trainee to stay in role until you interrupt them (after 20 minutes), or until they have reached a point of natural completion of Phase II. In the latter case, they may proceed to discuss what occurred, and, if they wish, may try a different (e.g., more prescriptive or confrontational) approach.

Debriefing:

Review progress in a large group, moving from one small group to the next, asking for observer reports and impressions from counselors and clients. Indicate that not every role play should necessarily have reached the point of resolution. Note useful key questions that were used, perhaps recording them on a display board. Highlight good examples in which counselors were able to successfully negotiate a decision with the client.

There are many other possible approaches in teaching motivational interviewing. Some we have tried, and still others that have never occurred to us may be obvious to you. What we have presented here are exercises that we have found to be quite reliably effective, and that work together well in sequence. We wish you success, creativity, and fun as you develop your own training approaches.

PART THREE

CLINICAL APPLICATIONS OF MOTIVATIONAL INTERVIEWING

Introduction

Since 1983, the concept of motivational interviewing has been applied in many creative ways and in a wide range of national, cultural, and clinical settings. For this final section, we have invited a number of colleagues who have been innovators in this field to describe ways in which they have adopted and adapted motivational interviewing in their clinical work. Their contributions, based on work in five different nations, span theory, research, and practice. These chapters are intentionally brief—"snapshots" of ways in which motivational interviewing can be adapted and applied, written with the practitioner in mind. Consistent with our usual approach, we suggest that you view this section as a menu, choosing from it the selections that interest you most. The following brief descriptions are meant to help you in this selection process.

Chapter 13 is written by Carlo DiClemente, whose work with James Prochaska has yielded the influential "transtheoretical" model of stages of change that is used throughout this book. He elaborates on the uses of motivational interviewing strategies at each stage of change, and provides helpful conceptual distinctions (e.g., "contemplation is not commitment"). He describes four different reasons why a client may be in precontemplation, and offers useful caveats for clinicians (e.g., "Being adamant about a change can be a sign of weak rather than strong determination to change"). Examples are drawn from DiClemente's clinical work in smoking cessation and employee assistance programs. A key point is that motivational interviewing strategies can be used at *all* stages of change.

In Chapter 14, Stephen Rollnick and Alison Bell describe how motivational interviewing can be applied in general medical settings by professionals who are not specialists in treating addictive behaviors. Primary health care workers have perhaps the greatest, earliest, and sometimes only access to individuals suffering from substance abuse, many of whom may never seek formal treatment. What can be done within the relatively brief contact of routine medical care? They address practical considerations of how to establish rapport, broach the subject, and negotiate change, drawing on their experience in counseling people in general practice and general hospital settings.

Can motivational interviewing be used in working with a really *tough* clinical population? "Yes," says Henck van Bilsen, on the basis of his work with heroin addicts in The Netherlands. Using verbatim case examples, he illustrates in Chapter 15 some of his own innovations, including the "Columbo" approach, for dealing with resistant court-referred addicts; he also describes a "motivational milieu therapy" currently being used in The Netherlands and the United Kingdom.

What about involving a client's spouse? Does this help or hinder the process of motivational interviewing? A seasoned marital and family therapist, Allen Zweben describes problems that can arise in working with couples, but argues persuasively that involving the spouse can greatly strengthen client motivation. Again, the focus of Chapter 16 is practical: how to engage and incorporate the spouse in motivational interviewing; how to handle an uncooperative or hostile spouse; how to evaluate the spouse support system and decide which of two ways to proceed. He offers more detailed commentary on how to deal in conjoint sessions with resistance encountered from the client, the spouse, or both.

When Steve Allsop and Bill Saunders began to apply "relapse prevention" strategies in Scotland, they found that the causes of relapse were often as much motivational as skill deficits. They developed, and now describe in Chapter 17, a set of "resolution enhancement" exercises useful in counseling severely dependent drinkers. Through case dialogue, they explain their client-centered strategies for dealing with resistant clients, and explain an interesting approach for counseling two clients together in a "buddy" system. Their approach also shows how motivational and skill-training strategies can be integrated.

Gillian Tober provides a case dialogue transcript in Chapter 18 to show how motivational interviewing can be applied with teenagers. She points out that some of the strategies that work well with adults (such as the assessment feedback described in Chapter 7) may be quite ineffective with young people; self-esteem may also be a special concern. Another complexity is that for teenagers, other people (e.g., parents, juvenile probation officers) have legal control over and responsibility for their actions, and these other parties must be considered in any plan for change. Nevertheless, the same basic principles can be adapted to precipitate change in young people.

In Chapter 19, W. Miles Cox, Eric Klinger, and Joseph P. Blount make the important point that drug use is only one behavior within the larger network of a client's life goals and motivations. Their "systematic motivational counseling" approach seeks to clarify how the problem behavior (in this case, drinking) fits into the client's bigger motivational picture. Where does drinking fit in the person's overall goal hierarchy? How does it serve or detract from other goals? The structured goal attainment counseling procedures described here nicely complement our more problem-focused discussion of motivational interviewing.

Precontemplators pose special challenges. In treatment settings, it is less common to encounter people who are genuine precontemplators; however, the more one reaches out into the community in a preventive manner, the more one finds at-risk drinkers who have not even considered changing. In fact, precontemplators probably constitute a *majority* of alcohol-impaired people in the community. In Chapter 20, Tim Stockwell describes the British system of "community alcohol teams," and provides two case examples from his work. He also shows how it is possible to work through a person's general practitioner, without ever engaging in formal specialist treatment.

It happens that, starting from the same idea, programs can evolve separately and rather differently. So it is that Bill Saunders and his colleagues, first in Scotland and then in Australia, started from the original paper on motivational interviewing (Miller, 1983) and developed their own clinical approach. In Chapter 21, they describe their approach to motivational intervention and its application to a population of Australian heroin addicts on methadone maintenance. Whereas we have described motivational interviewing as a *style* of counseling, the Saunders team has conceptualized it as a set of *techniques* that can be added to other approaches. There is truth in both views. This chapter, again rich in clinical dialogue, describes a seven-step approach to motivational intervention that the authors have found (in separately published outcome research) to be effective with heroin users being treated for the first time. They also rightly point out that different emphases are needed in different cultures. Our emphasis on a client-centered style has been strong, in part, because of the dominant American belief that aggressive confrontation is optimal in treating alcohol and other drug problems. Another factor to consider in this regard is the group being trained. Rollnick and Bell (Chapter 14) have found that in supervising primary care workers, it is easier to focus on a menu of concrete strategies than on improving the more subtle aspects of counseling style.

Chapters 22 and 23 explore novel applications of motivational interviewing. Amanda Baker and Julie Dixon have taken the logical step of moving from a focus on drug use itself to concern for the risk of being exposed to human immunodeficiency virus (HIV) and developing acquired immune deficiency syndrome (AIDS). Given the life-threatening nature of HIV exposure, motivating and retaining clients become crucial issues. It is simply not sufficient to turn away clients because they are "unmotivated." The prevention of AIDS involves altering behaviors that are highly reinforcing and notoriously resistant to change: intravenous drug use and unprotected sex. Baker and Dixon discuss in Chapter 22 how principles of motivational interviewing can be applied in this important task, and describe an illustrative case example.

Sex offenders have long been regarded as unmotivated and difficult to treat. Although effective treatment strategies are available, it has often been difficult to motivate and retain offenders in therapy, and motivation for change has been described as the single most important factor in outcome. Randall Garland and Michael Dougher, with long experience in treating sex offenders, began applying principles of motivational interviewing before and during treatment. In Chapter 23 they discuss motivational obstacles with this special population, and clinical strategies for overcoming them.

Finally, in Chapter 24, Rosemary Kent considers the importance of motivational interviewing even during the later phases of change—in what Prochaska and DiClemente have termed the "maintenance" stage. Although the primary focus of our work has been on preparing people for change (from precontemplation to determination and action), motivation remains a crucial issue during the challenging process of maintaining change. Self-motivational processes can be as important in avoiding relapse as in initiating change. Her chapter reminds us, then, that the wheel of change has a wholeness to it. Common factors affect each stage of change, and to some extent the boundaries we draw between the stages are arbitrary impositions on a continuous process. The skills of motivational interviewing can be useful throughout the course of counseling.

What is striking to us, from all of these descriptions, is the *similarity* of these clinicians' experiences across cultures, problem areas, and treatment settings. Their programs have ranged from specialized inpatient units to outpatient, aftercare, and general medical services, as well as community-based prevention. Their clients have included heroin addicts, teenagers, convicted sex offenders, at-risk or early problem drinkers, smokers, well-functioning employees, severely dependent "alcoholics," and intravenous drug users at risk for HIV exposure. Their clinical tasks have ranged from awareness raising with precontemplators to relapse prevention with revolving-door inpatients. Across this vast array of clinical experiences, motivational interviewing principles have been found to be useful, and clients have responded in rather similar ways. It persuades us of the obvious: that people are people. Although the addictive behaviors represent a wonderful medium for understanding and addressing ambivalence, the change processes involved here extend well beyond substance abuse. There is in each client a cotherapist to be engaged. Treatment strategies that place the client in a passive mode, making him or her a receptacle for dispensed wisdom and advice from an expert, fail to take advantage of these inner resources. Change is best accomplished, we believe, when the client's own motivations and decisional powers are awakened, and his or her own resources are tapped. Through the collective efforts of people like those who have contributed these clinical chapters, we are just beginning to understand how to do that.

13

Motivational Interviewing and the Stages of Change

CARLO C. DiCLEMENTE

A therapist can be understood as a midwife to the process of change, which has its own unique course in each case. The role for the therapist is to assist the individual, couple, or family in negotiating this process as efficiently and effectively as possible. In fact, the therapist can be a help or a hindrance to the process, as numerous previous examples in this book demonstrate. Skillful therapists will best facilitate change if they understand the process of change and learn how to activate or instigate the unfolding of that process. This is the task of motivational interviewing as it relates to the stages of change. The purpose of this chapter is to help counselors integrate more fully motivational interviewing with the stages-of-change model.

Chapter 2 gives a rather complete discussion of the stages of change. This model emerged while my colleagues and I were observing how individuals went about modifying problem behaviors. Thus, whether we are talking about changing drinking, eating, or smoking behaviors; poor marital communications and parenting; or problems with self-esteem, the structure of change appears to be the same. Individuals move from being unaware or unwilling to do anything about the problem to considering the possibility of change, then to becoming determined and prepared to make the change, and finally to taking action and sustaining or maintaining that change over time. Individuals come to counselors and therapists to seek help in negotiating one or more of these stages of change. Clients can come in at any point in this cycle, so the challenge to the therapist is first to understand where they are in the cycle and then to assist them. The stages of change have become a compelling concept for clinicians, researchers, and clients because the stages reflect this process of change.

Motivation for me involves both "motives" and "movement." These two notions are often confused. For many therapists the objective of motivation is action or specific behavioral change. Although the end point of motivational strategies is often behavioral change, it is important to remember that motives and motivation are needed in order to shift from one stage to the next for all stages, not simply for movement to the action stage. Thus, motivational considerations need to be stage-specific. Resistance, ambivalence, and commitment are most clearly understood in the context of the stages.

As I discuss some specific considerations concerning movement from one stage to the next, I use examples from my work with smokers and as an evaluator for an employee assistance program (EAP). Over the past 10 years my colleague Jim Prochaska, from the University of Rhode Island, and I have been examining how smokers go through the process of change and how to facilitate that change. Cigarette smoking is an interesting problem behavior because it is quite difficult to change and is a specific, nicely measurable behavior. My work with employees is quite different. Their problems or complaints are very diverse and diffuse. My involvement is limited to one to three evaluation sessions and referral to someone else if additional treatment is needed. What these two types of work have in common is that the motivational interviewing strategies described in the earlier chapters are very helpful in working with both groups of clients as they move through the stages of change.

Precontemplation: Resistance and "the Four R's"

Individuals in precontemplation about a problem behavior such as smoking are not even thinking about changing that behavior. In fact, they may not see the behavior as a problem, or at least they do not believe it is as problematic as external observers see it. With addictive behaviors, this group has often been labeled "resistant" or "in denial." However, it is clear that there are many reasons to be in precontemplation. These can best be summarized as the "four R's": reluctance, rebellion, resignation, and rationalization.

Reluctant precontemplators are those who through lack of knowledge or inertia do not want to consider change. For these people, the information or the impact of the problem has not become fully conscious. They are not as much resistant as they are reluctant to change; the technique of providing feedback in a sensitive empathic manner can be most helpful for them. Sometimes it also takes time, as it did with Helena.

Helena was a very successful businesswoman who had been promoted to senior vice president from a direct sales position. However, she found that managing others was much more difficult than doing the job herself, because of her problems in being direct with others. During the evaluation visits, we discussed many issues related to the job, the politics of the company, and her personal limitations. She was surprised to learn that she had difficulty being direct when it involved criticism of another, since she saw herself as an open, no-nonsense person. However, she chose to resign her management position rather than work on changing her interpersonal style. One year later, however, she returned asking for a referral to work on interpersonal issues. It seemed that the job change had relieved the immediate stress, but she had recently entered a romantic relationship where the problems we had discussed became quite apparent. She returned stating, "You know those problems we discussed last year? I am ready to tackle them now."

Rebellious precontemplators have a heavy investment in the problem behavior and in making their own decisions. They are resistant to being told what to do. The rebellion may be a residue of prolonged adolescence or the result of insecurity and fears. No matter what the source, the rebellious precontemplator will appear hostile and resistant to change. When we recruit precontemplators to participate in our smoking studies, it is easy to spot the rebels. They argue with the questions and make it very clear on the phone that they will participate only if we are not going to try to change them. Providing choices seems to be the best strategy for working with this type of person. Some paradoxical strategies and other techniques can also be used, as described in Chapter 8. However, I agree that these need to be used carefully and with rationales that make sense to the client. Although there is great resistance to change, this type of client does have a lot of energy invested in the problem behavior. The real task is trying to shift some of that energy into contemplating change rather than resistance or rebellion.

Lack of energy and investment, on the other hand, is the hallmark of the resigned precontemplators. These clients have given up on the possibility of change and seem overwhelmed by the problem. Many smoking clients begin by saying how many other attempts they have made to quit. They feel hopelessly addicted to cigarettes and out of control. The habit is in control, not the clients. Often these individuals will tell me that stopping young people from starting to smoke is the only way to deal with the problem. The clear message is that it is too late for them. Instilling hope and exploring barriers to change are the most productive strategies for this group. Without some hope of the possibility for change, the resigned precontemplator can never be motivated to contemplate change.

The rationalizing precontemplator has all the answers where the resigned precontemplator has none. These clients are not considering change because they have figured out the odds of personal risk, or they have plenty of reasons why the problem is not a problem or is a problem for others but not for them. For me, the key to identifying this type of client occurs when the interview begins to feel like a debate or a session of point–counterpoint. Although it may feel like rebellion, the resistance of the rationalizer lies much more in the thinking than in the emotions. Smokers who are convinced that they are really not at much risk because they started smoking after 21 years of age, are only smoking 15 cigarettes a day, have only smoked for 10 years, or have a 90-year-old grandfather who smokes are prime examples. Sometimes they want to discuss these issues, but discussion only serves to strengthen their side of the argument. Empathy and reflective listening seem to work best with this type of client. It seems to me that double-sided reflection would be particularly helpful here.

Before leaving the land of the precontemplator, I should mention several important additional considerations. First, the distinction between a reason and a rationalization can sometimes be quite unclear. A person who says, "I am well aware of the risks and problems associated with smoking and I choose to continue," may be a risk taker or an unreasonable individual, but has the freedom to choose this behavior. We must acknowledge the limits of any of our motivational strategies in the face of the client's informed choice to continue at least for the present what we consider a problematic behavior. However, the phrase "for the present" can give us hope of assisting a client to change in the future. Our work may have an impact some time later.

Another pitfall in dealing with precontemplators is to assume that "the problem" means the same thing to clients as it does to us. Often employees come to an evaluation session to discuss what the boss thinks is their problem rather than what they consider their problem. A classic example is that of the basketball player who had recently returned from a 4-week hospitalization at a drug treatment program. When asked in a TV interview about his drug problem, he responded that he had a "drug-testing" problem, not a drug problem. Clearly, his testing positive for cocaine, rather than its use, was the current focus even after weeks of treatment.

Finally, there is a myth among interviewers that in dealing with serious health-related addictive, or other problems, more is always better. More education, more intense treatment, more confrontation will necessarily produce more change. Nowhere is this less true than with the precontemplators. More intensity will often produce fewer results with this group. So it is particularly important to use careful motivational strategies, rather than to mount high-intensity programs or efforts that will be ignored by those uninterested in changing the particular problem behavior. It is just as false, however, to believe that precontemplators don't ever change and there is nothing we can do. We cannot make precontemplators change, but we can help motivate them to move to contemplation.

Contemplation: A Risk–Reward Analysis

Contemplation is often a very paradoxical stage of change. The fact that the client is willing to consider the problem and the possibility of change offers hope for change. However, the fact that ambivalence can make contemplation a chronic condition can be extremely frustrating. Contemplation is the stage when clients are quite open to information and decisional balance considerations. Yet it is also the stage where many clients are waiting for the one final piece of information that will compel them to change. The hope is that the information will make the decision for them. However, as we all know, individuals and not information make decisions, so the contemplator can be in for a very long, unproductive wait.

Motivational interviewing strategies are particularly important during the contemplation stage to assist in movement to decision making. It is important to realize that contemplation is not commitment. Clinicians and interviewers are often fooled by this distinction. A good example of this confusion is the workplace smoking cessation program. When surveys are taken in the workplace, large numbers of smokers (up to 70–80%) express interest in quitting. So programs are developed and offered. Typically, these programs are very poorly attended and are lucky to attract 3–5% of the smokers. Clearly, interest is not commitment. Most smokers wish to change or wish that they could stop smoking. Many are considering change in the near future. When confronted by a choice to sign up for a specific cessation program on a specific date, however, they can find many reasons why right now is not the right time. What are missing in most of these worksite programs are adequate motivational strategies to assist individuals in moving from contemplation to determination and being ready to take action.

Information and incentives to change are important elements for assisting contemplators. Although one piece of information will not make the decision for the individual, personally relevant information or feedback can have a real impact. When I talk with groups of smokers as part of their American Cancer Society quitting program, I try to give accurate information about the facts of smoking (e.g., there are over 1,000 different gases in cigarette smoke; smoking contributes not only to lung cancer, but also to heart disease and chronic obstructive lung disease; tar coats the cilia of the lungs, making them very inefficient in transferring oxygen). However, I also make this information personally relevant by asking about their smoker's cough, telling them to breathe out the smoke through a white handkerchief in order to see the residue, or discussing the number of colds or respiratory problems they are having. This information, which is visible and personally relevant, is more powerful in shifting the decisional balance toward action than all the scare tactics, general lectures, and nagging in the world.

"Accentuate the positive" takes a different twist when working with contemplators. Often individuals considering changing a problem behavior will concentrate on all the negative aspects of the behavior. "I know how bad my smoking or drinking is for me," they say. In fact, they can often produce a litany of reasons why what they are doing is bad for them. Clinician and client are often baffled by the fact that even with all these negatives, change does not occur. Part of the problem seems to be an underestimation of the pros or positive aspects of the problem behavior. As one employee put it, "I know I should be more assertive with my fellow workers and my wife, but I just can't seem to do it." Helping him to see how beneficial his passive, nonconfrontational way of dealing with work and spouse had been for him assisted in creating a more balanced perspective on the difficulties and losses he would face as he tried to become more assertive.

Decisional balance considerations should not be limited to the pros and cons of the problem behavior. There are pros and cons of the *change* that are often not fully considered by the contemplator. Clarification of the goals and removing barriers can best be done in this context. What will it mean for the individual to change the behavior? I have had smokers tell me that the reason they went back to smoking after quitting was that they were unable to work or were so angry and irritable that they viewed the cost of not smoking as worse than the risks of smoking. Sometimes this can only be realized in retrospect after making a change attempt. However, most people who come to a counselor for assistance have made one or more previous attempts to change. Exploring the problems with these previous attempts can offer valuable information about goals and barriers that can be used in motivational interviewing.

Information about past change attempts can also be very helpful for increasing self-efficacy. "Some success" rather than "a failure" can be a positive reframe of a change attempt, which can foster future action. One of the most helpful perspectives of the stages-of-change model is that of the cycle of change. Individuals who come to counselors are usually not naive novices with respect to changing this problem behavior. In fact, I like to see people who come to therapy as unsuccessful self-changers who need some assistance in negotiating the cycle of change in order to make a better and (everyone hopes) longer-lasting change. This perspective fits quite comfortably with the philosophy and perspective of motivational interviewing as proposed in this book.

Contemplators can be helped using all of the effective motivational strategies outlined in Chapters 2 and 6. These strategies seem most appropriate to assist the contemplator to move from a thorough consideration of change to a commitment to take action. Ambivalence is the archenemy of commitment and a prime reason for chronic contemplation. Helping the client to work through the ambivalence, to anticipate the barriers, to decrease desirability of the problem behavior, and to gain some increased sense of self-efficacy to cope with this specific problem are all stage-appropriate, effective strategies.

Determination: Commitment to Action

Deciding to take appropriate steps to stop a problem behavior or to initiate a positive behavior is the hallmark of the determination stage. Most individuals in this stage will make a serious attempt at change in the near future, and many have made an attempt to modify their behavior in the recent past. They appear to be ready for and committed to action. As such, this stage represents preparation as much as determination. The tasks for the counselor or therapist with clients in this stage of change are quite different but no less challenging.

It would seem to be a simple task to assist the client committed to action. In fact, motivational strategies may seem superfluous. However, commitment to change does not necessarily mean that change is automatic, that change methods used will be efficient, or that the attempt will be successful in the long term. Being determined or prepared for action does not mean that all ambivalence is resolved. The decision-making process continues throughout the determination stage.

The first task for the counselor is to assess the strength and levels of commitment. The techniques described in Chapter 9 seem best suited to this stage. The task is often one of increasing commitment to a particular plan of action. Strength of commitment is often difficult to assess simply from verbal self-report. Being adamant about a change can be a sign of weak rather than strong determination to change. Often smokers who insistently claim that they are committed to quitting are trying to convince themselves as much as me of their determination. A solid realistic assessment of the level of difficulty, and a calm dedication to making this change a top priority in the current life plan, are good indicators of commitment to change. This is not to say that those with insistent or lackadaisical approaches will never be successful. However, changing problem behaviors requires sustained action over time, which seems best accomplished with a solid, realistic commitment to change.

Barriers to successful action also play an important role during both the determination stage and the action stage. Anticipation of problems and pitfalls appears to be a solid problem-solving skill. Subjects who are ready for action would do well to examine these barriers. Often with these clients, I go over what the first week will be like once they have quit smoking. With employees who need to be more assertive in problem situations at work, I discuss various settings where they are likely to be challenged, who will be around, what office they will be in, and so forth. As they describe the specifics, the clients are able to generate their own options and solutions. This has the twofold benefit of making commitment more firm and solving the problems that may act as barriers to change.

Strong commitment alone does not guarantee change. Unfortunately, enthusiasm does not make up for ineptness. I often use stories of my attempts to be a handyman to illustrate the point. Plumbing is a particular area of ineptitude. The wrong size wrench will make a hexagonal nut smooth and circular with my aggressive attempts to loosen the nut. Conversely, my overly zealous, committed attempts to tighten a screw or nut securely will often strip the threads and make the task many times more difficult. Effort and energy expended with poor or misguided techniques will yield abortive attempts to change. Danger warnings of this sort are often effective; however, not all such warnings are heeded, as happened with Harvey.

Harvey came to a smoking cessation clinic for individuals who volunteered to be role models in a media-covered smoking cessation program. These volunteers agreed to be videotaped and interviewed over the course of their attempt to quit smoking. Their stories would be used in newspaper or TV ads to promote smoking cessation. Individuals in this program could be assumed to have rather strong commitment, since they would be making a public attempt to quit. Harvey was clearly one of the most committed. He smoked 40 cigarettes a day and wanted to quit completely. He was in his 40s and felt that health concerns and the dirtiness of the habit were the main reasons for his decision to quit. Harvey was dedicated to using a willpower approach to quitting. He did not want to examine difficult situations and kept simply saying that whatever the situation, he was just going to resist the urge to smoke. He had few alternative behaviors to replace the smoking habit. Despite the gentle proddings of the leader and some fellow group members to use skills as well as willpower, Harvey persistently pushed on, unwilling to consider situation-specific skills.

Immediately after quit day, Harvey reported that he was doing well. Willpower had helped him resist all urges, and he felt that quitting was rather easy. However, his whole day was dedicated to not smoking, and he kept a constant vigilance. This worked well in the early stages of action. The next session was 10 days after the quit day; Harvey arrived looking rather exhausted. He still had not smoked, but the constant drain on his willpower was taking its toll on his energy and his commitment. We discussed how he might need to use other coping activities. Other group members offered their own experiences. Harvey was able to shift to using other strategies and remained abstinent at 3- and 6-month follow-ups.

Commitment without appropriate coping skills and activities can create a tenuous action plan. Helping to explore the plan and focus on details can be a useful strategy for the client in the determination stage.

Action: Implementing the Plan

What do people in action need from a therapist? They have made a plan and have begun to implement it by the time they come to the session. Often, making a therapy appointment has coincided with other change activity. Clients in the action stage often use therapy to make a public commitment to action; to get some external confirmation of the plan; to seek support; to gain greater self-efficacy; and finally to create artificial, external monitors of their activity. These can be rather easy and quite rewarding roles for the therapist. In fact, clients at this stage represent many of our "miracle cures" who see us for one session, make significant and long-lasting changes, and tell everyone what great therapists we are.

Helping clients increase their sense of self-efficacy is an important task of this stage. Focusing on their successful activity, reaffirming their decisions, and helping them to make intrinsic attributions of success can affect self-efficacy evaluations. Offering information about successful models can also help, as long as the models have used a variety of action options. The purpose of the models is not to offer a rigid prescription for change (which would run counter to motivational interviewing principles), but to engender a sense that success is possible for people like this client.

There are some frustrations in working with action clients. Often they utilize therapy appointments only as a monitor, so they tend to cancel second and third appointments as they realize that they are making the changes on their own. The EAP clients are good examples. After one or two sessions where things are going well, they are often reluctant to make the third appointment too soon. One husband and wife were having trouble with their 8-year-old son. Much of the problem was the inconsistent discipline of the parents. Coming to therapy helped to reinforce their convictions to begin being firmer with their son and consulting with each other about discipline matters. After two sessions within 2 weeks, they wanted to schedule the next appointment 2 months later after school started again, to see whether they needed a referral for more extended treatment. However, when the time came, they canceled this appointment, stating that they would recontact me if they needed additional help. One year later, they still have not called. Therapists' needs to be needed may not be met with action clients, once the clients are comfortable and confident about the change.

Maintenance, Relapse, and Recycling

The action stage normally takes 3–6 months to complete. This time frame is supported in our research on addictive behaviors, but may vary with the type of problem. Since change requires building a new pattern of behavior over time, it takes a while to establish the new pattern. However, the real test of change for most problem behaviors, especially the addictive behaviors, is long-term sustained change over several years. This last stage of successful change is called "maintenance." In this stage the new behavior is becoming firmly established, and the threat of relapse or of a return to the old patterns becomes less frequent and less intense.

Relapse, however, is always possible in both the action and the maintenance stages. Relapse can occur for many different reasons. Individuals may experience a particularly strong, unexpected urge or temptation and fail to cope with it successfully. Sometimes relaxing their guard or testing themselves begins the slide back. Often the costs of the change are not realized until later, and the commitment or self-efficacy erodes. Most often relapse does not occur automatically, but takes place gradually after an initial slip occurs.

During what Saul Shiffman calls these "relapse crises," clients may turn to a therapist for help. Either they have slipped and are early into relapse, or they are scared and shaken by their desire to go back to smoking or drinking or drugs. They come to the therapist with a weakened self-efficacy and a fear that the old habit may be stronger than they are. They seek reassurance and some way to make sense of the relapse crisis. Understanding the cycle of change in a learning context can assist the therapist and the client at this point.

Feedback concerning the length of time it takes to accomplish sustained change, and the fact that some situations or cues can bring back a flood of memories associated with the problem behavior, may be quite helpful. Many EAP referrals concern marital or other relationship problems. At times the complaint is that the individual is experiencing an old problem in a new relationship. The client has begun to realize that there is a pattern to the problem and that as soon as there is physical intimacy, he or she feels angry and wants to break off the relationship. Here we can use the cycle of change to show how the client is learning from these repeated patterns what needs to be changed. For smokers and drinkers, relapse crises can uncover problems with commitment, coping, or environmental stress that are critical for successful sustained change. Exploration, information, feedback, and empathy are all important elements at this point in the cycle of change. Preventing relapse and helping clients successfully recycle through the stages are the goals for our motivational interviewing.

Summary

It should be quite apparent by now that motivational interviewing strategies can be integrated well with the stages-of-change model. In fact, knowing where a client stands in this model can be helpful in deciding which strategies to use and when to use them. Motivational interviewing approaches are appropriate for clients in all stages of change. The content and strategies will vary, but the objective remains the same. Clients need help to negotiate the passage from one stage to the next in the process of change. The ultimate goal is to help the individual make efficient and effective changes in his or her life. The assumption is that these changes will be life-enhancing and that they need to be sustained over time.

Although the strategies elaborated in this book are appropriate for dealing with individuals in all stages of change, they are most appropriate for the early stages of precontemplation, contemplation, and determination. These early phases of change are most affected by motivational considerations. Skills and self-efficacy are the primary foci of the later stages. The only caution I would give to counselors is that individuals in the action and maintenance stages may need skills training in addition to motivational strategies. If individuals are capable and competent to make the change, it is often quite sufficient to assist them with motivational strategies. However, lack of skills and abilities may necessitate a more directive and prescriptive approach.

In my own clinical and research work, I have found the motivational strategies described in this book to be extremely helpful. This approach treats the client as a fully functioning, managing partner in the process of change. Motivational interviewing respects the work that needs to be done in the early stages of change, and it does not assume that all clients come or must come to therapy ready for change. On the other hand, precontemplating clients are not judged as recalcitrant and incorrigible for their early status in the cycle of change. With both smoking and EAP clients, these strategies as I have employed them have been quite helpful. I have learned a great deal more about how the stages and motivational strategies weave together as I read the early chapters of this book. As I have written this chapter, my appreciation for these approaches has grown. Therapists, counselors, and all interveners can benefit from a fuller understanding of motivational interviewing and the stages-of-change model.

Suggested Readings

DiClemente, C. C. (1986). Antonio—more than anxiety: A transtheoretical approach. In J. C. Norcross (Ed.), *Casebook of eclectic psychotherapy*. New York: Brunner/Mazel.

DiClemente, C. C., McConnaughy, E. A., Norcross, J. C., & Prochaska, J. O. (1986). Integrative dimensions for psychotherapy. *International Journal of Eclectic Psychotherapy*, 5(3), 302–315.

DiClemente, C. C., & Prochaska, J. O. (1985). Processes and stages of change: Coping and competence in smoking behavior change. In S. Shiffman & T. A. Wills (Eds.), *Coping and substance abuse*. New York: Academic Press.

DiClemente, C. C., Prochaska, J. O., Fairhurst, S. K., Velicer, W. F., Velasquez,

M. M., & Rossi, J. S. (1991). The process of smoking cessation: An analysis of precontemplation, contemplation and preparation stages of change. *Journal of Consulting and Clinical Psychology, 59*(2), 295–304.

DiClemente, C. C., Prochaska, J. O., & Gibertini, M. (1985). Self-efficacy and the stages of self-change of smoking. *Cognitive Therapy and Research, 9*(2), 181–200.

Prochaska, J. O., & DiClemente, C. C. (1986). The transtheoretical approach: Towards a systematic eclectic framework. In J. C. Norcross (Ed.), *Handbook of eclectic psychotherapy*. New York: Brunner/Mazel.

Prochaska, J. O., & DiClemente, C. C. (1986). Toward a comprehensive model of change. In W. R. Miller & N. Heather (Eds.), *Treating addictive behaviors: Processes of change*. New York: Plenum Press.

14

Brief Motivational Interviewing for Use by the Nonspecialist

STEPHEN ROLLNICK

ALISON BELL

People struggling with substance use problems are more likely to encounter a nonspecialist—a family doctor, a nurse, a social worker, a probation officer, a member of the clergy, or a visiting nurse—than a specialist counselor. Empowering primary care workers to deal with these problems has been given prominence recently, particularly in the smoking and alcohol fields (see Heather, 1989; Stockwell & Clement, 1987). The rationale for the use of brief intervention (see Chapter 3) by these workers is that, since most substance users change their behavior without any help at all, a brief "motivational nudge" should suffice in the majority of cases. Nonspecialists are in a good position to do this work because they can maintain contact with clients over a period of time, however brief each session may be, and they are able to bypass the problem of stigmatization that so often prevents people from using specialist services.

One way of delivering brief intervention is to be perfectly straightforward—to give people information and advice about the need to change their behavior. Indeed, this may be all that is needed in some cases. There is a danger, however, that giving advice can easily take the form of confrontation; this may well lead to resistance from clients, particularly among those who are not sure whether they want to change their behavior (see Rollnick & MacEwan, 1991). The aim of this chapter is to show that it is possible for those of you who are nonspecialists to incorporate motivational interviewing strategies into brief intervention. In following the two basic principles of nonconfrontation and the eliciting of possible concerns from the client, you simply select strategies from a menu of options, providing information wherever appropriate.

This approach is well suited to your activity as primary care workers, since you may already spend a great deal of your time trying to persuade people to change their behavior. Motivational interviewing is a technique for doing just this. Ironically, it can be a lot easier than you may imagine, since you avoid the tiresome process of presenting good arguments for change only to find the client disagreeing with you. With a motivational approach, you do not have to have all the answers. The task is simply one of helping clients to do this work for themselves, using the kind of framework to be described below.

Another advantage of this approach is that it is suited to the majority of people whom you encounter in the primary care setting. They do not come forward asking for help with substance use problems; they are either "not ready" to change (the precontemplators) or "unsure" about it all (the contemplators). Motivational interviewing is specifically geared toward *preparing* people like this for change.

Finally (as described in Chapter 9), it is important to note that this process is not incompatible with giving someone information or advice, but simply forms the platform for this to be done in a sensitive manner, according to the needs of the client.

The Conduct of a Session

If you deliberately avoid presenting people with the reasons for concern or telling them what to do, there is an obvious danger that the session could lose its sense of direction. For this reason, we have found it helpful to use a menu of specific strategies to structure the session. You need to find the right balance between intervening actively on the one hand, and sitting back and listening on the other, letting the client do the work. This process is not unlike the interaction between a person learning to drive and an instructor, each of whom is behind a (dual-control) steering wheel. The pupil does most of the driving, but the tutor takes control at important junctions or at times when the pupil needs steering in another direction. To stretch the analogy a bit further, the opening, rapport-building phase of an interview is like getting into the car together, agreeing about where to go, and starting the engine. Exploring concerns can only take place once the car is moving and the client is feeling comfortable about the journey ahead.

Turning to the skills used by the interviewer, we find it helpful to distinguish between the use of "microskills" (e.g., open questions, summarizing, and reflective listening) on the one hand, and the use of broader strategies on the other. In motivational interviewing, these specific microskills are used in a continuous and often cyclical manner, yet need to be guided by broader strategies that allow the counselor to pursue the goal of exploring concerns in an appropriate manner. In supervising health workers, we teach these broader strategies as a first step. Within this framework, attention can then be turned to the use of microskills. The depth of focus on microskills depends on the experience of the trainees and the amount of training time available.

It is necessary to have access to a *menu* of these broader strategies, because clients vary in their readiness to express concerns. A strategy that is used appropriately with one person can involve jumping too far ahead with another. We provide our interviewers with a list that begins with the "safest" and least threatening strategies. Their task is simply to make a judgment about which strategy to choose. A useful guideline is this: If in doubt, choose a nonthreatening strategy first. They all lead logically to the use of the key tactic listed as Strategy 8 below—the exploration of concerns. With some clients, if they are ready to do this, you can start with the eliciting of concerns. With others (like some of the heavily drinking "precontempla-tors" we come across in the hospital setting), you may never get that far, and the session usually ends by raising awareness through providing them with information (see Strategy 7 below). We tend to view people as being on a "readiness-to-change" continuum, rather than as being in discrete stages. The aim of the brief motivational session is to help people move along this continuum toward decision making.

A session that is working well will usually proceed as follows: A new strategy is introduced by an open question from the interviewer. This will lead to elaboration from the client, which is best maintained by using reflective-listening statements and further open questions. At key junctions, however, when there is a need to change direction or use another strategy, the interviewer will summarize what has been said and then ask another open question; the session then proceeds through the cycle once again, with each strategy lasting between 5 and 15 minutes.

The Opening: Raising the Subject of Substance Use

Addictive problems do not necessarily present themselves to nonspecialists in a neatly packaged form. People may not expect or want to talk about their substance use, let alone to believe that they have a problem or need to change their behavior in any way. From the beginning, it is important to avoid labeling, confrontation, and giving advice. Ultimately, the clients are the ones who decide what is best. The goal is to encourage them to explore their substance use and possible reasons for concern, taking care to proceed at the clients' own pace. The question of action or behavior change, if they are ready for this, will arise naturally out of this discussion.

Some clients will be more reluctant than others, and broaching the subject of substance use will be an important first step. A direct question such as "Don't you think you might be drinking a bit too much?", no matter how well-meaning, will often lead to resistance. Even worse is to imply the need for behavior change with a question such as "What about your use of tranquilizers? Don't you think you should be doing something about this?"

Two simple strategies can be used to conduct the interview in a constructive way from the outset. One is to *establish rapport* for 5–10 minutes, and the other is to use appropriate *open-ended questions*. Rapport building not only serves to build up trust and empathy, but can also be used as a "way in" to discussing substance use. The interviewer simply chooses a topic for discussion that is of interest to the client, and that may be linked to substance use. The topic chosen will depend on the client and the context— health problems, fitness, stress at work or at home, looking after the children, recreation, and so on.

From this beginning, the interviewer will be in a better position to ask nonthreatening, open-ended questions: "Tell me, where does your use of tranquilizers fit into all this?" or "Can I ask you now, how about your use of alcohol? What sort of a drinker are you?"

Getting Going: Exploring Concerns and Options for Change

Once the subject has been raised, the goal should be to help clients express how they feel about their substance use and, most importantly, whether they have any concerns about it. Options for change, if appropriate, are best dealt with a little later. This stock-taking process does not have to take a long time. What follows is a summary of strategies that form a menu of options available to you as the interviewer. Since you may often have no idea about the person's readiness to change, it is best to start with nonthreatening strategies (those close to the top of the list). These strategies, and some other possibilities, are described in more detail in Chapters 6, 8, 9, and 10.

1. Ask about substance use in detail. Questions such as "What kind of drinker are you?" or "Tell me about your use of _____; what effect does it tend to have on you?" are good starting points for this kind of detailed discussion. They show your interest not just in behavior and consumption, but in the effect of substance use on mood as well. The client's concerns sometimes emerge quite naturally when this strategy is used.

2. Ask about a typical day/session. This is a variation of the first strategy. The crucial difference is that you keep to an account of specific events and experiences, building up a picture of substance use through questions such as this: "You say that you went into the pub and ordered your first drink. . . . What effect did this have on you?"

3. Ask about lifestyle and stresses. Talking about everyday routine and stresses can be used from the outset as a platform for subsequent discussion of drinking, smoking, or pill taking. Once the subject of substance use has been raised, people often say things like "It's nice just to have a drink/ smoke and relax." If timed correctly, this kind of statement can be turned around with a question like this: "You say that smoking is nice just to relax and unwind. Tell me about the times when you find yourself in this situation. What kind of pressures are you under?" This often opens up discussion about wanting the substance to deal with difficult situations—something that can lead naturally into a discussion about concerns.

4. Ask about health, then substance use. Most appropriate in health care settings, this strategy is particularly useful if someone's substance use is causing health problems. An inquiry about health and health-related problems thus leads to an open-ended question such as "I wonder, where does your use of _____ fit in here?" This often allows the person to articulate, sometimes for the first time, concerns about his or her substance use.

5. Ask about the good things, then the less good things. This strategy is fully described and illustrated in Chapters 4, 6, and 7. The challenge for the interviewer is to lead the session from talk about the "less good things" to talk about concerns. These are not equivalent. If a client says, "One of the less good things is that I spend $150 a week on alcohol," this does not mean that he or she is necessarily concerned about it. Your task as the interviewer will then be to find out whether this is a cause for concern, using an appropriate question (e.g., "I wonder, how much does that bother you?"). When using this strategy, we find it best to ask about the good/less good things about "having a drink," rather than about "your drinking."

6. Ask about substance use in the past and now. Questions such as "What's the difference between your use of _____ now compared to 10 years ago?" or "How has your drinking changed over the years?" can result in clients' describing areas of concern. If they do not, they often describe a history of increased tolerance—for example, "Well, I don't get drunk as easily as I used to. . . . I can hold my liquor better now," or "I drink more than I used to, but I can hold it fine. . . . I don't get drunk or anything like that." This can provide an ideal opportunity for working with such clients on the subject of tolerance, and reframing the meaning of this along the lines discussed in Chapter 8.

7. Provide information and ask, "What do you think?" How and when information is provided is as important as the information itself. Once you have chosen your moment, it is best to ask the client, in a low-key and curious tone of voice, something like this: "Would it be useful to spend a few minutes looking at this whole question of what is a safe level of consumption?" The information is then presented in the same nonjudgmental, low-key manner, and the presentation concludes with "What do you make of that?" or "I wonder, how does this apply to you?"

8. Ask about concerns directly. This direct strategy will only work if the client appears ready and willing to talk about this. Use an open-ended question ("What concerns do you have about your _____?"), rather than a closed question ("Are you concerned about your use of _____?"). Once the client begins to elaborate, encourage this process, being careful not to move on to the next concern too quickly. Then summarize the concern, and simply ask, "What other concerns do you have?" Build up a picture of concerns, share this with the client, and don't forget to summarize the "other side" (the positive aspects of substance use) as well.

9. *Ask about the next step.* The whole question of change can only be addressed if the client appears ready for this. This strategy is best used after the eliciting of concerns described in Strategy 8 above. Then you can simply ask open-ended questions such as these: "I wonder where this leaves you now? Where do you go from here?" or "It sounds like you are concerned about your use of _____. I wonder, what's the next step?" Often, there will be more silences at this point, and the person will be feeling uncomfortable. He or she may not be ready to make a decision. The negotiation that follows is best done by eliciting possibilities from the client. You can suggest a number of options for change or strategies for dealing with difficult situations, but ultimately the client should decide what is best (see Chapter 9). People often benefit from considering the consequences of change as part of this process—for example, "You say you want to stop using tranquilizers altogether. How will this turn out? What concerns do you have about coping without access to your tablets?" In the face of doubts about their ability to cope, people often withdraw from making a final decision; hence the importance of not rushing too quickly at this point.

Ending the Session

A brief session does not have to conclude with the person's agreeing to *do* something. Falling short of this goal does not imply failure. Success can be gauged by the extent to which the person has moved along the "readiness-to-change" continuum. Any time spent expressing concerns will be time well spent, whether or not a decision is made to initiate behavior change. A constructive way of winding things up is to summarize the progress made thus far, talking in "you" language and reiterating any concerns and intention to change expressed by the client. Emphasizing freedom of choice and your own willingness to provide further support, if possible, are most important at this stage. If the question of referral arises, the person should be informed about the options available and encouraged to make an active choice; offers to help organize this and to provide support in the future should be made, if appropriate.

Case Example

This case example illustrates the selective use of motivational strategies in a brief interview with someone dependent on nicotine. How to motivate someone to make a decision to stop smoking is a question that bedevils many a health care consultation. This case concerns a 42-year-old mother of two children who presents to her doctor with a throat infection. The underlying assumption of this intervention is that *telling* her that she *should* be concerned about stopping smoking will probably lead to resistance. Instead, the health worker needs to elicit from her any reasons for concern.

Commentary   The doctor's first tasks are to establish rapport, raise the subject of smoking, and then select an appropriate strategy from the menu of options. A decision is made from the outset to give this person 10–15 minutes to talk about health matters.

DOCTOR: (*5 minutes into consultation*) I've taken a swab of your throat, and I would like you to come back and see me in a few days so that we can have a look at the result together. In the meanwhile, try to get as much rest as you can. I know you have quite a busy household.

PATIENT: That's right. Rest in my house, it's impossible!

D: How are things going at home?

P: Well, as you know, I've got three children, and I have to work as well. It's all go. I only work 3 hours a day in the shop, but I've got to do a lot of the housework as well. It's like you never have time to just relax. I can't remember the last time my husband and I had any time to ourselves. It's go, go, go and then collapse into bed. All I needed was this throat business.

D: Now you have even less energy to cope with all this.

P: That's right. If I spend a day in bed, the whole show collapses, although my husband is trying his best now that I'm not well. He has a busy job himself.

D: How are you coping with it all?

P: Well, it's been hard since I started coughing and spluttering around the house, complaining of feeling ill (*laughs*). I've managed to get the children to help around the house, and I took 2 days off work. I just hope my throat gets better soon.

D: What else could you do to make things easier for yourself?

P: Well, I've thought about asking my mother to come down and help with making the evening meal. That would be a great help.

D: That's a good idea. It would be nice if you could look after yourself carefully these next few days.

P: I might phone her when I get back.

Commentary   The doctor chooses this moment to raise the subject of smoking, using a neutrally phrased open-ended question.

D: I wonder, you've talked about coughing around the house. Where does your smoking fit into all this?

P: I've cut my smoking down since my throat started hurting, because it just makes it worse.

D: Makes it worse.

P: Yes, I just have to slow down on the cigarettes at the moment. The thing is, I enjoy my smoking, it's one of the few relaxing things, like with my cup of tea or coffee.

Commentary   The doctor has a choice here: to focus on "negative" issues (e.g., her coughing), or to follow her reference to the more positive aspects. The latter is the safer route to follow.

D: Smoking can be a nice break from routine.

P: Yes, that's right. It's part of relaxing.

Commentary   Here the doctor chooses Strategy 2, asking about substance use in detail. The other obvious alternative is Strategy 5 (the good things and the less good things), which would also provide a solid platform for a discussion about concerns.

D: Tell me about your routine and where cigarettes fit in. Why don't you take me through a typical day, and tell me where and when you smoke?

P: Well, I don't smoke until the kids are out of the house. They would start moaning at me. But then it's into the living room with my cup of coffee and a cigarette. That's one of the best times in the day.

D: It's relaxing, and the cigarette is part of that.

P: That's right.

D: What about the next one?

P: Oh, that's not long after. . . . (*She continues.*)

Commentary   She describes most of the cigarettes she has during the day, with the doctor merely following her, taking care to ask her how she feels immediately afterwards. This takes 3–4 minutes. Now there is a need to change strategy. One possibility is to return to the issue of stress (Strategy 3). In this instance, the doctor decides to return to the coughing and to see whether she wants some information about smoking (Strategy 7). A summary and an open-ended question signal the change in strategy.

D: It sounds like these cigarettes do different things for you. After some of them, like the first one of the day and those after meals, you notice the biggest effect, and this can be relaxing. Others, like those in between, have less of an effect, and you even said it was like just keeping the habit going.

P: Yes, that's exactly right.

D: Where does the coughing come in?

P: Well, that's my smoker's cough. I've had it for years.

D: Do you know what that means about your lungs?

P: Yes, I know it's not good for me. It's like my lungs are telling me, "Stop it!"

D: What about some of the other effects of smoking on your body?

P: Well, they say it's not good for your heart and it can cause cancer and that sort of thing. I feel really guilty about my smoking; the kids are always going on at me about it.

Commentary It now becomes evident that this person does not really need information about smoking. She is aware of the main health effects. She spontaneously mentions feeling guilty about it. The doctor decides to follow this, knowing that soon it will be possible to elicit her concerns about smoking (Strategy 8). Again, a brief summary signals the change in strategy; this time, however, the doctor tries to capture both the positive and negative sides of her smoking.

D: You've told me quite a lot about your smoking this morning. It's relaxing sometimes, but it also makes you feel guilty.

P: Yes, I know it's bad for me. It costs so much each day, and the kids are always moaning about it.

Commentary Now the doctor uses the key strategy of exploring concerns.

D: Can I ask you, what really concerns you about your smoking?

P: I suppose I can put up with the coughing. Even the money is not too serious. It's really that I just feel hooked on the damned things, like I don't know where it's going to end.

D: You feel hooked on them.

P: Yes, as I told you earlier, I enjoy some of them, but most of them do nothing for me.

D: It's like you don't really know why you smoke some of them.

P: That's right.

D: What other concerns do you have about your smoking?

P: The health thing is a worry. I'm not getting any younger.

D: What exactly are you worried about?

P: Well, I don't feel healthy these days. I feel clogged up with smoking, and you should see me climb stairs. I'm like an old woman. I used to play sports, but I could never do that now. I'd collapse! And then there's my throat; I know it's made worse by smoking.

D: What other concerns do you have?

P: That's about it, really.

Commentary   The doctor decides to change strategies—to summarize both her concerns and the benefits of smoking (using "you" language) and to raise the question about change in a neutral way, without putting pressure on her to make a decision.

D: So, if I understand you correctly, sometimes when you smoke you feel relaxed, but you are concerned about being hooked on tobacco and its effect on your health and fitness. You've also mentioned concern about your throat. Where does this leave you now?

P: I don't know. It feels like a trap I'm in.

D: Like a trap.

P: Well, it's like this: I'd like to give up, but it just feels too much for me at the moment.

Commentary   Here the doctor makes a decision not to push things too far—to go along with her reluctance to consider change, but to raise the subject at a second visit. A summary is used to end the session, with emphasis being placed on the progress made.

D: I can understand that you are not feeling very well at the moment. It's really up to you. I can't force you to do anything, but I can certainly help you. You've told me about some of your concerns about smoking, and that's a very good first step. Perhaps you can think about it over for the next few days, and come back toward the end of the week so we can have a look at your throat and look at the result of the swab.

P: OK, I'll do that. Should I make an appointment now?

Conclusion

Negotiating behavior change with clients is part of nonspecialists' everyday work. People who are heavy users of such substances as alcohol, tobacco, tranquilizers, cocaine, and amphetamines often feel two ways about their behavior. Perhaps this is why many of them react against being told that they should be concerned or should change their behavior. Under this kind of pressure, they often answer, "Yes, but you see . . ." To put it another way, if such people are not ready to change their behavior, advising them to do this may not be the best way to proceed.

We believe that it is possible for nonspecialists to use the motivational approach described in this chapter. In our work with heavy drinkers in a medical setting, we have been able to distill the essential ingredients of motivational interviewing into a manageable brief intervention procedure that requires 6–12 hours of training.

Some clients will need more than just a brief session, particularly where other personal matters impinge upon their substance use. Referral may be necessary under these circumstances. Some clients will be happy to be *told* what to do, and some practitioners may feel uncomfortable with the framework presented in this chapter. However, we suspect that a large percentage of clients will react against a confrontational approach, and that the use of brief motivational strategies could well improve the success rate of brief intervention—which among smokers, for example, currently stands at roughly between 5% and 20% (Heather, 1987).

15

Motivational Interviewing: Perspectives from The Netherlands, with Particular Emphasis on Heroin-Dependent Clients

HENCK P. J. G. VAN BILSEN

In this chapter I discuss the application of motivational interviewing techniques in The Netherlands, particularly with heroin-dependent clients. First, I outline a practical framework for diagnosing the motivational level of clients, and then turn to the description of some special techniques that can be used in diverse settings. Finally, I discuss the specific application of motivational interviewing in work with heroin-dependent clients.

Understanding Motivation

I have found it helpful to define motivation in a very straightforward, concrete, and practical sense. This definition is based on the stages-of-change model described by Prochaska and DiClemente (Prochaska & DiClemente, 1984; van Bilsen, 1986, 1991).

People will be motivated to change their lifestyles in the following situation: They know what problems are caused by their behavior and are concerned about these problems; at the same time, they feel positive about themselves and competent to make a change. In short, a combination of "positives" (self-esteem and competence) and "negatives" (problem knowledge and concern) is needed. The first task of a therapist is to diagnose the client according to these four motivational areas. By listening carefully to the spoken words of a client and observing his or her nonverbal behavior, the therapist can observe small signs of problem knowledge, problem concern, self-esteem, and competence. If the therapist asks questions at all, these should be open-ended, nonprobing questions. My preference is to use reflections, positive restructurings, and summaries to guide the conversation. In such a way, clients are given an optimal opportunity to express their motives and feelings about their situation. Here is an example of a reflection and open-ended question:

CLIENT: Only when I use heroin I feel good. I am not saying I wouldn't want to cut down a bit, but how am I going to cope with life when I feel rotten all the time?

THERAPIST: On the one hand you don't want to exclude the possibility of decreasing your heroin use, but on the other hand you want to be able to cope with life's complexity. Could you tell me a bit more about this?

Here is an example of positive restructuring:

C: I couldn't decrease my cocaine use. If I did, the company would go bust. I need it to keep me going, I really need to work 80 hours a week.

T: You seem to be a very generous person, in a way. You are willing to risk damage to your health to save the company. Could you tell me a bit more about these pressures that are resting on your shoulders?

In traditional counseling, the first task of the therapist is often to diagnose the problems of the client. I have found it better to make this of secondary importance. Of primary importance are simply listening to the client's responses and taking note of the degree of knowledge and concern about the problem on the one hand, and the level of self-esteem and feelings of competence on the other. In general, therapists should direct their attention toward those areas in which clients show less "motivational behavior." Sometimes the problem knowledge and concern do not need to be increased (a client is already very worried about his or her problems), and the motivational efforts have to be directed toward self-esteem and competence.

An illustration of the beginning of a first session with a client is given below. The client is a 37-year-old managing director of a shipping agency. His wife and coworkers have been complaining about his drinking; after a second driving-under-the-influence accident, the client has decided to see a therapist.

THERAPIST: Welcome to my office. You have made an appointment to speak to me. What would you like to talk about?

Therapist gives client an opportunity to set the agenda.

CLIENT: Well, you see, my wife and my employer made me see you. It's not my choice to be sitting here and wasting my time.

T: You sound like a busy man. Despite that
fact, you agreed to come and talk to me
about something your wife and employer consider important. Could you tell me a bit more
about that?

*Positive restructuring: The
client is a busy man, and this
makes it even more admirable
that he sacrifices his time to
do something he considers
useless at the moment. Therapist empathizes with client but
at the same time elicits more
information from him.*

C: There is not much to tell. I have to work very
hard to keep the business going. I can hardly
find the time to spend an evening at home with
the wife and children. And they all nag at me
because I enjoy drinking a beer occasionally.

T: It seems as if you have two very important
issues in your life: the family and the job. You
really want to do both as best you can. Relaxing with a beer gives you the energy to do
both. It seems as if your wife and employer
have a different opinion. Could you tell me a
bit more about the differences of opinion?

*Again, positive restructuring
and reflection of a conflict.
Drinking beer is presented in
a positive context.*

C: Sometimes I can't stand all the pressures
that are put on me. Nothing seems to give me
a chance to relax. But I don't drink so much
that they should call me an alcoholic.

T: . . . An alcoholic.

Simple reflection (parroting).

C: (*Angry*) Yes, an alcoholic! I try to do my
best and this is what I get out of it—being accused of alcoholism.

T: Just to summarize: If I understand you correctly, you have come to see me in order to
discuss these differences of opinion between
you and your wife and employer. They seem
to think that there is a problem connected
with your drinking. You yourself think that
there is no problem whatsoever with your
drinking. Your wife and employer seem to
you to be completely out of line with these
accusations.

*Summarizing, empathizing
with client, and some amplified reflections.*

C: I am not saying that I shouldn't drink less,
but I am not an alcoholic.

In this example, it is clear that the motivational problem lies in the client's apparent lack of knowledge and concern. Positive restructuring, open questions, and (in the last therapist statement) amplified reflection are used to minimize resistance and encourage the client to express his concerns.

Special Techniques

I have found the following strategies helpful in dealing with various groups of clients, over and above the use of basic motivational skills described above.

Metaphors for Strategic Interviewing

People who suffer from severe and persistent behavior problems and are in the stages of precontemplation and contemplation tend to defend themselves against the possibility of a growing awareness that change is necessary. The word "defend" reminds us of warfare. In the same manner as an army general defends his positions from the enemy, a client defends himself or herself against the "enemy" therapist who unwillingly and unwittingly threatens to lower the client's self-esteem. A useful illustration of the value of metaphors for strategic interviewing in motivating and treating people with addictive problems comes from a treatise on war by an ancient Chinese general (Sun Tzu, 1963). Just as in war it is not wise to attack enemies in places where they have defended themselves at their best, it is often not wise as a therapist to work with a client on topics that are strongly defended against change. For instance, a client who is convinced that he or she has no drinking problem will defend this position very strongly, but will forget to "defend" the position concerning his or her lack of self-esteem and competence. Change should not be undertaken thoughtlessly, but has to be preceded by measures designed to make it easy to succeed. One of the guidelines used by Sun Tzu forms a useful piece of advice to the therapist trying to work with indirect strategies: "When capable he feigns incapacity; when near he makes it appear that he is far away; when far away he is near" (p. 107).

The primary task of a warlord is, according to Sun Tzu, creating changes and manipulating them to his advantage. Sun Tzu's theory of adaptability to existing situations is an important lesson for therapists. Just as water adapts itself to the configuration of the land, so in therapy one must be flexible. The therapist has to adapt to the client's way of thinking. If the client is given enough room to move, he or she will create a self-motivational situation. Under certain conditions in war, one yields a city, sacrifices a portion of one's force, or gives up ground in order to gain a more valuable objective. Similarly, a therapist seduces a client away from strongly defended positions (e.g., addictive behavior) and talks, for instance, about his or her being the parent of an adolescent who has just successfully completed secondary school (thus raising the self-esteem of the client in an indirect way!). To carry this example a bit further, what the therapist does is not to focus on the so-called problem behavior (the drinking or other addiction), but, directly or by way of positive restructuring, to focus on positive and successful components of the client's life. This in turn boosts the client's self-esteem and feeling of competence, apart from creating rapport between therapist and client. Under these circumstances, the client will loosen resistance and be less defensive in talking about the addictive problems.

The Incompetent Therapist, or the "Columbo" Technique

In my work with extremely difficult clients, I sometimes feel very incompetent as a therapist. The clients I feel incompetent with are those who try to engage me in a power struggle with them; clients who always have comments on what I say; clients who imply that I am incompetent. Through many failures, I have discovered a technique that sometimes works to motivate this kind of client to change. Thinking of the television series *Columbo* (starring Peter Falk), I have called this the "Columbo" technique. The therapist has to be able to lose face with the client. He or she has to act as a complete failure, to seem unable to provide any solution to the client's difficulties. The therapist listens to the client's problems with much empathy, and emphasizes how terrible it must be for the client to have to talk to such an incompetent therapist. The therapist also speaks in a low voice, makes notes all the time, and often asks for help or clarification ("I am not sure if I understand you well, but . . ."). The therapist can complain about a bad memory ("What were we talking about last time?") or can forget his or her notes.

The effect of this technique is sometimes amazing: The criticisms disappear, and the client becomes helpful toward the therapist. I remember one client, a very critical man, very much wanting to be in control, who had many problems connected with his alcohol drinking but did not see the need to enter treatment. For the next session with him, I prepared myself to act as the new psychologist in the team: "Everybody thinks I can't motivate clients for treatment. I have not been able to engage one client in treatment for 3 weeks. And I am sure you don't want treatment, because we have discovered that you can and will handle all the problems by yourself!" The client was very empathic with me as the "junior psychologist." Although he felt that he didn't need treatment at this moment, he agreed that we could still have a few sessions so that I could prove my motivational skills with my colleagues!

Strategic Use of Information

Providing objective information about the situations that clients find themselves in is a useful technique in motivational interviewing. But how does one get information from the client who doesn't want to give it, because "I don't have any problems, but nobody believes me"? This attitude is common among clients who have been sent to a therapist by the justice system or by their employers or partners.

I have found it very helpful to take the client's point of view in such situations (van Bilsen & Bennet, 1988), saying something like this:

> OK, I can see your point. You don't think there are any problems, and your main concern is how to convince [your wife, your boss, the judge, etc.] that there are no problems. I can congratulate you, because you have come to the right place. This institute specializes in helping people to get a clear picture of these confusing circumstances. I can help you to provide a clear picture of your situation. Do you think a report stating the facts would be of any use to you?

I have found that clients seldom refuse to cooperate with such a proposal. In order to get all the facts, the therapist needs to talk to the client several times. In these sessions, the therapist makes use of motivational interviewing techniques. When all the facts are assembled, the therapist may ask whether to include his or her own expert opinion about these facts in the first draft of the report. Again, I seldom find clients refusing this offer. In writing down the facts the therapist has to keep in mind the four motivational areas: The facts have to be stated, but not only the problematic side of the picture; the positive side should be stated as well.

Availability of a Range of Treatment Methods

All motivational interventions become completely useless if no suitable treatment methods are available for clients. Often treatment agencies have only a very narrow range of possibilities to offer, and expect their clients to become motivated not only for change but also for these specific change strategies as well. The specific treatment methods offered are often chosen on the basis of the therapists' beliefs and preferences, instead of being tailored to the clients' needs and preferences. In motivational milieu therapy (to be described below), clients can choose from a variety of change-directed interventions, and are also allowed to choose a treatment goal (including controlled use of substances) that is suitable for them.

Motivational Interviewing with Heroin-Dependent Clients

One thing is extremely important in applying motivational interviewing techniques with drug abusers: The therapist must be in contact with the clients. The treatment agency must create an optimum number of interactions between helping persons and the clients. If you never see a client, you can hardly motivate him or her. This is especially important at the present time, when we are encountering tremendous problems with human immune deficiency virus (HIV) and acquired immune deficiency syndrome (AIDS). We simply must persuade our clients to come to the clinics if we are to have any sort of influence. Depending on the facilities available, a drug treatment agency should aim to set up a motivational structure that maximizes its attractiveness to consumers. In such a program, methadone can help in attracting clients, but it is not a prerequisite. To create a contact point between clients and helping persons, a needle exchange service, free or cheap meals, coffee, advice, and medical services can all be used.

Problems with Traditional Outpatient Methadone Treatment

Giving methadone to heroin addicts is common practice in The Netherlands. A traditional outpatient methadone clinic is usually based on the "abstinence-only" treatment philosophy. Methadone is delivered to the client; Counseling often is mandatory. However, several experiences have led me to reconsider the value of this approach. I have found that staff members become preoccupied with arguing with clients instead of building therapeutic relationships with them. Clients are not half as eager to change their addicted lifestyle as the therapists are to have them do so. Burnouts among the staff and dropouts among the clients are frequent occurrences. Clients often seem dissatisfied with the treatment program. Finally, clients come to the clinic for 5 days a week; nevertheless, more could be done to make use of this opportunity to influence motivation. One mistake we have often made has been to assume that because clients are participating in a methadone program, they are therefore also motivated to change their addicted lifestyle.

Motivational Milieu Therapy: The Basic Principles

Motivational milieu therapy (MMT) is one example of the kind of motivational program that has been created by several treatment agencies in The Netherlands (van Bilsen & van Emst, 1986, 1989) and in the United Kingdom (Bolton & Watt, 1989; Fleming, 1989). In the MMT program, heroin addiction and heroin use are not looked upon as signs of an underlying disease, and heroin addicts are not seen as suffering from a disease that must be cured. Rather, the addiction is seen as learned behavior, which at present carries a high risk of creating problems for those who use heroin. These individuals run the risk of damaging their own lives and the lives of others. I view the prevention of (further) damage as the primary goal of treatment for heroin addiction. Consequently, the MMT program tries to give heroin users and heroin addicts a chance to learn survival skills that will enable them to live the life they want to lead, in a manner that results in the least possible damage to themselves and to other people.

The key principles of MMT are as follows:

- The client is accepted as he or she is, in a complete and unconditional way.
- Responsibility is left with the client for drug use and the problems connected with it.
- The client is treated as a grown-up, responsible person, capable of making his or her own decisions.
- Change efforts are not started before the client has committed himself or herself to particular goals and change strategies.
- Goals and treatment strategies are negotiated with the client.

The MMT Program

All the clients in the MMT program apply originally for methadone assistance. Most clients have to come to the clinic every day to collect their methadone during a specified hour, with bookings arranged so that the same group of about 15 clients is present for a given hourly period. A motivational milieu is provided in connection with the daily intake of methadone. In order to receive their methadone, clients have to pass through a space furnished like a living room. Here the clients can sit, talk, and drink coffee or tea for an hour every day.

Two staff members are always present; one staff member (preferably a nurse) works in the separate methadone delivery room, and the other (a social worker) in the MMT room. These people try to create the motivational milieu atmosphere. Their most important task is to use motivational interviewing skills (van Bilsen, 1986) in order to create a friendly, empathic atmosphere. The staff members encourage, elicit, and introduce discussions on topics of importance to the group (e.g., troubles with the rising price of heroin, worries about AIDS, etc.). The staff also tries to ensure that a few general rules are followed by all the participants. These rules are fairly straightforward:

- It is forbidden to bring guns, knives, or other weapons into the clinic.
- Dealing drugs on the premises is not permitted.
- Violence and threatening violence are forbidden.
- Time limits are strict.

Consequently, a steady, stable, and safe atmosphere is created. The climate is relaxed, open, and permissive. As noted above, clients are always treated by the staff as adults who are responsible for themselves.

The staff members "diagnose" which stage of change each client is in. Accordingly, a motivational plan is developed, depending on the client's stage of change. The goal of the intervention is to motivate the clients to move from precontemplation to decision. The staff members pinpoint certain desired behaviors for each client; whenever possible, they try to reinforce these behaviors.

An example may clarify the need for creativity in the process of pinpointing desired behaviors. It concerns a very shy, small heroin addict, whose only interaction with other people was complaining. Some days he went on complaining to another client or a staff member for the whole MMT hour. His complaints were about his health, his heroin use, and the like. We wanted him to take a more positive view of himself. We started by analyzing exactly what he did during the MMT hours, and discovered that he sometimes (about once a week) tried to tease staff members. He seemed to enjoy this, although he did not receive any particular attention or credit for it. We started reinforcing his staff-teasing behavior by paying attention to him when he did it, giving him credit for his teasing qualities in front of other clients, and so on. In doing so, we used pinpointing of behavior to raise the self-esteem and self-efficacy of the client. Giving positive attention in cases such as this one can be done in several ways:

- Sitting next to the client.
- Actively listening to the client.
- Complimenting the client.

- Giving the client "important" tasks (e.g., doing the shopping with the nurse) when he or she has engaged in these behaviors.

During the daily contact between staff and clients, the staff members use motivational interviewing techniques to reinforce desired behaviors, to elicit self-motivational statements from the clients, and to make sure that the rules of MMT are followed. Depending on the stage of change the client is in, there can be different goals: raising self-esteem (precontemplation); eliciting self-motivational statements and developing self-efficacy (contemplation); or changing attitudes and behavior (action). Staff members do not initiate discussions about changing the addicted lifestyle, but reinforce it when clients start talking about it by themselves.

Two further motivational strategies are useful in the MMT. The first of these is a 3-month evaluation system. All the clients are informed of their progress or deterioration. In each case, the therapist makes out a report stating all the facts about a client's participation in the program, and uses motivational interviewing principles in conducting the feedback session. The second strategy is leaving responsibility for drug use explicitly with each client. The staff members do not put pressure on the clients in any way to "motivate" them to change their heroin or methadone use. An example may clarify this.

CLIENT: I was using again last week. I think I'll never be able to stop using! I need some more methadone or I'll continue using heroin.

THERAPIST: Although you would like to change your heroin use, you doubt whether it will ever be possible for you.

The therapist reflects both the client's hidden wish to change and the feeling that it seems impossible.

C: Yes, I only want some more methadone, just for a little while. . . .

T: If I understand you correctly, your addiction is at the moment so intense that you need a large increase of methadone to control it. You have no strength left; your only chance of survival is getting more methadone.

Amplified reflection.

C: Well, it's not that bad. I suppose I could . . . You're not going to give me an increase, are you?

T: Of course we will allow you to increase your amount of methadone if you really feel that this is best for you. It seems that we didn't

Provocation.

realize the seriousness of your addiction and
your lack of willpower. How much did you
say you need?

C: I am not going to take this, man. Me not
having enough willpower? Go and ask on the
street! I can go for days without using once,
so don't talk to me about willpower. I don't
want your lousy methadone any more.

T: I am really sorry if I understood you wrong,   *The "Columbo" technique.*
but . . .

C: I'll see you tomorrow and I'll tell you all
about my willpower.

16

Motivational Counseling with Alcoholic Couples

ALLEN ZWEBEN

My interest in the problem of motivating patients for treatment stems from my initial involvement in conducting treatment outcome studies in an agency geared primarily to serving substance-abusing patients. While conducting the research, I learned that it was not uncommon for alcohol-dependent patients to abruptly cancel sessions without rebooking, and to arrive late or "not show" for appointments; eventually, a substantial number of these individuals prematurely terminated treatment. Increasingly concerned about motivational issues, I discovered that dropout from treatment is often linked with relapse among alcohol-dependent patients (Pickens, Hatsukami, Spicer, & Svikis, 1985).

At the time, the primary method of dealing with these compliance problems among practitioners in the setting was to overbook treatment appointments. The assumption here was that very little could be done to enhance the commitment or motivation of these reluctant alcoholics. These patients were considered to be highly "resistant" to change, or worse, "untreatable"; therefore, it was not felt to be surprising when a disproportionate number of these alcohol-abusing patients withdrew from treatment prematurely. These day-to-day frustrations in dealing with compliance issues led to an examination of data from my own research regarding factors that might be associated with a patient's commitment to change (as evidenced by the individual's inability or unwillingness to remain in treatment).

Through my research, I discovered that among socially stable problem drinkers, those assigned to an outpatient treatment were more likely to remain in treatment if their spouses were involved in the sessions than if they were not (Zweben & Pearlman, 1983; Zweben, Pearlman, & Li, 1983). Encouraged by these positive findings dealing with spouse participation, I reviewed other studies (as well as my own research) in which spousal involvement was considered an active ingredient of treatment. As expected, I discovered that the involvement of the spouse in treatment was associated with more favorable treatment outcomes, especially if positive ties existed between spouses prior to the initiation of treatment (Longabaugh, Beattie, Noel, Stout, & Malloy, in press; Sisson & Azrin, 1986; Zweben, Pearlman, & Li, 1988).

These experiences reflect a growing awareness of the importance of the spouse in helping to motivate the patient to change; they are incorporated into the present chapter. In attending the sessions, the spouse can obtain a better understanding of the alcohol problem, which in turn can help minimize his or her interference with treatment goals. The spouse can offer constructive input and feedback to the planning and implementation of treatment goals. More importantly, the spouse can provide requisite support for the patient while he or she is struggling with ambivalence about changing the drinking behavior. The remainder of this chapter is an elaboration of the spouse's role in motivational counseling.

Rationale for Involving the Spouse

The spouse can facilitate the motivational process in the following ways:

1. The spouse is allowed the opportunity to provide the patient with ongoing support for sobriety. Spousal support can be beneficial in helping the patient to become more committed and responsive to treatment. The spouse is encouraged to comment favorably on the patient's intentions and efforts to deal with the alcohol problem. It is expected that individuals provided with such support are more likely to sustain the benefits gained in the program.

2. The spouse can provide constructive feedback (i.e., information presented in a nonblaming manner) on the costs and benefits of the problem drinking behavior. In sharing concerns and expectations with regard to the drinking behavior, the spouse can become a powerful motivator for change. The underlying assumption here is that the alcohol-dependent person may become more committed to changing the drinking behavior when highly valued interpersonal relationships are threatened (Longabaugh & Beattie, 1985). For example, one client named John decided to "give up" drinking rather than cause further harm to his family, after listening to his wife, Joanne, discuss how the alcohol-abusing behavior had negatively affected the family milieu.

I should point out that it is not the intention of the present approach to provide intensive marital therapy; nor are spouses taught particular techniques or skills as conducted in cognitive–behavioral treatment.* These

---

*The use of motivational enhancement techniques does not preclude skill training for couples (e.g., changing communication patterns, reducing stress and anxiety, improving problem-solving skills, etc.). Some couples may lack the requisite skills to achieve the treatment goals, even though they are committed to resolving the presenting problem. In such instances, therefore, it might be appropriate to have motivational counseling follow skill training.

motivational strategies are aimed at encouraging the spouse to demonstrate support verbally and behaviorally, without providing specific training in order to accomplish these objectives. At the same time, the patient is asked to regard the spouse as one source of information to be considered among others (e.g., employer, legal advisor, friends, physician, etc.) in determining what to do about the drinking.

The Spouse's Role in Motivational Counseling: "Witness" versus Active Participant

How the spouse is utilized in treatment to influence the patient's decision to change will depend in part on the degree of interpersonal commitment between spouses to resolving the alcohol problem. In cases where the patient does not perceive spousal support as important in dealing with the problem, and/or the spouse has little or no investment in whether the patient attains sobriety, extensive involvement of the spouse may have little impact on subsequent outcome. In these situations, it may be useful for the spouse to become just a "witness" in the sessions; that is, specific input is *not* requested from the spouse in formulating treatment plans. In addition, the spouse is *not* asked to support decisions made by the patient. Instead, spousal involvement is limited to sharing and receiving information about the severity of alcohol problems. In contrast, in circumstances where interpersonal commitment is high, it may be beneficial for the spouse to play an extensive role in the motivational counseling sessions. That is, the spouse is asked to share relevant information in the planning and development of treatment goals; to collaborate constructively with the patient in determining how to attain the established goals; and, in general, to help promote the patient's commitment to change.

The manner of spouse involvement is also influenced by the degree of hardship for the spouse resulting from the drinking behavior (financial and legal difficulties, trouble with children, social isolation, etc.). The stress and impairment (depression, anxiety, sleeplessness, etc.) experienced by the spouse in attempting to cope with these alcohol problems may preclude her or him from becoming constructively involved in the motivational counseling sessions (Moos, Finney, & Cronkite, 1990). Therefore, it may be necessary for the spouse or other family members to attend first to their own difficulties before involving them in helping to instigate and sustain changes in the problem drinker. In such a situation, the spouse may need to be seen separately initially, for purposes of receiving support and concrete help for financial and legal difficulties as well as parenting issues (Zweben, 1986). At a later time, if warranted, the spouse may participate in the motivational counseling sessions.

Inviting the Spouse to Participate in Treatment

A patient is usually asked in the initial contact to involve the spouse in treatment. The rationale for involving spouses is presented. The patient is advised that the input of the spouse will be important in formulating goals and strategies, since changes the patient will be expected to make in relation to drinking and concomitant events will affect family members, and vice versa. If the patient appears to be hesitant about involving the spouse, then such involvement should be delayed until reasons are explored. Postponing such decision making allows the patient an opportunity to explore fully the potential benefits and consequences of spouse-involved treatment, and, in the long run, can help prepare him or her to work constructively with the spouse in the sessions. If no agreement can be reached concerning spouse participation, then the person should continue to be seen in individual sessions. Over time, the patient may become more agreeable to having the spouse involved in the sessions. Therefore, the issue of spouse attendance may be reconsidered at a later time in treatment.

In the initial session, you might comment favorably on the spouse's willingness to participate in the sessions. The rationale for the spouse's participation is again reviewed. Questions and comments are solicited from the spouse, in order to underscore his or her importance in helping to deal with the drinking problem.

Assessing the Spousal Support System

As mentioned earlier, in planning the interventions, you will need to consider the degree of positive regard and affection existing in the marital relationship. At the same time, you should determine whether the spouse is supportive of the treatment goals with regard to the drinking behavior. In addition, the present coping capacities of the spouse, in terms of his or her ability to participate in the conjoint motivational counseling sessions, should be evaluated. Information derived from standardized assessment measures such as the Revised Marital Relationship Scale (Zweben & Pearlman, 1983) can be used to assess the level of marital cohesion. The Significant Other Questionnaire (Longabaugh et al., in press) can be employed to determine the spouse's degree of support for the patient to overcome the alcohol problem. In addition, the Spouse Hardship Scale (Orford & Edwards, 1977) can be utilized to measure the number of alcohol-related difficulties currently experienced by the spouse. (For a full discussion on the utility of these assessment tools in treatment planning, see the references just cited.)

To gain a better understanding of the spousal support system, it is also important to examine the couple's interactional patterns. By observing interactions between the couple in the sessions, you can determine the degree of support available to the patient for changing the drinking behavior. The following questions should be kept in mind while observing the interactional patterns:

1. Are responses made by the patient to change the drinking behavior supported by the spouse?
2. Do comments made by the spouse concerning the patient's efforts or intentions to resolve the drinking problem seem to be exacerbating an already strained interpersonal relationship?
3. Is the spouse ready and motivated to make changes in his or her own everyday activities that might help to facilitate an improvement in the drinking behavior?

In acquiring a good familiarity with the couple's interactional style, you can develop a viable treatment plan for utilizing the spouse in helping to facilitate the motivational process.

Techniques for Spouse-Involved Motivational Counseling

Working with Supportive Couples

In a situation where both partners are committed to resolving the alcohol problem and where the nonalcoholic spouse's functioning has not been seriously impaired as a consequence of dealing with the problem, it may be suitable for the latter to be actively involved in building and strengthening a patient's commitment to change. The following strategies can be employed with such a couple:

Joining with the Couple

Initially, you should focus on creating a comfortable treatment environment; spouse and patient should feel free to share and explore concerns or questions about the need for alcohol treatment at this time. Efforts by the spouse to help the patient in the past should be affirmed. If appropriate, you should acknowledge and support steps undertaken by the spouse to initiate the treatment process. The spouse should also be complimented for his or her willingness to participate in the sessions. In attempting to join with the couple, you can ask the following:

Have you noticed any changes in your husband [wife] that you believe to be encouraging?

> Are you aware of times when your husband [wife] has been able to
> drink moderately or successfully abstain from alcohol? Explain.
> What have you found to be most helpful to your husband [wife] in
> terms of changing the drinking behavior?

In exploring these areas with the couple, you hope to instill an optimistic attitude toward change by reinforcing the patient's and spouse's beliefs about their ability to affect the drinking behavior positively.

Forming a Consensus about Treatment Goals

When the spouse is being asked to assist the patient in changing the drinking practices, it is important to forge a consensus between the spouses about the goals of treatment. Feedback on the assessment interview can be used to help formulate goals that are mutually agreeable to the partners. Information is provided for purposes of confirming or clarifying perceptions about the severity of the alcohol problems and the kind of treatment to be offered (e.g., abstinence-based approach). The assumption here is that such an understanding is essential for developing a consensus about the goals of treatment.

In presenting the material, attention is paid to using language relevant to the partner's education and background. A spouse may be asked:

> Is the material clear to you?
> Is anything unexpected?
> Do you agree?
> How do you see things differently?

By using techniques discussed in Part II of the book (such as reflective listening, clarifying, summarizing, taking a neutral stance, and avoiding arguments), you can obtain an agreement between the spouses about the goals of treatment. If a consensus cannot be arranged, it may be necessary to have further discussion about the unresolved issues in subsequent sessions.

Once an agreement is reached, the couple can begin to implement the necessary action steps to resolve the problem. The spouse can help build motivation by supporting the patient in his or her efforts to deal with the drinking behavior. For example, one spouse decided to join her husband each weekend at their summer cottage, a place where both spouses could relax without consuming alcohol. Another spouse suggested that she and her husband socialize only with friends who abstain or drink moderately.

Promoting Marital Cohesion and Satisfaction

Another aim of spouse-involved motivational counseling is to help the patient to draw upon natural helping relationships in supporting his or her desire and actions to deal with the abuse. Every effort should be made to enhance marital support and satisfaction, particularly between spouses who evidence strong interpersonal ties, in order to consolidate the patient's commitment to change (Edwards & Orford, 1977). Opportunities should be created to have the spouses confirm that a satisfactory relationship exists and to determine how to maintain or enhance marital cohesion during and after the course of treatment. Feedback on the assessment measures can be used to identify positive aspects of the marriage and to generate specific goals in relation to the marriage, such as improving the quantity and quality of marital interactions (e.g., spending more time in intimate activities, dining out, vacationing, etc.).

Dealing with "Difficult" Cases

When the Patient Is Resistant

The spouse can often play a significant role in helping a reluctant patient become more committed to change, especially if a satisfactory relationship is reported by the couple (see "The Spouse's Role in Motivational Counseling," above). As mentioned earlier, the threat of losing a supportive relationship can become a motivating force for change. The strategies below can be employed in a situation where the spouse is supportive of change while the patient remains hesitant or reluctant about modifying the drinking practices.

Eliciting Feedback from the Spouse. Feedback verbalized by the spouse can often be more meaningful to the patient than information presented by a practitioner. In requesting feedback from the spouse, the following line of questioning may be pursued:

How has the drinking behavior affected the situation at home?
Has anything changed to cause you to be more concerned about the drinking?

In conducting the feedback session, it is important to gauge the mood or state of the patient. There is a danger that the patient may begin to feel overwhelmed (i.e., "emotionally overloaded") by the spouse's negative feedback, and as a result may become even more resistant to change. Therefore, questions that may elicit a positive or supportive response by the spouse should be incorporated into the line of questioning. Such questions can be found in the earlier discussion on the technique of "joining." Having the spouse deliver these important messages can be valuable in motivating the patient to change. For example, one spouse pointed out in the session that her husband's inability to participate in family outings as a result of the drinking might be causing their children to become alienated from him. She also expressed concern about the stability of their marriage if the alcohol-abusing behavior did not change.

Exploring Alternatives with the Spouse. The spouse should be given the opportunity to explore other options in terms of dealing with the alcohol-abusing behavior if, despite your interventions, the patient refuses or is reluctant to recognize or address the presenting problem. At this juncture, it may be prudent for the spouse to "detach" herself or himself from the problem by allowing the patient to deal with the drinking problem in individual counseling. Otherwise, the responsibility for changing the drinking behavior may be shifted to the spouse. A spouse may be told:

> It can be frustrating when there is a disagreement between what your husband [wife] believes is best and what the program is recommending concerning the drinking behavior. In this situation you may have a number of options. You can keep coming to the sessions and talk about the drinking—an approach that has not had much success at this time. Yes? Or you can devote your energies to yourself and other family members while your husband [wife] is determining what to do about the drinking. Are you ready to do something different?

If the spouse agrees to try "something different" (i.e., discontinuing the conjoint motivational counseling), a plan should be developed with the spouse for carrying out these "alternatives" (e.g., attending Al-Anon, receiving individual counseling, etc.) while affirming his or her decision in this matter.

When the Spouse Is Resistant

As mentioned earlier, the involvement of a spouse in treatment may prove to be counterproductive if she or he appears to be uncommitted to change (Longabaugh et al., in press). It is important, therefore, to be sensitive to situations in which spousal involvement may seriously interfere with the motivational process. The strategies outlined below may be useful in preventing spouse disruptiveness.

Limiting the Spouse's Role to Information Sharing and Receiving. To minimize the spouse's negative impact on the motivational process, the involvement of the spouse should be limited to providing collateral information and acquiring knowledge about the severity of alcohol problems and the kind of changes that might be expected as a result of the patient's participation in the program. The interactions with the spouse should be restricted to clarifying relevant information about the alcohol problems and ensuring that the spouse has sufficient knowledge about the tentative treatment plans.

Maintaining a Focus on the Identified Patient. The focus should remain on the drinking partner in the sessions. The issues of how to attain and sustain sobriety should constitute the content of the sessions. Problems related to the marriage should be considered after the drinking behavior has been stabilized. Reframing, discussed in Chapter 8, may be employed in order to redirect the couple back to the individual's drinking behavior. Here is an example of such a reframe:

> I know that you are very concerned with you wife's [husband's] welfare. I am wondering whether your need to continue to talk about marital issues might be your way of protecting her [him] from facing the unpleasant struggle of changing the drinking behavior.

Despite your attempts to intervene, the couple may remain focused on interactional issues. If this occurs, it may be necessary to conduct the remainder of the sessions with the patient alone.

Limiting the Spouse's Input in Planning Treatment Goals and Strategies. In a situation where the involvement of the spouse may be having a negative impact on treatment (see "Assessing the Spousal Support System," above), little assistance is requested from the spouse in facilitating change. The spouse becomes primarily a "bystander" in the sessions. The spouse is not asked to share his or her thoughts or worries concerning the patient's plans for dealing with the drinking; nor is she or he asked to affirm any commitment made by the patient to modify the drinking practices. In general, the patient is asked to take full responsibility for examining and addressing the variety of concerns stemming from the abusive drinking behavior.

When Both Spouses Are Resistant

Couples who appear to be unresponsive to motivational interventions usually evidence a negative pattern of interaction. The spouses tend to blame, criticize, and harass each other in the sessions—a situation that can lead to increasing the patient's resistance to change, or worse, can cause him or her to leave treatment prematurely. Therefore, a primary objective in working with such a couple is to reduce negative interactions so that the patient will not be deterred from dealing with unresolved issues or conflicts about making a commitment to change. The strategies outlined below can be useful with these couples.

Reframing. Differences between spouses can be reframed as two different approaches to the same problem. Spouses' angry feelings can be redefined as (1) both spouses' firm commitments to their own solutions to the problem, and (2) demonstrations of concern for each other and for the future of the marriage if the drinking problem does not get resolved. In placing a positive connotation on the negative communication, you place the spouses in a more optimistic "frame" about their relationship, and thus they may become more amenable to resolving the problem.

Normalizing. The spouses are informed that their interactional difficulties may stem from residing in a stressful environment. They are told that living with stress is not unusual among families coping with a chronic disability, such as stroke, schizophrenia, or alcohol abuse. In normalizing these negative behaviors (e.g., excessive blaming), you can help to alleviate some of the anxiety and guilt that the spouses are feeling over their present situation, and thereby can contribute to the process of change.

Prescribing "No Change." The couple is advised to "go slow" in attempting to change the marital relationship. You can explain that, as a first step in dealing with the alcohol problem, the spouses may need to learn how to express and tolerate differences in each other without resorting to alcohol. In the past, alcohol may have served a protective function for them. It may have helped reduce conflict between each other and thereby to preserve stability in the household. In fact, you can point out to the spouses that their readiness to reveal these differences may actually be reflective of a strong commitment to sobriety—that is, they are now willing to *fight* rather than *drink*. Consequently, they may need to continue disagreeing or arguing in order to affirm their ongoing commitment to sobriety. Here is an example:

> Given the difficulties you have been living with, I do not believe that now is the time to make major changes in your relationship. It may be better just to keep on doing what you have been doing with respect to your marriage. (*The spouses have strong disagreements about a variety of issues.*) Sometimes the consequences of making a change in the relationship outweigh the benefits. What do you think might happen if you disengage from each other? (*Couple does not respond.*) In the past, feelings were expressed primarily while Gary was drinking. Consequently, the fighting right now may actually represent a "new beginning"—that is, a real willingness to reveal unpleasant emotions without

resorting to alcohol. Think about it, and let's discuss this further next week. OK?

Placing a positive connotation on the problem behavior can have a paradoxical effect on the couple (Haley, 1987). In this excerpt, the couple's resistance to change is reframed as compliance with treatment goals. The negative communication is redefined as a positive step toward resolving the alcohol problem. The counselor suggests that the couple may need to continue the arguing in order to sustain such improvement. Consequently, efforts to improve the marital situation while maintaining sobriety may signify "resistance" but may actually help promote the motivational process.

In sum, the motivational approach presented in this chapter is consistent with the principles outlined in Parts I and II of this book. This model, as applied to a couple, recognizes that the ultimate responsibility for change remains with the patient. Consequently, emphasis is placed in the treatment sessions on the patient's own decision-making capacities instead of relying on external motivators—namely, pressure from spouse, friends, employees, law enforcement officials, or others with respect to dealing with the drinking behavior. The primary role of the spouse is to assist the individual in generating his or her *own solutions* for change by providing constructive input and support, thereby helping the patient derive maximum benefit from treatment.

17

Reinforcing Robust Resolutions: Motivation in Relapse Prevention with Severely Dependent Problem Drinkers

STEVE ALLSOP

BILL SAUNDERS

Some Background

In early 1982, we were engaged in developing a research program to evaluate relapse prevention and management strategies. We were, of course, influenced by the work of Marlatt and his colleagues (Cummings, Gordon, & Marlatt, 1980; Marlatt, 1978), and indeed the experimental clinical program we initially favored was not dissimilar to that described by Chaney, O'Leary, and Marlatt (1978). Thus, the core of our program was originally envisaged as consisting of skills training to develop responses to high-risk situations.

In preparation for our investigation, we interviewed patients in an alcohol treatment unit (ATU—a specialist alcohol treatment service based in a psychiatric hospital) on the west coast of Scotland, eliciting from them information about recent "relapses." In the course of these interviews, we were struck by two observations. First, relapses were often reported as being enjoyable, even exciting; second, many of the patients' accounts indicated that they had taken active decisions to return to drinking, rather than having been overwhelmed by circumstances or situations. These impressions ran counter to the emphasis in the Marlatt model and the reports of counselors who often heard that relapses were the unfortunate consequence of breached defenses: "I couldn't cope," "I don't know what came over me," and so on. This observation—that clients actively set up and looked forward to their relapses—was also reported by Fulton (1983) in his investigation of the predictive value of "relapse fantasies." It seemed to us that the quality of the decision to change was as important in the relapse process as the high-risk situations people encountered. Rather than simply focusing on *how* to change, we also needed to focus on the *decision* to change.

Coincidentally, we were drawing similar conclusions from our teaching. One exercise we included involved asking participants to develop a model of why clients relapse. In designing this model, we asked participants to think of their own resolutions to change and what factors contributed to their success or otherwise. This emphasized an important point: that the processes involved in relapse are identical to those involved in the making and breaking of any resolution to change any behavior. Within these processes, decision making clearly has a crucial role: The quality of the initial decision to change has a direct bearing on the maintenance of that decision. Therefore, if we wanted to have any impact on relapse, we had to find a way of enhancing robust resolutions.

Fortunately for us, others in the addiction field were thinking about these issues, and indeed had given shape to them in ways that had clear clinical application. We were struck by the potential of motivational interviewing (MI), as described by Miller (1983), for enhancing robust decision making, and we made a decision to incorporate what we perceived as MI strategies into our program.

The Clinical Context

Our target group consisted of male problem drinkers attending the ATU. They were severely dependent, very heavy drinkers. In the 7 days prior to admission, the average consumption of the group was over 2,000 grams of absolute alcohol per week (approximately a bottle of spirits each day), with associated high levels of harm and social isolation. Most were unemployed and had a history of arrests for drunkenness, and more than one-third had liver damage. In order for patients to be able to take part in the program, we required that they be detoxified. This usually resulted in patients' attending the program 14 days after their last drink.

Although what follows is a description of a discrete section of a larger research program, it is important to stress that upon completion of the research, the techniques were adopted as standard clinical practice by the hospital staff. In addition, we continued to develop the techniques in clinical practice and other research, as outlined in Chapter 21.

The Program

In developing our clinical program we loosely constructed a model of behavior change, as outlined in Figure 17.1. In this model, we suggest that

FIGURE 17.1. A model of behavior change.

moving out of addiction behavior is a process that involves making an initial resolution to change, translating this into commitment, and then deploying strategies in line with this commitment. The maintenance of the resolution, we argue, is significantly influenced by lifestyle factors, especially the quality of life after change.

We have described the intervention program in detail elsewhere (Saunders & Allsop, 1991). However, in brief, it consisted of detailed assessment followed by eight 1-hour counseling sessions conducted over 2 weeks. The assessment included demographic information, descriptions of drinking patterns and related problems, identification of high-risk situations, and self-efficacy ratings. Although a substantial proportion of the counseling sessions was given over to performance-based strategies developed around problem-solving techniques, it was clear that an important first stage would require strategies that developed or enhanced a client's resolve to change. To this end, and using the Miller (1983) paper as a major reference point, we developed what we have called "resolution enhancement" (RE) exercises.

It was intended that the whole program would run on a platform of one-to-one counseling, with nurses (trained and supported by ourselves) acting as counselors. Early in the development of the procedures, however, we noted that working with two patients and one counselor had clear advantages. Each patient could act as a support or "buddy" to the other, and skills could be learned by modeling and observation. However, the initial stage of RE, lasting for approximately 40 minutes of the first session, involved one-to-one counseling to ensure that concerns could be explored in as nonthreatening a situation as possible. Other RE exercises, involving both patients, were conducted at various stages of the program.

The Meetings with Each Individual Patient

Introduction to the Program

Counselors commenced by describing the purpose and length of the program, followed by an explanation of the purpose of the session ("I'd like to try to explore how you see things just now"). It was noted that the patient would be joined by another later on ("After the first part of the session, I'll be asking John to join us, and then I'll explain where we go from there"). Confidentiality was stressed. The counselor noted that the first part of the session would take approximately 40 minutes and then, after a break, the second part (with the other patient) would last an additional 20 minutes.

A potential limitation of our RE exercises was that if concerns were not kept salient, the impact on behavior might be short-lived. Indeed, fading salience of the initial reasons for change may be a contributor to any relapse: Forgetting the pain may tempt people back in. This problem is especially relevant with a group whose memory functioning is often impaired. We therefore developed a manual that related to each session and consisted of self-completion sentences, with plenty of space for responses. For example, one page was headed: "Problems or concerns I have about drinking are _____." After establishing confidentiality, the counselor introduced the patient to the manual as follows: "You might find it useful to keep a record of the sessions. This may be a helpful reminder of what we come up with. It's yours to keep. You can refer to it or add to it at any time."

Eliciting the Positives

The counselor began the session by saying, "I'd like to start off by asking you about some of the good things about your drinking." Responses were summarized as follows: "So, you're telling me that the good things for you are . . . and . . . and. . . . Is there anything else?" Initially, this was used as a nonthreatening introduction to help the patient feel comfortable about talking. As we describe in Chapter 21, we later realized that this was an effective way to acknowledge and explore ambivalence.

Eliciting Concerns

Before we describe in detail the elicitation of the "other side" of the person's drinking, it is useful to note what we consider a crucial point: that simply and rationally extracting a list of costs and benefits was insufficient. These costs and benefits needed to have subjective values attached to them, and the values and concerns of the patients were far more important than those of the clinician. Two examples give substance to this observation.

One patient's records indicated that he and his partner were separating, his drinking behavior apparently being a significant contributor. He had also lost his job because of absenteeism and lateness. In relation to his health, he had sustained liver damage. Most clinicians associated with the case considered that the patient had a "classic case of denial"—an inability to recognize the reality of his situation. Closer examination, however, revealed that neither he nor his partner valued the relationship and even anticipated the separation with some relief (there was also a suggestion that both had lovers "waiting in the wings"). His previous job had been boring and tedious, and the termination included a substantial redundancy (severance) payment, which he was going to use to set up a small "market garden"—a personal ambition for over a decade. He did not understand the information given to him regarding his health. The tests might tell *us* that his liver was not coping well, but he had no subjective feedback about this— it had no personal meaning or relevance. In fact, his prime concern was his dog. Indeed, he eventually decided to quit drinking because when he did drink he neglected his pet, and this was the source of a great deal of personal sorrow. Thus what concerned the clinicians, what they valued, had little impact on the patient's behavior. What he valued did have impact.

Another patient arrived for counseling fresh from an alcohol education session that was run in the hospital. When asked, "'What sorts of problems do you think you might have with alcohol just now?", without pausing for breath he replied: "Marital, legal, housing, and health—heart disease, brain and nerve damage. . . ." This was an impressive array, perhaps, but it was devoid of any personal or emotional attachment for the patient. It was evident that one goal in RE would be to explore *concerns*, not just create lists of problems.

Consistent with Miller and Rollnick's suggestion that a clinician should avoid too immediate a focus on alcohol problems (see the discussion of the premature-focus trap, Chapter 6), we began this section by asking patients to describe general concerns: "OK, I'd like you to tell me about any of the things that might be problems or concerns for you right now." We found with our target group that patients immediately focused on alcohol. This may have been reflective of the extent and severity of alcohol-related harm in this group, the context of the treatment setting, or a combination of both. In addition, our introductory focus on "benefits of alcohol" may have "tracked" patients onto alcohol-related issues. Whatever the reason, we never encountered any difficulties with an early focus on alcohol. However, we concur with Miller and Rollnick that for other target groups (perhaps those less severely damaged and those in more generalist treatment settings), an early focus may be counterproductive.

Therefore, turning attention to alcohol-related issues, the counselor would ask, "What concerns might you have about drinking?" Occasionally a counselor would have to prompt a patient, but counselors were instructed to use broad examples:

PATIENT: I'm not sure what you mean.

COUNSELOR: Well, for example, some people are concerned about things to do with their health or relationships or finances. Do you have any concerns like these?

Conversely, patients' initial responses would often be very general (e.g., "Yes, I'm worried about my health"). In this situation the counselor always encouraged the patient to give a more specific response. Essentially, we considered it difficult to explore and express concern about a broad category, whereas it was easier if the counselor helped the patient to focus on some specific aspect. One useful way to do so was by encouraging patients to describe specific events in detail. Here is an example:

PATIENT: Well, finances are a worry.

COUNSELOR: In what way?

P: Well, you know, I just don't seem to have any money. I can't do anything. I can't even pay my bills.

C: Could you give me an example of when this caused you some difficulty?

P: Well, the last 2 months I've not been able to keep up my payments on the car. I'm going to lose it. And last week I couldn't even afford to buy petrol [gasoline].

C: How did you feel about that?

After exploring a concern in this way, the counselor would respond with simple reflection:

I can see how that might concern you. You're worried about being unable to pay the bills, and you might have your car repossessed.

The counselor then, in note form, wrote the concern on the whiteboard, checked with the patient that this was accurate, and then asked, "Is there anything else?" The counselor also regularly acknowledged the confusion or ambivalence experienced by the patient:

Being able to get about in your own car seems important to you. But at the same time you've spent so much of your money on drink that you can't afford it. Is this right?

Similar phrases would be used during minisummaries:

It seems like you feel two ways about this. On the one hand you've found . . . while on the other hand. . . . Other concerns you've expressed are . . . and. . . . Is there anything I've missed?

These minisummaries ensured that the counselor correctly heard what was being said, and were useful as a means whereby the patient heard his own concerns expressed back to him.

As described in Chapter 21, we did not develop a formal paradoxical interviewing technique until later. However, in training we had noted that counselors were easily convinced that patients had a problem. We therefore trained them to take on a role that was to some extent paradoxical. Thus, they attempted to have patients prove to them that a problem existed, rather than vice versa. The question "Why is that a concern for you?" was also useful in this regard. Indeed, in some cases, using such a question had a particularly powerful effect. An example from our program illustrates how the technique was applied.

COUNSELOR: What other concerns might you have just now?

PATIENT: (*Appearing unconcerned*) Well, I'm told my liver's damaged.

C: (*Clearly objective tone*) Does that concern you?

P: Pardon?

C: Does that concern you?

P: (*With a slight frown*) Yes.

C: Why?

P: *What*? What do you think? It's obvious. I'm going to die, you (*expletive*) idiot. Look, if I don't do something about my drinking I'm going to die. Do you think I want that? Of course I don't. I'm going to have to do something.

Those patients who had experienced more traditional confrontational responses to their situation were quite surprised at the methods used in the program. After being interviewed about his perceptions of the program, one patient said:

> I couldn't believe it. I'd never been asked what I thought before. There I was trying to tell this guy I had a problem. Like, what *I* thought was important.

Occasionally we employed the use of a mythical case study to elicit self-motivational statements. This case study included a range of concerns experienced by the imaginary person, and the patient was asked to identify what he thought this person might be concerned about. After exploring these for a little while, the counselor would then ask the patient whether he thought he had any similar concerns. We found this quite useful with some patients who might initially feel threatened. Introducing the subject in this way appeared to remove personal threat and encouraged a more comfortable atmosphere in which to begin exploring his own concerns.

Using Information from Assessment

When it appeared that the patient could think of no more adverse consequences, the counselor would offer relevant information that was available from the assessment. For example, the counselor might be aware that the patient's liver function tests were indicative of possible harm, or that a particular history of arrests was likely to result in a custodial sentence. It was stressed to counselors that such information should not be presented in a traditional confrontational manner, or indeed as some kind of objective reality. The patient was free to accept, reject, or modify, to be concerned or unconcerned. The counselor certainly should not attempt to "prove a point." The exercise was simply about raising awareness and providing the opportunity to explore and *perhaps* raise concerns. For example, the counselor might say:

> You may recall that a blood sample was taken the other day. I don't know whether this raises any concern for you or not, but it appears. . . . Does this concern you? (*If "Yes":*) Why?

The counselor would then summarize, providing the patient with the opportunity to add information to his manual.

The Future

The counselor then proceeded to elicit from the patient any concerns for the future:

> OK, we've looked at your present situation. If you were to continue drinking in the same way, what concerns might you have about the future?

The session then proceeded as described for current concerns. Exploring the future was important, especially in some cases. Although some patients appeared to be only moderately concerned about current events, they expressed a great deal of anxiety about *potential* future consequences of their drinking (e.g., "If I keep going like this I *know* my wife is going to leave me"). When future concerns had been identified and recorded in the manual, the counselor would draw together the whole session in a major summary:

> Let's see if I can pull all this together. The sorts of things you like about drinking are . . . and . . . and. . . . On the other hand, you're concerned about the fact that you're not as fit as you once were. This particularly worried you last month when you felt quite ill after going for a short bike ride—something you liked to do a lot in the past. You're also concerned about. . . . From the assessment, we talked about the possibility that you might go to jail. That didn't seem to bother you too much, but you were worried about the results of your blood test. . . . As far as the future goes, you're worried that some of these things will get worse, particularly your fitness and health. You're also particularly concerned about, as you put it, how much more of this your wife will take. Is that right? Is there anything I've missed or got wrong?

The first part of the session was then concluded, and the counselor advised that the next part would be conducted after a short break (1 to 1½ hours later) with the other patient. Counselor and patient negotiated that the latter would, in the break, spend about 20 minutes reviewing the record of the session and add anything that was left out. The responses to this last exercise were varied. Most patients did review their manuals, and a small number added to their list of concerns—one or two quite extensively. For example, one patient who was quite resistant in the first part of the session and who had come up with few concerns returned to the second part quite animated. He explained:

> Those questions you asked me. They really made me think. Nobody had asked me what I thought before. In fact, I'd never really thought about what bothered me. You really made me think. But you sitting there—it was hard to do with you there. Look at all this. It's like Pandora's box. Once I started I found lots of things. I'm going to have to think about all this. You know, I'm really going to have to do something.

As an aside, it is interesting to note that this patient had been in the unit several times before, was considered very resistant to change, and usually returned to heavy drinking within several days of discharge. He was followed up formally and informally over 18 months and was abstinent throughout this time. When we attempted to explore the factors associated with this change, he always replied:

> Those questions. Making *me* think. A large part of it was that. The first time anybody asked me what I thought so I had to think. And I realized things didn't look good. It was time to do something.

The Meetings with Two Patients

After the second patient had worked through the procedures and had been given time to review his manual, both patients were brought back together. Confidentiality was again stressed. Each was then asked to summarize his main concerns to the other, and was also asked to note any of the other patient's concerns that might be worries for him but not have been raised in the first part of the session. This technique was employed for several reasons: to help build up a recognition of common and distinct problems and concerns; to provide an opportunity to hear self-motivational statements again; and to pave the way for more "public" statements of intent.

Statement of Intent

After each patient had summarized his main concerns, the counselor asked:

I'd like you now to look over your manual and think for a moment. What are the main reasons you have for changing your drinking behavior?

Usually two or three major concerns would be identified, and these responses were reinforced by the counselor ("I can see how that might be a reason for you to think about changing"). The counselor then said:

What I'd like to do now is ask you to do a little homework. I'd like you to look over the day's work and carefully think through the reasons you have for cutting down, or stopping, your drinking. When you've done that, I'd like you to record the reasons in your manual.

From Resolution to Action

In the second part of the session on the following day, patients reported on their homework assignment and their main reasons for change. Patients valued this assignment and the opportunity to think through and hear their own statements of intent. The counselor summarized their reports:

OK, you both seem to have some reasons for changing your drinking. What we intend to do now is look at ways that might help you to do that.

The bulk of the remainder of the program then focused on developing coping skills. This procedure is described in detail elsewhere (Saunders & Allsop, 1991).

Reviewing Reasons for Change

A further component of RE was added in the eighth and final session. Patients were asked to reiterate their major reasons for changing. They were also introduced to decision matrices, which were included at the end of their manuals. These were based on those described by Marlatt and Gordon (1985). The counselor helped each patient to complete one of these, using it as an opportunity to highlight and explore ambivalence again:

> We can see some of the things that would encourage you to continue drinking heavily, and at the same time some of the things that would encourage you to avoid heavy drinking. If you find yourself feeling two ways about drinking, you might want to use this exercise to help you make your decision.

Although these exercises appeared to be a good idea, many patients found the matrices difficult to complete. We would suggest that a simpler method be developed for use when a counselor is not readily available to help a client complete them.

Self-Efficacy

Like other clinicians, we believe that the translation of resolution or intent into commitment and action is a function of three perceptions:

- My drinking or drug use is causing me problems (or there are things that I want and my drinking or drug use is preventing me getting them).
- If I change, things will get better.
- I can change.

Exclusive focus on the first perception may simply result in a client's believing that the situation is hopeless. Our experience was that RE should be followed by performance-based skills training, providing the opportunity for clients to change. It may also be necessary for clinicians to address how they can influence the environment to make it more conducive to change. These reflections are, of course, related to the target group we addressed. Those clients who have good internal and external resources may need very little assistance beyond changing their focus from "contemplation" to "action" (Biernacki, 1986; Billings & Moos, 1983).

Conclusions

Investigations of why people give up and why resolutions break down indicate that decision-making processes play a crucial role. Therefore, any technique that influences decision making, or that helps clients make more robust resolutions to change, is important in responding to the addictive behaviors. We believe that in our investigation we helped clients make more robust resolutions to change. We also offered a skills program that provided clients with both the confidence and means to change. The question now is this: What is the impact of the RE exercises on their own? To be able to answer this question we continued to develop the techniques, and this process we describe in Chapter 21.

Acknowledgments

Our clinical work described in this chapter was supported by a research grant from the Alcohol Education and Research Council of Great Britain. None of the work would have been possible without Vanda Brown, Pamela Marshall, Brian McCann, Sue McKenna, Brian McNamee, and Frank Rush. Thanks to Celia Wilkinson for comments on a draft of the chapter, and especially to Maureen Bright and Sandra Kelly for their word-processing skills and patience. Finally, thanks to Sandra Herrington for keeping work from our desk so that we could finish this.

18

Motivational Interviewing with Young People

GILLIAN TOBER

The aim of this chapter is to illustrate the application of motivational interviewing techniques to a growing clinical population—namely, young people (those in their midteens). The method used is an annotated verbatim report of a single motivational interview with a 15-year old girl. I conducted the interview at a community-based specialist addiction unit in England, funded by the National Health Service. Before presenting this interview, however, I should note that a number of factors peculiar to (or at least heightened in) this age group require some changes of emphasis in motivational interviewing. These factors are as follows:

1. *Time.* Interventions with young people, unless they are sources of fun or excitement (e.g., "Outward Bound" activities), are best planned on a short-term basis. As few as perhaps two counseling sessions may be appropriate. It is often claimed that motivational interviewing "takes a long time," but with increasing practice and the use of adequate preinterview information, the time taken may be greatly reduced.

2. *Low self-esteem and low self-efficacy.* Low self-esteem and low self-efficacy in young people will often be the results of a quite realistic perception that their views and desires are not taken into account in decisions that affect them. Rather than looking for examples of self-worth and mastery in their everyday lives, it may be more effective to create an opportunity for these feelings to be enhanced in the interview itself.

3. *Reactions to authority figures.* Expectations of disapproval and negative sanctions from people in authority are common among young people in difficulty. The opportunities afforded by motivational interviewing to enhance self-esteem and increase the clients' belief in their ability to have some control in their lives are likely to circumvent the traps of hostility and resistance resulting from the usual reaction to authority figures.

4. *The need to apply motivation to change at other levels.* In young people it is often the case that there is little evidence of dependence on a

substance, or much in the way of objectively identifiable substance-related physical or neuropsychological damage. The substance itself may be less relevant than the acting-out behavior. Often several substances will be involved. The dangers accrue from the riskiness of the behavior, but equally a greater amount of risk-taking behavior is considered quite normal and healthy in adolescence than in later adult life. These factors add up to a lessening focus on the problems of the substance use itself and a greater focus on problems in the social and interpersonal spheres. Third-party concerns and reactions may constitute as serious a problem as any actual substance-related effects. It is often the case, therefore, that the counselor needs to move between different levels of change, focusing on motivation to change at the level of social functioning or interpersonal relations in order to create the motivation to change at the substance use level.

5. *Peer group influences.* The drinking or drug taking often falls within the norms of behavior of a particular subculture and to some extent is reinforced by acceptance into a peer group. The counselor must take care not to be drawn into this ready-made opportunity for denying that there is a problem by repeatedly focusing on the unique circumstances and self-identified problems of the individual case.

Setting and Biographical Details

Lisa was nearly 16. Her mother had asked the local social services department to take her into care 8 months prior to this interview, describing her as uncontrollable. Lisa would steal money from her mother's purse and disappear for 3 days at a time, not attending school and being unable or unwilling to account for her whereabouts upon her return. Her mother claimed that Lisa was causing a great deal of family disharmony and threatening her second marriage (the mother had remarried 2 years earlier), as there were constant arguments in the home.

Lisa was first moved to a children's home; then, when she left school after 2 months and commenced a youth training program, she was moved to a hostel with 24-hour supervision. She had established a routine of not returning from work on Friday when she finished at lunchtime. She would reappear at the hostel late Saturday or Sunday and report to the hostel staff that she had been drinking. The staff referred her to a specialist addiction unit through a letter containing the aforementioned details. An appointment was arranged and Lisa was invited to attend, which she did, accompanied by her social worker. As the counselor, I requested, first of Lisa and then of the social worker, that I should see Lisa alone. Since it is the basis of the motivational interview that the client's contributions be guided by the counselor, it is advisable not to have any mediating influences. Unless there is more than one client (e.g., a couple, a family, etc.), it is preferable to conduct the session on a one-to-one basis.

The referral letter contained sufficient information to obviate the need for further information gathering at this stage. Had this not been the case, I would have requested the social worker to attend the first 5 minutes of the interview, in order to clarify the current situation and the reasons why the hostel staff had requested Lisa to be seen. This would have required a change in the opening sentences of the interview.

The Interview

Opening

In the interview excerpts that follow, the counselor (myself) is abbreviated as "GT"; the client (Lisa) is abbreviated as "LS."

GT: Good morning, Lisa. Thank you for coming to the addiction unit. Tell me, what can I do for you?

LS: I don't know. I didn't ask to see you.

GT: Who did ask you to see me?

LS: Don't know. Me social worker, probably.

GT: And what does he think the problem is?

LS: Staying out at weekends—not knowing where I am.

GT: So why did he ask you to come to *this* place?

LS: Because he thinks I drink too much.

Commentary   The aim in the opening sentences of such an interview is to get the word "alcohol" or "drinking" mentioned by the client and not by the counselor. In this way, the client is the one offering it for discussion; the counselor avoids the trap of the client's actively avoiding mentioning it or avoiding responding to the counselor's mention of it. A useful way to bring about the client's mentioning it is to ask for other people's perceptions of the situation.

Eliciting Concern

GT: And what do *you* think about your drinking?

LS: (*Shrugs*)

GT: Perhaps you could tell me about your drinking so I can get some idea of why it's a problem for your social worker, but also so we can see whether or not it's a problem for you.

LS: I only drink at weekends. I don't drink in the week, and me mates, they drink with me, and no one's bringing them to this place.

GT: You only drink at weekends. Could you describe a typical weekend to me—say, last weekend?

LS: Friday lunchtime when we get off work, we go to the pub.

GT: You go out with people from work.

LS: Yeah, that's what I'm saying. I don't drink by meself. I drink with me mates, so if I've got a problem, they've got one too.

GT: Could you go on describing the weekend?

LS: We stay in the pub till it closes at three, then we get a bottle of cider* and take it to me mate's house. Her mother works.

GT: So you'd be spending the afternoon drinking.

LS: Yeah, and in the evening we go to another pub and clubs after that.

GT: So you are drinking late into the night.

LS: Yeah, we might get a carry-out and go to someone's house after that.

GT: OK, Lisa, I am getting a good picture of your drinking on Fridays. You say you go straight out from work and drink through the afternoon and evening, and sometimes through the night. It must be difficult for you to remember how much you have to drink. Do you have any idea?

LS: (*Shrugs*) I just carry on till me money's gone.

GT: And how much money is that?

LS: It's me pay from work.

GT: Is that a week's pay?

LS: Yeah. Sometimes I have some left on Saturday, though, so we go out again and get some more to drink.

GT: And what about if there is none left? Does that mean it was all spent on alcohol on Friday night?

LS: I suppose so. Once me friend told me someone had nicked some money off me and I didn't even know.

Commentary This was Lisa's first expression of any concern about the consequences of her drinking, and it emerged spontaneously. In order to make progress in the interview, the next step was to focus immediately upon this expression of concern.

*alcoholic.

GT: Are you saying you don't even know because you can't remember what happens when you've been drinking?

LS: Yeah. Sometimes I don't remember how I got to where I am when I wake up. Me mates tell me all sorts of things about what I did, and I don't know whether they're just winding me up.

GT: That must be very unpleasant for you.

Dealing with Resistance

LS: Yeah. I hate it. But they've been with me all the time, so they must drink as much as I do. It's just they don't have social workers and all that.

Commentary This was the third time Lisa alluded to her friends' possibly drinking as much as she does, by way of attempting to claim that people were making an unnecessary fuss about her. This was an attempt to deny that she had an alcohol problem by blaming other people for singling her out, and to minimize the problem by equating her drinking with that of other people (see Chapter 8). However, in the same sentence she expressed a concern—namely, that she "hated" not remembering what happened. This provided an opportunity to reinforce the expression of concern about the drinking, but *not* the denial (by ignoring the latter part of the statement). The next step was to explore whether she had other concerns.

GT: So you have said that you hate not remembering what happened the night before. Tell me if there is anything else you dislike about your drinking.

LS: Well, I don't really like the stuff that much—do you know what I mean? But it gets me out of me head, than I don't think about not going home. You know, drugs can do that, but they ain't just across the road. I don't like spending all me money on alcohol; I mean, I don't like having none after I've stopped drinking. I get in trouble at the hostel for scrounging money for cigs and coffee and all that.

Summarizing

GT: OK, Lisa, you've told me two or three things about your drinking that *you* don't like: You don't like forgetting what you have done, not knowing how you ended up where you did, although you do want to get out of your head and forget about not going home. You don't particularly like alcohol, but it's "there," so it's the easiest way to get out of your head. And you don't like ending up with no money, whether it's because you spent it or because you were robbed.

LS: (*Nods*)

GT: These are all things that concern *you*. And would I be right in thinking that some of these are the same worries that your social worker had—namely, not knowing where you are on Friday night, and spending all your money so you have nothing left for the rest of the week?

LS: I suppose so. I just thought he didn't like me.

Commentary　This summary of concerns emphasized the negative side of Lisa's drinking, while not completely ignoring the positive side for her. The positive was de-emphasized through its juxtaposition with, and noted *after*, the negative side. Also, the summary returned to the original question: "What does your social worker think is the problem?" This was not an essential move, in that it could have shifted the emphasis away from Lisa's concerns. It was inserted, however, because it was becoming clear that negotiations with the social worker would be imperative; I was therefore attempting to show that there was some common ground.

The interview thus far had elicited a list of problems about Lisa's drinking. It was now time to consider ways to strengthen Lisa's perception of these problems—in other words, to identify the *conflict* in Lisa about her drinking and to strengthen the perception of this conflict.

It is my experience that objective feedback of the results of physical and psychological tests (Miller, Sovereign, & Krege, 1988) is not a useful technique with many young people, for several reasons. First, it is often very difficult, as it was in this case, to get anywhere near an accurate account of intake (whether of alcohol or of other drugs). Second, there will often be a short history of misuse, so that physical or neuropsychological impairment is unlikely to show up on tests. The most useful instrument is a decisional balance sheet, where the client can list the immediate advantages and disadvantages of continued drinking; he or she can come back to this when he or she is beginning to think about change.

GT: OK, Lisa, I'd like us just to jot down what we've said so far so we can keep a record of where we are at.

Good things	*Bad things*
Get out of my head	Forget what I did
Forget about not going home	Don't like taste
Don't have to go back	Get robbed
to the hostel	Spend all my money

GT: Is there anything else?

LS: Well, if I carry on drinking, I can't go home. Me social worker says I've got to stop drinking first.

Building Up Motivation to Change

GT: OK, Lisa, now tell me what it is that makes you go out on Friday after work and not go back to the hostel.

LS: Well, me mates are going out drinking after work, like, you know. And then I don't want to go back there, it's not home.

GT: Are you saying you dislike it at the hostel?

LS: It's all right sometimes. It's just not home. The others don't stay long, and you have social workers coming in telling you what to do and hostel staff on your back. I just wanna go home to me mam [mother].

Commentary   These questions elicited an expression of motivation to change at the level of family functioning (Prochaska & DiClemente, 1984); this motivation to change now needed to be applied at the substance use level. One way to do this was to express empathy and concern about the family and social situation, and *also* about Lisa's description of her drinking.

GT: So let's check up what it is you want. You are saying that you want to go home to live with your mother rather than stay at the hostel.

LS: Yeah.

GT: But isn't it the case that soon you will be old enough to live wherever you choose?

LS: Yeah, except me mam won't have me back to live at home unless the social workers tell her that I don't go out getting drunk any more, and me social worker says he won't even talk about it till I stop getting drunk at the weekend.

GT: So your mother is concerned about your drinking and wants you to stop. Is that right?

LS: Yeah.

GT: Tell me what she doesn't like about your drinking.

LS: She says it makes me rough, and steal, and she gets worried 'cause she don't know where I am.

GT: So your mother is worried about some of the same things as you are—namely, that you don't know where you get to when you are drinking, and you use up all your money and need more. You are saying that because of your drinking *then* you were taken into care, and because of your drinking *now* you can't go home again.

LS: (*Nods*)

GT: (*Adds these factors to the decisional balance sheet and shows it to Lisa*)

LS: (*Nods*)

Eliciting Expression of Desire to Change

GT: How is this looking to you? Have we got everything on it? (*Shows Lisa balance sheet with "Can't go home" added to right-hand column*)

LS: Makes drinking look pretty stupid.

GT: Well, the way you've described it to me, it sounds like it might feel like the only thing to do at the time. So, really, you've got to come up with a better idea.

LS: (*Looks at decisional balance sheet and smiles*) If you take away Fridays I wouldn't drink.

GT: Given that we can't take away Fridays, what else could you do?

LS: Get out of the hostel.

GT: And how do you do that?

LS: By stopping drinking.

GT: So this must seem like a very difficult situation to you. You drink because you don't want to go back to the hostel, and you have to stay at the hostel because you drink.

LS: If I stopped drinking, though, I could go home.

GT: Is that what you want to do?

LS: Yes.

GT: Well, Lisa, it seems from the letter I got from your social worker that you were drinking *before* you left home.

LS: Yeah. It was me new dad. I didn't like him. He'd get drunk and throw us out of the house in the middle of the night. He was nasty when he wasn't drinking, too. It was like being in the army, told off all the time for me clothes and everything I did.

GT: I see, so it felt quite unpleasant to be at home.

LS: Yeah, when he was there.

GT: So what would be different if you went home now?

LS: Me mam told me he's left and he ain't never coming back. She won't have him.

GT: So you are saying that things have changed at home—the problems have been removed, so it won't be difficult not drinking when you get home. It's just a problem how to stop when you are still at the hostel.

Commentary   At this point, it seemed important to know whether the details of the situation were as Lisa describes them: Was her mother prepared to have her at home if she stopped drinking? Had the stepfather really left home? Did the social service department see the situation in the way Lisa described it? This was important because, although Lisa had expressed a number of concerns about her drinking, a major concern was the way in which it had contributed to the disruption of her family life, and so reparation of this disruption was high on her list of motivating factors to change. The motivation to change the course of events in her family life would be applied to the process of expressing a commitment to stop drinking and strengthening that commitment. However, I did not want to stop the interview at this stage in order to check the accuracy of Lisa's account, because I did not think we had achieved enough to finish the interview. Although the discussion had elicited concern about Lisa's drinking, statements of a desire to change her social situation, and an expression of a desire to stop drinking, I felt that the initial interview must get to the point of establishing a concrete plan of action, so that Lisa would have achieved something tangible by coming to the appointment. I therefore took a chance that Lisa's account of her mother's position and the position of the social service department was accurate.

What were the relative advantages and disadvantages of taking this chance? During the interview, Lisa had visibly relaxed her initial stiff posture; her statements were less offhand and defensive in tone; she was clearly becoming convinced that she was being listened to. There was now opportunity to bolster her self-esteem, which was low, as was her belief in her ability to influence events and decisions that affected her. Hitherto, her drinking had been the only means of influencing what happens, albeit in a way she did not want. I decided that bolstering Lisa's self-esteem and self-efficacy were essential first steps to planning any change. Rather than accomplishing these goals through specific gestures and cognitive restructuring, I intended to accomplish them through the whole process and outcome of the interview. In the event that Lisa's account was not accurate, I might lose credibility by being "taken in," and any plan we made clearly would not work. The safeguard for the risk of taking this chance was to refocus on the drinking as quickly as possible and to make a plan that could be applicable to a variety of situations.

GT: So am I right in saying that you think you will be happier when you get home and you won't need to get out of your head?

LS: Yeah, there'll just be me and me mam and the little 'uns.

GT: OK, well, perhaps we can worry about first things first. Are you ready to make a plan for stopping drinking in the hostel?

LS: How do I know it will work?

GT: Because we are going to work out a deal with the social worker and with your mother—one where it's agreed that if you stick to your side of the bargain, he and your mother will stick to their sides of the bargain.

LS: OK.

Commentary   This statement made it clear that I was going to take an active role in this bargaining by being the mediator. I was not asking Lisa to go and set it up herself; this active helping illustrated to Lisa that we were embarking upon the proposed strategy together. Implicit in this was the assumption that if the plan did not work, we would try a different strategy. This was construed as a partnership, however temporary.

The dialogue continued. First, I asked Lisa what would be a reasonable time for her to stop drinking before she was offered the opportunity of going home on a trial basis. She offered 4 weeks; she said she wanted a trial weekend at home at the end of this period. If this worked, she wanted trial weekends at home once a fortnight for another 4 weeks, with the agreement that she would then be allowed to go home. This would take her beyond her 16th birthday.

Next, the planning focused on the details of how Lisa would avoid drinking on Friday. She got paid on Thursday. She would arrange with the hostel worker *she liked most* to open a bank account and pay in the money saved after buying some provisions for the week. She would buy these on Thursday evening and would have no more than her bus fare in her pocket on Friday. She would arrange to meet someone she did not work with on Friday at lunchtime, and together they would go to meet her social worker for a progress report. She would arrange to play table tennis in the early afternoon with someone from the hostel. She decided to organize a tournament—they were all "into" table tennis at the moment. The winner would get to choose the evening video, would take all the entry fees, and so on. The principles of drawing up the action plan were as follows:

1. The suggestions were Lisa's; they were *concrete* suggestions of *realistic* activities that she would gain some reward for doing. She could check up that she had accomplished each part of the plan.

2. She had a number of accomplices, and had some trust in each of them. I negotiated the whole scheme with Lisa and all other parties; her "chosen" hostel worker (the one she liked) would carry out the interim plans with her, and her mother and the social worker would ensure that the plan,

if successfully executed, would have the intended consequence (i.e., she would go home).

The details of the plan highlighted the need to ensure that the change strategy was acceptable (it was suggested entirely by Lisa, with only some prompting and direction from me), accessible (I checked that it was possible to carry out the plan and that there were no obstacles), appropriate (I checked that the alternatives suggested would not in themselves introduce new problems), and effective (all parties agreed that successful completion of the plan would bring about the desired goal, which was for Lisa to avoid drinking in the short term in order to go home in the longer term).

Sequel

I convened the meeting to activate this agreement. Separately, I arranged a further appointment with Lisa once the plan was underway. If the plan failed, it was to be decided why it failed: Was the problem accurately defined? Was Lisa's motivation to change adequate? Were the plans made concrete, realistic, and achievable? If the plan succeeded, the second appointment would constitute a further motivational interviewing session, whose aim would be specifically to focus on the drinking itself, using the decisional balance sheet (this time to highlight the advantages of continued abstinence and the disadvantages of relapse).

Discussion

In some ways Lisa's case was an "easy" one; she had been dealt with quite harshly, with coercive measures that afforded scope for negotiation. Coercive measures have been shown to be effective in precipitating change (Prochaska & DiClemente, 1984; Vaillant, 1988) and it is likely that some will already have been applied in the case of young people seen for substance misuse problems. Clearly, when these measures have already included removal to a penal institution for compulsory detention, negotiation may not be possible; where they *are* negotiable, however, the opportunity to use them in planning and decision making should not be missed. The coercive measures are construed as negative consequences of the drinking or drug taking and will be essential in completing the decisional balance. As mentioned above, negative consequences in the shape of objectively identifiable drug-related harm may not be evident, because it is likely that the client will have a short history of use and show little dependence. Not only may the "punishment" that followed the drinking or drug taking be the dominant negative consequence, but it may well be the one the client cares most about.

In Lisa's case, there were nonetheless a number of consequences of her drinking per se that she disliked. These were important in strengthening the conflict about drinking, and also in any subsequent negotiation for continuing abstinence. It may be argued that too much weight was put upon Lisa's motivation to move back home—that if stopping drinking were a means to this end, it is unlikely that the decision would be sustained beyond the accomplishment of this objective. This was clearly a risk that needed to be addressed; it was addressed here by the arrangement of an appointment after the first part of the plan had been accomplished. It should be emphasized, however, that Lisa would have learned a number of important things that might assist her in sustaining motivation to be abstinent. Her self-esteem was boosted by the focus in the motivational interview on Lisa's needs; her self-efficacy was enhanced by her position as decision maker and focus of the negotiating procedure; and successfully carrying out her side of the plan would illustrate to her that drinking was *not* the only way she could affect other people's responses.

19

Alcohol Use and Goal Hierarchies: Systematic Motivational Counseling for Alcoholics

W. MILES COX
ERIC KLINGER
JOSEPH P. BLOUNT

Alcoholics who can lead emotionally satisfying lives without alcohol tend to stay in recovery. Current studies show that people are more resistant to relapses if they do the following:

1. Report more positive changes and fewer negative changes in their lives (Tucker, Vuchinich, & Harris, 1985).
2. Develop substitute activities (Vaillant, 1983, p. 190).
3. Express greater life satisfaction (Polich, Armor, & Braiker, 1981, p. 86 ff).
4. Encounter environmental factors that enhance their satisfaction with life (e.g., Moos & Finney, 1983).
5. Experience less frustration of goal-directed activities or deal with these frustrations more effectively (Marlatt & Gordon, 1985; Sanchez-Craig, Wilkinson, & Walker, 1987).
6. Have more nonalcoholic activities they enjoy and fewer constraints that inhibit access to them (Vuchinich & Tucker, 1988).

For these reasons, a treatment technique that specifically helps alcoholics to find sources of emotional satisfaction as an alternative to drinking alcohol would appear to be highly promising. Nathan Azrin and his colleagues recognized this possibility a number of years ago when they developed the community reinforcement approach for treating alcoholics (Azrin, 1976; Hunt & Azrin, 1973). They helped alcoholics develop a rewarding life without alcohol by teaching them the skills needed for marital and social interactions, finding jobs, and enjoying recreational activities. Considering the phenomenal success of their approach, it is surprising that it is not more widely used.

At the same time, it is important to recognize that whether or not recovering alcoholics can find emotional satisfaction through nonchemical means is not due simply to the "good" and "bad" events that befall them. Rather, it is due largely to the way their life realities mesh with their motivational patterns, such as (1) the kinds of goals they set (e.g., whether these focus on healthy, positive incentives that might serve as alternatives to drinking alcohol); (2) the manner in which alcoholics strive for their goals; (3) negative incentives that cause them discomfort and that they want to remove; (4) incentives whose pursuit will almost certainly prove frustrating or unsatisfying; and (5) subgoals that they have formed (or have failed to form) as steps toward obtaining positive incentives or removing negative and frustrating incentives. Our approach, therefore, focuses on changing alcoholics' *motivational patterns* that interfere with their developing a satisfying life without alcohol.

We use the term "motivation" in a technical sense different from its common meaning, which would seem to refer to alcoholics' "unwillingness" to change. Thus, like Miller (1985b, 1989a), we view alcoholics' lack of motivation for treatment as a characteristic that treatment personnel can change. Patients' motivation depends on the relative amount of satisfaction they expect to find by drinking alcohol, as compared with the emotional satisfaction they expect to obtain nonchemically. A "motivational intervention," therefore, is one that shifts the balance between these sources of satisfaction, thereby increasing "the probability of [patients'] entering, continuing, and complying with an active change strategy" (Miller, 1985b, p. 88). Our "systematic motivational counseling" (SMC) technique focuses specifically on patients' motivation for recovery.

Motivational Model of Alcohol Use

The SMC technique is based on our motivational model of alcohol use (Cox & Klinger, 1988, 1990), which in turn is derived from a more general motivational model (Klinger, 1975, 1977, 1987b). The model recognizes that alcohol use is fueled by complex biological, psychological, and environmental influences. Nonetheless, the final common pathway to alcohol use is *motivational*.

Alcoholic drinking occurs when factors that contribute to the decision to drink (e.g., an individual's positive biochemical reactivity to alcohol) strongly outweigh factors that contribute to the decision *not* to drink (e.g., positive, nonchemical incentives with which drinking interferes). The alcoholic may, for instance, have an inadequate number of sufficiently positive incentives to pursue; the available incentives may have lost positive value through habituation or the build-up of opponent processes (Solomon, 1980); or the alcoholic's pursuit of positive incentives may be unrealistic or inappropriate, making goal attainment unlikely. Alternatively, the alcoholic's positive goals—even if appropriate, realistic, and sufficient in number— may conflict with one another, making goal attainment unlikely or impossible. In addition, a patient whose life is burdened by aversive incentives may be unable to make progress toward removing these noxious elements. Due in part to the alcoholic's ineffective motivational patterns, drinking alcohol may be his or her most attractive source of emotional satisfaction. Our intervention for alcoholics seeks to increase their nonchemical sources of emotional satisfaction that can replace drinking, thereby shifting the balance in favor of decisions *not* to drink.

Assessing Motivational Structure

In order to study the interrelationships between people's pursuit of nonchemical incentives and their motivation to use alcohol, we constructed a questionnaire to assess motivational structure. This instrument, the Motivational Structure Questionnaire for Alcoholics (MSQ-A), was developed to measure subjects' *current concerns* (Klinger, 1975, 1977, 1987b). It asks alcoholics to name and describe their current concerns, and to make judgments about the goal pursuit corresponding to each concern along various dimensions that will reveal the structure of each patient's motivation. These judgments include, for example, (1) the alcoholic's degree of commitment to pursuing each goal; (2) the amount of positive affect the alcoholic expects to experience upon reaching the goal, as well as the amount of unhappiness associated with reaching it; (3) the perceived probability of success and amount of time urgency associated with pursuing the goal; and (4) the impact of continued alcohol use on attaining it.

From a patient's completed MSQ-A, we derive quantitative indices that indicate (among other things) the value, perceived accessibility, and imminence of the alcoholic's goals, as well as patterns of commitment to these goals and the nature of the patient's desires and roles in regard to them. From these indices, we construct a profile to depict each patient's motivational structure. In separate papers (Cox, Klinger, Blount, Thaler, & Thurman, 1989; Klinger, 1987a), we have presented data on the reliability and validity of these and other MSQ-A indices. The MSQ-A test booklet and response sheet and information about the quantitative indices are available from us.

The Counseling Technique

Our initial studies using the MSQ-A with alcoholics indicated not only that people's motivation to use alcohol is linked to their incentives in other life areas, but also that their motivation to *change* their drinking behavior is likewise tied to these incentives (Klinger & Cox, 1986). Therefore, we went on to develop a counseling technique for alcoholics, based on the MSQ-A, that seeks to modify directly the motivational basis for problem drinking. The SMC technique focuses on the alcoholic's nonchemical incentives, aiming to maximize the emotional satisfaction that he or she derives from these incentives, and thereby to reduce the motivation to seek emotional satisfaction by drinking alcohol. SMC is a highly individualized procedure. Thus far we have used it only in individual counseling, but in the future we plan to explore the feasibility of using the technique in a group format.

Getting Started Working with Patients: Issues to Address Early

During the first session, it is important to get to know your patient and establish rapport, building a therapeutic relationship. Nevertheless, even this early, you can begin to understand the patient's motivations for drinking. Attempt to establish (1) why drinking alcohol has a high incentive value for this particular patient, and (2) what it is about the nonchemical incentives in this patient's life (and the patient's goal striving for incentives) that motivates him or her to bring about affective changes by drinking alcohol.

You need to address several issues during the early sessions with a patient. Although the relevance of each issue will vary from one patient to another, you should explore each of the following questions:

What Are the Circumstances Surrounding Your Patient's Entering Treatment?

A good opening line is "What brings you into treatment?" The intent in asking this (or a similar) question is to determine why the patient has entered treatment at this particular time. This information can serve as a powerful early lever for identifying characteristics of the patient's motivational structure; it may also provide examples of obvious relationships between the patient's nonchemical concerns and the motivation to drink alcohol, before you are able to identify more subtle relationships as you proceed with the SMC technique. You will want to establish, for instance, whether your patient initiated the decision to enter treatment, or whether somebody else (e.g., a spouse, the courts) was the immediate impetus.

Patients often finally decide to enter treatment and do something about their alcohol problem only after some crisis has occurred vis-à-vis their nonchemical incentives. Common reasons include an actual or threatened divorce, separation, or dismissal from a job, or having been "ordered" into treatment by the courts. Even if there is no single event that patients can link to the decision to enter treatment, they have usually reached the general conclusion that things are going so badly in their lives as a result of their drinking that they feel they must do something about it. In beginning to work with a patient, start by identifying those incentives whose actual or potential loss moves your patient to change his or her drinking patterns.

What Is Your Patient's Perception of the Problem?

Patients differ widely in what they perceive their "problem" to be, what they think caused it, and how they expect to "cure" it. People solve problems in accordance with the goals they conceive of as affected by the problem. Therefore, the way they formulate the problem—in other words, the way they conceptualize the goals that the problem frustrates—plays an integral role in their efforts to rebuild their lives. Therefore, SMC must assess their goal formulations and work from there.

It is also important to determine what patients think "caused" their problem. For instance, believing that they have inherited a disease may interfere with patients' ability to see relationships between their use of alcohol and the status of their nonchemical concerns, and this perception needs to be changed. It is also important to know what patients perceive "treatment" to be. If, for instance, they believe themselves to be passive recipients of some kind of "fix," this perception needs to be changed, for patients are active participants in the SMC technique. They make decisions jointly with the counselor, and actively participate in homework that the counselor assigns. These issues all bear on the *stage of change* that the patient is in. According to Prochaska and DiClemente (1986), in changing an addictive behavior, patients pass through identifiable stages, including precontemplation, contemplation, determination, action, maintenance, and relapse. The different components of SMC correspond with varying relevance to the various stages of change that your patient may be in. For example, if your patient is in the contemplation stage, then the diagnostic functions of giving and interpreting the MSQ-A may be particularly important, whereas if your patient is in the action stage, the most applicable part of SMC may be developing goal ladders.

What Is the History of Your Patient's Use of Alcohol?

Exploring your patient's history will help to clarify the relative contributions of biological, psychological, and environmental factors to his or her motivation to drink, and the ways in which these have changed during the course of the patient's drinking career. One way to explore a patient's history of alcohol use is in chronological order, beginning with the very first drinking occasion and what the experience was like. For instance, was it strongly reinforcing, or did he or she become sick? (One patient whom we recently saw reported that in the beginning he found drinking aversive and had to "teach" himself to drink in order to socialize with his peers.) How did your patient's alcohol use progress from then until the present? When did your patient first notice that he or she had a problem with alcohol? What problems has drinking alcohol caused? Has your patient sought help for a drinking problem previously? What does your patient perceive that he or she gets out of drinking (e.g., why does he or she do it, and how has this changed during the course of the patient's drinking career)? In order to answer the last questions, try to identify specific examples of how your patient's motivation to use alcohol has been related to his or her nonchemical incentives. Consider how this information may affect your patient's goals for treatment.

What Are Your Patient's Goals for Treatment?

Explore the patient's goals with regard both to drinking and to changes in other aspects of his or her life. Does the patient intend not to drink at all, or just to cut down? When patients say that they simply want to moderate their drinking, how realistic and appropriate is that goal? To start helping patients rebuild their lives, two questions addressed to patients can yield fruitful information: (1) What is it about your life that you would like to change? (2) What is it about your life that would have to change in order for you not to drink again? At the end of the first session, it is a good idea to have your patient complete a balance sheet (Janis & Mann, 1977; Marlatt, 1985) whose columns consist of the gains and losses that the drinker expects to accrue from continued drinking, and whose rows consist of the gains and losses that the drinker expects to accrue from not drinking. Later on, when your patient begins to waver in the commitment not to drink, the balance sheet can serve as a tangible reminder of the advantages of not drinking.

What Are the Sources of Your Patient's Motivation for Drinking?

Which variables from the motivational model are the most salient ones for your patient? After the initial interview(s), try to draw some preliminary conclusions as to the patient's motivation for drinking. For one thing, you might determine whether there is any evidence that the patient is genetically predisposed to problem drinking. For example, do other members of the patient's family have an alcohol problem? Did the patient get a strong positive biochemical reaction to alcohol on the first drinking occasion? In addition to biological factors, you should also identify the psychological factors that have promoted your patient's drinking. For instance, has your patient drunk to enjoy the camaraderie of others, or has he or she drunk alone? Has your patient drunk more heavily when he or she was in situations (e.g., in the military) that promoted drinking?

Changing Alcoholics' Motivational Structure

There are two major phases of the SMC technique. First, we assess motivational structure with the MSQ-A, constructing a profile for each patient. Second, we undertake a multicomponent counseling procedure to modify patients' motivational structures, helping them to develop meaningful lives without alcohol. In this section, we describe the SMC components and provide clinical examples to illustrate how we have applied each component. The technique does not adhere to a prescribed session-by-session agenda that is identical for all patients. Although certain components of the technique are in fact utilized with all patients, other components may or may not be, depending on patients' particular motivational structures. The sequence in which the individual components are used may also vary.

Preliminary Counseling Components

Review of MSQ-A. Together with your patient, review the information he or she has provided on the MSQ-A, so that you can understand the patient's goals and concerns and can assess whether the ratings of them are accurate, appropriate, and realistic. Patients, for instance, may not be aware of how much value they actually have invested in their goals, and so they may have underestimated or overestimated it on the MSQ-A. Or patients may have unrealistically optimistic or pessimistic beliefs about their ability to achieve their goals. Or they may accord too much or too little value to their goals for the degree of emotional satisfaction that they will ultimately derive from them. The discussion between you and the patient helps to identify such discrepancies and enables your patient to begin to re-evaluate inaccurately described, inappropriate, and unrealistic goals. The discrepancies also serve as "flags" for the subsequent counseling sessions.

Discussion of one patient's completed MSQ-A revealed, for example, that he placed great value on acquiring material possessions, wanting especially to have a new car and expensive clothes. Although these incentives might be emotionally satisfying in their own right, this patient exaggerated the extrinsic implications of having them, believing that people would rebuff him if he did not drive a new car and wear expensive clothes. Because currently he could not afford these material possessions, he avoided social contacts. This pattern, in turn, interfered with a number of the patient's interpersonal goals that he had named on the MSQ-A (e.g., "obtain true, honest friends," "keep friendly toward people," "establish a healthy, caring relationship") and promoted his tendency to drink to cope with his present loneliness. As the patient said, "I might as well be drinking if I have to live like this." Hence, one goal of the subsequent counseling sessions was to help the patient place less value on material possessions and to help him reach his *interpersonal* goals without first acquiring a new car and expensive clothes.

Analysis of Goal Interrelationships. People get more satisfaction from life if their personal goals facilitate rather than conflict with one another (Emmons, 1989). In fact, conflict among goals is associated with high levels of depression and other negative affect, neuroticism, and psychosomatic complaints (Emmons & King, 1988). In order to examine interrelationships among your patient's goals, help the patient complete a goal matrix, similar to the Personal Strivings Matrix used by Emmons (1986) and the Personal Projects Matrix used by Palys and Little (1983). When you identify appropriate and realistic goals that facilitate the attainment of other such goals, encourage your patient to pursue them. When, on the other hand, you identify goals that interfere with the attainment of other goals, you will need to help your patient find a suitable resolution of the conflict.

For instance, one patient's completed goal matrix revealed that one of his goals, "get back to having a meaningful relationship with a woman," critically facilitated the attainment of a number of his other goals (e.g., "spend more time with my younger sister," "keep commitments," "maintain watching my weight," "prevent my emotions running amok," "accumulate some money in the bank," "become more dependable," "begin exercising more," "get back to going out more," "get my father to have a better understanding of alcoholism"). With the support of the subsequent counseling sessions, this patient did, in fact, attain his goal. He established a meaningful relationship with a woman, whom he later married, and with whom he continued to have a very satisfying relationship. Attaining this goal, moreover, had the expected positive impact on attaining the patient's other goals.

Goal-Setting Components

Goal setting constitutes an integral part of SMC. This includes setting immediate and long-range goals, formulating plans for reaching those goals, and reviewing patients' success or lack of success in reaching goals that have been set. There are three goal-setting components: (1) setting treatment goals, (2) constructing goal ladders for these and other long-range goals, and (3) setting goals for patients to complete between counseling sessions.

Setting Treatment Goals. From the long-range goals that your patient has named on the MSQ-A, help the patient put together a list of appropriate, realistic, and nonconflicting goals toward which he or she wishes to work during the course of counseling. The goal of attaining abstinence is specifically dealt with at the time that treatment goals are set. Because the goal of giving up alcohol itself is a conflictual goal for the alcoholic, explore with your patient the motivational conflicts associated with reaching it. After completing the list of goals, you might use "goal attainment scaling" (Smith, 1981, pp. 429–434) to set expected levels of outcome for each goal and, later, to evaluate the degree to which each goal was actually achieved.

Constructing Goal Ladders. For each of your patient's major long-range goals that have been judged to be appropriate and realistic and not to conflict significantly with the achievement of other such goals, construct a "ladder" that consists of a series of hierarchical subgoals—the necessary steps leading to attainment of the patient's final goal. As discussed below, during subsequent counseling sessions, the patient works to achieve successive subgoals from the ladders.

Setting Between-Session Goals. Throughout counseling, help your patient formulate activities directed at goal attainment to undertake between counseling sessions. There are two kinds of these activities: (1) healthy activities that are gratifying in their own right and that are sources of immediate pleasure, and (2) activities aimed at reaching subgoals that serve as steps toward achieving the patient's long-range goals. Between counseling sessions, your patient works to achieve successive subgoals from his or her goal ladders (described above) that will lead to the ultimate goal. At each session, discuss the list of goals that was constructed at the previous session and the progress (or lack of progress) made toward achieving them.

Subsequent Counseling Components

Having identified appropriate and realistic goals for your patient to work toward and motivational structures to change, help the patient reach those goals and change the style of his or her goal striving by using the following counseling components:

Improving the Ability to Meet Goals. Help your patient to improve his or her ability to reach the appropriate and realistic long-range treatment goals that have been identified through the preliminary counseling components described above. There are two ways in which this objective is achieved: (1) by identifying subgoals underlying the achievement of long-range goals, and (2) by identifying and developing skills needed for achieving these subgoals. Within the framework of cognitive–behavioral therapy (e.g., Kendall & Hollon, 1979), give your patient "homework" assignments for trying new behaviors and testing hypotheses related to them.

One patient wanted to "become a good father," a goal that needed to be operationalized. Thus, this patient was helped to define specific, concrete behaviors (e.g., "get dressed up and go to a nice restaurant with my wife and daughter") that to him would indicate that he was being a good father. The same patient wanted to "buy a house," but to him this goal seemed financially out of reach. Accordingly, after exploring with him different neighborhoods and types of houses in which he might live, the patient's counselor helped him devise a plan to save enough money for a down payment on a house.

Resolving Conflicts between Goals. Help your patient explore ways to resolve conflicts between goals identified through the goal matrix. This objective is achieved by finding alternative means for the patient to satisfy one or the other (or both) of the conflicting goals.

One of our patients completed a goal matrix indicating that his goal to perform well in his present job strongly interfered with his goal to complete his associate's degree at a vocational school. This patient held a full-time job as a mechanic, to which he devoted considerable energy. Consequently, he was able to take only one evening course per semester, had very little time to study, and had received below-average grades in most of his courses. Having explored with his counselor various alternative ways to achieve his two goals, the patient eventually decided to take a half-time job that would permit him to devote more time to his studies and complete his degree requirements in a reasonable length of time.

Disengaging from Inappropriate Goals. Help patients disengage from goals when (1) a conflict between goals is unresolvable, (2) a goal is judged to be unachievable, or (3) a patient overvalues a goal that does not contribute much to the satisfaction he or she derives from life. After you and your patient have jointly decided that a goal is inappropriate, help the patient to endure and work through the immediate pain and frustration accompanying relinquishment of the goal.

One patient whom we saw was recently divorced from his wife but was still very much emotionally attached to her. Despite the fact that there was no chance for the couple to be reconciled (the wife, in fact, was about to remarry), the patient was obsessed with thoughts of reuniting with his former wife. Requiring considerable emotional support, this patient was strongly encouraged to put his past behind him and to find new sources of pleasure to replace his loss.

Identifying New Incentives. One way in which we help patients discover new incentives is by exploring with them the pleasurable activities that they have enjoyed in the past and the activities that they imagine would bring satisfaction in the future. We also attempt to identify the categories of activities that seem to bring them satisfaction and to find other activities in each category in which the patients might enjoy engaging. Finally, we also use the Pleasant Events Schedule (Lewinsohn, Muñoz, Youngren, & Zeiss, 1978) to help patients identify pleasurable activities to try.

One patient in our program, now that he had given up drinking alcoholic beverages, thought that he would enjoy trying new and interesting nonalcoholic beverages. He decided that each week he would go to a "fancy" grocery store and choose either some gourmet coffee beans to sample or an exotic fruit (e.g., a mango or papaya) with which to make a nonalcoholic drink.

Shifting from an Aversive to an Appetitive Lifestyle. When people are mostly absorbed in avoiding negative, aversive goals (e.g., failure, divorce, humiliation) rather than in achieving positive, attractive goals (e.g., accomplishment, good times, and friendships), they are more likely to attempt to cope by using alcohol than if the reverse were true (Klinger, 1977). Thus, you need to help patients eliminate or reconceptualize negative goals in their lives and replace them with positive, attractive ones. For example, the goal "get rid of my weight problem" might become "develop an attractive, healthy body through good nutrition and exercise." "Avoid making a fool of myself around other people" could be reformulated as "learn to enjoy having other people appreciate me for the person I really am." "Escape from my present boring job situation" could be recast as "find a job where I really enjoy going to work."

Re-Examining Sources of Self-Esteem. People with alcohol problems often hold high standards for achieving goals that are not inherent sources of emotional satisfaction, and they are unduly harsh on themselves when they are unable to achieve their high standards (Cox, 1983; Klinger, 1977). Therefore, you should help your patients to find new sources of self-esteem related to goal attainment, to eliminate sources of self-condemnation, and to develop the capacity to forgive themselves when they have not attained a goal.

For example, one of our patients stressed how important it was for him to "keep on striving to be even better." He pursued this goal relentlessly, and in doing so neglected other incentives that he might have pursued and enjoyed, thereby placing himself in a perilous "all-or-none" situation. Discussion revealed that the patient's constant striving to improve himself had apparently arisen from his relationship with his grandfather. The grandfather had always worked hard to "make something out of himself," had become a "self-made man," and had successfully instilled his own values in his grandson. Wanting to live up to his image of his grandfather, the patient felt compelled always to better himself. Accordingly, the patient's counselor strove to help him not to equate his self-esteem with accomplishments and to find new ways to feel good about himself.

Conclusions

The SMC technique, as we currently practice it, is an adjunct to an inpatient and aftercare alcohol rehabilitation program. We have used the technique with more than a dozen patients during brief counseling, usually lasting about six sessions. We have seen four additional patients for extended counseling that ranged from several months to 2 years. Patients have responded favorably to the technique, and have often spontaneously told us that merely completing the MSQ-A helped them to articulate their important concerns in life and served as an impetus for them to prioritize their goals. Moreover, during the course of the counseling sessions, our patients have appeared to make progress toward rebuilding their lives through nonchemical goals and incentives. Except for one patient who experienced a "slip" (which turned out to be a temporary setback), none of our patients resumed drinking for the duration of our contacts with them. Despite the promise that the SMC technique holds, it now awaits formal, systematic evaluation.

20

Dealing with Alcohol Problems in the Community

TIM STOCKWELL

The reflections contained in this chapter are mainly based on my experiences of applying motivational interviewing (MI) procedures while working as a full-time member of a community alcohol team (CAT) in southwest England. It is likely that if the principles and techniques so clearly outlined in this volume are properly understood, they can help us to perform better in almost any situation that involves negotiation and attempts to influence another person to take a particular course of action. I am convinced that as a result of learning and applying MI principles, I am now better at negotiating access to confidential research files, supervising student dissertations, and even buying secondhand cars (to name but a few personal fringe benefits!). Perhaps of slightly greater relevance to this chapter is my conviction that MI principles are of immense value to a community-based practitioner concerned with the treatment and prevention of alcohol-related problems—a view that I now attempt to substantiate.

Community Alcohol Teams

A few words of explanation are in order about the nature of that peculiarly British animal, a CAT. In the United Kingdom in the 1980s, it is fair to say that CATs became the radical alternative to the traditional inpatient, medically dominated, and mainly abstinence-oriented services that had been available for people with drinking problems since the early 1960s. Some of the radical features of CATs are as follows:

1. The guiding philosophy in most CATs is that specialist alcohol services will only ever directly encounter a tiny minority of a community's alcohol-related problems (Orford, 1987).

2. As a consequence, most CATs have attempted to make their services as *accessible* as possible to problem drinkers and those concerned about problem drinkers—whether they be family members, friends, general prac-

titioners (GPs), social workers, or representatives of other agencies. Direct treatment services have been made more accessible by being centrally located, open to self-referrals, available at no or minimal waiting time, and often offered to clients in their own homes (Stockwell & Clement, 1989).

3. In addition, CATs have attempted to influence primary care workers to take a greater interest in the role alcohol plays in the presenting problems of their clientele. The great majority of people who experience alcohol-related problems will come into contact with a GP, probation officer, or other community agent; they will often be prepared to discuss their drinking with such an agent, but will refuse to attend a specialist clinic perceived as being "just for alcoholics." Most CATs have offered training to primary care workers to help them identify and respond better to people with alcohol-related problems. There is encouraging evidence that such efforts can be successful (e.g., Clement, 1987).

4. Most CATs have espoused the goal of intervening early in a problem drinking career, and even with heavy drinkers who are merely "at risk" of developing subsequent problems. As a consequence, they have usually advocated controlled drinking for many of their clients (Stockwell & Clement, 1989).

5. All CATs have been multidisciplinary, and several have included representatives of multiple agencies. It has been the exception rather than the rule for them to be under the direction of a medical practitioner, and several have experimented with "democratic" management structures (Stockwell & Clement, 1989).

The Relevance of Motivational Principles to Community-Based Alcohol Work

Rather than just describing in general terms how MI principles are of crucial relevance to CAT work, I attempt to illustrate their value in relation to the resolution of two common dilemmas facing community-based alcohol workers.

Dilemma 1: Focusing on a Client's Drinking versus Other Life Problems

The question "To what extent should I focus on a client's drinking and to what extent on the client's other life problems?" will be familiar to anyone who has worked in a specialist alcohol and drug treatment or counseling setting. I would argue that this issue needs to be handled with special sensitivity when the client is at the stage of "precontemplation." A successful community-based service will contact many such individuals in a *proactive* way—whether by screening for problem drinkers in a general hospital, persuading primary care workers to ask their clients routinely about their alcohol use, or assisting relatives to influence a problem drinker in their family toward change. In each instance, a drinker is likely to see other life problems as more pressing and more in need of resolution than any negative consequences of the drinking. To illustrate this dilemma, I now present an account of such a case that is based upon a former client of mine, though with certain details altered to protect his identity.

John was a man in his 50s who had once held a senior management post in a large multinational company. Because of a personal dispute, he had been fired; at about the same time, his marriage of 15 years had come to an end. Always a heavy social drinker, he began to drink a bottle or more of spirits some days, and never a day passed without his having at least four pints of beer. He was unable to regain a job at his previous salary or level of seniority. He was unable to accept the authority of his managers in the jobs he did gain, and he expressed his resentment by drinking on the job, causing scenes, and (inevitably) being fired once more. He was first persuaded to attend for counseling by his *de facto* wife of some 4 years. She was threatening to leave him if he didn't "do something about his drinking." The first occasion on which John attended counseling (about 4 months before I saw him) he was extremely resentful about any suggestion that his drinking constituted "a problem," and he failed to attend his next appointment. The question in this case was as follows: What, on MI principles, should be the focus of the counseling session at John's second contact?

In this instance, the counselor John saw on the first occasion happened to be someone who naturally adopted both a confrontational and an abstinence-only approach. Because this counselor was also considerably younger than John, this approach was particularly likely to antagonize him, with his recent history of being managed by younger and less well-qualified people than himself. (It should be noted that this particular counselor was highly successful with many other, different clients!) I was allocated to see John when he contacted our service on the second occasion. Adopting an MI standpoint, I focused on the following issues both in making requests for information and in subsequent summarizing:

1. Initially, I felt it to be important to acknowledge the pressure exerted on him by his *de facto* wife to attend for counselling. This was achieved by inquiring about the process of deciding to make the appointment ("Who first suggested your coming here?" "What led up to your wife suggesting you came?" "How do you feel about being pressed into attending a place for counseling problem drinkers?"). I also used some mild paradox, along these lines: "So would it be true to say that the only difficulty caused by your drinking is your wife's insistence that you drink too much?"

2. It was evident that John's recent heavy drinking bouts had occurred in response to situations he had difficulty with at work. A good proportion of the first interview was spent in exploring these situations, the events leading up to them, and his subsequent reactions to them. Rather than offering any opinions or judgments, I focused on his emotional responses and their link to his drinking (e.g., "What effect did the alcohol have on the anger you felt toward your boss?").

3. It seemed important to acknowledge the extent of John's status and achievement earlier in his career if he was to trust me (e.g., "It must be demeaning for you to have better qualifications than your boss," or "What sorts of responsibilities did you have in your previous [high-status] job?").

4. I did my best to show John that I understood that in his view drinking was not causing any difficulties. I did this mainly by not focusing very much at all on his alcohol use and focusing more on his work and relationship problems.

No further appointment was made after this session; to have done so without John's requesting it would have been to insist covertly that he really did have a drinking problem. I did, however, suggest instead that he might like to consider whether he would like to discuss his work and relationship difficulties with me further, and for him to contact me if he did. Two weeks later he did request this, and I suggested he come along with his *de facto* wife. During their subsequent attendance at several counseling sessions (conducted with the assistance of a female colleague), the nature of their relationship difficulties was explored. During the course of these discussions, the full extent of John's drinking emerged. He eventually acknowledged the severity of this—in fact, he had developed a severe degree of alcohol dependence—and he decided to stop drinking completely for a period of time, in order to help resolve the problems between him and his wife.

This example is generally representative of my experiences with various clients who attended the CAT with varying degrees of unwillingness. The main point I wish to make is that John was not an uncommon kind of client: He was resentful about being "forced" to see a counselor, and any mention of the word "alcohol" would trigger off an angry reaction. Confrontational tactics by the first counselor only served to make him angrier. Before it was possible for him to discuss his drinking openly, it was necessary to defuse his assumption that an alcohol counselor was yet another person who would attribute all his problems to drink. It should be noted, however, that his wife's confrontational tactics (viz., threatening to leave him) were essential to his contacting our service in the first place. I have frequently observed that constructive confrontation by another person—whether a family member, a friend, or a professional "helper"—can combine very well with a more gentle, nonjudgmental MI style from a neutral counselor.

The short answer to this first dilemma, then, is that you should focus upon a client's alcohol (or other drug) use to the extent that the client permits you to. I do not side with those who believe that alcohol use is nearly always irrelevant, since it is only symptomatic of "deeper" psychological problems. I have argued elsewhere that, according to the research evidence, whatever "deep" problems may have preceded a period of problem drinking are almost invariably worsened by the heavy drinking, and hence the alcohol use is ignored at a therapist's peril (Stockwell & Bolderston, 1987). However, it is often strategically necessary to downplay, minimize, and even totally ignore the client's alcohol use early in counseling, in order to establish sufficient trust to do so effectively at a later stage.

Another point that this example suggests is the importance of acknowledging the existence of the client's right *not to change the drinking at all*— and, also, not ever to darken the doors of the alcohol counseling agency again! To press an ambivalent client into agreeing to a period of counseling may only set the client up to fail.

Dilemma 2: Accepting a Referral from a Primary Care Worker versus Providing Guidance to the Worker

While investigating the cause of Mr. Tate's gastritis, Dr. Stevens, his GP, conducted a number of tests, including one of liver function; she discovered an elevated gamma-glutamyltransferase (GGT) score of 160—indicating the early signs of (probably reversible) alcoholic liver damage. At his next visit to the office, Dr. Stevens relayed this information to her patient, who flatly denied drinking more than 2 pints of beer a day. Dr. Stevens phoned the CAT for advice on how to refer Mr. Tate for counseling about his drinking. The question here, then, was this: How should the CAT respond?

As the counselor "on call" that day, I spoke to Dr. Stevens and rapidly decided that this was an instance in which a referral to a specialist agency such as ours would be disastrous. She agreed that it was unlikely that Mr. Tate would willingly see a member of the CAT, even in his home or at her office. She said that she had known him as a patient for over 2 years and would be interested in attempting brief counseling with him if someone could give her guidance about how to go about this. I made an appointment to see her the next day to discuss the case in more detail.

Carefully avoiding some of the psychological jargon associated with Prochaska and DiClemente's (1986) model of motivation, I suggested that Mr. Tate had probably never considered his drinking to be a serious problem, even if he *was* drinking more than he said he was. It was possible that he was someone who was highly susceptible to liver disease at even a low level of intake. Were he drinking a great deal more than he was admitting to, he might still be able to reduce his drinking to a harm-free level, after a period of abstinence to allow his GGT to normalize. We agreed on the following strategy, which was to put into action at Mr. Tate's next visit to the office: It was to be explained to him that he was one of those unfortunate people who are highly susceptible to liver disease. As a consequence, her medical advice should be that he stop drinking completely for an experimental period of 2 weeks, to see whether his abnormal liver function would recover.

When Dr. Stevens presented this advice to Mr. Tate, he expressed dismay and amazement at this suggestion, but promised to try. Two weeks later the test was repeated, but his score was slightly higher than before—175. When this was relayed to him in a carefully nonjudgmental way, along with the question "How did you manage about not drinking?", he admitted he had found it too hard and that in reality he was drinking at least 5 pints of beer a day. Following a further consultation with me, Dr. Stevens helped him to complete a drinking diary for the previous week to get a clearer picture of this. She then outlined some options: that he could continue to drink if he chose and risk liver disease; that he could stop drinking completely and for good; or that he could stop drinking until his GGT reading was within normal limits. If he chose either of the latter two, Dr. Stevens indicated that she would offer to perform liver function tests on a regular basis to check on his progress. Mr. Tate decided to try to stop completely for the next 2 weeks, which he succeeded in doing. In fact, he subsequently maintained virtual abstinence until he had a normal liver function result some 6 weeks later, whereupon he resumed drinking, but at a much lighter level than before.

Anyone who has carefully read the principles of MI outlined earlier in this volume will readily recognize where they were applied in this case. I have usually found primary care workers to be very receptive to these basic principles—whether relayed during an individual consultation as in this example, or in a formal training situation. In this instance, the principle of avoiding the twin traps of "labeling" the client and getting involved in an argument were successfully avoided by the GP. Instead of simply conducting a medical investigation and telling the patient the result, the patient was invited to take part in an experiment in order to see whether a particular course of action would improve the liver function result. The various options (including that of not changing) and their consequences were spelled out to Mr. Tate, and he was made to take responsibility for choosing a plan of action. The medical nature of the mild liver damage gave Dr. Stevens far more credibility than an alcohol counselor would have had. Her acknowledgment of the possibility that he *was* really drinking as little as he initially said avoided the possibility of an argument about this. An attempted referral to the CAT would have been interpreted by him as tantamount to a diagnosis of alcoholism.

Mr. Tate's case is similar to those of many other mildly dependent heavy drinkers who see GPs for relatively minor problems, which are often caused by their drinking. Referral to a specialist agency not only may be unnecessary, but may be positively harmful. The most appropriate and acceptable (to the client) person to intervene will usually be the GP himself or herself; very often, a brief intervention with a few follow-up visits is all that is required (Anderson, 1987).

Summary and Conclusions

I have suggested that resistance to changing a problematic drinking pattern is frequently encountered both directly and indirectly by community-based alcohol workers. Prochaska and DiClemente's (1986) model of motivation to change, and Miller's principles of MI, are particularly helpful to the task of dealing with this resistance. I believe this to be especially true when attempting to assist primary care agents to work more effectively with drinkers—a major function of CATs. It has been well documented (e.g., Clement, 1987; Shaw, Cartwright, Sprately, & Harwin, 1978) that primary care workers tend to have a pessimistic view about the value of addressing their clients' drinking; that is, they show "low therapeutic commitment" (Shaw et al., 1978). However, what is rarely acknowledged is that the bulk of their clientele who are adversely affected by drinking will be classifiable as "precontemplators." Thus having high expectations of being instantly effective by means of drug therapy, intensive counsling, or even brief advice will quickly lead to disillusionment. The MI approach teaches us not to underestimate a drinker's reluctance to change (or even to discuss his or her drinking openly), and offers a range of techniques for dealing with this reluctance as a necessary precursor to tackling the drinking itself.

Of equal importance is the applicability of MI techniques to the unwilling GP, social worker, or other primary care worker (i.e., a worker who is unwilling to discuss or respond to a client's drinking). Each group experiences genuine difficulties in doing this, which have to be acknowledged and dealt with if such workers are to be persuaded to develop a more positive attitude and effective response to alcohol-related problems (Lightfoot & Orford, 1987).

21

Motivational Intervention with Heroin Users Attending a Methadone Clinic

BILL SAUNDERS
CELIA WILKINSON
STEVE ALLSOP

"But," said Steve Rollnick, "your view of motivational interviewing is idiosyncratic." These words confirmed our past, sneaking suspicions that what we thought constituted motivational interviewing was not necessarily what everyone else thought it was. Once we had had the opportunity to attend separate workshops run by Bill Miller and Steve Rollnick, it became very apparent that instead of being motivational interviewing adherents, we were deviationists (albeit accidental and amicable ones). In our clinical and research work—ostensibly work on motivational interviewing—we had unwittingly evolved a different *modus operandi* and understanding of motivational interviewing.

For us, motivational interviewing had become a distinct intervention, a cluster of useful strategies that could be deployed in therapeutic work to test out, assess and augment a client's potential for change. This conceptualization was especially noticeable in our teaching, where we described motivational interviewing as a "bolt-on" extra, which any clinician could usefully incorporate into his or her therapeutic stance. What was evident in Miller's and Rollnick's workshops was that for them motivational interviewing was a counseling *style*, an overall way of interacting with clients, rather than an adjunct to one's overall therapeutic approach.

It is perhaps important to stress again that we are not captious deviationists. Rather, we are teachers, researchers, and clinicians who have evolved, from Miller's (1983) seminal paper, a way of working with problem drug users that we feel does encapsulate the central tenets of "motivational interviewing" in a pragmatic and portable form. However, given that our use and understanding of motivational interviewing can be viewed as "idiosyncratic," we ought perhaps to differentiate our deviation by labeling what we do as "motivational *intervention.*" This gives emphasis to the different focus of our endeavors, and stresses that the strategies outlined below do constitute a discrete therapeutic package that can be of considerable value when incorporated into one's counseling format.

The Nature of Our Research

From this perspective we undertook a controlled evaluation of motivational intervention in a Western Australian methadone clinic, in which 122 clients were randomly allocated to receive either a motivational or a placebo ("educational") intervention. The fact that we viewed motivational intervention as a counseling component rather than a counseling style was clearly shown in the study design, in which clients received two discrete sessions of motivational work—the first about 1 hour long, and the second a follow-up session 1 week later of some 15–25 minutes. This brief motivational intervention was given in addition to the routine counseling offered by the clinic, and the research allowed us to test the impact of this intervention against the control (educational) procedure. The results, which we believe to demonstrate the value of this approach, are reported in detail elsewhere (Saunders, Wilkinson, Philips, Allsop, & Ryder, 1991).

The purpose of this chapter is to outline the key principles on which the two sessions of motivational intervention were based. In summary, the therapist worked according to a therapeutic agenda that included the following seven areas:

1. Assess the client's perception of the good things about heroin and other drug use.
2. Facilitate the generation of the client's inventory of the less good things about the behavior.
3. Elicit the client's current satisfaction with her or his lifestyle, vis-à-vis that previously envisaged and that anticipated for the future.
4. Have the client enunciate which, if any, of the elicited problems are real concerns to the client.
5. Compare and contrast with the client the benefits and costs of continuing the behavior (a type of cognitive review of the current situation).
6. Highlight and reflect on areas of greatest concern and discrepancy, thereby generating discomfort for the client with the current behavior (an emotional review of drug use and related problems).
7. Elicit and agree on future intentions regarding the behavior.

It is important to stress that although this was the clinician's working agenda for motivational intervention, the various areas of work were not rigidly demarcated. Thus an examination of, for example, less good things could easily flow into and involve aspects of other areas of the agenda.

It is relevant to comment briefly on the clients who were involved in this study. All were "new" attenders at the clinic (i.e., they had not been on the methadone program in the previous 3 months), and all reported that heroin use was their primary drug problem. Males constituted 65% of the sample, and the average age was 28. Approximately half of the subjects were married or in *de facto* marital relationships, and one in four were in full-time employment. Approximately 80% had left school at year 10 (i.e., at 15 years of age), and their average age at first use of heroin was 19.

Part of the research assessment involved completion of the stages-of-change questionnaire developed by Prochaska, Velicer, DiClemente, and Zwick (1986). This showed that at the time of admission 6% of the client group were "precontemplators" (i.e., untroubled users), 38% were "contemplators," 38% were in the "action" phase, and a surprising 17% were in the "maintenance" phase. It must be stressed that all of the clients in the experimental group complied well with the motivational intervention; indeed, many wished to extend the session beyond the time allowed. It is possible that this perhaps unusual degree of cooperation by clinic-attending heroin users was due to so few of them being precontemplators. We also think that having the sessions conducted by someone who was a researcher, and not a member of the clinical team and thus not responsible for ongoing management, may have prompted more open disclosure of the problems, concerns, and benefits of drug use. It has to be noted also that the counselor conducting the interviews was highly skilled in the application of motivational intervention, and quickly established good rapport with the clinic clients and staff.

The remainder of this chapter is given over to examples of clinical dialogue (derived from our research study and other clinical work) relevant to each area on the therapeutic agenda, with each being prefaced by a rationale for working in this way.

The Good Things about Drug Use

As noted in our preceding discussion (see Chapter 17), we originally included questioning regarding the good things about drug use as an empathic opening stance, which we hoped would put the respondents "at ease." Our experience with problem alcohol users indicated that many of them welcomed the opportunity to talk of the good things, since an overwhelming burden of their clinical contact was to talk only of the gloom and doom of drinking. We also found that in addition to establishing rapport, such an opening quickly indicated the nonjudgmental perspective of the counselor. Such questioning also allowed outside reality to intrude into the clinical arena—the fact that drug use does bring benefits (it is enjoyable, sociable, and exciting).

Especially with heroin users, establishing the benefits of use was found to be important because the conflicted nature of their lives ("I really want to use heroin very much" vs. "I know I really shouldn't use it") became blatantly clear. For many individuals, being encouraged to articulate the benefits and then the costs established for them that, rather than being out of control, they were being subjected to strong opposing forces. Thus, instead of being made to feel that they had no choice, the clients came to see that the matter was really one of choosing between two powerful *competing* choices—the benefits and costs of using, versus the benefits and costs of stopping.

It has to be noted that elicitation of the good things can sometimes constitute a surprise for a counselor, since what a client may value may not accord with the counselor's view of the world. The requirement not to disapprove or express dislike of what the client sees as benefits is therefore an essential skill.

A typical "good-things" dialogue could go as follows:

COUNSELOR: Tell me, John, what for you are some of the things you like about using heroin?

CLIENT: Well, I dunno. I mean, it's nice, using is good, especially at the beginning—I like the effect, it's great.

COUNSELOR: So you like how heroin makes you feel?

CLIENT: Yeah, it's fantastic, it's a real buzz, and it takes all the worries away. Makes you feel really full, really good, nothing matters, sort of on top of the world. And I just like being a user.

COUNSELOR: What do you particularly like about being a user?

CLIENT: Well, using smack is something real different. I like it 'cause it's illegal—the straight people, the ordinary people wouldn't dream of it, my brother-in-law like, a real stiff. The people I use with are different—we can all get out of it together. And I like doing the deals.

COUNSELOR: Tell me about that.

CLIENT: Dealing?

COUNSELOR: Yes.

CLIENT: Well, it's funny, people think it's the three-piece suits who are the wheelers and dealers, but some of the toughest people are out there dealing. It's very exciting—you're dealing and you don't know until it's done whether you're going to get away with it, whether the drug squad pigs will get you, or whether the buyers will pay up. One good deal and you know you're set up for days.

The Less Good Things

The objective of taking the "good-side" inventory is not to overprolong such examination, but rather to establish a framework of benefits before studying the negative things in detail. Doing this clarifies the rational nature of drug use, and emphasizes the volitional rather than the compulsive (out-of-control) nature of the behavior. Furthermore, many of the clients in this study genuinely welcomed the opportunity to weigh up and reflect upon what had become an increasingly chaotic but habitual behavior.

We have found that introducing the examination of the debit side by a question such as "Well, what are some of the less good things?" or "Well, these are the pluses, what about the negatives?" is preferable to direct questions such as "What are the bad things about your heroin use?" In essence, in order to facilitate open discussion, the gentler the opening the better.

It is relevant to note that over the course of some 60 sessions undertaken as part of our research (and many other clinical interviews), the majority of users spontaneously, as part of the inventory of good things, generated "less good" things. In fact, they often did the therapist's job by arguing that although there might be good things, there were bad things too. It was easy to pick up this lead and introduce the client-generated inventory of debits in a manner such as the following:

COUNSELOR: Well, you're saying there are things you don't like about heroin use, such as getting hepatitis. Can you tell me how that happened?

CLIENT: I'd been using quite heavily, four or five times a day for several weeks, and I was getting careless. I knew things were snowballing a bit, and I guess I was less careful about who I was sharing with. When I started to get ill, I went and saw a doctor, and she said that I had hepatitis.

COUNSELOR: How did you feel about that?

CLIENT: I was pissed off, a bit disgusted with myself, but angry that someone could do it to me. I'd always said to myself that I wouldn't use like a junkie, that I was different, but here I was with a junkie problem.

COUNSELOR: A junkie problem?

CLIENT: Well, things weren't going well—junkies get hepatitis, junkies get sick. Things were beginning to get on top of me. I was spending much more than before, far more than I could afford, and the bank was on my back, the folks were refusing to bail me out. The money hassles meant that I ended up nicking and hocking things, and not being able to get them back.

COUNSELOR: So you're saying there are money troubles, family problems, health issues—such as the hepatitis—but also this junkie thing. Can you tell me a bit more about that?

CLIENT: I'd always prided myself that I wouldn't get in a mess with heroin like junkies I know have. No dirty flats, abscesses, cold baked beans, and runny noses for me. But the hepatitis, and, well, I was also getting greedy on it.

With regard to this negative inventory, the objective is to facilitate discussions so that the client is able to give voice to a wide scope of issues. In our practice, we rely more on the clients' generating their own individual inventories of problems than on using objective tests such as blood results, urine analysis, or dependence inventories. Thus, rather than trying to persuade clients that they have "markers" of a syndrome or a disease, the rationale of this exercise is to give the clients free rein and see what they generate. In this way, each client's appreciation of her or his problems can be gauged. What seems to be important is not the total "truth," but rather having the clients listen to themselves describe a range of problems in detail. The clients thus begin to convince themselves of their problems. We have found that a useful questioning technique is to ask for specific examples of problems:

COUNSELOR: So you're worried about the effect of your heroin use on your relationship?

CLIENT: Yeah.

COUNSELOR: Can you give me a recent, specific example of that?

CLIENT: Well, last week I said I'd be in about 4 P.M. to look after the kids so that Josie could visit a friend, but, well, I got involved and it was more like 4 A.M. when I got in. Josie was really pissed off, and the argument hasn't really stopped yet. And I know that I'm running her patience out— she's left a couple of times before, and it's going to happen again.

Another issue that frequently appears is that clients distance themselves from problems, as in this example:

CLIENT: Well, the doctor said that needle sharing was dangerous—you know, AIDS, hepatitis, that sort of thing.

COUNSELOR: Yes, but what do you think?

CLIENT: Well, I've done it a lot, and I've never got anything—but I know people who've got hepatitis, and the AIDS thing is making some people a bit more careful. But I don't know anyone who's AIDS-positive—I don't think there's anyone in my circle who is, though I wouldn't share with a gay, nor anyone who's been in Africa! Yeah, so I suppose I'm more careful than I was—most of us do clean our works before sharing. I usually try to use first—you know, when it's clean. "Me first" is my motto.

Life Satisfaction

Increasingly, we have found that inviting clients to reflect on what they envisaged for themselves in the past and what they anticipate for the future is useful in raising issues or concerns that otherwise may not be disclosed. For example:

COUNSELOR: So, from what you're saying, your heroin use has become more troublesome of late. Tell me, is this what you envisaged for yourself when you were, say, 18? Did you think then that at 26 you'd be on a methadone program?

CLIENT: Eh, who would? At 18 I didn't really know what I was going to do, but I thought I'd be making good money—probably up north on the rigs or in mining. I'd always been practical, and I thought, time up north, then back with money to spend and no worries, no ties, being tough and independent! Didn't work out like that, though, did it?

COUNSELOR: How do you feel about that?

CLIENT: Well, it didn't happen, so I suppose no use worrying about it, but the last couple of years particularly I've not been going anywhere—round in circles, really. And with my convictions and my work record, I'm not really a good bet for a job, am I? So, no, I guess I haven't done what I thought I might.

COUNSELOR: What of the future? If you carry on using, what do you think will happen?

CLIENT: More of the same, I guess. More methadone, back into using, detoxes, attempts to stop, more pressure from the police—they know me well now—hassles from the family, no job; but some bright-lights-and-big-city stuff; with, I guess, sort of time going by and me with it. But stopping won't change that much—last time I was off, things were much the same. I was bored, no job, no money, nothing happened, so I used again. At least this way there are some good times.

COUNSELOR: How do you feel about that?

CLIENT: Well, pretty hopeless, I guess. It doesn't seem to matter what I do.

Comments such as this client's raise a host of issues regarding the format of any ongoing therapeutic involvement. Rather than to challenge such statements, the task is to acknowledge the client's perception of future reality and to reaffirm that the client is confronted by difficult options, but options over which he or she does have control. The issue to be appreciated here is that reflection exercises such as this one may not result in the client's immediately giving up, but rather gradually coming to view continued use as more negative. Thus, the possibility of a decision to stop sometime in the future is at least established. Our experience is that many heroin users view continued use as a very mixed blessing, and many acknowledge that at some stage quitting is inevitable.

Problems or Concerns

A lesson we learned early on is that clients can acknowledge an aspect of drug use as being problematic, without its necessarily being deemed a concern. This is illustrated in the following dialogue with a female heroin-using client.

COUNSELOR: So you're saying that in order to pay for your heroin, you work as a prostitute?

CLIENT: Yes, I've done that for the past 2 years. I work four nights a week at Sarah's, and occasionally during the day, if the demand is there—you know—if the American Navy is visiting or something like that.

COUNSELOR: How do you feel about being a prostitute?

CLIENT: Well, at first it was difficult—a lot of the men are awful, fat, smelly, rude—but after a while I found that I got used to it, and funnily I found I'm good at it. I can sort of cut off, but also the other girls came to rely on me to help them and to handle the worst clients. And you realize that a lot of the clients are pitiful—they come and demand what their wives won't give them. This may sound strange, but often I feel quite powerful. I can excite men, and they want me but they have to pay for it, and in spite of the heroin, I've got more than them. I might use heroin, but I don't have to pay for a screw. So it's, well, OK really, and it pays for the heroin, which nothing else could. And I like the other girls.

COUNSELOR: So your prostitution doesn't worry you much?

CLIENT: Well, you can't really tell people what you do for a job. There are risks too—some guys refuse to wear condoms, but we've got tricks for that. Look it's not what I'd choose to do, but it hasn't caused me any grief and, as I said, I like the money. I like being good at something, and I like the power it gives me. Anyway, it's not something you can do forever—I'll get a day job sometime, eventually.

COUNSELOR: So which of the other problems we discussed concerns you?

Cost–Benefit Analyses

At one level, doing a cost–benefit analysis is a straightforward exercise—a summary of the positive things contrasted with the negatives, plus a review of the major concerns and some consideration of the future. This can and does often work well, with clients acknowledging that they had not really conceived of their difficulties in this way before, and that they are confronted with the task of making a decision one way or the other.

However, some clients can tote up the good things, recite the less good things, and be unmoved by the apparent troubles and turmoil even when a large debit is obvious. It is as though they are inured to the problems and are quite detached from them. In any cost–benefit analysis, therefore, it is important to invite the client to "own" the problems. This can be done by encouraging the client to list the pros and cons as part of a homework exercise, and then to discuss the list at a follow-up session. A valuable technique, if used sparingly and with a keen sense of the risk, is to encourage the client to argue that she or he really does have a problem by the use of paradoxical questioning.

COUNSELOR: Well, you seem concerned about your health—but why do you think your heroin use is involved in all that?

CLIENT: I'm losing weight, my sex life is nonexistent, and I'm always getting the flu. And if heroin's so harmless, what about John who overdosed, and Lisa who got syphillis from sharing? No wonder I'm worried about it. You never know quite what you're getting, and recently the shit's been really poor, really dirty. I used to be fit, a footballer; now I'd be lucky to run 100 yards, and it's all to do with heroin, one way or another.

COUNSELOR: One way or another?

CLIENT: Come on, you know. You hit up, you can't be bothered to eat, you don't have money to eat, you've got to score, you get careless when hanging out, dirty needles, sores—health and beauty aren't what heroin's about.

It has to be acknowledged that such paradoxical questioning does not always engage the client in owning the negatives and seeing the case for giving up. Reviewing the pros and cons can sometimes remain a detached appraisal of the issues. As Tam Stewart (1987) has adroitly expressed it in her autobiographical account of heroin use, logic is not always enough:

> Hunting for a reason to stop that outweighs the drive to stay hooked is the major problem. During one soul-searching session I neatly listed advantages and disadvantages of taking smack. Potential consequences of using heroin including being charged with an offence, starring in a scandal, losing home, job, health, wealth, friends, and credibility of every kind. Advantages were impossible to find. The following statements appeared on the list of reasons not to stop: "It [heroin] makes life easy"; "I'm scared to stop" and "I don't feel like it." A moment's thought contradicted the first two and left me confronted by the third. I did not "feel like it." I did not stop, but logic had not assisted the choice.

Our experience confirms that logic does not always help. We have become increasingly aware that robust decisions to quit often come out of emotional discomfort, and that distress is in many ways a better harbinger of change than is cool cognitive appraisal.

Emotional Reviews

We have therefore become increasingly interested in tapping into, exploring, and exploiting those concerns that appear to be the most uncomfortable for a client. Although an intent to cause patients psychological distress may appear to be the antithesis of good counseling, we deploy what we have colloquially termed "the psychological squirm" only within the context of rapport and empathy. Furthermore, rather than being a callous exploration of a client's vulnerability, the exercise is directed at allowing patients to acknowledge and experience any latent discomforts with their current behavior. Few of us like to examine aspects of ourselves about which we are disquieted or even ashamed. Tapping into the discrepancy that can exist between public persona and subjective assessment can be valuable. Here is an example:

COUNSELOR: So you're telling me that a prime concern is that your heroin use is having a bad impact on your family. Can you tell me more about that?

CLIENT: Well, just last week—you know the police have been giving me a lot of attention recently, and we've been raided twice. Last week it was 5 A.M. and my wife and daughters were confronted by pickaxes, sledgehammers, and armed cops. And Maxine, my wife, got hurt. She didn't realize they were cops at first and tried to protect the baby. It was all a fiasco. I wasn't even there. Maxine didn't know where I was, whether the cops had me or not. She was upset for days, and it was all because of what I do.

COUNSELOR: How did you feel about that?

CLIENT: Terrible. My kids aren't getting a good deal. My own childhood was shitty, and now I'm giving them much of the same. I hated my father—he was a drunk—for what he did to Mum and to us, and was pleased when he got killed. Now I'm doing the same.

COUNSELOR: So you think you're not a very good father?

CLIENT: I'm lousy. I'm never there, I leave it all to Maxine, and I'm spending too much money. And the youngest won't have anything to do with me—she cries all the time. I lose my temper with them a lot and . . . (*distressed*). Maxine blames me, I know she's thinking of leaving—I heard her talking to her mate the other day. The last time she left it was terrible.

COUNSELOR: You found it difficult when she left you?

CLIENT: It was terrible. She took the kids, and she started to do all right. She got a job, and I saw her in the street one day—she was looking really good and happy, and now she's all withdrawn, cheap-looking, she's sort of given up.

COUNSELOR: How do you feel about that?

CLIENT: Not good. Some of it's about me. I promised to stop using and dealing, but I just couldn't, and I know that when she came back I felt so good, all the worries went away, and now she's sort of got them all, and I'm OK. I think she's probably better off without me—I don't like thinking that. I used to make her feel good, but not now. She often just sits and cries, and the house is shit, and our oldest daughter is having troubles at school. Maxine blames me for that too—the arguments, never having any money—but I can't stop using. If I did there'd be nothing. I can't win. If I carry on using and dealing, Maxine will leave; if I stop, there's nothing. I don't know what to do. I can't stop—I can't go on.

A technique that we have also found to be of value on occasion is to invite clients to contrast themselves as individuals with themselves as drug users. For example:

COUNSELOR: Steve, tell me what words might you use to describe yourself—you know, the characteristics that you like about yourself.

CLIENT: Eh, what do you mean?

COUNSELOR: Well, if you think about yourself, your good qualities, what words come to mind?

CLIENT: Um, that's difficult—good qualities. Well, I'm happy-go-lucky, I guess, and I am humorous—a good sense of humor—and, well, I'm not sure. . . .

COUNSELOR: Happy-go-lucky, humorous—anything else?

CLIENT: Well, it may sound funny, but I'm kind and, well, easy-going—I get on well with most people.

COUNSELOR: So, happy-go-lucky, humorous, kind, and easy to get along with—is that right?

CLIENT: Yeah—that's about it, I guess.

COUNSELOR: Well, what about you, you the heroin user? What words come to mind then?

CLIENT: Ah, greedy, definitely greedy and unreliable—not to be trusted. . . .

COUNSELOR: Greedy, unreliable, not very trustworthy—anything else?

CLIENT: I suppose the word that really came to mind first was tense—me the heroin user is tense, harassed, worried—well, unless I'm using, that is!

COUNSELOR: So how do these things go together—you know, you as a happy-go-lucky, humorous, easy-to-get-along-with person, versus the greedy, unreliable, untrustworthy, worried person?

CLIENT: Well, they don't really go together, do they? I used to think that heroin was me, suited my character, but I know that the things I do to get heroin aren't good. It's not like "take it or leave it" any more. I've got to have it, and I'd steal from my best friend to get it. In fact, I have done that.

Again, the trick is to allow clients every opportunity to examine those aspects of their drug taking with which they are unhappy. The old adage of "stewing in one's own juice" is apposite for this aspect of our motivational intervention.

Future Intentions

Given the limited time allowed in our research for motivational intervention, a key skill was the ability to pull the various threads together and then invite clients to consider their future intentions. Sessions were generally brought to a close by the therapist's recapping what she considered the central issues to be, and then asking what it all meant for the client. Here is an example:

COUNSELOR: Well, Joe, from what you've been saying, it would appear to me that while you still enjoy using heroin and you find dealing exciting, there are things you increasingly don't like. You're worried by your physical health, your mother's concern about you, the possibility of another overdose, and going to jail. Also, the negative changes that have happened in the local drug scene. Is this right?

CLIENT: Yeah. It's really not what it was any more.

COUNSELOR: Well, what do you think you're going to do?

CLIENT: I guess I'll give it a bit of a rest for a while. When I was on methadone before, I stayed clean for 3 months—the longest time since I was 18. So I can do it when I want to.

COUNSELOR: Do you want to?

CLIENT: Well, I need to, for a while at least. Give me and the family a bit of a break. Who knows, I might even get a job. What about that?

Concluding Comment

We have begun this chapter by noting that our approach to motivational interviewing has departed from that espoused by Miller and Rollnick. It is important to stress in conclusion that this departure is more one of emphasis and application than one of overall philosophy. We endorse unreservedly the central tenets of motivational interviewing, especially the call to "roll with resistance" and perceive the world from the client's standpoint. Perhaps the differences that do exist (and the reader can make up her or his own mind about the extent of these) have more to do with personality and culture than with anything else. And by that we mean our own personality and culture. The American addiction scene is markedly different from its British or Australian counterpart. In the latter countries addictions are not universally regarded as diseases, and notions of confrontation have never been a central part of the counseling *Zeitgeist* of either.

Furthermore, the reliance on ex-users as counselors is less in evidence in the United Kingdom and Australia than it is in the United States. In British or Australian clinics, clients are more likely to encounter professionally qualified workers, many of whom bring to their day-to-day work a client-centered approach. Thus, reflective listening, paraphrasing, avoidance of labeling, being where the client is, and seeing clients as responsible for their behavior are nothing new. Indeed, one of our colleagues, a senior social worker who is well versed in motivational interviewing in the mode of Miller and Rollnick, commented that in essence it is nothing more than the application of good counseling skills to the addictions arena. We agree with this statement, inasmuch as motivational interviewing represents the application of a client-centered counseling style to addictions; however, we believe that the specific strategies outlined above constitute a refinement, an additional "edge"—one that has evolved from the application of good counseling principles to addictions practice.

As far as personality goes, some of us engage the world around us in a more head-on way than others. Therefore, we have to amend our personal interactional style when counseling problem drug users, so that we are more in tune with the principles of motivational interviewing. Mind you, in retrospect there have often been occasions in everyday life when rolling with resistance and avoiding arguments might well have served us better than the head-on collisions that did occur! Perhaps as well as being a practical, straightforward, and essentially useful addition to our therapeutic armentarium, motivational interviewing may be a valuable way of engaging the world in general.

Acknowledgments

The research study referred to in this chapter was funded by the Research into Drug Abuse Advisory Committee, Commonwealth Department of Community Services and Health. The cooperation of the Western Australia Alcohol and Drug Authority, especially the William Street Clinic, in undertaking the study was much appreciated. The word-processing skills of Robyn Taylor are gratefully acknowledged, as are the helpful comments on the first draft of this chapter made by Sue Helfgott, Jan Herrington, and Steve Rollnick.

22

Motivational Interviewing for HIV Risk Reduction

AMANDA BAKER

JULIE DIXON

Our motivational interviewing approach is evolving through a program of research that has been underway for several years (see Stallard & Heather, 1989). The general approach has been strongly influenced by Miller's work (e.g., Miler, 1989a). The actual strategies have been refined over time during our work with clients who are intravenous drug users (IVDUs). We hope that readers working with IVDUs and other clients at risk for human immunodeficiency virus (HIV) infection will be able to apply relevant aspects of our approach in their everyday work.

Philosophical Framework for the Approach

> The individual or agency which offers intervention to the dependent person inevitably bases the intervention upon philosophic premises relevant to the intervenor. . . . The addicted person must be wooed in an acceptable way. And if we see him at a crisis point when he is susceptible, then we must be flexible enough to use the right bait. If we are overly concerned with our own philosophy and ego, we may turn off the customer. And however righteous we feel, we may have stuffed up his chance of finding a way out. (O'Neill, 1985, p. 103)

Before attempting motivational interviewing with a person at risk of transmitting or acquiring HIV, it is crucial for the counselor to examine his or her own philosophical basis of treatment. This is not an easy task; these are confusing times for drug and alcohol workers. Drew and Taylor (1988) have pointed out that many countries seem to be adopting contradictory approaches to preventing the further spread of HIV. On one hand, governments are declaring wars on drugs; on the other, the same governments are allowing the establishment of such services as needle exchange programs. The traditional curative philosophy coexists with the more recent harm reduction model. Counselors have largely been expected to make their own sense of this confusion, even though many of them have worked entirely from the traditional curative philosophy for many years.

A number of problems may arise during the interview process if the counselor has not adequately resolved this conflict. If, for example, the counselor is only prepared to accept a goal of abstinence for the client, a confrontation–denial trap (see Chapter 6) may well arise early in the interview. Sooner or later, it is likely that the client will begin to experience a lack of genuine empathy in the counseling relationship. Alternatively, the client may feel pressured into expressing a desire for abstinence, and may then not return for any further sessions. This process of "turning off the customer," as O'Neill describes it in the quotation above, has many potentially serious consequences for clients at risk for HIV and their significant others. In addition to the usual dangers to the drug user (e.g., overdose, hepatitis B, etc.), the client is at risk of transmitting the virus to his or her sexual partners; to fellow users, if they share injecting equipment; and, in the case of women, to the fetus and breast-fed child. Drew and Taylor (1988) have argued that if the counselor is genuinely concerned about the well-being of the client, then he or she can only accept that harm reduction must have a higher priority than eliminating drug use. Flexibility is obviously important here. In sum, before attempting to interview a client at serious risk for HIV, the counselor needs to analyze his or her counseling philosophy and to feel comfortable working with the client on the goal of his or her own choosing: harm reduction or abstinence. The potential risks involved in not taking this basic first step are too great to be ignored.

Much of the counselor's confusion may be resolved by identifying his or her own assumptions and challenging any that conflict with the public health model of drug use (Stimson, 1990). This model assumes that (1) the main problem with drug use is not the drug user per se, but the administration of drugs by injection; (2) the drug user is concerned about his or her health and is willing to reduce HIV risk-taking behaviors; (3) the aim is to promote change in health and risk behaviors—specifically, to help clients stop needle sharing and adopt safer sexual practices; (4) drug workers need to be skilled in medicine, counseling, and community action; and (5) relationships with clients must be nonjudgmental and "user-friendly." This model obviously fits in well with the principles of motivational interviewing outlined in Chapter 5. If the counselor cannot come to terms with any one of these assumptions, we believe that it is not in the best interests of clients for him or her to attempt motivational interviewing for HIV risk reduction.

Clinical Population

In both the United States and Europe, IVDUs represent the second largest risk group infected with HIV after homosexual men, and the trend is for an increasing proportion of cases to occur in this group. They are generally considered to be the most likely transmission route for HIV to the general community. Little is known about the occasional or regular IVDUs who are not receiving treatment. Much more is known about addicts, especially those on methadone programs, because of their high retention rates. This is the group we are currently working with. A recent review of clients applying to enter public methadone programs in Sydney (Bell, Fernandes, & Batey, 1990) reports that they lead very disrupted lives. Most have long histories of illicit drug use and previous attempts to stop, and are involved in crime and prostitution and a drug subculture. Most do not live with a partner, and many of those with children do not have custody of them. Our clients certainly fit this picture. We have found that our motivational interviewing procedures are equally effective with heterosexual and gay IVDUs, and are readily generalized to intravenous use of drugs other than heroin.

Aims of the Motivational Interview

In terms of the prevention of the further spread of HIV, it is necessary for IVDUs to change two types of long-standing, immediately gratifying behaviors that are often cued by partners and significant others: the sharing of injection equipment and unprotected sexual intercourse. Within the context of a research study, we are conducting single 90-minute motivational interviews with IVDUs attending methadone clinics. Clients are assessed and offered an interview if they have injected any kind of drug in the previous 6 months. The aims of the motivational interview are to help the client review and evaluate injecting and sexual behaviors that place him or her at risk for infection and/or transmission; for the client to express concerns about this risk; and for the client to express a desire to change needle use and unsafe sexual practices.

Rapport

Having come to terms with a harm reduction philosophy, the first task for the counselor is to establish a good working relationship with the client. The client must feel that the counselor can be trusted, genuinely cares, and is interested in trying to understand and help him or her.

How can a non-IVDU counselor establish rapport with IVDUs? First, the counselor must realize that he or she may need to take more time than with most clients in establishing a working relationship. Second, the counselor must reassure the client that everything they discuss will remain completely confidential and will not affect the current treatment. Many clients arrive at the session reluctant to be entirely truthful because of fears regarding confidentiality. They may be worried about possible legal and treatment implications if they reveal their illicit drug use or unprotected sexual behavior. Possibly added to these concerns are fears of ostracism because of their suspected or confirmed HIV antibody status. In one case, outlined later in this chapter, a client had to endure the experience of other methadone clients' taking up a petition to have her removed from the program when they discovered that she was antibody-positive. The client was reluctant to disclose her serostatus to the counselor and remained very wary about telling others.

Third, with regard to establishing good rapport, possessing a harm reduction philosophy and a public health paradigm on a cognitive level is a necessary but not a sufficient condition for a good therapeutic relationship. The counselor should clearly state that the purpose of the session is to help prevent the further spread of HIV among IVDUs, and that he or she would like to discuss the client's current injecting and sexual behavior in order to conjointly assess whether the client is at risk for HIV. The client should be reassured that he or she will not be forced into making any decisions. Fourth, we believe that an assertive approach to engaging clients helps to establish a good rapport. If a client arrives for a session intoxicated, he or she is seen briefly, and the appointment is rescheduled. We consider it inappropriate to turn away clients because of their "lack of motivation"; after all, that is why we are there. Similarly, clients are reminded about sessions with handwritten letters and/or telephone calls, and missed appointments are rescheduled in the same way. On the whole, clients seem to appreciate this approach and often remind us to remind them!

Interview Strategies

We employ a number of "core" strategies in our interviews. They are presented below in a roughly chronological sequence. However, we do not always employ every strategy with each client, nor do we follow this sequence rigidly. We consider these strategies to be items on a menu; it is up to the counselor to select the most appropriate strategy at the most appropriate time. A snippet of information put forth by the client may best be "stored" with the counselor until the counselor can put that snippet together with another. In this way, more complex strategies highlighting relationships between behaviors, especially discrepancies in behavior change (so crucial to HIV transmission), can be comfortably incorporated into the interview.

Assessing Stages of Change for Needle Sharing, Injecting, and Unprotected Sex

The vast majority of clients show a high level of knowledge about HIV and its routes of transmission. Nevertheless, they typically report high levels of needle sharing (particularly with sexual partners), injecting, and unprotected sex. Many report that they have greatly reduced their sharing practices (though they often still share with their sexual partners) and are currently trying to stop injecting altogether. Very few use condoms with their casual or regular partners. Thus, most of our clients are at least at the contemplation stage for injecting and sharing practices, but are at the precontemplation stage for using condoms.

Encouraging Contemplation

One of our first aims is therefore to help the client to personalize the risks associated with unprotected sex, and thus to bring him or her to the contemplation stage for condom use. This is usually effectively achieved by raising the virus's most salient feature: HIV is transmissible. This is most often raised during discussion of the pros and cons of using condoms. Expectations of longevity are also often discussed, along with hopes for the future. Discussion of the transmissible nature of HIV is especially valuable in generating client discomfort, usually feelings of guilt regarding his or her behavior and the danger in which he or she is placing significant others. It is necessary at this point in the interview to reassure the client that his or her past reluctance and current ambivalence regarding the use of condoms is normal and completely understandable. In the case study presented below, the client's failure to use condoms was related to her grief reaction following her diagnosis as antibody-positive. To her, unprotected sex was one of the few remaining things in her life that she felt allowed her to experience intimacy with other people; it was also one of the few remaining pleasures in her life. In this way, the generation of discomfort and empathic discussion are extremely useful in generating contemplation of condom use.

Negotiating Client Goals

When the client is aware of the risks to himself or herself and others, and has at least thought about the possibility of change, goals can then be negotiated. As mentioned previously, it is necessary for IVDUs to change two types of immediately reinforcing behaviors: the sharing of injection equipment and unprotected sexual intercourse. The client chooses whether he or she wishes to prevent relapse to sharing injection equipment or to injecting itself. Use of condoms is very often an important goal, as it is impossible to be absolutely certain that the client's partner has been entirely monogamous or has not shared injection equipment. The aim here is not to eliminate sexual behavior itself, but for clients always to use condoms.

Deploying Discrepancy

Sexual behavior is traditionally seen as difficult to change. Nevertheless, we have found that once the client has entered the contemplation stage for using condoms, motivational interviewing techniques can often be extremely useful in increasing clients' stated intentions and subsequent condom use. Since most IVDUs have made at least some behavior change (usually a reduction in needle sharing with an occasional lapse), we attempt to create the conditions in which the client will recognize the discrepancy and continued risk in changing one behavior but not the other (commonly, not using condoms). This discrepancy in behavior change often seems to be at least partly due to the client's failure to make any personal link between sharing injection equipment and the possibility of transmission of HIV during sex. Double-sided reflection (see Chapter 8) is often useful here. For example, the counselor may say, "Your husband is very important to you. On the one hand, you've just about stopped sharing, and on the other, you haven't been using condoms." In addition to helping the client recognize his or her discrepant behaviors, this sort of reflection is also useful in that it avoids raising the potentially delicate issue of monogamy early in the interview, which may lead to reactance. This can often be raised later without problems, once the client has recognized condoms as protective for what he or she considers a more likely (and less hurtful) reason. Once the client has recognized the discrepancy between his or her behaviors, he or she often begins to express the desire to at least try using condoms. Thus, the counselor, although seemingly facing a very difficult task in attempting to help the client seek to change multiple behaviors at a number of levels, can make use of this complexity by increasing the client's awareness of his or her interactions.

In addition to deploying discrepancy between behaviors, it is also useful to emphasize inconsistencies within the same behavior. For example, many clients initially report that they no longer share injection equipment to avoid acquiring HIV. These same clients, though, will later mention that they do pass on their injection equipment to others. As most do not use condoms, these clients are at risk of acquiring the virus sexually and transmitting it by lending their injection equipment. Other inconsistencies include sharing only with lovers or close friends; lapsing to sharing only "rarely"; and, in one case, refusing to share but using injection equipment found discarded on the street. Inconsistencies in condom use are also important. Prostitutes, for example, often use condoms with clients but not with their primary partners. These inconsistencies often come to light after stages of change have been assessed and in the course of discussion during the interview. When snippets of information can be put together to reveal inconsistencies in behavior (which are surprising to the client), double-sided reflection is again helpful in increasing awareness and discomfort regarding risk for HIV.

Discussing Longevity to Encourage Determination

Another useful exercise to encourage determination to change is to discuss the client's expectations of longevity with him or her. Being antibody-positive can be seen as a reason to improve one's own health care in order to prolong life, as well as to protect others from the virus. Clients at risk of acquiring the virus often talk at some length of their wish to see their children grow up. Sometimes they also mention a desire to help others avoid the same life that they find themselves living. Clients can become quite distressed when discussing this material, indicating the recognition of the personal risks they are taking and the possible danger to others.

Providing Personal Risk Feedback

Personal feedback regarding the client's level of risk for HIV, based on his or her sharing, injecting, and sexual behaviors, is given. Again, it is important to provide the client with factual information about the risk in which he or she is placing others, as well as his or her own risk of acquiring the virus. As mentioned above, the client who has decided not to use other people's injection equipment after they have used it may nevertheless pass on his or her equipment to other people. In this case, the client would be seen to be at greater risk of unknowingly transmitting the virus than of contracting it from someone else. If, however, he or she is in a sexual relationship with another IVDU and is not using condoms, then the personal risk for HIV is also possible. Knowledge regarding the degree of risk for infection must depend on information (which is often unreliable) regarding monogamy and abstinence from sharing behavior. This feedback can be very powerful and can serve to reinforce the client's recognition of risk to himself or herself and others, as well as the interconnections between risk behaviors.

Encouraging Action

Once the client has expressed commitment to reduction of specific injecting and sexual risks, possible strategies for change are discussed. The IVDU population is not a supportive subculture. Many seem to hold the belief that "once a junkie, always a junkie." Obviously, such a belief is not conducive to change, and we feel it is very important to point out to the client that past failed attempts at drug abstinence are largely irrelevant to the behavior change required to reduce the risk for HIV. Strategies that may be useful to the client are discussed, and a booklet summarizing the session's content and the client's responses is given to him or her. This is especially useful if the client has been under the influence of drugs during the session or is showing signs of forgetfulness (possibly related to HIV infection). The booklet also contains diaries for the client to begin to record his or her injecting and sexual behavior. The hope is that the client's new level of motivation, discussion of appropriate change strategies, and this booklet will help the client to reduce his or her HIV risk-taking behaviors, and thus to prevent the further spread of infection. We are currently evaluating the clinical effectiveness of this approach.

The Case of Kerry

The following account of a motivational interviewing session with an IVDU conducted by one of us (Amanda Baker) is given to illustrate the material presented above, rather than the entire interviewing process.

Kerry was a 31-year-old woman whose *de facto* husband was in prison, but due to be released at any time. Kerry shared a house with another woman and that woman's children. She was bonded to that address by the courts on charges of breaking and entering, stealing, and assaulting police; she had served a prison term in the past. Kerry's two children lived several hundred miles away with her mother. She was receiving sickness benefits.

Kerry was on methadone and remained abstinent from heroin, but injected amphetamines several times a week using her own injection equipment. She had not shared equipment since being diagnosed as HIV-positive 18 months earlier (she was in the maintenance stage in regard to sharing). Her partner was aware of her HIV status and, before he was imprisoned, had regularly undergone antibody tests. The couple did not use condoms. During her primary partner's prison term, Kerry had had three casual sexual partners, again without using condoms.

At the beginning of the session with Kerry, she was at the contemplation stage for injecting amphetamines and at the precontemplation stage for using condoms. The session progressed smoothly into a discussion of her injecting, and Kerry soon stated that she would like to stop injecting altogether. This discussion included the pros and cons of injecting; its dangers; her view of herself as a noninjector as opposed to an injector; her expected longevity; and her main reasons for giving up injecting. During this time, she had talked about the acquired immune deficiency syndrome (AIDS) virus and about wanting to see her children grow up.

It was not until the discussion moved to the subject of condom use, however, that the power of the motivational interviewing techniques became evident. When the counselor (Baker) introduced the topic to her, in terms of preventing the spread of HIV, she angrily said she had refused to use them in the past ("Never, ever!"). Having reassured her that any decision she made to change in any way would be up to her, the counselor suggested that they talk about condoms and the virus as they had done about injecting. To this she was agreeable. They began to discuss the pros and cons of condoms, and Kerry said that the reason she and her partner did not use condoms was because she felt it interfered with the intimacy between them. She admitted at this stage that condoms offered protection against HIV, but she said that they took precautions not to have intercourse during menstruation. In any case, she said her partner had suggested they use them, but he respected her wish to continue unprotected sex.

It was when Kerry and the counselor began to discuss the dangers of unprotected sex in more detail that Kerry began to cry. She admitted that her partner had been at risk; when the counselor questioned her about the regularity of her menstrual cycle, she became very emotional. It became evident that her cycle was extremely irregular and that she really could not be sure that her partner would avoid contact with menstrual blood. She began to sob, crying that she had lost so much through being antibody-positive. She described how her whole life had changed—how her former sharing practices had been "lost," as had many other things in her life. She especially singled out having had to endure a petition against her by other clients on the methadone program, and how she took great care with her hygiene now, so as not to place anyone in danger. She seemed, essentially, to be suffering a grief reaction to the loss of her former lifestyle. She felt that to start using condoms would remove the last remaining experience of intimacy. She had lost so much, she felt, she was not going to allow the virus to cause her to lose any more.

Having experienced this level of emotion, Kerry concluded that she would suggest using condoms to her partner after she was posed with this dilemma. "On the one hand, the worst thing that could happen for you is the loss of your partner, and on the other, you've lost so much you don't like the idea of using condoms. . . . What can you do in your situation?" Possible alternatives were discussed, and Kerry arrived at her own plan, whereby she would speak with her partner while he was still in prison and tell him she wanted to protect him. She also decided to have a range of different condoms available for their use, in order to make condom use more fun. She agreed to work on her attitude that condoms interfered with intimacy, and to try thinking of them as protection from further loss.

Kerry, having reached these decisions, then admitted that she had had unprotected sex with three casual partners while her regular partner was in prison. She stated that she felt guilty about this and that she had been with these partners to relieve sexual frustration. When questioned about masturbation, she stated she felt too inhibited to masturbate, as she had always been taught that it was wrong. She was concerned, too, about appearing to be promiscuous to her casual partners if she carried condoms with her. Earlier in the session, Kerry had mentioned that her flatmate's teenage daughter had begun to take the contraceptive pill, and added that it was better to be prepared than pregnant. When the counselor pointed out to Kerry that she seemed to be saying it was OK for someone else and not for her, the client stated that she would work on that attitude too, as well as carry condoms with her.

Important Elements

The most important elements of motivational interviewing in this session were (1) assurance of confidentiality; (2) an empathic attitude to behavior that placed sexual partners at risk for HIV; (3) moving on with the interview, past initial resistance without confrontation; leaving any decision making to the client; (4) increasing the client's level of discomfort with regard to being antibody-positive and placing another person at risk, and using that discomfort to generate statements of intention to change; (5) deploying discrepancy—working with the continued risk in changing one behavior (sharing), but not another (using condoms); and (6) discussing possible action and barriers to action, such as beliefs about condoms and interference with intimacy.

Using these strategies with Kerry was challenging and difficult at times. In a case such as Kerry's, the counselor has to remain alert to any possible means of helping to motivate the client. The temptation to confront the client directly has to be resisted, as does the temptation to become enmeshed in grief counseling. The latter may be appropriate at another time, but not during the motivational interview. As for confrontation, there are no short cuts. It is the client who has to recognize and state the need for change. When this is accomplished, risk reduction is all the more likely.

23

Motivational Intervention in the Treatment of Sex Offenders

RANDALL J. GARLAND

MICHAEL J. DOUGHER

Not everything that is faced can be changed; but nothing can be changed until it is faced.

—James Baldwin, *Notes of a Native Son*

Motivation is widely recognized as a key issue in the treatment of sex offenders (Abel, Becker, Cunningham-Rathner, Rouleau, Kaplan, & Reich, 1984; Knopp, 1984; Langevin, 1988; Langevin & Lang, 1985; Salter, 1988). Sex offenders typically present as unmotivated for treatment and uninterested in changing their deviant behavior. They frequently deny, minimize, rationalize, or justify their actions. For example, one study reported that 54% of 100 consecutive cases of men accused of child sexual abuse initially denied the criminal charges, refused evaluation, or denied any problems related to children (Hucker, Langevin, Bain, & Handy, 1987). Another study, using what was admittedly a biased sample of members of a Dutch pedophile organization, reported that 45 out of 50 pedophiles did not want to change their pedophilic orientation (Bernard, 1975). Not surprisingly, many sex offenders go untreated because they are deemed unamenable to treatment due to poor motivation (Dougher, 1988a; Knopp, 1984; Schwartz, 1988a). In addition, high dropout rates from treatment programs are typically attributed to poor motivation (Knopp, 1984).

Given how crucial motivation for treatment is in working with sex offenders, it is disturbing, perplexing, and even tragic that there is almost no systematic research on this issue. Many untreated sex offenders will reoffend; recidivism rates for untreated sex offenders have been estimated to be as high as 60% within the first 3 years of release from prison (Krauth &

Smith, 1988). This figure, though perhaps an overestimate, also implies that incarceration per se does little to deter reoffending. Consequently, many sex offenders who go untreated because of poor motivation are likely to reoffend, creating new victims whose anguish is becoming increasingly well understood. Furthermore, sexual abuse, in conjunction with other variables, may predispose some individuals to act out sexually, thus perpetuating the problem (Garland & Dougher, 1990). This is all the more unfortunate when one considers that there are a number of promising treatment approaches with sex offenders, such as hormonal and antiandrogen treatments; behavioral treatments to modify sexual preferences; and cognitive–behavioral approaches, including relapse prevention models (Laws, 1989; Marshall, Laws, & Barbaree, 1990).

Motivational interventions can be useful in getting sex offenders to contemplate change, to work at change, and to maintain change. This, at least, has been our experience in both community-based and residential treatment settings. The purpose of this chapter is to articulate and integrate a variety of interventions that address treatment motivation with sex offenders.

Motivation for treatment is conceptualized here as dynamic and interactive in nature—a function of personal, environmental, and temporal variables (cf. Miller, 1983, 1985b). Thus, consideration is given to where the offender is on the "wheel of change" and what interventions are appropriate. Factors undermining treatment motivation are discussed first, followed by strategies and interventions for engaging the sex offender in treatment, keeping him in treatment, and strengthening his desire to change.

At the outset, we should note that sex offenders are referred to in the masculine gender in this chapter. This is not intended to be sexist, but reflects the fact that the vast majority of indentified sex offenders are male (Finkelhor et al., 1986). In addition, the clinical experiences upon which our motivational interventions are based involved male offenders. Presumably, many of the principles and interventions described could (at least in principle) be used with female sex offenders.

Factors Undermining Treatment Motivation

Client Dissimulation

If an alleged offender has not yet been convicted of a sex offense, he may believe that his credibility and reputation will withstand the allegations against him (Langevin, 1988). Furthermore, he may believe that circumstances make it advantageous for him to conceal his problem (e.g., he may believe that the victim will be a poor witness) (Langevin, 1988). Moreover, his family and social network may support his dissimulation (Salter, 1988).

Cognitive Distortions

The sex offender often has a set of distorted beliefs that support and maintain his deviant sexual activities (Abel, Becker, & Cunningham-Rathner, 1984; Abel, Becker, Cunningham-Rathner, Rouleau, et al., 1984; Murphy, 1990; Segal & Stermac, 1990). These beliefs, or "cognitive distortions" as they are typically called, may pre-empt the sex offender's recognition that he (rather than others) has a serious, intractable problem, and may shield him from guilt or distress about his behavior. Thus, the offender may feel that he has overcome his problem prior to engaging in treatment, perhaps through sheer willpower or perhaps through some form of moral or religious conversion (Langevin, 1988; Salter, 1988). Complicating matters is the fact that he actually may be experiencing a temporary suppression of his deviant sexual urges as a result of discovery, arrest, or incarceration. In addition, the offender may externalize responsibility for his sexually deviant behavior or may minimize the seriousness of the effects of his behavior.

Inappropriate Therapist Expectations and Behaviors

There are a number of ways in which a therapist can contribute to the sex offender's lack of or tenuous motivation for treatment. First, the therapist may underestimate how difficult it is to acknowledge to oneself and others that one is, in fact, a sex offender—a "pervert." Consequently, the therapist may have unrealistic expectations about when and to what extent the sex offender will admit his problems. Unrealistic expectations about disclosure, in turn, can lead the therapist prematurely to write off the offender as being "in denial," and therefore unamenable to treatment. However, it is typical that sex offenders begin to disclose more fully the extent of their problems only after several months of treatment (Langevin & Lang, 1985; Salter, 1988).

Second, the therapist may underestimate the sex offender's ambivalence about changing his sexually deviant behavior. This may result in involving the offender in treatment activities for which he is not yet ready. However, many sex offenders, especially pedophiles, may value their deviant sexuality for reasons that are difficult for the average person to comprehend.

Third, the therapist may prematurely and forcefully confront the sex offender. Although confrontation is often seen as a part of sex offender treatment, it may not be useful when used too soon or too aggressively (Murphy, 1990; Salter, 1988). This is especially true in the absence of strong extrinsic motivation for treatment. Under these circumstances, the offender may more energetically disagree with the therapist and minimize his problem; he may insincerely accept the therapist's points; or he may simply drop out of treatment.

An additional danger of aggressive confrontation is that it is easily abused and may serve the countertransference needs of the therapist. Aggressive confrontation can often be disguised, rationalized therapist hostility. Although the therapist obviously should not collude with the sex offender's deviance, some degree of empathy and acceptance is necessary for working with the offender.

Finally, the therapist may fail to be straightforward with the sex offender. By not adequately informing the sex offender about the parameters of confidentiality, the nature and purpose of evaluation and treatment procedures, or the therapist's role in the legal or institutional system, the therapist may undermine the sex offender's willingness to discuss his problems (e.g., Aubrey & Dougher, 1990). This can be damaging not only to the offender's initial motivation for treatment, but also to any treatment he undergoes. For example, the sex offender may underreport the extent and nature of his sexual deviance, and thus may receive inadequate treatment.

Environmental Barriers and Inadequate Resources

In community-based treatment, the sex offender may have inflexible working hours, transportation problems, or inadequate funds to pay for treatment. Although the therapist needs to be skeptical of these obstacles to treatment, he or she should assist the offender in dealing with them. For example, the therapist may provide evening hours for treatment or arrange for transportation with another treatment client.

In residential treatment settings, especially prisons, the therapist needs to ensure that an environment exists in which sex offenders can safely seek treatment and in which dissimulation and avoidance of treatment are not reinforced by the prison culture (Knopp, 1984). This can be accomplished in part through the creation of semiautonomous therapeutic communities within the prison and through the education of prison staff (Schwartz, 1988b; Smith, 1988).

Inadequate Behavioral Contingencies

Still another major factor undermining treatment motivation consists of absent or inadequate behavioral contingencies. Initially, at least, there need to be differential consequences associated with participating or not participating in treatment (e.g., outpatient treatment vs. incarceration, placement at one institution vs. another; cf. Miller, 1985b). This is necessary inasmuch as sex offenders typically enter treatment because of pressure from third parties (e.g., their families, social service or community correction agencies, the court) and because they work to avert negative consequences, not because of intrinsic motivation.

While the sex offender undergoes treatment, behavioral contingencies are still important. The sex offender's motivation for treatment can be diminished if contingencies involving treatment behavior are not established and maintained. This would include failure to communicate expectations about treatment participation and about consequences for noncompliance; inadequate goal setting; inadequate behavioral contracting; inadequate feedback about treatment progress; and failure to provide differential consequences for treatment participation versus nonparticipation.

Now, it may appear that emphasizing the use of external behavioral contingencies in motivating sex offenders for treatment is antithetical to the approach advocated in this volume—that of cultivating client motivation for treatment. This is a partially accurate perception. However, what needs to be considered is that in many cases sex offender treatment has a direct or indirect goal of creating and enhancing motivation for change (e.g., through increasing victim empathy, reducing the desirability of sexually deviant behavior, etc.). Behavioral contingencies are useful for holding the sex offender in place until treatment interventions take effect and intrinsic motivation begins to develop. In the interim, behavioral contingencies supplement the client's treatment motivation, especially during difficult periods.

Engaging the Sex Offender in Treatment

Sex offenders present with a variety of behaviors that challenge the therapist's motivational intervention skills. The therapist may be faced with an offender who denies or minimizes sexually deviant behavior and/or the need for treatment. The therapist may also encounter an anxious or remorseful individual who has referred himself in anticipation of being discovered or in reaction to psychological discomfort following an episode of offending. In any event, it is most likely that the sex offender is highly resistant to or ambivalent about changing his behavior; that is, he is in the precontemplation or contemplation stage of the Prochaska and DiClemente (1982) model of change. Even when he is determined to change, it must be realized that this determination probably will be very short-lived as the demands of treatment unfold. Therefore, the initial task of the therapist is to engage the sex offender in treatment. Toward this end, there are several identifiable strategies and interventions.

Providing Information

Initially, the therapist should inform the sex offender about the limits of confidentiality, the nature and purpose of any evaluation to be performed, and the therapist's role in the offender's case (cf. Aubrey & Dougher, 1990). The therapist also should describe what treatments are available and what the requirements of those treatments are.

Short-Circuiting Dissimulation

It is helpful for the therapist to expect dissimulation as a high-probability behavior from the offender facing treatment. The therapist may short-circuit dissimulation by communicating his or her empathic understanding of the reasons for it (e.g., difficulty in self-labeling, loss of self-esteem, etc.), by noting how common it is, and by predicting that the offender may be tempted to engage in it. Subsequently, the therapist may describe the consequences of persistent denial (e.g., being found unamenable for treatment, reoffending) and the tragedy of this, since there are a number of promising treatment approaches. The therapist may also want to undermine the sex offender's confidence in the efficacy of his dissimulation (e.g., by noting how common it is for "pillars of the community" to be convicted as sex offenders).

Using Motivational Interviewing Strategies

Several of the interviewing strategies described earlier in this volume can be very helpful for engaging the sex offender in treatment.

Asking open-ended questions enables the offender to begin talking about his problem and helps communicate an interest in the offender. This approach will also assist the therapist in evaluating the offender's motivational state (e.g., complete denial of sexually deviant behavior, minimization, etc.).

With an offender who partially admits to a problem with sexual deviance, the therapist can elicit self-motivational statements. For example, a convicted rapist was interviewed recently for his treatment amenability in a residential sex offender treatment program. The rapist initially admitted to having sex with his victim, but denied that it was rape. Rather, he said, he had bartered with a prostitute for sex and she had later accused him of rape. The interviewer, instead of directly confronting the rapist's minimization, said only, "That sounds like soliciting prostitution to me, not a sex offense," and then elaborated on this remark. The more the interviewer doubted whether the rapist had a problem with sexual deviance, the more the rapist provided reasons that he did indeed have a problem. Thus, the interviewer elicited self-motivational statements from the offender regarding his acknowledgment of a problem. (We would like to thank Paul Victor for this example.) What is especially important to note about this example, however, is that a powerful contingency was in effect. Persistent minimization on the part of the offender would have resulted in his transfer to a less attractive prison because he would have been deemed unamenable to treatment.

Another technique that can be used profitably is reframing. For an offender who claims that he did not plan his sex offense but that it just occurred spontaneously, the therapist can point out how dangerous that makes him, since he acts so unpredictably (Knopp, 1984). For the offender who views treatment as an imposition, the therapist can reframe it as a "privilege." For the offender who sees treatment as a sign of deficiency, the therapist may reframe it as "heroic." For the offender who presents as confident that he will not reoffend and is not in need of treatment, the therapist can reframe his certainty as a "bet" with very high stakes and very poor odds. And last, early in treatment, the therapist may reframe the offender's deviant sexual behavior as being like "addictions," although later the therapist will want to get the offender to own more and more responsibility for his actions.

Using Assessment Results

The therapist should use assessment results to confront the offender indirectly and to increase discrepancy. Commonly, assessments of sex offenders involve the physiological measurement of sexual arousal patterns (Dougher, 1988b; Knopp, 1984; Langevin, 1988). In addition, polygraph procedures are sometimes used (Knopp, 1984). These assessment results can be used to challenge the sex offender's dissimulation or minimization of deviant sexual arousal and behavior (Knopp, 1984; Langevin, 1988). Furthermore, if there are clear differential consequences associated with concealing versus admitting a problem, the anticipated use of these procedures may motivate the offender to begin discussing his sexually deviant behavior.

The therapist may also note inconsistencies between the offender's self-presentation and official documentation regarding his deviant sexual behavior (e.g., police reports, presentencing investigations). There may also be inconsistencies in his self-presentations across time, or between his verbal reports and psychological test results. Rather than aggressively confronting the sex offender at the outset, though, the therapist may doubt the offender's ability to benefit from treatment, inasmuch as he seems incapable of providing reliable information about himself and his cycle of sexual deviance. Another approach may be to permit the offender to correct his self-presentation by acknowledging the stress he must be under and the way in which this has apparently muddled his thinking. This communication may elicit a more reliable self-report while allowing the offender to save face.

Using Contingencies and Enlisting the Support of Others

The therapist should identify or create any potential behavioral contingencies relevant for the offender's participation in treatment. Furthermore, the therapist needs to communicate these contingencies to the offender in a tactful yet explicit manner. To assist this process, the therapist should involve others who may exert important and persuasive influences on the offender (e.g., spouse, attorney, peers). Many of the strategies and interventions used to engage the offender in treatment (e.g., motivational interviewing techniques, assessment results) can be applied to others in the offender's social network. In addition, if it is practical and safe to do so, the therapist may tentatively involve the offender in group therapy with offenders who are further along in treatment. Such group involvement with peers, if appropriately managed, may help the offender to acknowledge his problems and his need for treatment.

Motivation During Treatment

After the offender has acknowledged a problem with sexual deviance and a need for treatment, treatment can begin. As treatment progresses, the therapist should always keep in mind the offender's ambivalence about treatment and his potential for resistance. It is helpful to conceptualize the offender as constantly fluctuating among the stages of change in the Prochaska and DiClemente (1982) model. Because sexual deviance is typically deeply ingrained and ego-syntonic, it is always possible for the offender to slip from a treatment-motivated to an unmotivated state.

The following are various strategies and interventions that can be specified for treating the sex offender.

Appropriately Structuring Treatment Activities

Resistance to treatment can be diminished by appropriately structuring the various treatment activities in which the sex offender will be involved.

Initially, this means that the therapist provides an overview and rationale for the treatment modalities the offender will undergo.

In addition, the therapist should sequence treatment modalities in such a way that resistance is minimized. Both we and Abel, Becker, and Cunningham-Rathner (1984) have found that behavioral treatment to reduce deviant sexual arousal is best administered early in the course of treatment, following physiological assessment of sexual arousal. If introduced later in treatment, the techniques often engender client resistance. Furthermore, with the exception of the behavioral techniques, the therapist generally should sequence treatment activities according to difficulty. Thus, treatment modalities that may be easier for the offender to engage in (e.g., psychoeducation, assertiveness training, stress management, individual or group therapy) should be administered prior to more difficult modalities (e.g., victim confrontation groups, aversive behavioral rehearsal, drama therapy).

Another aspect of appropriately structuring treatment activities is to balance more and less difficult treatment modalities. For example, the therapist may want to conduct stress management training simultaneously with behavioral treatment to reduce deviant sexual arousal.

Using Motivational Interviewing Strategies

A number of motivational interviewing strategies are helpful in strengthening the offender's commitment to change and in dealing with resistance.

It is generally useful for the therapist to ask questions evoking self-motivational statements (e.g., about the offender's concerns about his problem, his intentions to change, his treatment goals). This material may be used subsequently with double-sided reflection (i.e., reflecting both sides of the client's ambivalence) to deal with client resistance. For example, when a sex offender claims that he cannot participate in an important form of treatment (e.g., behavioral treatment), the therapist can reflect this and can also remind him of his previously stated treatment goals (e.g., to control his deviant sexual urges).

Another helpful strategy is paradox, or the "creation of resistance in the service of therapeutic change" (Watzlawick, 1990, p. 89). This strategy can be used repeatedly by the therapist throughout the course of treatment with the sex offender. It consists of explaining the value of a treatment intervention for the sex offender, but then immediately doubting that the offender can maintain his motivation and follow through with the treatment. Often this will challenge the offender and motivate him to prove the therapist wrong.

Affirming and framing the offender's successful coping efforts are important not only for enhancing his self-efficacy, but also for dealing with those times when his treatment motivation sags. The therapist should acknowledge and remind the offender that he has made progress, especially when his self-esteem is low and he is considering giving up.

When the offender is considering dropping out of treatment, it is helpful to delay him from making any impulsive decisions, while emphasizing that dropping out is a choice he can make. This is especially appropriate when the offender is predicting future difficulty with some treatment modality. The therapist may respond, for example, "I hear what you're saying about how difficult doing this will be for you, but you don't really need to decide now about quitting. You can make that decision later if you want to." This intervention may buy time for the therapist and allow the offender to change his mind.

Next, reframing can be used to encourage the offender to adopt a different perspective about some issue and to undermine his resistance. For example, the therapist may reframe the offender's justifications for sexually deviant behavior as attempts to maintain self-esteem, rather than just excuses for bad behavior. Another example is for the therapist to reframe the offender's sexual assaultiveness as an act of weakness rather than power.

Finally, confrontation is often necessary. However, confrontation is apt to be more successful when the therapist has discussed it with the offender at the beginning of treatment as an occasional necessity, and when it is done with tact, warmth, and sometimes a sense of humor (Salter, 1988).

Reducing the Desirability of Sexually Deviant Behavior and Increasing Discrepancy

The most significant aspect of strengthening the sex offender's motivation for change and for preventing relapse is to reduce the desirability of sexually deviant behavior and to make it discrepant with the offender's beliefs, feelings, and self-image. If successful, this process is what will facilitate intrinsic motivation for change and the maintenance of such change.

A variety of interventions are useful for this purpose, including psychoeducational behavioral treatments; hormonal and antiandrogen treatments; therapy for sexual victimization; cognitive restructuring; role play, psychodrama, and drama therapy; and group therapy focusing on sexual deviance cycles, relapse prevention, and victim empathy (Bradford, 1990; Dougher, 1988b; Green, 1988; Knopp, 1984; Langevin & Lang, 1985; Murphy, 1990; Pithers, 1990; Quinsey & Earls, 1990; Ruben, 1989).

Using Contingencies and Enlisting the Support of Others

In treating the sex offender, it is important to establish and maintain contingencies around treatment behavior. To minimize client resistance, it is helpful to involve the offender in this process to some extent (e.g., setting treatment goals). The therapist also needs to communicate these contingencies to the client; to provide differential consequences for treatment participation versus nonparticipation; and to provide feedback as to how well the offender is satisfying these contingencies.

Again, it is important to enlist others (e.g., spouse, family, peers, community corrections or institutional personnel) to monitor the offender's behavior outside the treatment context, to establish and maintain behavioral contingencies, and to provide support for the offender's treatment.

Conclusions

Sex offenders present a difficult treatment challenge, and constitute a group for whom motivational interventions are particularly warranted. Although specific treatment goals differ across offenders, the general goals for all offenders include giving up a highly reinforcing and typically long-established pattern of behavior. The offender's motivation for change is the most important determinant of treatment outcome, which means that motivation-enhancing strategies are absolutely critical in working with this population. This chapter has outlined various obstacles and intervention strategies for working with offenders at different stages of treatment. At this point, many of the suggestions are based only on our clinical experience and have not yet been empirically tested. However, most of the propositions are testable; considering the devastating effects of sexual abuse and assault, the empirical analysis of these propositions seems to be an important and worthy endeavor.

24

Motivational Interviewing and the Maintenance of Change

ROSEMARY KENT

Nearing the End of the Journey

Various images have been used in this book to help the reader to understand motivational interviewing. One of these is that using motivational interviewing to help someone overcome a drinking problem is like accompanying him or her as a guide on a journey. The guide needs the qualities of a companion and the skills of someone who knows the route. Once on the road, there will be unexpected obstacles that the traveler will have to learn to cope with or avoid. The guide, in turn, will need to encourage and assist, and to recognize where there may be hidden dangers. There will be different stages on the journey, and the traveler and the guide may want to pause and reflect before embarking on each new stage. So it is with the counseling process.

This chapter looks at how motivational interviewing can be used after the initial stages of the "journey" have been completed. Problems may arise as client and counselor reflect on the action stage, and obstacles appear to prevent a move on to the maintenance stage. Indeed, the "traveler" may be tempted to stop completely—perhaps with mixed feelings about the need to go on with the guide, or with the belief that the destination has in fact been reached. Motivational interviewing approaches can help the client/traveler to get back on the right road.

Ambivalence about Moving On

"Maintenance is not an absence of change, but the continuance of change" (Prochaska & DiClemente, 1984, p. 28). This can be very uncomfortable for some people to accept, and counselors need to recognize that these people may give out mixed messages. Some clients seem to use premature self-efficacy as a way of resisting this continuance of change. Their ambivalence may manifest itself as verbal assurances that they are managing satisfactorily on their own, while their behavior suggests that they are struggling. One of the counselor's first priorities is to provide a safe environment in which mixed feelings can be expressed. Following this, the clients will necd to consider how changes in thinking, feeling, and behavior all need to be adopted if new, healthy habits are to be maintained and relapse prevented.

Clients who have achieved what they have for a long time desired—controlled use or abstinence—may at first feel extremely pleased with having done so. They may appear to the counselor to be almost superstitious in how they act: Nothing must be altered, they believe, lest it break the "spell" of their sobriety or their new behavior pattern. Prochaska and DiClemente (1984) point out that this rigid and structured way of thinking is not unusual. However, people may also find it hard to deal with unfamiliar thoughts, feelings, and behaviors. There may be a part of them that wants to retreat, or at least to stand still. Clients may need to be helped to retake personal responsibility for their own behavior—specifically, the prevention of relapse—and to accept positive and negative feelings about themselves.

Ambivalence and Premature Self-Efficacy

Some clients may believe that they have gone as far on their journey as they want to or need to when they have reached the action stage. Their "guide" or counselor, however, may believe that they have further to go. Sometimes the changes in behavior that occur following the contemplation and determination stages may be very short-lived or superficial, or the alert counselor will detect that there is a discrepancy between what a client has done and what he or she feels and says about these changes. Clients may make unexpectedly confident statements, such as "Well, things really are different," "I know I can do it this time," or "Everything is going to be better from now on."

There are other clients who, although they have changed their behavior, have feelings and thoughts more typical of the contemplation stage. They may be reluctant to consider that they need further help, because they expect counseling or treatment to cease once they have made initial changes. This can be recognized as ambivalence, because clients are normally eager to admit their fears and wishes for further help once they are given permission by the counselor. This can happen early or late in the maintenance stage. This kind of ambivalence tends to emerge as a result of pressure from other people (or society's expectations in general), or of resistance within the client himself or herself.

Pressures from Other People

Many people believe that treatment for alcohol problems ceases as soon as a drinker shows that he or she can stop drinking and remain abstinent for a longer period of time than after the previous attempt. In traditional approaches to alcohol problems, we sometimes find that treatment programs are based on the idea of a "dose" of treatment (often on an inpatient basis), and then exhortations to go to Alcoholics Anonymous (AA) meetings, to participate in hospital reunions, or perhaps to attend a clinic for follow-ups or a chat with a nurse. Clients or patients, it is often believed, will keep to their new resolutions if the right mixture of encouragement, peer pressure, occasional reminders, threats, willpower, and luck is available. This belief exists among the general population, as well as among some helping professionals and drinkers themselves. In contrast, the counselor who is familiar with a motivational approach will be aware that clients go through a number of stages in resolving their problems, and will probably feel that a more systematic program of counseling help may be appropriate.

A counselor may find that working on ambivalence at the maintenance stage may be at odds with popular beliefs or those of clients themselves. Families, friends, or employers may explicitly discourage clients from seeing themselves as still having any difficulties, or from expressing doubts about what they have achieved thus far. The view of a client's family, helping agencies, or the court my be that as soon as the client achieves sobriety, for instance, he or she should feel totally committed to the new behavior at all times. He or she may also feel pressure into making immediate changes, such as getting a job or seeking reconciliation with family members. In addition, there may be pressure to be grateful for, and not to make further demands on, help provided by counselors or professional agencies. All this can contribute to clients' reluctance to express their needs directly, or to articulate the ambivalence they might be feeling. The principles of motivational interviewing can be applied to enable clients to sort out for themselves some of these mixed messages.

Another difficulty arises when clients are assumed to be at the action or maintenance stage by those in a helping role, when in fact they have only stopped drinking or radically reduced their drinking in order to prove something to others. (This was the case with George in the example given below.) They may be responding directly to a threat or the promise of a reward. Some practitioners make inaccurate assumptions because the practical consequences of this *not* being the case are too messy or problematic to contemplate! For instance, someone may be bullied or cajoled into entering a "dry house" because a welfare officer wants to solve the client's homelessness problem. Any problem drinker can respond to threats (e.g., prison, family disruption) or inducements (e.g., a place in a hostel, promotion at work) by a short-lived change in behavior, such as temporary abstinence, without having had the chance to weigh things up, reflect, and take personal responsibility for choices. The counselor may need to work with a client as if he or she is in the contemplation stage, even though a shift in the behavior has taken place.

An example of this is a probation officer's work with a client called George. George had to appear in court for sentence on a burglary charge. Prior to this, he had contacted AA and had had an assessment interview at an alcohol counseling center. The judge was impressed that he appeared to be tackling his underlying drinking problem by doing these things, and he was given a probation order. At his next interview with his probation officer, George reported that he had cut down to a pattern of very occasional drinking and that he was having no problems. He was impatient with the suggestion that his previous and current patterns of drinking should be discussed. He believed that he had done what was required of him.

George and the sentencing judge believed that the action stage had been reached, but the probation officer was not so sure. She believed that George had not really internalized the need for change, and that he had not adequately worked through the thoughts and feelings that normally characterize the contemplation stage. Had she confronted him about this, however, he would have become even more reluctant to discuss his drinking. To avoid falling into this trap, she acknowledged his reluctance to discuss his "drinking problem," but remarked, "Perhaps you could tell me a little more about how you achieved the recent reduction in your drinking." Similarly, she avoided commenting on the apparent fragility of his new behavior, but encouraged him to acknowledge any current ambivalence he had about it. For example, she asked him, "What is it like when your friends see you at the bar with a nonalcoholic drink in your hand?"

The probation officer also enabled George to identify discrepancies in some of the things he said. For instance, he remarked that it was "no big deal to cut down," but also admitted at another point that he had never been able to put any limits on his drinking previously. She commented, "You say you've not had any difficulty cutting down your drinking. For some reason, in the last week it's been quite easy, but in the past it's been a big problem for you." Through expressing empathy, avoiding argumentation, and supporting self-efficacy, she enabled George to recognize that the changes he had made were important and worth sustaining. For example, she stated, "You feel that people have been pushing you to get your drinking sorted out, and that's what you've done. You're quite proud of what you've achieved, especially because nobody seemed to believe you could do it."

Many of the probation officer's interventions were reflective, which provided George with the time and permissive atmosphere he required to reach his own decisions. Here is an example:

GEORGE: I can't understand what I'm supposed to discuss with you. Everyone kept saying that it was the drinking that got me into trouble. I've stopped getting drunk, so where's the problem now?

PROBATION OFFICER: It's all quite confusing. You've been told that I'm here to try to help you sort yourself out, but yet people have been saying that you're the only one who can actually change your drinking. You've done that, so what now?

GEORGE: Yeah. I feel pretty confused by it all.

The probation officer explained the choices open to George in terms of what kind of help she could offer him—for example, relapse prevention training, a social skills group, or goal-setting counseling. Through this and other motivational interviewing strategies, she was able to help him consolidate the action stage and negotiate the transition to the maintenance stage.

Resistance from the Clients Themselves

Clients at the maintenance stage may feel ambivalent about whether it is legitimate to have further help, and about whether they need it. We also know that they may have received mixed messages from other people about whether or not it is "normal" to continue with counseling. A motivational interviewing approach encourages clients to articulate any ambivalence they might be experiencing, focusing on the "here and now." For example, a client called Liz attended counseling sessions for many months and had many ups and downs in her attempts to achieve a goal of controlled drinking. She learned some basic techniques about harm-free drinking and stuck to them for a month. After careful discussion, Liz and the counselor agreed that it would be a good thing for her to be referred to a specialist alcohol treatment unit, where she could address the more deep-seated difficulties that could precipitate a relapse. Liz attended one session at the unit but then returned to her counselor, saying that the treatment program would interfere with her job and she didn't know if it was worth going through with it. She thought, after all, that she could make it on her own. Liz's counselor pointed out possible discrepancies between what she was *doing* and what she was *feeling*, using what has been called a "double-sided reflection" (see Chapter 8): "On the one hand you can't really see the point of having any further help with the problems around your drinking, but on the other hand you felt it may be worth continuing to talk things through. Perhaps you're here now to try to do that."

Another example is that of Tom. Tom had complained to his doctor about gastric problems and had been helped to recognize that this was a result of prolonged heavy drinking. He agreed that it would be best to give up alcohol completely and went into a hospital for detoxification. While he was on the ward, a psychiatrist had visited him briefly and suggested that he come and talk to her when he was discharged. He did so, having remained abstinent for 3 weeks, but she was concerned that he was unwilling to admit he had any further problems, and she felt sure he would soon relapse. In talking to Tom, the psychiatrist used amplified reflection (see Chapter 8) as a way of dealing with his resistance about returning for a further session: "It seems to you that you've achieved your goal and there is nothing further to discuss." This enabled Tom to acknowledge some contradictory feelings: "Well, not really. . . . I know it might not be that easy to keep off the booze completely."

Counselors need to help clients to talk through their feelings about whether or not they believe they are able to "make it" on their own. A counselor can use key questions to focus a client's attention on aspects that he or she may avoid or be unaware of. For instance, has the client adequately explored what functions drinking served in the past, and therefore what alternative ways of coping he or she may need to develop? Thus Liz's counselor said to her, "You often used to talk about getting drunk as being a way of running away. What ideas do you have about finding less harmful ways of 'escaping'?" Open-ended questions can also be used to invite a client to consider what situations may make him or her feel vulnerable, and thus need to be thought through to avoid relapse. One question put to Tom, for example, was "What sort of situation in the future might make you feel you really 'need' to have a drink?"

While clients are feeling confident, healthy, and encouraged by friends and family members, it is entirely possible that they will not be in the mood for reflecting on how or when they have "gone wrong" in the past. Alternatively, they may go through unexpected phases of low self-esteem and low self-efficacy. In either case, they may be resistant to making plans to avoid relapse in the future, or to considering ways of minimizing harm if a relapse occurs. Motivational interviewing techniques can help clients feel more willing to set appropriate goals in these areas. Liz, for instance, remarked that she saw no point in trying to anticipate what she might do if she felt really depressed; she believed that it would just be "luck" whether she poured herself a drink or not. The counselor, using a reflective statement, said, "You're pessimistic about your ability to control what you do when you're feeling really bad. It's hard for you to believe that this could ever change. I guess it's tempting to avoid thinking about exactly what it is that you may need to learn to do differently." A counselor's task is to encourage such a client to be realistic and systematic, and to avoid taking refuge in overpessimistic or overconfident assumptions.

Differing Expectations

Dealing with clients at the maintenance stage can present the counselor
with two dilemmas about how situations are perceived. First, there is the
question of whether or not to take at face value what clients say about how
secure they believe their new achievements are. The counselor needs to try
to understand whether clients are genuinely free of any ambivalent feelings
(both about wanting to maintain their new behavior and about needing no
further counseling help) or whether they are resistant about expressing
them. Sometimes the counselor's own feelings can interfere with recognizing and helping clients with their ambivalence. Particularly when a counselor has been working with certain clients over an extended period of time,
the counselor may have specific fears, hopes, or expectations that prevent
him or her from allowing the clients to express themselves in their own way
at their own pace. When faced with comments such as "I'm OK now, I can
do it by myself," the unwary counselor may (1) totally accept without
further exploration that the client has reached a plateau or an end point,
and that he or she neither wants nor needs any further contact with a
helping agency; or (2) confront the client with the statement that he or she
ought to have more help, that relapse will inevitably occur without it, and
that overconfidence at this stage is a warning signal. In some situations, the
counselor may feel despairing, impatient, angry, or shocked by the client,
and may become punitive or didactic. Failure to recognize ambivalence can
also occur when the counselor is listening only to the *words* of the client,
and not what lies behind them. It is vital to pick up on nonverbal cues, such
as voice tone, hesitation, body language, and facial expression, in order to
obtain a full picture of what is happening for the client.

A second dilemma concerns the possibility that a counselor and a
client will have different expectations regarding their contact. When this
happens, it is easy for the counselor to become either collusive or confrontational. Thus, for example, Liz's counselor needed to be aware that Liz
might expect to be "rescued" from her dilemma of whether to enter a
formal treatment program or not. The counselor had to be on guard
against doing so, lest Liz should use this to avoid taking personal responsibility for her decisions, however tricky she might be finding it. Tom's
counselor might have felt irritated by his assumptions that he could cope
on his own now, while in fact the client's own understanding of the
situation was simply this: He was assessed as needing treatment; he stopped
drinking and went into the hospital; he was now cured; and he was going to
speak to someone only in order to have a final check-up and to be given
good wishes for the future. In George's situation, the probation officer
might have been feeling eager to start some in-depth therapeutic work with
him, whereas George's expectations were that he had done what was

required of him, and that having to talk about his problems would be a punishment, not a help.

The question of differing expectations between a counselor and client often emerges if the client enters what is sometimes referred to as a "honeymoon period," normally immediately after the action stage, when self-efficacy seems to be high. The counselor may have a dilemma about how or whether counseling should proceed during this time. It is entirely appropriate to say this to the client, in a nonjudgmental way. If it is indeed a "honeymoon period," surely the client should be allowed to enjoy it while it lasts! If the suggestion of future appointments comes from the counselor, he or she should make it clear that talking about achievements or setbacks will be equally acceptable, and that it will be up to the client if he or she wishes to negotiate additional counseling help after that.

Conclusion

Clients who make important changes are likely to have mixed feelings about the experience, particularly when their whole lifestyle is affected. Counselors can play an important role in helping them both to embark on these changes and to sustain them. Often there will be pressures from families, courts, or social welfare agencies that carry the clients along, with little chance to reflect on whether they are truly ready to make changes, or on how they feel about having made them. This chapter has aimed to show how motivational interviewing can provide a helpful framework for these concerns to be explored by clients and counselors together.

References

Abel, G. G., Becker, J. E., & Cunningham-Rathner, J. (1984)). Complications, consent, and cognitions in sex between children and adults. *International Journal of Law and Psychiatry, 7,* 89–103.

Abel, G. G., Becker, J. V., Cunningham-Rathner, J., Rouleau, J. L., Kaplan, M., & Reich, J. (1984). *The treatment of child molesters.* (Available from Gene G. Abel, M.D., Behavioral Medicine Institute, Paces Pavilion, Suite 202, 3193 Howell Mill Road, N.W., Atlanta, GA 30327)

Addiction Research Foundation. (1985). *A Structured Addictions Assessment Interview for Selecting Treatment* (ASIST). Toronto: Author.

Alcoholics Anonymous. (1976). *Alcoholics Anonymous: The story of how many thousands of men and women have recovered from alcoholism* (3rd ed.). New York: Alcoholics Anonymous World Services.

American Psychiatric Association. (1987). *Diagnostic and statistical manual of mental disorders* (3rd ed., rev.). Washington, DC: Author.

Anderson, P. (1987). Early intervention in general practice. In T. Stockwell & S. Clement (Eds.), *Helping the problem drinker: New initiatives in community care* (pp. 61–82). London: Croom Helm.

Anderson, P., & Scott, E. (1990, February). Randomised controlled trial of general practitioners' advice to heavy drinkers to cut down on their drinking. In G. Elvy (Chair), *Brief intervention.* Symposium presented at the Fifth International Conference on Treatment of Addictive Behaviours, Sydney, Australia.

Annis, H. M., & Chan, D. (1983). The differential treatment model: Empirical evidence from a personality typology of adult offenders. *Criminal Justice and Behavior, 10,* 159–173.

Annis, H. M., & Davis, C. S. (1989). Relapse prevention. In R. K. Hester & W. R. Miller (Eds.), *Handbook of alcoholism treatment approaches: Effective alternatives* (pp. 170–182). Elmsford, NY: Pergamon Press.

Appel, C.-P. (1986). From contemplation to determination: Contributions from cognitive psychology. In W. R. Miller & N. Heather (Eds.), *Treating addictive behaviors: Processes of change* (pp. 59–89). New York: Plenum Press.

Aubrey, M., & Dougher, M. J. (1990). Ethical issues in outpatient group therapy with sex offenders. *Journal for Specialists in Group Work, 15*(2), 75–82.

Azrin, N. H. (1976). Improvements in the community-reinforcement approach to alcoholism. *Behaviour Research and Therapy, 14,* 339–348.

Babor, T. F., Korner, P., Wilber, C., & Good, S. P. (1987). Screening and early intervention strategies for harmful drinkers: Initial lessons from the Amethyst Project. *Australian Drug and Alcohol Review, 6,* 325–339.

Babor, T. F., Kranzler, H. R., & Lauerman, R. J. (1989). Early detection of harmful alcohol consumption: Comparison of clinical, laboratory, and self-report screening procedures. *Addictive Behaviors, 14,* 139–157.

Bandura, A. (1977). Self-efficacy: Toward a unifying theory of behavioral change. *Psychological Review, 84,* 191–215.

Bandura, A. (1982). Self-efficacy mechanism in human agency. *American Psychologist, 37,* 122–147.

Bateson, G. (1971). The cybernetics of self: A theory of alcoholism. *Psychiatry, 34,* 1–18.

Baugh, J. R. (1988). Gaining control by giving up control: Strategies for coping with powerlessness. In W. R. Miller & J. E. Martin (Eds.), *Behavior therapy and religion: Integrating spiritual and behavioral approaches to change* (pp. 125–138). Newbury Park, CA: Sage.

Baumann, D. J., Obitz, F. W., & Reich, J. W. (1982). Attribution theory: A fit with substance abuse problems. *International Journal of the Addictions, 17,* 295–303.

Bell, J., Fernandes, D., & Batey, R. (1990). Heroin users seeking methadone treatment. *Medical Journal of Australia, 152,* 361–364.

Bernard, F. (1975). An enquiry among a group of pedophiles. *Journal of Sex Research, 11,* 242–255.

Biernacki, P. (1986). *Pathways from heroin addiction: Recovery without treatment.* Philadelphia: Temple University Press.

Billings, A., & Moos, R. (1983). Psychosocial processes of recovery among alcoholics and their families: Implications for clinicians and program evaluators. *Addictive Behaviors, 8,* 205–218.

Bolton, K., & Watt, R. (1989, March–April). Motivating change. *Druglink.*

Bradford, J. M. W. (1990). The antiandrogen and hormonal treatment of sex offenders. In W. L. Marshall, D. R. Laws, & H. E. Barbaree (Eds.), *Handbook of sexual assault: Issues, theories, and treatment of the offender* (pp. 297–310). New York: Plenum Press.

Brehm, J. W. (1966). *A theory of psychological reactance.* New York: Academic Press.

Brehm, S. S., & Brehm, J. W. (1981). *Psychological reactance: A theory of freedom and control.* New York: Academic Press.

Brown, S. A. (1985). Reinforcement expectancies and alcoholism treatment outcome after a one-year follow-up. *Journal of Studies on Alcohol, 46,* 304–308.

Brown, S. A., Christiansen, B. A., & Goldman, M. S. (1987). The Alcohol Expectancy Questionnaire: An instrument for the assessment of adolescent and adult alcohol expectancies. *Journal of Studies on Alcohol, 48,* 483–491.

Brown, S. A., Goldman, M. S., & Christiansen, B. A. (1985). Do alcohol expectancies mediate drinking patterns of adults? *Journal of Consulting and Clinical Psychology, 53,* 512–519.

Brown, S. A., Goldman, M. S., Inn, A., & Anderson, L. R. (1980). Expectations of reinforcement from alcohol: Their domain and relation to drinking patterns. *Journal of Consulting and Clinical Psychology, 48,* 419–426.

Brownell, K. D., Marlatt, G. A., Lichtenstein, E., & Wilson, G. T. (1986). Understanding and preventing relapse. *American Psychologist, 41,* 765–782.

Burnum, J. F. (1974). Outlook for treating patients with self-destructive habits. *Annals of Internal Medicine, 81*, 387–393.

Cahalan, D. (1987). *Understanding America's drinking problem: How to combat the hazards of alcohol.* San Francisco: Jossey-Bass.

Cahoon, D. D. (1968). Symptom substitution and the behavior therapies: A reappraisal. *Psychological Bulletin, 69*, 149–156.

Cartwright, A. K. J. (1981). Are different therapeutic perspectives important in the treatment of alcoholism? *British Journal of Addiction, 76*, 347–361.

Cavaiola, A. A. (1984). Resistance issues in the treatment of the DWI offender. *Alcoholism Treatment Quarterly, 1*, 87–100.

Chafetz, M. E. (1959). Practical and theoretical considerations in the psychotherapy of alcoholism. *Quarterly Journal of Studies on Alcohol, 20*, 281–291.

Chafetz, M. E. (1961). A procedure for establishing therapeutic contact with the alcoholic. *Quarterly Journal of Studies on Alcohol, 22*, 325–328.

Chafetz, M. E. (1968). Research in the alcohol clinic of an around-the-clock psychiatric service of the Massachusetts General Hospital. *American Journal of Psychiatry, 124*, 1674–1679.

Chafetz, M. E., Blane, H. T., Abram, H. S., Clark, E., Golner, J. H., Hastie, E. L., & McCourt, W. F. (1964). Establishing treatment relations with alcoholics: A supplementary report. *Journal of Nervous and Mental Disease, 138*, 390–393.

Chafetz, M. E., Blane, H. T., Abram, H. S., Golner, J., Lacy, E., McCourt, W. F., Clark, E., & Meyers, W. (1962). Establishing treatment relations with alcoholics. *Journal of Nervous and Mental Disease, 134*, 395–409.

Chamberlain, P., Patterson, G., Reid, J., Kavanagh, K., & Forgatch, M. (1984). Observation of client resistance. *Behavior Therapy, 15*, 144–155.

Chaney, E. F., O'Leary, M. R., & Marlatt, G. A. (1978). Skill training with alcoholics. *Journal of Consulting and Clinical Psychology, 46*, 1092–1104.

Chapman, L. J., & Chapman, J. P. (1967). Genesis of popular but erroneous psychodiagnostic observations. *Journal of Abnormal Psychology, 72*, 193–204.

Chapman, P. L. J., & Huygens, I. (1988). An evaluation of three treatment programmes for alcoholism: An experimental study with 6- and 18-month follow-ups. *British Journal of Addiction, 83*, 67–81.

Chess, S. B., Neuringer, C., & Goldstein, G. (1971). Arousal and field dependence in alcoholics. *Journal of General Psychiatry, 85*, 93–102.

Chick, J., Lloyd, G., & Crombie, E. (1985). Counselling problem drinkers in medical wards: A controlled study. *British Medical Journal, 290*, 965–967.

Christiansen, B. A., & Goldman, M. S. (1983). Alcohol related expectancies versus demographic/background variables in the prediction of adolescent drinking. *Journal of Consulting and Clinical Psychology, 51*, 249–257.

Christiansen, B. A., Goldman, M. S., & Inn, A. (1982). The development of alcohol-related expectancies in adolescents: Separating pharmacological from social-learning influences. *Journal of Consulting and Clinical Psychology, 50*, 336–344.

Christiansen, B. A., Smith, G. T., Roehling, P. V., & Goldman, M. S. (1989). Using alcohol expectancies to predict adolescent drinking behavior after one year. *Journal of Consulting and Clinical Psychology, 57*, 93–99.

Clancy, J. (1961). Procrastination: A defense against sobriety. *Quarterly Journal of Studies on Alcohol, 22*, 269–276.

Clancy, J. (1964). Motivation conflicts of the alcohol addict. *Quarterly Journal of Studies on Alcohol, 25*, 511–520.

Clement, S. (1987). The Salford experiment. In T. Stockwell & S. Clement (Eds.), *Helping the problem drinker: New initiatives in community care* (pp. 121–144). London: Croom Helm.

Condiotte, M. M., & Lichtenstein, E. (1981). Self-efficacy and relapse in smoking cessation programs. *Journal of Consulting and Clinical Psychology, 49*, 647–658.

Costello, R. M. (1975). Alcoholism treatment and evaluation: In search of methods. *International Journal of the Addictions, 10*, 251–275.

Council for Philosophical Studies. (1981). *Psychology and the philosophy of mind in the philosophy curriculum*. San Francisco: San Francisco State University.

Cox, W. M. (Ed.). (1983). *Identifying and measuring alcoholic personality characteristics*. San Francisco: Jossey-Bass.

Cox, W. M. (Ed.). (1987). *Treatment and prevention of alcohol problems: A resource manual*. New York: Academic Press.

Cox, W. M., & Klinger, E. (1988). A motivational model of alcohol use. *Journal of Abnormal Psychology, 97*, 168–180.

Cox, W. M., & Klinger, E. (1990). Incentive motivation, affective change, and alcohol use: A model. In W. M. Cox (Ed.), *Why people drink: Parameters of alcohol as a reinforcer* (pp. 291–314). New York: Gardner Press.

Cox, W. M., Klinger, E., Blount, J. P., Thaler, D. K., & Thurman, B. J. (1989, August). *Concurrent validity of the Motivational Structure Questionnaire for Alcoholics*. Paper presented at the 97th Annual Convention of the American Psychological Association, New Orleans.

Cronkite, R. C., & Moos, R. H. (1980). Determinants of the posttreatment functioning of alcoholic patients: A conceptual framework. *Journal of Consulting and Clinical Psychology, 48*, 305–316.

Cummings, C., Gordon, J. R., & Marlatt, G. A. (1980). Relapse: Prevention and prediction. In W. R. Miller (Ed.), *The addictive behaviors: Treatment of alcoholism, drug abuse, smoking, and obesity* (pp. 291–321). New York: Pergamon Press.

Davidson, R., Rollnick, S., & MacEwan, I. (Eds.). (1991). *Counselling problem drinkers*. London: Tavistock/Routledge.

Davies, P. (1979). Motivation, responsibility and sickness in the psychiatric treatment of alcoholism. *British Journal of Psychiatry, 134*, 449–458.

Davies, P. (1981). Expectations and therapeutic practices in outpatient clinics for alcohol problems. *British Journal of Addiction, 76*, 159–173.

Deci, E. L. (1975). *Intrinsic motivation*. New York: Plenum Press.

Deci, E. L. (1980). *Self-determination*. Lexington, MA: Lexington Books.

DiCicco, L., Unterberger, H., & Mack, J. E. (1978). Confronting denial: An alcoholism intervention strategy. *Psychiatric Annals, 8*, 596–606.

DiClemente, C. C. (1981). Self-efficacy and smoking cessation maintenance: A preliminary report. *Cognitive Therapy and Research, 5*, 175–187.

DiClemente, C. C., & Hughes, S. O. (1990). Stages of change profiles in outpatient alcoholism treatment. *Journal of Substance Abuse, 2*, 217–235.

DiClemente, C. C., Prochaska, J. O., & Gilbertini, M. (1985). Self-efficacy and the stages of self-change in smoking. *Cognitive Therapy and Research, 9*, 181–200.

Donovan, D. M., & Marlatt, G. A. (Eds.). (1988). *Assessment of addictive behaviors.* New York: Guilford Press.

Donovan, D. M., Rohsenow, D. J., Schau, E. J., & O'Leary, M. R. (1977). Defensive style in alcoholics and nonalcoholics. *Journal of Studies on Alcohol, 38*, 465–470.

Dougher, M. J. (1988a). Clinical assessment of sex offenders. In B. K. Schwartz (Ed.), *A practitioner's guide to treating the incarcerated male sex offender* (pp. 77–84). Washington, DC: U.S. Department of Justice.

Dougher, M. J. (1988b). Behavioral techniques to alter sexual arousal. In B. K. Schwartz (Ed.), *A practitioner's guide to treating the incarcerated male sex offender* (pp. 109–114). Washington, DC: U.S. Department of Justice.

Drew, L. R. H., & Taylor, V. K. (1988). *The second AIDS epidemic: Spread via needle-sharing to the general community. A review.* Unpublished manuscript.

Edwards, G., & Gross, M. (1976). Alcohol dependence: Provisional description of a clinical syndrome. *British Medical Journal, i*, 1058–1061.

Edwards, G., & Orford, J. (1977). A plain treatment for alcoholism. *Proceedings of the Royal Society of Medicine, 70*, 344–348.

Edwards, G., Orford, J., Egert, S., Guthrie, S., Hawker, A., Hensman, C., Mitcheson, M., Oppenheimer, E., & Taylor, C. (1977). Alcoholism: A controlled trial of "treatment" and "advice." *Journal of Studies on Alcohol, 38*, 1004–1031.

Egan, G. (1982). *The skilled helper: A model for systematic helping and interpersonal relating* (2nd ed.). Monterey, Ca: Brooks/Cole.

Elkins, R. L. (1980). Covert sensitization and alcoholism: Contributions of successful conditioning to abstinence maintenance. *Addictive Behaviors, 5*, 67–89.

Elvy, G. A., Wells, J. E., & Baird, K. A. (1988). Attempted referral as intervention for problem drinking in the general hospital. *British Journal of Addiction, 83*, 83–89.

Emmons, R. A. (1986). Personal strivings: An approach to personality and subjective well-being. *Journal of Personality and Social Psychology, 51*, 1058–1068.

Emmons, R. A. (1989). The personal striving approach to personality. In L. A. Pervin (Ed.), *Goal concepts in personality and social psychology* (pp. 87–126). Hillsdale, NJ: Erlbaum.

Emmons, R. A., & King, L. A. (1988). Conflict among personal strivings: Immediate and long-term implications for psychological and physical well-being. *Journal of Personality and Social Psychology, 54*, 1040–1048.

Ewing, J. A. (1977). Matching therapy and patients: The cafeteria plan. *British Journal of Addiction, 72*, 13–18.

Festinger, L. (1957). *A theory of cognitive dissonance.* Stanford, CA: Stanford University Press.

Fillmore, K. M. (1975). Relationships between specific drinking problems in early adulthood and middle age: An exploratory 20 year follow-up study. *Journal of Studies on Alcohol, 36,* 882–907.

Finkelhor, D., Araji, S., Baron, L., Browne, A., Peters, S. D., & Wyatt, G. E. (1986). *A sourcebook on child sexual abuse.* Beverly Hills, CA: Sage.

Finney, J. W., & Moos, R. H. (1979). Treatment and outcome for empirical subtypes of alcoholic patients. *Journal of Consulting and Clinical Psychology, 47,* 25–38.

Fleming, P. (1989, March–April). A low threshold methadone programme. *Druglink.*

Fox, R. (1967). A multidisciplinary approach to the treatment of alcoholism. *American Journal of Psychotherapy, 123,* 769–778.

Frank, J. D. (1973). *Persuasion and healing* (2nd ed.). Baltimore: Johns Hopkins University Press.

Frankl, V. E. (1960). Paradoxical intention: A logotherapeutic technique. *American Journal of Psychotherapy, 14,* 520–535.

Freedberg, E. J. & Johnson, W. E. (1978). Effects of various sources of coercion on outcome of treatment of alcoholism. *Psychological Reports, 43,* 1271–1278.

Freud, A. (1948). *The ego and the mechanisms of defence.* London: Hogarth Press.

Fuller, R. K. (1989). Antidipsotropic medications. In R. K. Hester & W. R. Miller (Eds.), *Handbook of alcoholism treatment approaches: Effective alternatives* (pp. 117–127). Elmsford, NY: Pergamon Press.

Fuller, R. K., Branchey, L., Brightwell, D. R., Derman, R. M., Emrick, C. D., Iber, F. L., James, K. E., Lacoursiere, R. B., Lee, K. K., Lowenstam, I., Maany, I., Neiderheiser, D., Nocks, J. J., & Shaw, S. (1986). Disulfiram treatment of alcoholism: A Veterans Administration cooperative study. *Journal of Nervous and Mental Disease, 256,* 1449–1455.

Fulton, A. (1983). *Relapse fantasies.* Unpublished postgraduate diploma dissertation, Paisley College of Technology, Paisley, Scotland.

Gallant, D. M., Bishop, M. P., Mouledoux, A., Faulkner, M. A., Brisolara, A., & Swaanson, W. A. (1973). The revolving door alcoholic. *Archives of General Psychiatry, 28,* 633–635.

Garfield, S. L., & Bergin, A. E. (Eds.). (1986). *Handbook of psychotherapy and behavior change* (3rd ed.). New York: Wiley.

Garland, R. J., & Dougher, M. J. (1990). The abused/abuser hypothesis of child sexual abuse: A critical review of theory and research. In J. R. Feierman (Ed.), *Pedophilia: Biosocial dimensions* (pp. 488–509). New York: Springer-Verlag.

Glaser, F. B., Annis, H. M., Skinner, H. A., Pearlman, S., Segal, R. L., Sisson, B., Ogborne, A. C., Bohnen, E., Gaxda, P., & Zimmerman, T. (1984). *A system of health care delivery* (3 vols.). Toronto: Addiction Research Foundation.

Godding, P. R., & Glasgow, R. E. (1985). Self-efficacy and outcome expectations as predictors of controlled smoking status. *Cognitive Therapy and Research, 9,* 583–590.

Gordon, T. (1970). *Parent effectiveness training.* New York: Wyden.

Gottheil, E., McLellan, A. T., & Druley, K. A. (Eds.). (1981). *Matching patient needs and treatment methods in alcoholism and drug abuse.* Springfield, IL: Charles C Thomas.

Green, R. (1988). Psychoeducational modules. In B. K. Schwartz (Ed.), *A practitioner's guide to treating the incarcerated male sex offender* (pp. 95–100). Washington, DC: U.S. Department of Justice.

Greenberger, R. S. (1983, January 13). Sobering method: Firms are confronting alcoholic executives with threat of firing. *The Wall Street Journal,* pp. 1, 26.

Greenwald, A. F., & Bartmeier, L. H. (1963). Psychiatric discharges against medical advice. *Archives of General Psychiatry, 8,* 117–119.

Griffith, R. M. (1961). Rorschach water percepts: A study in conflicting results. *American Psychologist, 16,* 307–311.

Haley, J. (1963). *Strategies of psychotherapy.* New York: Grune & Stratton.

Haley, J. (1987). *Problem-solving therapy.* San Francisco: Jossey-Bass.

Hall, S. M. (1979). The abstinence phobia. In N. A. Krasnegor (Ed.), *Behavioral analysis and treatment of substance abuse* (pp. 55–67). Rockville, MD: National Institute on Drug Abuse.

Harris, K. B., & Miller, W. R. (1990). Behavioral self-control training for problem drinkers: Mechanisms of efficacy. *Psychology of Addictive Behaviors, 4,* 82–90.

Hazelden Foundation. (1985). You don't have to team 'em down to build 'em up. *Hazelden Professional Update, 4*(2), 2.

Heather, N. (1987). Psychology and brief interventions. *British Journal of Addiction, 84,* 357–370.

Heather, N. (1989). Brief intervention strategies. In R. K. Hester & W. R. Miller (Eds.), *Handbook of alcoholism treatment approaches: Effective alternatives* (pp. 93–116). Elmsford, NY: Pergamon Press.

Heather, N., Campion, P. D., Neville, R. G., & Maccabe, D. (1987). Evaluation of a controlled drinking minimal intervention for problem drinkers in general practice (the DRAMS scheme). *Journal of the Royal College of General Practitioners, 37,* 358–363.

Heather, N., Whitton, B., & Robertson, I. (1986). Evaluation of a self-help manual for media-recruited problem drinkers: Six month follow-up results. *British Journal of Clinical Psychology, 25,* 19–34.

Hester, R. K., & Miller, W. R. (Eds.). (1989). *Handbook of alcoholism treatment approaches: Effective alternatives.* Elmsford, NY: Pergamon Press.

Holder, H. D., Longabaugh, R., Miller, W. R., & Rubonis, A. V. (in press). The cost effectiveness of treatment for alcohol problems: A first approximation. *Journal of Studies on Alcohol.*

Horn, J. L., Wanberg, K. W., & Foster, F. M. (1987). *Guide to the Alcohol Use Inventory.* Minneapolis: National Computer Systems.

Hucker, S., Langevin, R., Bain, J., & Handy, L. (1987). *Provera therapy for sex offenders against children.* Unpublished manuscript, University of Toronto.

Hughes, R. (1987). *The fatal shore: The epic of Australia's founding.* New York: Knopf.

Hunt, G. M., & Azrin, N. H. (1973). A community-reinforcement approach to alcoholism. *Behaviour Research and Therapy, 11,* 91–104.

Institute of Medicine, National Academy of Sciences. (1989). *Prevention and treatment of alcohol problems: Research opportunities*. Washington, DC: National Academy Press.

Intagliata, J. (1976). A telephone follow-up procedure for increasing the effectiveness of a treatment program for alcoholics. *Journal of Studies on Alcohol, 37,* 1330–1335.

Ivey, A. (1980). *Counseling and psychotherapy: Skills, theories and practice.* Englewood Cliffs, NJ: Prentice-Hall.

Ivey, A. (1982). *Intentional interviewing and counseling.* Monterey, CA: Brooks/Cole.

Jacobson, G. R. (1989a). A comprehensive approach to pretreatment evaluation: I. Detection, assessment, and diagnosis of alcoholism. In R. K. Hester & W. R. Miller (Eds.), *Handbook of alcoholism treatment approaches: Effective alternatives* (pp. 17–53). Elmsford, NY: Pergamon Press.

Jacobson, G. R. (1989b). A comprehensive approach to pretreatment evaluation: II. Other clinical considerations. In R. K. Hester & W. R. Miller (Eds.), *Handbook of alcoholism treatment approaches: Effective alternatives* (pp. 54–66). Elmsford, NY: Pergamon Press.

Janis, I. L., & Mann, L. (1977). *Decision-making: A psychological analysis of conflict, choice, and commitment.* New York: Free Press.

Jellinek, E. M. (1960). *The disease concept of alcoholism.* New Haven, CT: Hillhouse Press.

Johnson Institute. (1987). *How to use intervention in your professional practice.* Minneapolis: Johnson Institute Books.

Johnson, V. E. (1973). *I'll quit tomorrow.* New York: Harper & Row.

Jones, R. A. (1977). *Self-fulfilling prophecies: Social, psychological and physiological effects of expectancies.* Hillsdale, NJ: Erlbaum.

Kanfer, F. H. (1987). Self-regulation and behavior. In H. Heckhausen, P. M. Gollwitzer, & F. E Weinert (Eds.), *Jenseits des Rubikon* (pp. 286–299). Heidelberg: Springer-Verlag.

Kanfer, F. H., & Gaelick, L. (1986). Self-management methods. In F. H. Kanfer & A. P. Goldstein (Eds.), *Helping people change* (3rd ed., pp. 283–345). Elmsford, NY: Pergamon Press.

Karoly, P. (1980). Person variables in therapeutic change and development. In P. Karoly & J. J. Steffen (Eds.), *Improving the long-term effects of psychotherapy* (pp. 195–261). New York: Gardner Press.

Kendall, P. C., & Hollon, S. D. (Eds.). (1979). *Cognitive–behavioral interventions: Theory, research, and procedures.* New York: Academic Press.

Kissin, B., Platz, A., & Su, W. H. (1971). Selective factors in treatment choice and outcome in alcoholics. In N. K. Mello & J. H. Mendelson (Eds.), *Recent advances in studies of alcoholism* (pp. 781–802). Washington, DC: U.S. Government Printing Office.

Klinger, E. (1975). Consequences of commitment to and disengagement from incentives. *Psychological Review, 82,* 1–25.

Klinger, E. (1977). *Meaning and void: Inner experience and the incentives in people's lives.* Minneapolis: University of Minnesota Press.

Klinger, E. (1987a). The Interview Questionnaire Technique: Reliability and validity of a mixed idiographic–nomothetic measure of motivation. In J. N. Butcher & C. D. Spielberger (Eds.), *Advances in personality assessment* (Vol. 6, pp. 31–48). Hillsdale, NJ: Erlbaum.

Klinger, E. (1987b). Current concerns and disengagement from incentives. In F. Halisch & J. Kuhl (Eds.), *Motivation, intention and volition* (pp. 337–347). Berlin: Springer-Verlag.

Klinger, E., & Cox, W. M. (1986). Motivational predictors of alcoholics' responses to inpatient treatment. *Advances in Alcohol and Substance Abuse, 6*, 35–44.

Knopp, F. H. (1984). *Retraining adult sex offenders: Methods and models.* Syracuse, NY: Safer Society Press.

Knupfer, G. (1972). Ex-problem drinkers. In M. A. Rodd, L. N. Robins, & M. Pollack (Eds.), *Life history research in psychopathology* (Vol. 2, pp. 256–280). Minneapolis: University of Minnesota Press.

Kogan, L. S. (1957). The short-term case in a family agency: Part II. Results of study. *Social Casework, 38*, 296–302.

Kopel, S., & Arkowitz, H. (1975). The role of attribution and self-perception in behavior change: Implications for behavior therapy. *Genetic Psychology Monographs, 92*, 175–212.

Koumans, A. J. R., & Muller, J. J. (1965). Use of letters to increase motivation for treatment in alcoholics. *Psychological Reports, 16*, 11–52.

Koumans, A. J. R., Muller, J. J., & Miller, C. F. (1967). Use of telephone calls to increase motivation for treatment in alcoholics. *Psychological Reports, 21*, 327–328.

Krauth, B. & Smith, R. (1988). *Questions and answers on issues related to the incarcerated male sex offender: An administrator's overview.* Washington, DC: U.S. Department of Justice.

Kristenson, H., Ohlin, H., Hulten-Nosslin, M. B., Trell, E., & Hood, B. (1983). Identification and intervention of heavy drinking in middle-aged men: Results and follow-up of 24–60 months of long-term study with randomized controls. *Alcoholism: Clinical and Experimental Research, 7*, 203–209.

Kurtz, E. (1979). *Not-God: A history of Alcoholics Anonymous.* Center City, MN: Hazelden Foundation.

Langevin, R. (1988). Defensiveness in sex offenders. In R. Rogers (Ed.), *Clinical assessment of malingering and deception* (pp. 269–290). New York: Guilford Press.

Langevin, R., & Lang, R. A. (1985). Psychological treatment of pedophiles. *Behavioral Sciences and the Law, 3*, 403–419.

Laws, D. R. (Ed.). (1989). *Relapse prevention with sex offenders.* New York: Guilford Press.

Leake, G. J., & King, A. S. (1977). Effect of counselor expectations on alcoholic recovery. *Alcohol Health and Research World, 11*(3), 16–22.

Lean, G. (1985). *Frank Buchman: A life.* London: Constable.

Lemere, F., O'Hollaren, P., & Maxwell, M. A. (1958). Motivation in the treatment of alcoholism. *Quarterly Journal of Studies on Alcohol, 19*, 428–431.

Lettieri, D. J., Nelson, J. E., & Sayers, M. A. (Eds). (1985). *Alcoholism treat-*

ment assessment research instruments (NIAAA Treatment Handbook Series, Vol. 2). Rockville, MD: National Institute on Alcohol Abuse and Alcoholism.

Lettieri, D. J., Sayers, M. A., & Nelson, J. E. (Eds). (1985). *Summaries of alcoholism treatment assessment research* (NIAAA Treatment Handbook Series, Vol. 1). Rockville, MD: National Institute on Alcohol Abuse and Alcoholism.

Leventhal, H. (1971). Fear appeals and persuasion: The differentiation of a motivational construct. *American Journal of Public Health, 61*, 1208–1224.

Lewinsohn, P. M., Muñoz, R. F., Youngren, M. A., & Zeiss, A. M. (1978). *Control your depression.* Englewood Cliffs, NJ: Prentice-Hall.

Lieberman, M. A., Yalom, I. D., & Miles, M. B. (1973). *Encounter groups: First facts.* New York: Basic Books.

Lightfoot, P., & Orford, J. (1987). Attitudes of helping agents towards alcohol-related problems: Situations vacant? *British Journal of Addiction, 81*, 749–756.

Locke, E. A., Shaw, K. N., Saari, L. M., & Latham, G. P. (1981). Goal setting and task performance: 1969–1980. *Psychological Bulletin, 90*, 125–152.

Longabaugh, R., & Beattie, M. (1985). Optimizing the cost-effectiveness of alcoholism treatment. In *Future directions in alcohol abuse treatment* (ADAMHA Research Monograph, No. 15, DHHS Publication No. ADM 85-1322, pp. 104–136). Washington, DC: U.S. Goverment Printing Office.

Longabaugh, R., Beattie, M., Noel, N., Stout, R., & Malloy, P. (in press). The effect of social investment on treatment outcome. *Journal of Studies on Alcohol.*

Luborsky, L., McLellan, A. T., Woody, G. E., O'Brien, C. P., & Auerbach, A. (1985). Therapist success and its determinants. *Archives of General Psychiatry, 42*, 602–611.

Malcolm, A. I. (1968). On the psychotherapy of alcoholism. *Addictions, 15*(1), 25–40.

Mann, M. (1950). *Primer on alcoholism.* New York: Rinehart.

Manohar, V., (1973). Training volunteers as alcoholism treatment counselors. *Quarterly Journal of Studies on Alcohol, 34*, 869–877.

Martlatt, G. A. (1978). Craving for alcohol, loss of control and relapse: A cognitive–behavioral analysis. In P. Nathan, G. A. Marlatt, & T. Løberg (Eds), *Alcoholism: New directions in behavioral research and treatment* (pp. 271–314). New York: Plenum Press.

Marlatt, G. A. (1985). Cognitive assessment and intervention procedures for relapse prevention. In G. A. Marlatt & J. R. Gordon (Eds.), *Relapse prevention: Maintenance strategies in the treatment of addictive behaviors* (pp. 201–279). New York: Guilford Press.

Marlatt, G. A., & Gordon, J. R. (Eds). (1985). *Relapse prevention: Maintenance strategies in the treatment of addictive behaviors.* New York: Guilford Press.

Marlatt, G. A., & Rohsenow, D. J. (1980). Cognitive processes in alcohol use: Expectancy and the balanced placebo design. In N. K. Mello (Ed.), *Advances in substance abuse: Behavioral and biological research* (Vol. 1, pp. 159–199). Greenwich, CT: JAI Press.

Marshall, W. L., Laws, D. R., & Barbaree, H. E. (Eds.). (1990). *Handbook of sexual assault: Issues, theories, and treatment of the offender.* New York: Plenum Press.

Mayfield, D., McLeod, G., & Hall, P. (1974). The CAGE questionnaire: Validation of a new alcoholism screening instrument. *American Journal of Psychiatry, 131,* 1121–1123.

McLellan, A. T., Woody, G. E., Luborsky, L., O'Brien, C. P., & Druley, K. A. (1983). Increased effectiveness of substance abuse treatment: A prospective study of patient–treatment matching. *Journal of Nervous and Mental Disease, 171,* 597–605.

Miller, W. R. (1976). Alcoholism scales and objective assessment methods: A review. *Psychological Bulletin, 83,* 649–674.

Miller, W. R. (1978). Behavioral treatment of problem drinkers: A comparative outcome study of three controlled drinking therapies. *Journal of Consulting and Clinical Psychology, 46,* 74–86.

Miller, W. R. (Eds.). (1980). *The addictive behaviors: Treatment of alcoholism, drug abuse, smoking, and obesity.* New York: Pergamon Press.

Miller, W. R. (1983). Motivational interviewing with problem drinkers. *Behavioural Psychotherapy, 1,* 147–172.

Miller, W. R. (1985a). *Living as if.* Philadelphia: Westminster Press.

Miller, W. R. (1985b). Motivation for treatment: A review with special emphasis on alcoholism. *Psychological Bulletin, 98,* 84–107.

Miller, W. R. (1986). *Client-Therapist Behavior Code.* Unpublished manuscript, University of New Mexico.

Miller, W. R. (1987). Motivation and treatment goals. *Drugs and Society, 1,* 133–151.

Miller, W. R. (1989a). Increasing motivation for change. In R. K. Hester & W. R. Miller (Eds.), *Handbook of alcoholism treatment approaches: Effective alternatives* (pp. 67–80). Elmsford, NY: Pergamon Press.

Miller, W. R. (1989b). Matching individuals with interventions. In R. K. Hester & W. R. Miller (Eds.), *Handbook of alcoholism treatment approaches: Effective alternatives* (pp. 261–271). Elmsford, NY: Pergamon Press.

Miller W. R., & Baca, L. M. (1983). Two-year follow-up of bibliotherapy and therapist-directed controlled drinking training for problem drinkers. *Behavior Therapy, 14,* 441–448.

Miller, W. R., & Brown, J. M. (1991). Self-regulation as a conceptual basis for the prevention and treatment of addictive behaviours. In N. Heather, W. R. Miller, & J. Greeley (Eds.), *Self-control and the addictive behaviours.* Sydney: Pergamon Press.

Miller, W. R., Gribskov, C. J., & Mortell, R. L. (1981). Effectiveness of a self-control manual for problem drinkers with and without therapist contact. *International Journal of the Addictions, 16,* 1247–1254.

Miller, W. R., Hedrick, K. E., & Orlofsky, D. (1991). The Helpful Responses Questionnaire: A procedure for measuring therapeutic empathy. *Journal of Clinical Psychology.*

Miller, W. R., & Hester, R. K. (1986a). The effectiveness of alcoholism treatment methods: What research reveals. In W. R. Miller & N. Heather (Eds.), *Treating addictive behaviors: Processes of change* (pp. 121–174). New York: Plenum Press.

Miller, W. R., & Hester, R. K. (1986b). Matching problem drinkers with optimal treatments. In W. R. Miller & N. Heather (Eds.), *Treating addictive behaviors: Processes of change* (pp. 175–203). New York: Plenum Press.

Miller, W. R., & Jackson, K. A. (1985). *Practical psychology for pastors: Toward more effective counseling.* Englewood Cliffs, NJ: Prentice-Hall.

Miller, W. R., Leckman, A. L., Delaney, H. D., & Tinkcom, M. (in press). Long-term follow-up of behavioral self-control training. *Journal of Studies on Alcohol.*

Miller, W. R., & Marlatt, G. A. (1984). *Manual for the Comprehensive Drinker Profile.* Odessa, FL: Psychological Assessment Resources.

Miller, W. R., & Muñoz, R. F. (1976). *How to control your drinking.* Englewood Cliffs, NJ: Prentice-Hall.

Miller, W. R., & Muñoz, R. F. (1982). *How to control your drinking* (rev. ed.) Albuquerque: University of New Mexico Press.

Miller, W. R., & Page, A. (in press). Warm turkey: Other routes to abstinence. *Journal of Substance Abuse Treatment.*

Miller, W. R. & Pechacek, T. F. (1987). New roads: Assessing and treating psychological dependence. *Journal of Substance Abuse Treatment, 4,* 73–77.

Miller, W. R., & Sanchez, V. C. (in press). Motivating young adults for treatment and lifestyle change. In G. Howard (Ed.), *Issues in alcohol use and misuse by young adults.* Notre Dame, IN: University of Notre Dame Press.

Miller, W. R., & Saucedo, C. F. (1983). Assessment of neuropsychological impairment and brain damage in problem drinkers. In C. J. Golden, J. A. Moses, Jr., J. A. Coffman, W. R. Miller, & F. D. Strider (Eds.), *Clinical neuropsychology: Interface with neurologic and psychiatric disorders* (pp. 141–195). New York: Grune & Stratton.

Miller, W. R., & Sovereign, R. G. (1989). The Check-up: A model for early intervention in addictive behaviors. In T. Løberg, W. R. Miller, P. E. Nathan, & G. A. Marlatt (Eds.), *Addictive behaviors: Prevention and early intervention* (pp. 219–231). Amsterdam: Swets & Zeitlinger.

Miller, W. R., Sovereign, R. G., & Krege, B. (1988). Motivational interviewing with problem drinkers: II. The Drinker's Check-up as a preventive intervention. *Behavioural Psychotherapy, 16,* 251–268.

Miller, W. R., & Taylor, C. A. (1980). Relative effectiveness of bibliotherapy, individual and group self-control training in the treatment of problem drinkers. *Addictive Behaviors, 5,* 13–24.

Miller, W. R., Taylor, C. A., & West, J. C. (1980). Focused versus broad-spectrum behavior therapy for problem drinkers. *Journal of Consulting and Clinical Psychology, 48,* 590–601.

Milmoe, S., Rosenthal, R., Blane, H. T., Chafetz, M. E., & Wolf, I. (1967). The doctor's voice: Postdictor of successful referral of alcoholic patients. *Journal of Abnormal Psychology, 72,* 78–84.

Montgomery, H. A., Miller, W. R., Tonigan, J. S., Meyers, R. J., Hester, R. K.,

Abbott, P. J., & Delaney, H. D. (1990, November). *SOCRATES as presage: Validation of a new instrument for assessing motivation for behavior change in problem drinkers.* Paper presented at the annual meeting of the Association for Advancement of Behavior Therapy, San Francisco.

Moore, R. C., & Murphy, T. C. (1961). Denial of alcoholism as an obstacle to recovery. *Quarterly Journal of Studies on Alcohol, 22,* 597–609.

Moos, R. H., & Finney, J. W. (1983). The expanding scope of alcoholism treatment evaluation. *American Psychologist, 38,* 1036–1044.

Moos, R. H., Finney, R. C., & Cronkite, R. C. (1990). *Alcoholism treatment: Context, process and outcome.* New York: Oxford University Press.

Moskowitz, J. M. (1989). The primary prevention of alcohol problems: A critical review of the research literature. *Journal of Studies on Alcohol, 50,* 54–88.

Murphy, W. D. (1990). Assessment and modification of cognitive distortions in sex offenders. In W. L. Marshall, D. Laws, & H. E. Barbaree (Eds.), *Handbook of sexual assault: Issues, theories, and treatment of the offender* (pp. 331–342). New York: Plenum Press.

National Council on Alcoholism, Criteria Committee, (1972). Criteria for the diagnosis of alcoholism. *American Journal of Psychiatry, 129,* 127–135.

Nirenberg, T. D., Sobell, L. C., & Sobell, M. B. (1980). Effective and inexpensive procedures for decreasing client attrition in an outpatient alcohol treatment progrm. *American Journal of Drug and Alcohol Abuse, 7,* 73–82.

O'Farrell, T. J., & Cowles, K. S. (1989). Marital and family therapy. In R. K. Hester & W. R. Miller (Eds.), *Handbook of alcoholism treatment approaches: Effective alternatives* (pp. 183–205). Elmsford, NY: Pergamon Press.

O'Leary, M. R., Rohsenow, D. J., Schau, E. J., & Donovan, D. M. (1977). Defensive style and treatment outcome among men alcoholics. *Journal of Studies on Alcohol, 38,* 1036–1040.

O'Neill, P. (1985). The patient—where should I go for help? *Australian Drug and Alcohol Review, 4,* 103.

Orford, J. (1973). A comparison of alcoholics whose drinking is totally uncontrolled and those whose drinking is mainly controlled. *Behaviour Research and Therapy, 11,* 565–576.

Orford, J. (1985). *Excessive appetites: A psychological view of addictions.* New York: Wiley.

Orford, J. (1986). Critical conditions for change in the addictive behaviors. In W. R. Miller & N. Heather (Eds.), *Treating addictive behaviors: Processes of change* (pp. 91–108). New York: Plenum Press.

Orford, J. (1987). The need for a community response. In T. Stockwell & S. Clement (Eds.), *Helping the problem drinker: New initiatives in community care* (pp. 4–32). London: Croom Helm.

Orford, J., & Edwards, G. (1977). *Alcoholism: A comparison of treatment and adivce, with a study of the influence of marriage* (Institute of Psychiatry, Maudsley Monograph No. 26). New York: Oxford University Press.

Orford, J., & Hawker, A. (1974). An investigation of an alcoholism rehabilitation halfway house: II. The complex question of client motivation. *British Journal of Addiction, 69,* 315–323.

Palys, T. S., & Little, B. R. (1983). Perceived life satisfaction and the organization of personal project systems. *Journal of Personality and Social Psychology, 44,* 221–230.

Panepinto, W. C., & Higgins, M. J. (1969). Keeping alcoholics in treatment: Effective follow-through procedures. *Quarterly Journal of Studies on Alcohol, 30,* 414–419.

Parker, M. W., Winstead, D. K., & Willi, F. J. P. (1979). Patient autonomy in alcohol rehabilitation: I. Literature review. *International Journal of the Addictions, 14,* 1015–1022.

Parsons, O. A., Butters, N., & Nathan, P. E. (Eds.). (1987). *Neuropsychology of alcoholism: Implications for diagnosis and treatment.* New York: Guilford Press.

Patterson, G. R., & Forgatch, M. S. (1985). Therapist behavior as a determinant for client noncompliance: A paradox for the behavior modifier. *Journal of Consulting and Clinical Psychology, 53,* 846–851.

Peele, S. (1985). *The meaning of addiction: Compulsive experience and its interpretation.* Lexington, MA: Lexington Books.

Peele, S., & Brodsky, A. (1975). *Love and addiction.* New York: Taplinger.

Pickens, R. W., Hatsukami, D. K., Spicer, J. W., & Svikis, D. (1985). Relapse by alcohol abusers. *Alcoholism: Clinical and Experimental Research, 9,* 244–247.

Pithers, W. D. (1990). Relapse prevention with sexual aggressors: A method for maintaining therapeutic gain and enhancing external supervision. In W. L. Marshall, D. R. Laws & H. E. Barbaree (Eds.), *Handbook of sexual assault: Issues, theories, and treatment of the offender* (pp. 343–361). New York: Plenum Press.

Polich, J. M., Armor, D. J., & Braiker, H. B. (1981). *The course of alcoholism: Four years after treatment.* New York: Wiley.

Premack, D. (1970). Mechanisms of self-control. In W. A. Hunt (Ed.), *Learning mechanisms in smoking* (pp. 107–123). Chicago: Aldine.

Prochaska, J. O., & DiClemente, C. C. (1982). Transtheoretical therapy: Toward a more integrative model of change. *Psychotherapy: Theory, Research, and Practice, 19,* 276–288.

Prochaska, J. O., & DiClemente, C. C. (1984). *The transtheoretical approach: Crossing traditional boundaries of therapy.* Homewood, IL: Dow Jones/Irwin.

Prochaska, J. O., & DiClemente, C. C. (1986). Toward a comprehensive model of change. In W.R. Miller & N. Heather (Eds.), *Treating addictive behaviors: Processes of change* (pp. 3–27). New York: Plenum Press.

Prochaska, J., Velicer, W., DiClemente, C., & Zwick, W. (1986). *Measuring processes of change.* Unpublished manuscript, University of Rhode Island.

Prue, D. M., Keane, T. M., Cornell, J. E., & Foy, D. W. (1979). An analysis of distance variables that affect aftercare attendance. *Community Mental Health Journal, 15,* 149–154.

Quinsey, V. L., & Earls, C. M. (1990). The modification of sexual preferences. In

W. L. Marshall, D. R. Laws, & H. E. Barbaree (Eds.), *Handbook of sexual assault: Issues, theories, and treatment of the offender* (pp. 279–295). New York: Plenum Press.

Raynes, A. E., & Patch, V. D. (1971). Distinguishing features of patients who discharge themselves from psychiatric ward. *Comprehensive Psychiatry, 12*, 473–479.

Rimmele, C. T., Miller, W. R., & Dougher, M. J. (1989). Aversion therapies. In R. K. Hester & W. R. Miller (Eds.), *Handbook of alcoholism treatment approaches: Effective alternatives* (pp. 128–140). Elmsford, NY: Pergamon Press.

Ritson, B. (1986). Merits of simple intervention. In W. R. Miller & N. Heather (Eds.), *Treating addictive behaviors: Processes of change* (pp. 375–387). New York: Plenum Press.

Robins, L. N., Helzer, J. E., & Davis, D. H. (1975). Narcotic use in Southeast Asia and afterward: An interview study of 898 Vietnam veterans. *Archives of General Psychiatry, 32*, 955–961.

Rogers, C. R. (1957). The necessary and sufficient conditions for therapeutic personality change. *Journal of Consulting Psychology, 21*, 95–103.

Rogers, C. R. (1959). A theory of therapy, personality, and interpersonal relationships as developed in the client-centered framework. In S. Koch (Ed.), *Psychology: The study of a science. Vol. 3. Formulations of the person and the social context* (pp. 184–256). New York: McGraw-Hill.

Rogers, R. W., & Mcwborn, C. R. (1976). Fear appeals and attitude change: Effects of a threat's noxiousness, probability of occurrence, and the efficacy of coping responses. *Journal of Personality and Social Psychology, 34*, 54–61.

Rokeach, M. (1973). *The nature of human values.* New York: Free Press.

Rollnick, S. (1985). The value of a cognitive–behavioral approach in the treatment of problem drinkers. In N. Heather, I. Robertson, & P. Davies (Eds.), *The misuse of alcohol: Clinical issues in dependence treatment and prevention* (pp. 135–147). New York: New York University Press.

Rollnick, S., & MacEwan, I. (1991). Alcohol counselling in context. In R. Davidson, S. Rollnick, & I. MacEwan (Eds.), *Counselling problem drinkers* (pp. 97–114). London: Tavistock/Routledge.

Rosenberg, C. M., Gerrein, J. R., Manohar, V., & Liftik, J. (1976). Evaluation of training of alcoholism counselors. *Journal of Studies on Alcohol, 37*, 1236–1246.

Rosenberg, C. M., & Liftik, J. (1976). Use of coercion in the outpatient treatment of alcoholism. *Journal of Studies on Alcohol, 37*, 58–65.

Rosenberg, C. M., & Raynes, A. E. (1973). Dropouts from treatment. *Canadian Psychiatric Association Journal, 187*, 229–233.

Ruben, D. (1989, January–February). Jailhouse dramas. *New Age Journal*, p. 16.

Russell, M. A. H., Wilson, C., Taylor, C., & Baker, C. D. (1979). Effect of general practitioners' advice against smoking. *British Medical Journal, ii*, 231–235.

Saint-Exupéry, A. (1943). *The little prince.* New York: Harcourt Brace.

Salter, A. (1988). *Treating child sex offenders and victims: A practical guide.* Newbury Park, CA: Sage.

Sanchez-Craig, M. (1990). Brief didactic treatment for alcohol and drug-related problems: An approach based on client choice. *British Journal of Addiction, 85,* 169–177.

Sanchez-Craig, M., & Lei, H. (1986). Disadvantages of imposing the goal of abstinence on problem drinkers: An empirical study. *British Journal of Addiction, 81,* 505–512.

Sanchez-Craig, M., & Wilkinson, D. A. (1989). Brief treatments for alcohol and drug problems: Practical and methodological issues. In T. Løberg, W. R. Miller, P. E. Nathan, & G. A. Marlatt (Eds.), *Addictive behavior: Prevention and early intervention* (pp. 233–252). Amsterdam: Swets & Zeitlinger.

Sanchez-Craig, M., Wilkinson, D. A., & Walker, K. (1987). Theory and methods for secondary prevention of alcohol problems: A cognitive approach. In W. M. Cox (Ed.), *Treatment and prevention of alcohol problems: A resource manual* (pp. 287–331). Orlando, FL: Academic Press.

Saunders, B., & Allsop, S. J. (1991). Helping those that relapse. In R. Davidson, S. Rollnick, & I. MacEwan (Eds.), *Counselling problem drinkers* (pp. 73–91). London: Tavistock/Routledge.

Saunders, B., Wilkinson, C., Phillips, M., Allsop, S., & Ryder, D. (1991). *Motivational intervention with heroin users attending a methadone clinic* (Report to the Research into Drug Abuse Advisory Committee, Department of Community Services and Health, Canberra). Perth, Australia: Addiction Studies Unit, Curtin University of Technology.

Saunders, J. B. (1987). The WHO project on early detection and treatment of harmful alcohol consumption. *Australian Drug and Alcohol Review, 6,* 303–308.

Saunders, W. M., & Kershaw, P. W. (1979). Spontaneous remission from alcoholism: A community study. *British Journal of Addiction, 74,* 251–266.

Schmidt, M. M., & Miller, W. R. (1983). Amount of therapist contact and outcome in a multidimensional depression treatment program. *Acta Psychiatrica Scandinavica, 67,* 319–332.

Schorer, C. G. (1965). Defiance and healing. *Comprehensive Psychiatry, 6,* 184–190.

Schuckit, M. A. (1984). *Drug and alcohol abuse: A clinical guide to diagnosis and treatment* (2nd ed.). New York: Plenum Press.

Schwartz, B. K. (1988a). Decision-making with incarcerated sex offenders. In B. K. Schwartz (Ed.), *A practitioner's guide to treating the incarcerated male sex offender* (pp. 43–49). Washington, DC: U.S. Department of Justice.

Schwartz, B. K. (1988b). Interpersonal techniques in treating sex offenders. In B. K. Schwartz (Ed.), *A practitioner's guide to treating the incarcerated male sex offender* (pp. 101–107). Washington, DC: U.S. Department of Justice.

Segal, Z. V., & Stermac, L. E. (1990). The role of cognition in sexual assault. In W. L. Marshall, D. R. Laws, & H. E. Barbaree (Eds.), *Handbook of sexual assault: Issues, theories, and treatment of the offender* (pp. 161–174). New York: Plenum Press.

Selzer, M. L. (1971). The Michigan Alcoholism Screening Test: The quest for a new diagnostic instrument. *American Journal of Psychiatry, 127*, 89–94.

Shapiro, A. K. (1971). Placebo effects in medicine, psychotherapy, and psychoanalysis. In A. E. Bergin & S. L. Garfield (Eds.), *Handbook of psychotherapy and behavior change: An empirical analysis* (pp. 439–473). New York: Wiley.

Shaw, S., Cartwright, A., Sprately, T., & Harwin, J. (1978). *Responding to drinking problems*. London: Croom Helm.

Simon, S. B. (1988). *Getting unstuck: Breaking through the barriers to change*. New York: Warner Books.

Sisson, R. W., & Azrin, N. H. (1986). Family-member involvement to initiate and promote treatment of problem drinkers. *Journal of Behavior Therapy and Experimental Psychiatry, 17*, 15–21.

Sisson, R. W., & Azrin, N. H. (1989). The community reinforcement approach. In R. K. Hester & W. R. Miller (Eds.), *Handbook of alcoholism treatment approaches: Effective alternatives* (pp. 242–258). Elmsford, NY: Pergamon Press.

Sisson, R. W., & Mallams, J. H. (1981). The use of systematic encouragement and community access procedures to increase attendance at Alcoholics Anonymous and Al-Anon meetings. *American Journal of Drug and Alcohol Abuse, 8*, 371–376.

Skinner, H. A., & Allen, B. A. (1983). Differential assessment of alcoholism. *Journal of Studies on Alcohol, 44*, 852–862.

Skutle, A., & Berg, G. (1987). Training in controlled drinking for early-stage problem drinkers. *British Journal of Addiction, 82*, 493–502.

Smith, A. (1981). Goal attainment scaling: A method for evaluating the outcome of mental health treatment. In P. McReynolds (Ed.), *Advances in psychological assessment* (Vol. 5, pp. 424–459). San Francisco: Jossey-Bass.

Smith, R. C. (1988). Program planning and implementation. In B. K. Schwartz (Ed.), *A practitioner's guide to treating the incarcerated male sex offender* (pp. 31–41). Washington, DC: U.S. Department of Justice.

Sobell, L. C. (1991). Natural recovery from alcohol problems. In N. Heather, W. R. Miller, & J. Greeley (Eds.), *Self-control and the addictive behaviours*. Sydney: Pergamon Press.

Sobell, L. C., Sobell, M. B., & Ward, E. (Eds.). (1980). *Evaluating alcohol and drug abuse treatment effectiveness*. Elmsford, NY: Pergamon Press.

Solomon, K. E., & Annis, H. M. (1990). Outcome and efficacy expectancy in the prediction of post-treatment drinking behavior. *British Journal of Addiction, 85*, 659–665.

Solomon, R. L. (1980). The opponent process theory of acquired motivation: The cost of pleasure and the benefits of pain. *American Psychologist, 35*, 691–712.

Stallard, A., & Heather, N. (1989). Relapse prevention and AIDS among intravenous drug users. In M. Gossop (Ed.), *Relapse and addictive behaviour* (pp. 133–145). London: Tavistock/Routledge & Kegan Paul.

Stanton, M. D., Todd, T. C., & Associates. (1982). *The family therapy of drug abuse and addiction*. New York: Guilford Press.

Stewart, T. (1987). *The heroin users*. London: Pandora Press.

Stimson, G. (1990). AIDS and HIV: The challenge for British drug services. *British Journal of Addiction, 85,* 329–339.

Stockwell, T., & Bolderston, H. (1987). Alcohol and phobias. *British Journal of Addiction, 82*(9), 971–980.

Stockwell, T., & Clement, S. (Eds.). (1987). *Helping the problem drinker: New initiatives in community care*. London: Croom Helm.

Stockwell, T., & Clement, S. (1989). *Community alcohol teams: A review of studies evaluating their effectiveness with special reference to the experience of other community teams*. London: Department of Health and Social Security.

Sun Tzu. (1963). *The art of war* (S. B. Griffith, Trans.). London: Oxford University Press.

Swenson, C. H. (1971). Commitment and the personality of the successful therapist. *Psychotherapy: Theory, Research, and Practice, 8,* 31–36.

Syme, S. L. (1988, September). *Changing difficult behaviors: How to succeed without really trying*. Paper presented at the Advancing Health Education Symposium, Mills College, Oakland, CA.

Tarter, R. E., McBride, H., Buonpane, N., & Schneider, D. U. (1977). Differentiation of alcoholics: Childhood history of minimal brain dysfunction, family history, and drinking pattern. *Archives of General Psychiatry, 34,* 761–768.

Thornton, C. C., Gottheil, E., Gellens, H. K., & Alterman, A. I. (1977). Voluntary versus involuntary abstinence in the treatment of alcoholics. *Journal of Studies on Alcohol, 38,* 1740–1748.

Tiebout, H. M. (1953). Surrender vs. compliance in therapy: With special reference to alcoholism. *Quarterly Journal of Studies on Alcohol, 14,* 58–68.

Tiebout, H. M. (1954). The ego factors in surrender in alcoholism. *Quarterly Journal of Studies on Alcohol, 15,* 610–621.

Tomlinson, T. M. (1967). The therapeutic process as related to outcome. In C. R. Rogers (Ed.), *The therapeutic relationship and its impact* (pp. 315–335). Madison: University of Wisconsin Press.

Trice, H. M. (1957). A study of the process of affiliation with Alcoholics Anonymous. *Quarterly Journal of Studies on Alcohol, 18,* 39–54.

Truax, C. B., & Carkhuff, R. R. (1967). *Toward effective counseling and psychotherapy*. Chicago: Aldine.

Truax, C. B., & Mitchell, K. M. (1971). Research on certain therapist interpersonal skills in relation to process and outcome. In A. E. Bergin & S. L. Garfield (Eds.), *Handbook of psychotherapy and behavior change: An empirical analysis* (pp. 299–344). New York: Wiley.

Tucker, J. A., Vuchinich, R. E., & Harris, C. V. (1985). Determinants of substance abuse relapse. In M. Galizio & S. A. Maisto (Eds.), *Determinants of substance abuse: Biological, psychological, and environmental factors* (pp. 383–421). New York: Plenum Press.

Vaillant, G. E. (1983). *The natural history of alcoholism: Causes, patterns, and paths to recovery*. Cambridge, MA: Harvard University Press.

Vaillant, G. E. (1988). What can follow-up teach us about relapse? *British Journal of Addiction, 83,* 1147–1157.

Valle, S. K. (1981). Interpersonal functioning of alcoholism counselors and treatment outcome. *Journal of Studies on Alcohol, 42*, 783–790.

van Bilsen, H. P. J. G. (1986). Heroin addiction: Morals revisited. *Journal of Substance Abuse Treatment, 3*, 279–284.

van Bilscn, II. P. J. G. (1991, April). *Linking training and service development.* Paper presented at the conference "Training Excellence," Canterbury, England.

van Bilsen, H. P. J. G., & Bennet, G. (1988). *Motivational interviewing: A videotape demonstration* [videotape]. Bournemouth, England: East Dorset Health Authority.

van Bilsen, H. P. J. G., & van Emst, A. J. (1986). Heroin addiction and motivational milieu therapy. *International Journal of the Addictions, 21*(6), 707–714.

van Bilsen, H. P. J. G., & van Emst, A. J. (1989). Motivating drug users. In G. Bennet (Ed.), *Treating drug abuse.* London: Routledge & Kegan Paul.

Vuchinich, R. E., & Tucker, J. A. (1988). Contributions from behavioral theories of choice to an analysis of alcohol abuse. *Journal of Abnormal Psychology, 97*, 181–195.

Wallace, P., Cutler, S., & Haines, A. (1988). Randomised controlled trial of general practitioner intervention in patients with excessive alcohol consumption. *British Medical Journal, 297*, 663–668.

Watzlawick, P. (1990). *Munchhausen's pigtail, or psychotherapy and "reality."* New York: Norton.

Wedel, H. L. (1965). Involving alcoholics in treatment. *Quarterly Journal of Studies on Alcohol, 26*, 468–479.

Wilkinson, D. A. (Ed.), (1979). *Cerebral deficits in alcoholism.* Toronto: Addiction Research Foundation.

Wilkinson, D. A. (1991). The neuropsychology of self-control in addictive behaviours. In N. Heather, W. R. Miller, & J. Greeley (Eds.), *Self-control and the addictive behaviours.* Sydney: Pergamon Press.

Wilkinson, D. A., & LeBreton, S. (1986). Early indications of treatment outcome in multiple drug users. In W. R. Miller & N. Heather (Eds.), *Treating addictive behaviors: Processes of change* (pp. 239–261). New York: Plenum Press.

Wilkinson, D. A., & Sanchez-Craig, M. (1981). Relevance of brain dysfunction to treatment objectives: Should alcohol related cognitive deficits influence the way we think about treatment? *Addictive Behaviors, 6*, 253–260.

Wilson, W. H. (1977). Sobriety: Conversion and beyond. *Maryland State Medical Journal, 26*(4), 85–91.

Winokur, G., Reich, T., Rimmer, J., & Pitts, F. N., Jr. (1970). Alcoholism: III. Diagnosis and familial psychiatric illness in 259 alcoholic probands. *Archives of General Psychiatry, 23*, 104–111.

World Health Organization. (1982). Shortened memorandum: Nomenclature and classification of drug- and alcohol-related problems. *British Journal of Addiction, 77*, 3–20.

Yablonsky, L. (1965). *Synanon: The tunnel back.* New York: Macmillan.

Yablonsky, L. (1989). *The therapeutic community: A successful approach for treating substance abusers.* New York: Gardner Press.

Zweben, A. (1986). Problem drinking and marital adjustment. *Journal of Studies on Alcohol, 47*, 167–172.

Zweben, A., & Li, S. (1981). The efficacy of role induction in preventing early dropout from outpatient treatment of drug dependence. *American Journal of Drug and Alcohol Abuse, 8*, 171–183.

Zweben, A., & Pearlman, S. (1983). Evaluating the effectiveness of conjoint treatment of alcohol complicated marriages: Clinical and methodological issues. *Journal of Marital and Family Therapy, 9*, 61–72.

Zweben, A., Pearlman, S., & Li, S. (1983). Reducing attrition from conjoint therapy with alcoholic couples. *Drug and Alcohol Dependence, 11*, 321–331.

Zweben, A., Pearlman, S., & Li, S. (1988). A comparison of brief advice and conjoint therapy in the treatment of alcohol abuse: The results of the marital systems study. *British Journal of Addiction, 83*, 899–916.

Index